Jamaican Place Names

Jamaican
Place Names

B. W. Higman

and

B. J. Hudson

University of the West Indies Press
Jamaica • Barbados • Trinidad and Tobago

University of the West Indies Press
7A Gibraltar Hall Road   Mona
Kingston 7   Jamaica
www.uwipress.com

13 12 11 10 09   5 4 3 2 1

Higman, B. W., 1943–

Jamaican place names / B. W. Higman and B. J. Hudson.

p. cm.

Includes bibliographical references.

ISBN: 978-976-640-217-4

1. Names, Geographical – Jamaica. 2. Jamaica – History, Local.
I. Hudson, Brian J. II. Title.

F1864.H446 2009   917.292'003

Cover illustration: Detail from Thomas Craskell and James Simpson, *A Map of the County of Middlesex in the Island of Jamaica* (*surveyed 1756–61*).

Book and cover design by Robert Harris.

Set in Bembo 11/15 x 24

Printed in the United States of America.

Contents

List of Illustrations / *vi*

List of Tables / *viii*

Preface / *ix*

Abbreviations / *xii*

1 Place Names and History / *1*

2 Names and Name-Givers / *21*

3 Common Names / *60*

4 Topographical Names / *85*

5 Hydrological Names / *110*

6 Coastal Names / *138*

7 Enterprise Names / *155*

8 Settlement Names / *196*

9 Route Names / *223*

10 Conclusion / *245*

Notes / *259*

Bibliography / *279*

Index / *295*

Illustrations

1.1   Jamaica: Modern parishes and counties / *2*

2.1   Jamaica: Taino and Spanish names / *25*

2.2   Jamaica: Parishes, 1841 / *33*

2.3   Jamaica: Districts, main towns and places, 1950 / *34*

2.4   Jamaica: Transfer names from England / *36*

2.5   Jamaica: Transfer names from Scotland / *36*

2.6   Jamaica: Transfer names from Wales / *37*

2.7   Jamaica: Transfer names from Ireland / *37*

2.8   British Isles: Places named in Jamaica, cadastral series / *39*

3.1   Jamaica: *Content*, habitation and settlement names, 1760, 1800 and 1950 / *64*

3.2   Jamaica: *Content*, habitation names, 1834 / *65*

3.3   Jamaica: *Friendship*, habitation names, cadastral series / *68*

3.4   Jamaica: *Prospect*, habitation names, cadastral series / *70*

3.5   Jamaica: *Hope* and *Good Hope*, habitation names, cadastral series / *71*

3.6   Jamaica: *Belvedere*, *Bellevue* and *Mount Pleasant*, habitation names, cadastral series / *73*

3.7   Jamaica: *Retreat*, *Retirement* and *Hermitage*, habitation names, cadastral series / *76*

4.1   Jamaica: *Mountain*, settlement names, 1950 / *91*

4.2   Jamaica: *Hill*, settlement names, 1950 / *93*

4.3   Jamaica: *Valley*, settlement names, 1950 / *96*

4.4   Cockpit Country / *101*

4.5   Jamaica: *Savanna* names, 1680, 1760 and 1800 / *105*

4.6   *Savañas*: Redrawn from Bochart and Knollis, 1680 / *106*

4.7   Jamaica: *Grove*, settlement names, 1950 / *108*

5.1   Jamaica: *River* and *rio* names, 1800 (as on Robertson's map) / *113*

5.2   Rio Grande and tributaries, redrawn from Robertson, 1800 / *115*

5.3 Roaring River and tributaries, redrawn from Robertson, 1800 / *116*

5.4 Jamaica: *Spring*, *well* and *hole* names, 1800 (as on Robertson's map) / *122*

5.5 *Black Grounds* district, 1800, redrawn from Robertson's map / *123*

5.6 Jamaica: *Gully* and *gut* names, 1800 (as on Robertson's map) / *128*

5.7 Black River *morasses*, redrawn from Robertson, 1800 / *133*

6.1 Coastal features and terms / *139*

6.2 Jamaica: *Bay*, *cove*, *harbour* and *port*, 1800 (as on Robertson's map) / *142*

6.3 Hanover coastline, 1800 (as on Robertson's map) / *144*

7.1 Jamaica: *Estate*, habitation names, cadastral series / *158*

7.2 Jamaica: *Hall*, habitation names, cadastral series / *160*

7.3 Jamaica: *Castle*, habitation names, cadastral series / *161*

7.4 Jamaica: *Plantation*, habitation names, cadastral series / *166*

7.5 Jamaica: *Park*, habitation names, cadastral series / *172*

7.6 Jamaica: *Pen*, settlement names, 1950 / *173*

7.7 Jamaica: *Crawl*, habitation names, cadastral series / *176*

7.8 Jamaica: *Farm*, habitation names, cadastral series / *177*

7.9 Jamaica: *Settlement*, habitation names, cadastral series / *179*

7.10 Jamaica: *Walk*, habitation names, cadastral series / *181*

7.11 Jamaica: *Garden*, habitation names, cadastral series / *183*

7.12 Jamaica: *Mountain*, habitation names, cadastral series / *187*

7.13 Jamaica: *Land* and *run*, habitation names, cadastral series / *189*

8.1 Jamaica: *Village* and *–ville*, settlement names, 1950 / *198*

8.2 Jamaica: *Town*, settlement names, 1950 / *201*

8.3 Jamaica: *Shop*, *store*, *tavern* and *market*, settlement names, 1950 / *207*

8.4 Jamaica: *Hall* and *castle*, settlement names, 1950 / *209*

8.5 Kingston: *Pen*, *farm*, *estate*, *gardens*, *park*, *hall*, *town* and *city* names, 1900 / *212*

8.6 Kingston: *Pen*, *estate*, *gardens*, *park*, *meadows*, *hall*, *hill/heights*, *town* and *city* names, 2000 / *216*

9.1 Jamaica: *Corner*, *turn*, *cross*, *junction*, *roads* and *bridge*, settlement names, 1950 / *225*

9.2 Jamaica: *Gate*, *pass*, *paths*, *lane* and *street*, settlement names, 1950 / *230*

9.3 Kingston: *Road*, *avenue*, *street*, *lane*, *close*, *drive*, *way*, *crescent* and *place*, route names, 2000 / *235*

vii

Tables

3.1 Types of Names on Maps, 1680–1950 / *61*

3.2 Top Ten Settlement Place Names, Including Extension: 1950 Topographical Map / *62*

3.3 Top Ten Habitation Place Names, Including Extension: Cadastral Database / *63*

3.4 Habitation Place Names, Not Counting Extensions in Combination, Frequency Five or More: Cadastral Database / *78*

3.5 Settlement Place Names, Not Counting Extensions in Combination, Frequency Five or More: 1950 Topographic Map / *82*

Preface

THIS BOOK IS A STUDY OF the place names of Jamaica and of what they can tell us about the history and culture of the island. It is not a gazetteer or dictionary of the names that can be found on a map. Readers hoping to find here the story of a particular Jamaican place name can look for it in the index, but many names, important and not so important, are omitted from the narrative or treated only as part of a larger group. Nor do we seek to give the meaning or origin of each particular place name mentioned, because we are often interested only in some of its elements. Certainty about meaning and origin is difficult to assert in specific instances, even when a self-proclaimed name-giver left a written account of why a name was given, because words can change their meaning over time and can be understood only in context. The same words can mean different things to different people, even contemporaries. It is equally true that effective communication and naming depends on a vocabulary of agreed meanings for classificatory terms, and it is these that receive the most attention in this book. The reason for this approach is that our major objective is to study the composition and distribution of Jamaican place names, and to see what they have to tell us about the cultural, political and social history of Jamaica and the changing physical and economic topography of the island. To achieve this goal requires the study of names in general rather than specific, individual cases.

The first three chapters of the book set out the general principles and significance of the study of place names, the relative frequencies of names of different types and the sources of the names that were transferred to Jamaica from other parts of the world. The next three chapters focus on the names given to specific features in the physical landscape: landforms, hydrological features and coastal features. Chapters 7, 8 and 9 deal with the names given to habitation sites, both rural and urban, and the names associated with routes.

The place names mentioned in the text are generally identified by their locations within the modern parish boundaries. The parishes multiplied and contracted over time and shifted their boundaries, resulting in apparent anomalies and anachronisms, but the modern parishes are the best-known system of reference and have been fixed since 1867. In the text, place names are generally followed by an abbreviated form of the parish name in small capital letters. Where a place name had more than one occurrence within a parish, this is noted only when appropriate, so the parishes may add up to a number smaller than the total for a name. The parish names are listed from west to east across the island. References to the counties of the British Isles are to those that existed before the reforms of the 1970s. The 1972 (England and Wales) and 1973 (Scotland) Local Government Acts greatly altered county boundaries. Some counties disappeared while new ones were created. Before the reforms, the pattern of counties changed relatively little over many centuries, and it is these units that provided transfer names for Jamaica.

The meanings of words used in Jamaican place names and speech are generally taken, without reference, from the *Dictionary of Jamaican English*, edited by F.G. Cassidy and R.B. Le Page, in its first and second editions (1967 and 1980). Frank Cundall was the pioneer of place-name studies in Jamaica. To his publications can be added a series of articles by "Graeme" on "Names and Legends of Jamaica" that appeared in the *West Indian Review* in the late 1940s, and another on "Jamaica Places" by Alex D. Hawkes published in the *Gleaner* in the 1970s, though both of these writers depended substantially on the findings and opinions of Cundall. The most comprehensive work is Inez Knibb Sibley's *Dictionary of Place-Names of Jamaica*, published in 1978, and this may be supplemented by the more recent *Encyclopedia of Jamaican Heritage* (2003) by Olive Senior. The work of these authors has been essential to the preparation of this study, and we trust that they will regard this general acknowledgement as sufficient thanks. These and other reference works and alphabetical compendiums have been used throughout the preparation of this book, generally without specific citation except where direct quotation has been used or where the material cannot be easily identified. These works are listed in the bibliography in the section headed "Dictionaries, Directories, Gazetteers and Encyclopedias". The meanings of British place names are taken from the dictionaries listed in the bibliography, and specific references have not generally been provided.

The work for this book began when we were at the University of the West Indies, Mona, Jamaica. There, one of us (Higman) was in History and the other (Hudson) in Geography. The work was completed in Australia, where one of us (Higman) is located in the History Program of the Research School of Social Sciences, Australian National University, Canberra, and the other (Hudson) in the School of Urban Development, Queensland University of Technology, Brisbane. We are grateful for the institutional support we have received. Parts of the work made use of a grant from the Australian Research Council to one of us (Higman) for the Discovery Project "A Creole Landscape: Jamaica in Space and Time". Kay Dancey prepared the maps and William Murray the drawings. For assistance in the preparation of databases we thank Gregory Bowen, Jan Conant, Nalini Moorthi, Lawrence Niewojt, Elizabeth Pigou-Dennis and Jane Salter. Trevor Burnard kindly obtained for us a copy of Craskell and Simpson's map. For advice and guidance over many years we thank Mervyn Alleyne, Sir Roy Augier, Jean Besson, Gertrud Aub-Buscher, Pauline Christie, Howard Johnson, Joyce Johnson, Trevor MacClaughlin, James Robertson, Veront Satchell, Verene Shepherd, Barry Smith, Jean Stubbs, Mary Turner and Swithin Wilmot. We thank Anne Hickling-Hudson for her helpful comments, and Merle Higman and Woodville Marshall for reading the complete manuscript.

B. W. HIGMAN

B. J. HUDSON

Abbreviations

PARISHES

NOTE: Parish locations are indicated in small capitals, as, for example, Constant Spring AND. All places are located within the modern parish boundaries, whatever the period. Where a place name occurs more than once within a parish, the parish is identified only once.

AND	St Andrew
ANN	St Ann
CLR	Clarendon
CTH	St Catherine
ELZ	St Elizabeth
HAN	Hanover
JAS	St James
KGN	Kingston
MAN	Manchester
MRY	St Mary
PLD	Portland
THS	St Thomas
TRL	Trelawny
WLD	Westmoreland

SOURCES

DCEU	Dictionary of Caribbean English Usage, Richard Allsopp, 1996
DJE	Dictionary of Jamaican English, F.G. Cassidy and R.B. LePage, 1967/1980.
OED	Oxford English Dictionary

CHAPTER ONE

Place Names and History

ONE AFTERNOON IN JUNE 1988 FAMILY and friends filled a small church at Dundee in the district of Maroon Town, parish of St James, western Jamaica, and waited patiently for the commencement of the funeral of Jane Reid. Meanwhile the hearse carrying her body was on its way to Dundee in the neighbouring parish of Westmoreland, fifty kilometres away, the drivers from the funeral home having mistaken this to be their proper destination. The service started two and a half hours late.[1] Apart from the Dundee of Westmoreland, the drivers of the hearse might have set out for Dundee in Trelawny, the neighbouring parish to the east, or even a Dundee in Hanover, the parish to the west (Figure 1.1). Why so many Dundees in Jamaica?

The trouble created by the duplication of place names had been noted often enough and long before. For instance, James G. Sawkins, reporting on the geology of Portland parish in 1869, observed that "The former inhabitants of this island appear to have been very fond of applying the same name to residences and rivers; in this parish Belle Views, Cliftons, and Groves prevail, while in the adjacent parish [St Mary] there are no less than three 'White Rivers'. In this [parish] we have two Barbecues, two Mammee, and two Falls Rivers. As distinctions prevent confusion and doubt[,] this is to be regretted."[2] Even earlier, in the 1840s, it was remarked that Jamaican property owners had adopted a limited range of "favourite" names, which they sprinkled across the island, in imitation or affection.[3]

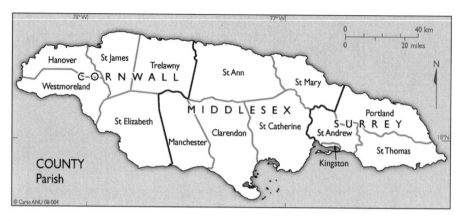

Figure 1.1 Jamaica: Modern parishes and counties

Giving names to persons, places and things serves very practical purposes in everyday life. Above all, names serve to identify, distinguish and differentiate, to help us know who, what or where we are talking about, and to locate those persons and things when they cannot be touched or pointed to. Duplication subverts this purpose. Naming is particularly significant for the understanding of space and place because it requires the identification of units within a continuum. Whereas human beings and buses, for example, are perceived as discrete units separated from nature and characterized by mobility, the naming of places is vital to their very creation by distinguishing them as bounded units extracted from the never-ending landscape. Landscape terms are not natural but segment the continuous surface of the earth in ways that differ from culture to culture, and in some languages there are no words for the objects that seem so obviously to be *mountains*, *cliffs* or *rivers*. It is necessary also to distinguish *objects* from *places*. For example, in the expression "The plantation was large", *the plantation* is an object, whereas in "The sugar mill on the plantation", *the plantation* becomes a place, with specific semantic properties.[4]

In every case, naming depends on the perception of an existing bounded unit, which can be understood to have a separate and individual existence, and for which a number is inappropriate or shows insufficient respect. This is true of naming of all sorts, from personal naming to the naming of boats, buses, handcarts and hurricanes (which became formal in 1950). Thus a Jamaican cartman told David De Camp shortly before independence: "I wouldn't paint only a number on a cart. I'd never get to know the cart then. A good cart deserves more."[5] On the other hand, social circumstances might compel people to endure being called by the wrong name. Thus one morning in July 1804 Maria Nugent recorded in her journal that her husband, Jamaica's governor, had been "attended home by a large party to breakfast; among whom were a lady and gentleman, that he called Donellan or Donaldson; but we found when they were gone, that the name was Campbell. However, the hospitality was the same, and they seemed much pleased."[6]

The things most likely to be named are those which are themselves distinctive, are not overwhelmingly numerous, and have valued functions in everyday life. In order to achieve these useful purposes, two major types of terms are employed. The first identifies the individual, as, for example, *Postmistress Icilda Campbell of Kirkpatrick Town*, whereas the second principle operates to group individuals into categories by giving them generic labels, as in *postmistress* or *town*. Generic terms or labels identify the type or class of a named person, place or thing, rather than describing the individual. Only in small places with small populations – with one postmistress and one town – can generics be functional by themselves, without specifiers.[7] The process is not foolproof, of course, and confusion and misidentification can take place when two people with the same set of names are mistaken for each other or when a *town* is referred to as a *village*. Generally, the more information the better, but if too much information is required in order to know for certain who or what we are talking about, then the system of naming is not working efficiently and names begin to sound like slogans or abstracts.[8] Two people or places with the same name can play havoc, as in mistaken identity or the hearse going to the wrong church. Inappropriate use of generic labels can equally cause trouble. Thus Nugent expressed her bemusement when a baby was "christened *Doctor* George William David, to the great astonishment of the clergyman and us all; but his father [William Robert Burrowes, assistant staff surgeon to the regiment] very sagaciously accounted for it, by saying, he intended him for his own profession, and it might save a diploma".[9]

In everyday life, place names are taken for granted, as necessary guides to identification and navigation. However quaint, familiarity means that names can be used without self-consciousness. In a more reflective mode, however, names are a source of interest and amusement. Lorna Clarke, in a playful article published in 2001, claimed, "As in everything else, we [Jamaicans] are the leaders, way out front when it comes to intriguing and interesting place names."[10] Whether Jamaica is truly unusual in having a large stock of intriguing names is hard to measure, but well-worn examples, all of them inscribed on the modern map, come easily to mind: Wait-a-Bit, Gimme-Me-Bit, Me No Sen You No Come, District of Look Behind, Bog Walk, Slippery Gut, Fat Hog Quarter.

Apart from the practical functions of place names in daily life, and the amusement they may offer, their study has much to tell the historian, linguist and cultural geographer. The fact and idea of place deeply affect the ways people relate to space, so that a "sense of place" is associated with a mental map or visualization of the contents of that site, and "place attachment" similarly identifies the emotional bond between people and their environment. The social and aesthetic experience of place gives the concept a larger role in history. Thus the value of place-name study derives from the fact that, although names may appear quaint and quirky, mischievous and whimsical, even these are applied with patterned regularity and change over time in accordance with rules and fashions. They are worth studying systematically.[11]

PLACE-NAME STUDY

In every type of naming, the first essential is the perception that the thing observed possesses some kind of unity. Although place names always name units of space or the location of points in space, the boundaries and extent of these units or points can range from the very precise, as in the fence or wall built along a property edge, to the vague and constantly shifting, as in the edge of a morass or a sprawling village. The identity of place and location can be challenged in some contexts, as in, for example, a camp, which is constantly moving but maintains its internal integrity and relationship to landscape as a place, as does a ship at sea, or the topological continuum of global air travel that connects airport and plane cavity as a single place apparently disconnected from geodetic coordinates.[12] Similarly, a stream can be a rapidly moving, bubbling concatenation of water droplets and other matter (soil in solution, leaves, dead insects and the like) flowing over rocks and soil, cutting into its banks, and changing its course with drought and flood. It must be seen to exist as a physical feature before it can be named. Further, places can be defined according to their internal uniformity or homogeneity, as in a coconut plantation or tourist village, or according to their functional unity, as in a river or road system. These features provide scope for individuals and groups to define places differently, recognizing different principles and elements.

Places can also be internally differentiated and these internal units given their own names, as in the naming of fields within a plantation or farm, or the streets within a town. They can be packed into larger nested units that gain new names, or an existing name can be applied to a larger zone or district thought to have similar or unifying characteristics. The history of naming can therefore shed light on the principles used in selecting natural features for attention – what is named and what is not, and how cultures differ in what they choose to distinguish. This principle applies to human settlement and architecture as much as it does to natural landscape features, though the notion of intent in human construction may mean that there is often a prior perception of the thing as a unit – a road or plantation – in spite of its many internal elements and the fuzziness of its boundaries.

Place names often consist of more than one word or element. Those identified by a single word and element – *farm* or *tavern*, for example – are called *simplex* place names. Such names cannot be broken down into elements. *Compound* place names, on the other hand, are made up from two or more elements joined together in a single word, as in Springfield or Heartease, which bring together *spring* and *field*, and *heart* and *ease*. The separate elements often make sense only in terms of their sequence and must be studied in context. Compound names are much more common than simplex names, in Jamaica as elsewhere.[13] In some cases, such as Heartease, the creation of the compound name occurred in Jamaica, but in many cases the compound name was transferred to Jamaica ready-made and therefore carried with it primary characteristics of a *simplex* name, as, for example, Springfield, which is a common place name in Britain and North America, found in at least six different locations. All of the elements are capable of yielding significant historical information.

In the study of Jamaican place names, rooted as they are in the process of colonialism, the distinction between simplex and compound names is less important than that between descriptive and generic elements. As noted above, generic terms or labels are used to classify landscape features and to place them in a hierarchy, whereas descriptive elements are applied to particular, individual places. Thus *river* is by itself a generic term but not a place name, whereas Black River is a place name containing both the generic classifier *river* and the specific descriptive *black*. Similarly, a settlement might be labelled a *town* or *village*, as in Browns Town and Central Village. Jamaica developed a refined system of classification for types of rural enterprises, including *estate, pen* and *mountain*, for example, which had precise meanings. A looser variety of labelling reflected notions of status, as when a settlement or enterprise included in its name terms such as *hall, castle* or *hut*. All of these generic terms functioned as labels, serving to locate specific places and place names within an accepted hierarchy of classes. Only occasionally did a generic term become a complete place name, as in the Jamaican examples *tavern, cottage* and *farm*.

Generic terms can be arranged as a system of types according to the things they label. The first division is between physical (sometimes called topographical) and habitative (or human settlement). Next, the names applied to physical features can be divided first between land and water, and the latter between streams (hydrological) and marine (littoral, coastal).[14] It is important to note that the study of place names is closely associated with an older branch of geography known as topography (from the Greek *tópos*), in which the objective was a detailed descriptive account of the physical form and contents of particular geographical regions. From this association is derived *toponym* as a synonym for *place name*, and *toponymy* as the study of place names.[15] Here, *topography* is used strictly to refer to the physical shape of the land, not the total contents of geographical space.

In analysing generic terms, the first thing to ask is how particular cultures select physical features for naming. Why are some features ignored? Second, why do different cultures use different terms for the same thing or the same word for different things? These questions are particularly interesting in colonial settings, where people from the same background encounter different kinds of environments, or where a creole language develops parallel to the perception of a previously unknown physical world, as in Jamaica. Descriptive elements in a name may refer to a variety of perceptions and features, such as ownership, land tenure, land use, climatic conditions, social status, settlement history, sentiments and the origins of the name-givers. In the case of Jamaica, the names can tell how a succession of colonizing peoples perceived and assessed the physical environment, what they found valuable within that environment and how they exploited the resources. The place names can also tell how settlement spread and was organized, and how it was integrated through lines of communication. Place names give clues to the colonizers, their hopes and aspirations, and their view of themselves in the social hierarchy. They enable an understanding of the structure of social power that restricted different styles of naming to different groups of name-givers.

Although place names serve a very particular purpose, their construction is often closely related to other varieties of name-giving, and they frequently contain elements derived from the names of people and things. For example, the Brown of Browns Town ANN is derived from the name of Hamilton Brown, the Irish-born reactionary penkeeper of the early nineteenth century who founded the town, calling it first Hamilton Town. This type of place name is termed an *eponym* and the style of naming is *eponymous*.[16] Such naming is not always obvious, as elements are lost over time and associations forgotten. The modern May Pen of Kingston and the May Pen of Clarendon parish were both once known as May's Pen, meaning simply that they were located where a Mr May owned a livestock-raising property called a *pen*.

The creation of eponymous place names can be traced through the cartographic surveys of Jamaica. Maps of the seventeenth and eighteenth centuries typically identified habitation sites by the names of the property owners. This could take the form of the name itself, as in "W. Dawkins" or "Elletson", simply locating the place of residence of the person named, or it might indicate the beginnings of continuity by identifying a specified piece of land as belonging to an individual or family, as in "Dawkins's" or "Taylor's". Such identifications often coexisted with descriptive names and generic labels. Thus Dawkins might own a plantation called "Caymanas", referring to a larger descriptive term for an area, to which was added the generic label "estate" to distinguish the property as a sugar-producing enterprise, rather than a plantation or pen, for example. Other proprietors owning estates in the same area might use the same descriptive term, and eventually the full name of a property might become "Dawkins Caymanas Estate" or "Taylors Caymanas Estate". Other properties were fully eponymous, taking the name of an original owner to name a place, as in "Dawkins Estate". In some cases, eponym plus generic label eventually named a district or town, as in May Pen.

The evidence of place names derived from other places is more precise. Names of this sort are termed *transfer names*, meaning that they are imported fully formed from some other place, distant or nearby, rather than being local creations. Many of Jamaica's place names come from the British Isles. Generally, it can be assumed that these names were applied to Jamaica in memory of those British places. Thus *Oxford* seems most likely to refer to the well-known university town, and was chosen because the name-givers had been residents of the town or had been students there, or thought it added status or seemed whimsical or even paradoxical or ironic, or perhaps even a little of all of these. The particular reasons for the choice are not vital in this context. The important thing is the assumption that the name was taken directly from the name of the English town. The alternative would be to argue that the name reflected its etymological origins in Old English, combining *ox* and *ford* in a compound name, meaning a stream-crossing used by oxen, and that the Jamaican name-givers referred to that meaning. Certainly, Jamaica had many fords, and, down to the early twentieth century, oxen were widely used to pull heavily laden wagons along the island's roads and across its streams. Within the English context, it is the Old English meaning that would count as useful evidence in place-name study, providing both linguistic clues to the namers and topographic and land-use clues to past activity. The name was not used in this way in Jamaica. Even where a name such as Oxford can be shown to fit the landscape, the possibility remains that the original reference was to the English town rather than to these local features. Another possibility is that the image in the name-giver's mind was not so much of the town and its dreaming spires but of the landscape setting, with the river running through the landscape and oxen still very much an important part of the scene – remembering that comparison must be with the Oxford of circa 1700 rather than the modern semi-industrial city.

The case of Oxford might appear misleading in that its elements, *ox* and *ford*, remain strongly emphasized in the modern English spelling, and easily interpreted. Much the same applies to Springfield, already mentioned, which seems most likely to have been a transfer name. Less difficult is a name like Kildare HAN ELZ PLD, which recalls the Kildare of Ireland that was derived from *kil* (church) and *dare* (oak), meaning "church of the oak", and alluded to the supposed site of the cell of St Bridget who lived between AD 452 and 523, and thus pointed to the Irish *cill* and *dara*. Here we can much more easily agree that the Jamaican Kildares came from the Irish place, without needing to test the etymology against any local landscape features or religious traditions. The oak does not grow in Jamaica.

Another problem in the analysis of place names is the difficulty of establishing original spellings and meanings. The meaning of words, and hence names, is not self-evident and can only be established through an understanding of context. It is possible to follow the changing meaning of words only by locating them within past contexts, and it is therefore essential not to apply present usage without consideration of alternatives and variants. This creates difficulty for place-name studies in that names are not always found in context – as, for example, when they are available only from historic lists or maps – hence it is necessary to seek help in other contemporary sources.[17] The problem is greatest where the documentary source is far removed from the giving of the name and where linguistic "corruption" has been active. Related to these problems is the difficulty of establishing chronological sequences in the giving of names. Unlike the precise dates that can be applied to most of the documentary sources that list personal names, used in studies of early modern migration, place names are often slow to appear on cartographic and other sources, making it hard to trace changes over time. In St Catherine, for instance, a place called Simmers Valley in 1834 and owned by Jane Simmers became known by the end of the nineteenth century as Sinners Valley. Similarly, patents of 1846 stated that disputed lands of Sally Carter Cheese and William Cheese were properly known as "Cheesefield and Criterion Hall" but "commonly known as Cheesefield Penn or Plantation".[18]

Many surnames, including ones of British origin, had their ultimate origins in place names, so that in analysing the use of such a name in Jamaica it may be difficult to distinguish between an eponym and a transfer name. For example, a person living in the English place York might take the name of the town as a surname. Occurrences of York in Jamaica could thus be attributed to either a person or a place. In the absence of evidence that the Jamaican place name was derived from a surname, it must generally be assumed that the place name is a transfer name. The choice is based on the greater recognition of places compared to persons, and the directness of naming a place after another place. In any case, even if the place name is in fact derived from a surname, the link goes back indirectly to a particular place, and the name is a strong indicator of regional genetic origins.[19] The problem is less than it might seem. A list of common Jamaican surnames reads very differently from a list of the island's place names.

For the study of place names, a vital starting point is the collection of names and their organization, in the form of gazetteers and geographic indexes. Lists of this sort have often been created by governments and cartographers for practical purposes and may exist in accessible published and unpublished forms. Generally, however, these sources lack the completeness needed for systematic place-name study. For Jamaica, there is no comprehensive published list at the cadastral or landholding level. Similarly, at the beginning of the twenty-first century the United States was still in the process of constructing an electronic gazetteer, the National Geographic Names Database, and in the United Kingdom a computerized database remained under construction from the numerous published volumes of the English Place-Name Society.[20]

In the public sphere, naming has become increasingly formal and official. In Jamaica, children must be registered soon after birth and identified by their personal names and those of their parents. In legal matters, it is these names that count, though the individual may have many aliases and alternatives. Changing names formally requires a legal process, such as a deed poll or marriage certificate. In earlier times, before the civil registration of births, deaths and marriages began in Jamaica in 1878, naming was generally much looser and less official. In the last decades of slavery, between 1817 and 1834, the owners of enslaved people were required by the state to make registration returns for these people, listing names (sometimes with surnames), and in some cases these names copied those already found in plantation records or the baptism records of churches. These were the names known to, and often imposed by, the owners of the enslaved people, rather than those used within the community. In the long term, Jamaicans have resisted pressures to standardize spelling, though with more success for birth or given names than for surnames.[21]

The formal recording of place names has followed a different route. Places change in character over time, becoming differentiated or consolidated, but they tend to have long-term continuity rather than the brief lives of human beings. This continuity contributes to stability in formal naming, though alternatives, abbreviations and localisms may exist in parallel. Many of Jamaica's place names have great longevity. This applies not only to the names of administrative units such as the parishes and counties but equally to the names of habitations and properties. Place names derived from plantations established in the seventeenth century have survived successfully for more than three hundred years. This stability is not a product of state regulation but simply reflects the utility of retaining names.

The United States Board on Geographic Names was established as early as 1890, assuming its present form in 1947, and the British set up a Permanent Committee on Geographical Names in 1919. Although the US board had responsibility initially for settling internal name problems, it later took an interest in other countries. The aerial photography undertaken over Jamaica during World War II and the subsequent topographic mapping exercise were associated with this growing interest, and in 1947 the US board published a series of guides for regions of the Caribbean, including *Directions for the Treatment of Geographical Names in Jamaica*. This publication listed decisions on many names, designed to provide "a geographical nomenclature as uniform and accurate as is possible", and included "about 150 names approved by the Place Names Committee in the office of the Director of Surveys, Jamaica". This committee had been established by the director of surveys, E.D. Stanfeld, who left the island in 1947. As well as approving particular names, the Jamaican Place Names Committee decided, *inter alia*, to avoid the use of the apostrophe in almost all names and to anglicize most non-English terms, so that, for example, *río* become *rio*.[22]

Collaboration between the British and US agencies led to a concern for international standardization and the creation by the United Nations of the Group of Experts on Geographical Names, which held conferences beginning in 1967. A principal objective was the standardization of orthography, including the romanization of all scripts, but there was also an effort to encourage nations to create their own authorities. In Jamaica, the Place Names Committee continued the task after independence, becoming known as the Geographical Names Committee and providing advice from local geographers and historians on questions relating to place names that were to be used on official maps and documents. The details of official naming practice were, however, not always transparent.[23]

Standardization of place names has followed several routes. Governments have sought to impose a single name and agreed orthography, and to ensure consistency between different documents such as maps and legislation. Further, there have been efforts to apply standard generic labels to particular landforms, applying a hierarchy of measurable definitions to *hill* and *mountain*, for example. In spite of these efforts, and in spite of success in establishing agreement in naming between series of published maps and official documents, the names found on these maps and documents may not be the ones in everyday local use. People cling to older forms or pass down names by word of mouth over several generations, the names persisting in oral culture but never appearing on maps.[24] If the corpus of place names as used in everyday speech is not recorded, it is impossible to study the lexicon.

SOURCES AND METHODS

Systematic place-name studies depend on the existence of documentary records over a long period of time. For analytical purposes, it is necessary also to relate name data to contextual metadata that describe features of the location of a place name, particularly its physical setting. In summary, the analysis of Jamaican names offered here rests on five large-scale databases for the years circa 1680, 1760, 1800, 1880 and 1950. These databases are derived from the names recorded on contemporary maps and surveys, supplemented by data describing the physical landscape taken from modern maps. They contain a total of roughly twenty-two thousand names, including the personal names shown on the earliest of the maps. A separate database of street names in the Kingston Metropolitan Area has been constructed, as at circa 2000. Field names cannot be reconstructed systematically on an island-wide basis and are excluded from the analysis.[25] Readers satisfied by this summary of the sources and methods used in the book may choose to skip the following paragraphs, which set out some of the more technical details underlying the creation of the databases.

The maps chosen for close study are not the only potential sources. Alternative cartographic sources of place names include maps of the entire island of Jamaica, maps of districts and coastlines, cadastral maps and maps of particular individual landholdings.[26] The early maps of Jamaica lacked geodetic control, so that even the outline shape of the island is poorly represented. Their small scale meant that only a few place names could be included, and often it was the coastline that received the most names. Cartography based on "actual surveys" became common only in the middle of the eighteenth century, with Patrick Browne's 1755 map claiming a firm foundation in surveys made between 1730 and 1749. In spite of their inadequacies, the better maps of the late seventeenth century offered a fair level of accuracy in the settled regions of the island, at least in the relative location of names.

All of the place-name databases depend on sets of island maps. The shorthand titles given below are meant to generalize the dates of the maps, all of which depended on land surveys and cartography preceding the map's date of publication. Their dates have been rounded to match this relationship.

The first of the databases depends on the 1680 Bochart and Knollis map. This useful map seems to be little known and is missing from Kit S. Kapp's list of Jamaican maps, published in 1968. Its full title is *A New and Exact Mapp of the Island of Jamaica, with the true and just scituation of the several townes, and churches, and alsoe the plantations with their names and the names of their proprietors.* The map was dedicated "To his Excellency Sir Thomas Lynch Knight Captain Generall and Commander in Cheife of his Majesties Island of Jamaica and other the Territories depending thereon" by Charles Bochart and Humphrey Knollis. This helps to date the map, as the governorship of Lynch ran from 1682 to 1684, matching the date 1684 attributed by the British Library. The copy of Bochart and Knollis in the British Library was "printed for Charles Harper", London, at about the scale 1:180,000. It recorded 1,139 names, including personal names. The latter are the names of individuals shown on the map at the location of properties. Many of these were owners or tenants at the time of survey, but some refer to people formerly associated with these places. As well as names, there were symbols denoting towns, churches, sugar works, indigo works, cotton works and provision plantations, cacao walks and "craules for hoggs and pens for cattel".

For the pattern at the middle of the eighteenth century, the 1760 Craskell and Simpson map has been used. Consisting of separate sheets for each of the three counties, the elaborate cartouche of the Cornwall map reads: "To the Right Honorable Robert Earl of Holdernesse, this map of the County of Cornwall, in the Island of Jamaica; (laid down from the papers, and under the direction of Henry Moore Esquire His Majesty's

Lieutenant Governor, and Commander in Chief of that Island, (in the years 1756, –57, –58, –59, –60, and –61;) and from a great number of actual surveys performed by the publishers) is humbly inscribed by His Lordship's most obedient and humble servants Thomas Craskell Engineer and James Simpson Surveyor." The map was engraved and published in London in 1763, and drawn at the scale 1:100,000. Symbols distinguish different types of activity, particularly the works of sugar factories, with names attached, but without indicating the boundaries of landholdings. The total number of names on Craskell and Simpson's maps is 2,276, including personal names.

The most complete map of Jamaica during the period of slavery was that produced by James Robertson, referred to here as the 1800 Robertson map.[27] Based on surveys undertaken between 1796 and 1799, Robertson's map was published in 1804 at the scale 1:63,000, and as on the maps of Craskell and Simpson each county occupied a single large sheet. Places were identified simply as points, with symbols identifying different types of settlements, as was done by Craskell and Simpson. Robertson systematically employed varied fonts to identify the different styles of naming. His symbols include: water mill (sugar), cattle mill (sugar), wind mill (sugar), house (coffee estates, grass pens and all other settlements) and church. Robertson identified a total of 4,595 names, including personal names.

Unlike the preceding maps, the 1880 cadastral series represents a first attempt to identify the boundaries of landholdings as well as their names and (generally separately) the names of the owners. This parish-by-parish map series consists of thirty-five sheets, at the scale 1:15,840, constructed by Thomas Harrison between 1876 and 1891. Harrison was a practising land surveyor who also collected plans of landholdings made by other surveyors, and compiled them into his general cadastral map without always carrying out fresh surveys of the land. This means that the information on his maps reflected former naming as well as the pattern at the end of the nineteenth century. These maps remain the most complete and accessible source of property names for Jamaica, recording a total of 9,554 names. Fresh cadastral surveying was not carried out until the 1960s.

The fifth database derives from the 1950 topographical map that consists of twelve sheets, at the scale 1:50,000, "compiled and drawn by Directorate of Overseas Surveys from air photographs, incorporating some plotting by 1st Marine Survey Company, and revision material (1950) by Survey Dept., Jamaica". A detailed reference to symbols used for features is provided. The total number of places named on this series of maps is 4,586, including natural features, which are distinguished from districts and settlements by variations in typography. Aerial photography greatly improved spatial accuracy and the drawing of contours (at 250-foot intervals) but contributed no names. Very few personal names were included. How exactly the place names on the maps were gathered is not explained, and it can only be assumed that information from earlier maps and reports was added to local knowledge. In Barbados the names for the equivalent map were collected by an individual enthusiast, but the task for Jamaica was far larger.[28] New editions appeared from time to time, after the first of 1950.

Other maps used less systematically in this book include the Jamaica Automobile Association's *Road Map of Jamaica* (referred to here as the 1960 JAS map) and the 1970 topographical map. The former was published in 1960 at the scale 1:250,000 and based on a map produced by the Directorate of Overseas Surveys, London. An index is attached with a total of 795 names. The 1970 topographical map, produced at the scale 1:12,500 and covering more than one hundred sheets, was "prepared using photogrammetric methods by the Survey Department of Jamaica with assistance from the United Nations Development Programme", and based on air photography performed in 1968. Preliminary editions of the sheets began to appear in 1971, and later revisions were made for some areas. The density of contours is greater than on the 1950 map but relatively few additional place names appear.

The 2000 *Jamaica Road Map* was first published by Macmillan Caribbean in 1999, at the scale 1:250,000 for the island at large. Kingston was drawn at 1:30,000 and other towns at various scales. The map built on earlier editions of the 1:356,000 Esso Jamaica road map, which was in turn based on the 1:50,000 topographical map of the Survey Department and designed for use by motorists. The 2000 Jamaica road map includes a

"Town Index", listing 1,113 names, as well as separate indexes to the streets of Kingston and Portmore, and to "Places of Interest" and "Sugar Factories and Estates". Gridlines are imposed on the map of Kingston to enable reference to the street index, and the grid units created by these lines have been employed in the analysis of route names.

Of the five databases used in this study, the largest is that derived from the 1880 cadastral series. Using the words in the names themselves, place-name elements are classified and described by the following variables and elements: type (estate, pen and so on); personal name; physical feature (hill, stony); aesthetic (fair, lovely); soil (marl, salt); scale (little, grand); location (halfway, summit,); physical quality (cool, dry,); flora (bamboo, copse); colour (green, black); fauna (dolphin, ringtail); status (hall, hut); sentiment (content, endeavour); religion (paradise, pilgrim); state (constitution, royal); stage (new, old); classical (arcadia, lethe); ethnicity (African, Irish); and site (bridge, gate). To identify the original sites for which Jamaican places were named from outside the island (transfer names), the descriptive names in the 1880 cadastral series were searched for in gazetteers and dictionaries, as listed in the bibliography. It is assumed that any name with a possible foreign origin was in fact transferred from that place and that in every case the transfer was from the original source. Thus, Newcastle (the name of several places in Jamaica) is assumed to be transferred from the well-known city Newcastle upon Tyne in northeastern England rather than the smaller English Newcastle-under-Lyme or the Newcastle Emlyn in Wales, and, further, that it has not been created independently in Jamaica from the elements *New* and *Castle* (the form New Castle also naming several Jamaican places). Place names which are common and widely dispersed – such as Newton, Sutton and Weston – have been rejected as potential transfer names, while names which are not common but occur more than once were attributed to the largest of the originals. The great majority of names are in fact unique, and many are associated with small places.

In the cadastral database, place names are allocated according to a system of quadrats or grid squares, namely the square grid units on the 1950 topographical map, with three-kilometre sides. Approximately one thousand of these quadrats contain land. In addition to the place-name data described above, a number of common variables are applied to the quadrats, such as elevation, slope and rainfall. The quadrat-grid used for the 1880 cadastral series has been applied also to the Bochart and Knollis 1680 map, the Craskell and Simpson 1760 map, the Robertson 1800 map, and the 1950 topographical map. The last-named four maps were coded for named natural topographic features, both on land and at sea, whereas this was not done for the 1880 cadastral series.

Additional sources of place names are found in lists of various sorts. For the period of slavery, there are the crop accounts, returns of registrations of slaves, and claims for compensation made by slaveowners at the abolition of slavery in 1834. The last of these lists is the most valuable, because it is comprehensive and links the personal names of slaveowners to place names – specifically property and town names – and provides more complete versions of the names than are supplied by Robertson's 1800 map. Most importantly, these lists are the most complete sets of data that include generic labels, such as *estate, pen* and the like.[29]

Whereas the generic terms are typically explicit, the descriptive words used in place names are sometimes more difficult to interpret. Complete and unique personal names applied to routes, such as Marcus Garvey and Mandela, are straightforward, but Cherry, Diamond, Temple, West and York might or might not be derived from surnames. Similarly, Montgomery (Avenue, Close, Road, Terrace, Way) could refer to a personal name, surname or given name, or to a Welsh town or former county, or even to somewhere in the United States. All descriptives and, indeed, generic terms must be considered in context in order to allocate them to the most probable category.

MEANINGS

How might a study of Jamaica's place names contribute to a more complete understanding of the island's history? The naming of places directly reflects power relations within a community, and the maps and other documents which record place names are without doubt social constructions.[30] The documentary, visual and oral sources available for Jamaican history are rich and diverse but say less than might be hoped for on a number of significant subjects, such as perceptions of the environment and the origins of its colonial settlers. It is particularly in areas such as these that place-name studies have much to contribute.

Differences in cultural patterns and principles of environmental perception, as well as variations in population density and mobility, affect the overall frequency of place names. In terms of place-name density, Jamaica falls somewhere between Old World European and New World continental American patterns. George R. Stewart, in the 1940s, estimated that the United States had three million known place names with another one million obsolete terms. Stewart found this to be a very low density by comparison with European countries. He recognized that the comparison was affected by variations in what was identified as a place name, but the difference was so great that it could be assumed to reflect a reality. Jamaica, with roughly one place name per square kilometre, has a density about three times as great as is found in the United States but still less than the European pattern. These differences in place-name density not only reflect variations in economy and settlement but also illuminate contrasting understandings of the landscape and its definable elements.[31]

More obviously, a historical study of place names enables analysis of change over time or, equally interesting, a lack of change that demonstrates the conservative virtues of not changing names. An advantage of place names as a type of historical evidence is that their inertia provides a reading of the perceptions and attitudes of the initial name-givers and thus of the earliest periods of colonization. The great value of place-name study for an understanding of very long periods of time lies in this inertia and the existence of the past in the names that can be collected now. In the short term, the too-frequent changing of names creates confusion, but in the longer term archaic names can come to appear inappropriate, even patently racist or otherwise offensive, and the failure to change may come to be seen as the greater fault.

Modern Jamaicans speak a variety of English referred to by linguists as Jamaican English. In recognition of its distinctiveness, *Dictionary of Jamaican*

English (*DJE*) was published in 1967, edited by F.G. Cassidy and R.B. Le Page, and a revised edition appeared in 1980. The purpose of this dictionary was to record those words which did not appear in the *Oxford English Dictionary* (*OED*) and that could be regarded as distinctively Jamaican in their meaning or usage. Thus an interesting question is how far the place names of Jamaica make use of these Jamaican words and how "Jamaican" they might be. Similarly, how far can the creole combining of vocabulary and grammar from English and African languages be identified in the island's place names? Looked at another way, it may be asked how much the study of Jamaica's place names might contribute to studies of Jamaican language from a linguistic point of view.[32]

The current repertoire of Jamaican place names remains heavily dominated by British names. The same applies to other forms of naming, most obviously personal names which similarly remain largely British or, more recently, Anglo-American or Afro-American. Place names are less subject to fashion than personal names, because people are relatively short-lived and new generations can easily be given new – fashionable – names. Although some place names contain strong elements of Jamaican English, derived often from African language, it is the British tradition of naming that has persisted, effectively undisturbed by the ending of slavery in 1838 or by political independence in 1962. Why has this "British" system survived so well whereas Taino and, to a somewhat lesser extent, Spanish place names were both unable to withstand their respective onslaughts? The most obvious reasons for this difference lie in the continuity of colonial government and population. Equally important were the relative completeness of settlement achieved by the end of the eighteenth century and the continuity of ownership of large landholdings that commonly gave names to districts. Further, the place names of Jamaica, whatever their origins, became naturalized and accepted as part of the creole culture that marked Jamaicans as a people with a particular identity. Thus the names of the island ceased to sound foreign but rather came to be heard as indigenous – rooted in the environment – not as words introduced from some other place. The names became part of the natural language of place, Jamaican.

CHAPTER TWO

Names and Name-Givers

ALL OF THE PEOPLES WHO SETTLED JAMAICA brought with them not only their own personal names but also a particular knowledge of naming practices and an inventory of names. They arrived with a vocabulary and a grammar of space. Although all of them contributed, the ability of the different contingents of arrivals to apply these norms to the Jamaican landscape varied quite dramatically, and the place names, rather than giving explicit clues to the origins of the Jamaican people, reflect much more strongly the origins of the name-giving population. Economic and political power went together with the domination of land and people, and the power to give names to places.[1] The way the process worked out in Jamaica meant that a large proportion of the island's place names derived from the European colonizers' personal names and homelands rather than from the African places from which most of the people came.

The inventory of modern Jamaican place names includes a significant proportion derived directly or indirectly from the personal names of colonizing people. These are the eponyms, most of them drawn from surnames rather than first names. In the cadastral series of habitation place names, compiled at the end of the nineteenth century, as many as 42 per cent were eponyms. When a colonizing name-giver chose not to use a personal name, a second strong inclination was to give a Jamaican place a name already known from somewhere else. These are the transfer names. Of the place names in the cadastral series that were not eponymous, 44 per cent were transfers from places outside the island, making 2,373 names of this type. Together, the eponyms and the transfer names dominated the settlement landscape around 1880 but, individually, none of them was among the most common of the Jamaican place names. The common names are discussed in the next chapter, whereas in this one the names discussed almost all belong to the transfer type.

In some cases, the choice of a name reflected a simple, direct transfer of the name of the place the name-giver had left behind. In other cases, the name-giver chose a place name because it had some resonance in the Jamaican landscape, such as a perceived similarity of physiography or climate. There was also the possibility of irony, that the choice might be decidedly inappropriate or paradoxical. But choice was always limited by knowledge, even when irony was the objective, and the large number of known place names and the small scale of reference encourage confidence in the ability of the samples to provide useful clues to origins. The decision to name a new place by reference to a place left behind represented a conscious choice, a rejection of alternative modes of naming.

Of the 2,373 transfer place names in the 1880 cadastral series, 86 per cent derived from Great Britain and Ireland and another 6 per cent from continental European places. Thus the European and specifically British element is dominant. After these, the minor contributors were Asia (2.5 per cent), North America (2.4 per cent), Africa (1.9 per cent), South America (0.9 per cent) and other places in the Caribbean (0.3 per cent). These patterns varied relatively little across the different kinds of economic enterprise, except that livestock pens were marginally more likely to have British names and small-farming places less likely to be named in this way. Of the 802 sugar estates identified on Robertson's 1800 map, 38 per cent had names potentially derived from other places, a higher ratio than for all property names. Of the 304 sugar estates named for other places, 85 per cent took their names from Britain and Ireland, 7 per cent from Europe, 2 per cent from each of North America, South America and Asia, 1 per cent from Africa, and just 0.3 per cent from the Caribbean. The broad outlines of the pattern are clearly drawn and had great continuity. The British naming of the land left little trace of what had gone before.

The process and pattern of place-naming in Jamaica was not simply a matter of colonialism. In some of the many regions of the world that were heavily colonized by Europeans since Columbus, substantial numbers of indigenous place names were retained. Elsewhere, place names chosen by founder colonizers were retained when new colonial powers replaced them. In Jamaica few indigenous names and only a sprinkling of Spanish ones survived, though several of the survivors have a prominent place in the landscape. The reasons for this lack of continuity are that the Spanish quickly decimated the Taino population and had no great respect for the aboriginal names, and that Spanish settlement of Jamaica remained sparse and undeveloped. The English conquest found a thin population and a poorly developed system of place names. Rapid expansion of the plantation economy under the English resulted in a much greater population density and a system of governance and settlement that gave power to landed proprietors and established large-scale landholdings as the basis of a network of routes and central places. It was within this ferment that a large proportion of the place names emerged from personal names, transfers from other places (short and long distance) and local creations.[2]

Jamaica's experience was broadly similar to that of most of the Caribbean islands colonized by the British and similar to that of British North America, where the home places of governors and colonists in the British Isles were favoured sources. This contrasted with the practice of the Spanish, Portuguese and French colonies, where the names of saints and national heroes were more likely to provide inspiration. Jamaica, however, has a higher proportion of "British" place names than is now found in North America, even in the eastern coastal regions most heavily colonized by the British.[3]

Within the Caribbean, the Jamaican pattern can be contrasted with the unusual case of Trinidad. As argued by the linguist K.M. Laurence, modern Trinidad possesses "a plethora of Amerindian, Spanish and French toponyms" that survive from the period before the beginning of British colonization at the very end of the eighteenth century. Trinidad remained a backwater of Spanish settlement much longer than did Jamaica, and missions had a much larger role, assimilating Amerindian names into the language. Although Trinidad was never a colonial possession of France, the great inflow of French immigrants in the late eighteenth century had a profound and lasting impact on the language and toponymy of the island, including the gallicization of pre-existing Amerindian and Spanish names. The British influence was injected into this powerful linguistic ferment, with an acceptance of what was already in place largely determined by the continuity of ownership and of demography. This contrasted with the case of Jamaica where, in the seventeenth century, the English assumed a relatively blank slate after the Spanish were driven from the island.[4] Other late-settled British colonies in the eastern Caribbean had a range of experience, with the role of British place names reflecting the "language affiliation" of each island rather than demographic weight. Tobago has the most English names and Dominica and St Vincent a polyglot heritage derived from Amerindian, French and English names, while Grenada changed the least after British settlement. In all of these islands, as in Jamaica, the weakness of African influence is striking.[5]

TAINO PLACE NAMES

Columbus heard and recorded Jamaica's name – *Yamaye* or *Xamaye* – even before he reached the island. In the course of his second voyage, he sailed west from Hispaniola to Cuba and coasted along the southern end of that island towards Guantanamo (named by Columbus Puerto Grande) and Santiago de Cuba. It was there that he was first told of the large island lying to the south, *Jamaica*.[6] The people who offered the name called themselves Taino, as did the first people of Jamaica.

The Taino of Jamaica shared language and culture with the ancient peoples of the Greater Antilles, being part of the same migration stream out of the South American mainland that brought them to the island as late as AD 700. The naming of the island was relatively straightforward. The *ca* of *Jamaica* is a locative suffix typical of Amerindian languages, identifying *Jamaica* as a word meaning the place or location where the Jamai (or Yamaye) people lived, much as in the *ca* of the Mexican *Oaxaca* and the *go*

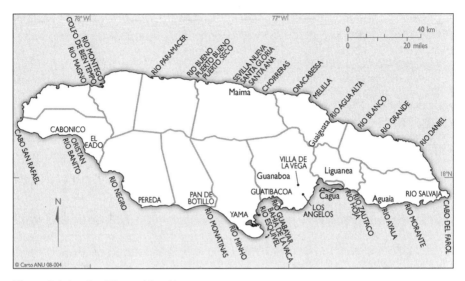

Figure 2.1 Jamaica: Taino and Spanish names

of *Tobago*. Alternative, often poetic, interpretations translated *Jamaica* as "land of springs" or "island of springs", but the former attribution is more convincing.[7]

Jamaica has always been the proper name of the island, challenged only briefly in the early sixteenth century. The name's longevity may seem surprising in the context of colonization, but the example is not unique. All of the neighbouring islands – Cuba, Cayman and the Bahamas – retained their Amerindian names, and Haiti (meaning "rugged, mountainous") was regained following the revolution. In contrast, the Dominican Republic, Puerto Rico and most of the eastern Caribbean islands took new names.[8] In Jamaica, the retention of the Taino island-name was not matched by the names applied to places within the island. Although the Taino named many places, few of these are known and few have survived in common use in the landscape (Figure 2.1). Even fewer of the people survived the devastation that followed European colonization.

Among the Taino place names, an important survivor is *Liguanea*, which names the sweeping plain that slopes evenly down to the harbour of

Kingston and provides the site for the city. The name derives from *iguana*, a once common reptile, and has survived in several forms – Liguanea Plain AND, Liguanea Ridge AND, Liguanea Villa AND – and found new life in Liguanea Plaza AND. In the middle of the eighteenth century, Patrick Browne referred to "the mountains of New Liguanea". Another long-term survivor is *Guanaboa*, perhaps derived from a word for the fruit soursop, now used with an English extension to make it Guanaboa Vale CTH. Although Guanaboa has an equivalent and perhaps original place name in Hispaniola, the possible direct reference to the soursop tree makes it difficult to conclude that it can be counted as a transfer name.[9] In general, it seems certain that although the Taino brought their language with them from South America, they brought few place names intact. This pattern contrasts with that for the later Spanish and British colonization, perhaps because of the long-extended process of migration for the Taino but equally a product of the invasive character of the European settlement that sought to write on a clean slate with an imperial pencil.

The modern river known as the Wag Water derives from the Taino *Guaiguata*, and it appeared on sixteenth-century maps in that form. Early English attempts to employ the name led to the Spanish-sounding Agua Alta, meaning deep water, and the second part of *Guaiguata* was later resolved to the English *water*. What the Taino intended by the original name remains uncertain. Similarly, Cassidy has argued that "*Yallahs* has gone through two distinct changes, first in Spanish from *Aguaia*, perhaps Arawak, to *Ayala*, then in English to *Yallahs*, which was for a time understood, following a common pronunciation, as *Yellow River* and district".[10]

Where the Spanish attempted substantial settlement, the Taino place names disappeared quickly and are now unknown. Columbus, during the nine months he spent marooned near St Anns Bay in 1503 and 1504, noted other villages, including Aguacadiba and Ameyro. The first significant Spanish site, Sevilla Nueva, commenced in 1508, was above the large coastal Taino town called Maima.[11] None of these Taino place names survived. Other Taino names persisted through the relatively light settling by the Spanish, only to be swept aside by the British. The place now known as Port Royal was called by the Taino *Caguay* or *Caguaya*. The Spanish accepted this name, and the English first rendered it as *Cagway* but quickly replaced it. Long argued in 1774 that *Cagua* or *Cagway* was "a corruption probably of caragua, the Indian name for the coratoe, or great aloe, which overspreads the adjacent Saltpan Hill".[12]

Recent rather than historic naming which uses Taino vocabulary has been rare. An exception is the village of Arawak ANN, which first appeared on the Jamaica Automobile Association map of 1960, located behind Mammee Bay between Ocho Rios and St Anns Bay. Inez Knibb Sibley argued that it "received this name from the fact that Arawak remains were once found there". The Arawak Hotel was constructed nearby and, when it opened its doors in 1957, was the largest in the island, but in less than ten years it was renamed the Jamaica Hilton Hotel. Similarly drawing on the archaeological heritage, the Coyaba River Garden and Museum was opened near Ocho Rios in 1993. It was said then that "To the Arawaks, Coyaba was a special word, it meant paradise, or heaven". The Taino did not in fact share this eschatological understanding but rather thought of life after death as another form of life on earth. *Coyaba* was used by the novelist Peter Abrahams to name his home in the Red Hills AND in the 1950s, identifying it as a "secluded, tranquil" place, not easily reached, the type of place the Arawaks chose to bury their dead.[13]

SPANISH PLACE NAMES

Columbus first set foot on Jamaica on 5 May 1494, describing it as "darkly green Xamayca . . . the fairest island that eyes have beheld". According to Cassidy, the correspondence of the king of Spain between 1519 and 1526 expressed a preference for the name St Iago by making many references to "the Island of St. Iago, called Jamaica".[14] Neither St Iago nor Santiago ever appeared on a map as the island's name. Charles Leslie in 1739 claimed that Columbus had named Jamaica "St. James's Isle; but that name it soon lost, and was generally called Jamaica, which it still retains".[15] The full modern form – Jamaica – appeared as early as 1512, on Peter Martyr's chart.

Acceptance of the Taino name for Jamaica was rarely paralleled by retention of names for places within the island. The imposition of Spanish names commenced almost immediately, as an important symbolic means of installing the imperial presence. However, although the Spanish practised a harsh system of exploitation, their colonization and settlement of Jamaica were of a relatively weak variety because the island lacked the precious metals that dazzled the Spanish and lured them to the mainland. The population of Spanish colonists and enslaved people brought from Africa was never large. Jamaica effectively became a backwater of empire, with a thin spread of population and economic activity, and a weak system of Spanish place names.

Columbus made landfall at what is now known as St Anns Bay but was first called by him Santa Gloria "on account of the extreme beauty of its country" and later Santa Ana. He sailed west along the north coast, naming Puerto Bueno (now Rio Bueno) and Golfo de bien Tiempo (Fair Weather Gulf, now Montego Bay, derived from the Spanish *manteca*, lard), then along the south coast Bahia de la Vaca (Cow Bay, now Portland Bight) and Cabo del Farol (Cape of the Lighthouse or of the Signal Fire, now Morant Point).[16]

Under the Spanish, from 1494 to 1655, the Jamaican landscape was dominated by names of Spanish derivation (see Figure 2.1). As well as the first major settlement at Sevilla Nueva, another short-lived town was established as Melilla, but the capital was soon relocated to Villa de la Vega (Spanish Town). Sevilla, Santa Ana and Morante were place names transferred from Spain, whereas Melilla (most probably at the site of Port Maria) came from a Spanish-ruled town on the Barbary Coast, and Oristan (the southwestern district of Jamaica running from Savanna la Mar to Bluefields) took its name either from a municipality in the province of Barcelona or perhaps from a town in Sardinia.[17]

The Spanish names of natural features, particularly rivers, survived more successfully than the habitation names. As will be seen in chapter 5, streams often retain the Spanish form *rio*: Rio Cobre and Rio Minho, for example. Edward Long in his 1774 *History of Jamaica* argued that the first European settlers had been a mixture of Spanish and Portuguese and that therefore Jamaica contained mountains and rivers that had been named in both of these languages. He believed, for instance, that "the river Minho was probably so called after one of the same name in Portugal". Other names taken from Portugal that appear in the cadastral series are Pera THS and Madeira THS. Most often, the British settlement meant a fundamental replacement, so that Rio Zautaco became Hope River.[18]

Some of the place names that derived from the Spanish occupation were anglicized rather than corrupted. Near Spanish Town, the *Los Angeles* of the Spanish became The Angels. The Round Hill of Vere had been called by the Spanish *Pan de Botillo*. But name changes did not always persist – for instance, it seems odd to hear Long say in 1774, "Ocho Rios, or, as it is now more commonly called, Chereiras Bay".[19] In 1890 Edgar Mayhew Bacon and Eugene Murray Aaron observed that "The ch in Ocho is pronounced soft by the inhabitants, in violence to its Spanish origin. *Chereras* it used to be – the Bay of the Waterfalls; a name certainly as descriptive as it was poetic. The present appellation, 'Eight Rivers,' does not do justice to the many streams that rush foaming down the slopes and cool their boiling little bodies in the sea."[20] Although the notion that Ocho Rios means simply Eight Rivers seems obvious now, the corruption of the Spanish *chorreras* does point to the many waterfalls, some of which tumble into the sea. The usual Spanish words for waterfall are *la cascada* or *catarata* or *salto de agua*. *Chorrera* means "spout" but is occasionally applied to waterfalls. Of Black River, Long said, "The Eastern side retains its antient name of Palléta, or Parratee Bay." The town of Lacovia ELZ, he said, "has its name perhaps from a corruption of the Spanish words la-agua-via, the watery way, or lago-via, the way by the lake; for this part of the country, being very low and flat, is sometimes overflowed with water, from the large morass which surrounds it".[21]

The name of Columbus appears in no significant Jamaican place names. Columbus Heights ANN was built only in the 1970s, as a residential complex above the tourist town of Ocho Rios. Earlier, in the 1960s, the Kaiser Bauxite Company set up Columbus Park TRL as a tourist and craft site overlooking Discovery Bay, but this was not a place where people lived. Spanish Town provides a clear-cut memory of the Spanish presence, but modern townhouse developments with names like Santa Fe simply sound American.[22]

BRITISH PLACE NAMES

When the English took Jamaica from the Spanish in 1655 they commenced a radical transformation of the economy, introducing a plantation system that quickly came to be dominated by large-scale sugar production based on the labour of enslaved Africans. The total population grew rapidly, from about 50,000 in 1700 to 350,000 in 1800, and Jamaica became a major world producer of sugar and coffee. The Atlantic slave trade to Jamaica ended in 1808 and the institution of slavery was abolished in 1838, follow- ing a four-year interim period called the Apprenticeship. With a few important exceptions, the land was by then fully settled. Thus the giving of names to particular places within Jamaica was largely complete by the end of the period of slavery, and throughout that period the people with power to give names were the British colonists, particularly the wealthy men who owned the land and the people. The pre-existing names applied by the Taino and the Spanish were largely forgotten or obliterated, except for some notable physical features, such as rivers and mountains.[23]

By the end of the nineteenth century, as measured by the cadastral series, "Spanish" place names made up barely 1 per cent of the total stock of transferred names in Jamaica. The thirty Spanish names did no better than equal the number from Germany, and both of these countries con- tributed fewer than the thirty-five transferred from France. This poor showing resulted from the lack of respect the English colonists had for the names the Spanish had given to places, problems of language that meant Spanish names lacked the descriptive qualities (and hence the meaning) enjoyed by places named in English, and the more general enmity between British and Spanish people down to the end of the eighteenth century. In the cadastral series, a large proportion of the "Spanish" names in fact had a strong British association. One-half (fifteen) of the places were called Gibraltar and another one-quarter (seven) Trafalgar, both celebrating British victories. Gibraltar, attached to the Spanish mainland, had been taken by the British in 1704 and withstood a long siege from 1779 to 1783. Cape Trafalgar is a headland near the Straits of Gibraltar and the scene of Nelson's naval victory over Napoleon and the French fleet in 1805. The names Gibraltar and Trafalgar were widely scattered across Jamaica at the end of the nineteenth century, and appeared also in the names of streets, with Gibraltar's presence reinforced during World War II when some of its people were given refuge at camps in the island. Apart from Gibraltar and Trafalgar, the only Spanish names in the cadastral series were Carthagena JAS, Castile Fort Pen AND, La Caridad CTH, Madrid PLD, Navarre TRL and Seville ANN.

The heavy imprint of British names on Jamaica reflects both the dominance of a British class of planter-settlers and the imposition of an essentially English system of local government within the context of a slave society. Jamaica was divided into primary administrative units called parishes, and these were later combined into counties, on the English model. Three counties were established in 1758, to expedite the holding of courts: Cornwall in the west (matching the westernmost county of England), Middlesex, appropriately in the middle, and Surrey in the east (probably because it contained Kingston, as did the English county) (see Figure 1.1). Kingston was the county town of Surrey, Spanish Town of Middlesex, and Savanna la Mar of Cornwall.[24] The county names remained fixed and undisputed, and of no great consequence. They were rarely applied to places within the county boundaries. Cornwall county had a Cornwall Estate and a Cornwall Mountain in each of Westmoreland and St James, but Cornwall Pen was located in faraway Portland. The modern institutions Cornwall College and Cornwall Regional Hospital are both located in Montego Bay, within the county. Only one of the five places called Middlesex was found in the county, the other four all in distant parts of Cornwall. Surrey had no places named for the county. In modern times, county names were used occasionally to serve as a label for a company or corporation, most often in Cornwall, sometimes in Middlesex, but rarely in Surrey.

The number and arrangement of the parishes was changed often between the English conquest and the establishment of Crown Colony government. The first seven parishes were created by the Assembly in 1664: St Thomas, St David, St Andrew, St John, Clarendon, Port Royal and St Catherine. A further division in 1677 increased the number of parishes to fifteen.[25] Westmoreland was carved out of St Elizabeth in 1703. Twenty years later, Westmoreland was in turn reduced by the creation of Hanover, and Portland was created from parts of St George and St Thomas in the East. In 1770 Trelawny was extracted from St James, and in 1814 Manchester was created from sections of Clarendon, Vere and St Elizabeth.

Immediately after the abolition of slavery, a scheme was advanced in the House of Assembly for a subdivision of the existing parishes and the creation of a new level of governance. For example, St Andrew was to be divided into five new parishes, named St Joseph, St Christopher, Liguanea, Stoney Hill and St James. Confusingly, the old parish of St James was to be made up of St James, Marley, Rose Hall, Springfield, Montpelier and Bellefont. Clarendon was to be divided simply into north, south, east and west sections. The new names generally came from existing regional place names, together with the well-established tradition of honouring the saints. Westmoreland was the most saintly of all, subdivided into Savanna la Mar, St Pauls, St Peters, St John, Trinity and St Thomas. All of these new subdivisions, numbering eighty-four, were in future to be known as parishes, while the old parishes became twenty-one counties, and the three former counties became "provinces". Part of the logic of the new scheme was to ensure that one clergyman was allocated to each parish. Diagrams of the new boundaries were drawn and population statistics collected, but the only concrete outcome of the plan was the creation of the new parish of Metcalfe in 1841, formed from parts of St Mary and St George.[26] The proliferation of parishes was now at an end (Figure 2.2). In 1867 they were reduced to the present fourteen and finally fixed.

Jamaicans often think of themselves as parishioners and inhabitants of named districts, but hardly ever as defined by the counties. The fixity of the parish names since 1867 has remained strong and a common reference for individual identity, as the parishes are characterized in distinct ways. Few parish names developed aliases, though St Ann did become known as the "garden parish". Pronunciation has been disputed. For example, modern speakers refer regularly to Cla-*ren*-don, with the emphasis on the second syllable rather than the first as preferred by the more refined, while the occasional modern emphasis on the first syllable of Han-over or

Figure 2.2 Jamaica: Parishes, 1841

Man-chester is considered equally deplorable. The argument for particular pronunciations is sometimes based on supposed English practice.

One dispute over the spelling of a parish name occurred in the late twentieth century. Westmoreland had maintained its spelling, apparently without question, until it was argued that the parish was named for Lord Westmorland and should be spelled the same way, though it may be equally plausible that the Jamaican parish was named for the English county, which was spelled alternatively with and without the *e* throughout the seventeenth and eighteenth centuries. Whatever the merits of the case, government agencies accepted the argument that Westmorland was correct and began using this spelling, and it was this form that appeared on the topographic survey maps of the 1950s. In 1984 Howard Wedemire, member for South Eastern Westmoreland, brought to the House of Representatives copies of official census publications, the *National Physical Plan* and the *Statistical Yearbook*, in all of which the parish was spelled "Westmorland", and asked, "Why is it that nobody can spell Westmoreland?" The matter might seem trivial, said Wedemire, but he thought it indicated the way in which recent governments had neglected the parish, though it had carried great weight when the economy rested on sugar. He added, "I don't know how many people are familiar with the fact that Westmorelites and

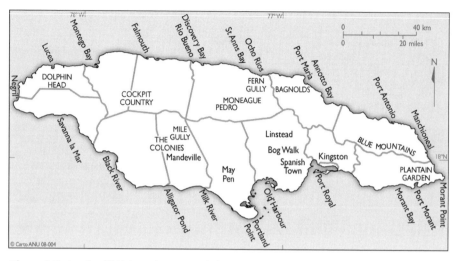

Figure 2.3 Jamaica: Districts, main towns and places, 1950

Westmorelanders often refer to themselves not as Westmorelites. Not as Westmorelanders. But as belonging to the Cow Tail."[27]

In addition to the formal regions of government, some areas of Jamaica are known as districts, and these are often associated with a sense of local identity. The 1950 topographical map named several districts, partly recognizing defunct parishes but also recording areas which identified with these descriptive titles. These districts were strongly concentrated, only partly because most of the reduction of parishes had taken place in the eastern end of the island (Figure 2.3). Districts named – sometimes using antique orthography – to match the old parishes were St Thomas in ye/the Vale, Vere, St Dorothy, St George, Port Royal, St David and Upper St David. Important towns and ports that gave their names to districts were Moneague, Retreat, Richmond, Port Maria, Annotto Bay, Morant and Manchioneal. Others marked less well-known areas but places that had come to have a regional identity, as in Mile Gully, Grove Place, Davyton, Lime Savanna, Pedro, Bagnolds and Salt Pond. More comprehensive was the District of Plantain Garden River and Port Morant, which drew together a functional region rarely referred to in this way in other media.

Different again was the District Known By the Name of Look Behind, which referenced a kind of folk rather than cartographic naming. Located on the southeastern edge of the Cockpit Country – beyond Me No Sen You No Come and Quick Step – Look Behind was used in 1957 by Mona Macmillan, an English visitor, for the title of her book *The Land of Look Behind: A Study of Jamaica*. Macmillan saw it as a metaphor for island society. The idea struck her, she said, when she "saw that blank space on the map (in the Cockpit country) across which is written 'district known as the land of look behind'" and she applied the attitude to social distrust, fear of thieves and an unwillingness to confront the past.[28] The map she was looking at was the 1950 topographic sheet. By the end of the twentieth century, most maps called it simply District of Look Behind. Cockpit Country, discussed in chapter 4, may be regarded as another variety of regional identity, but it lacked a substantial human population. Another variety was shown on the 1950 map as the Locality Called The Colonies. Neither The Colonies nor Look Behind appeared on Robertson's 1800 map, but they were well known by the end of the nineteenth century.

Related to the idea of *district* was *quarter*, the term applied most famously to Middle Quarters ELZ, now known as a settlement at a significant intersection but shown as an extensive district on Robertson's 1800 map as well as on the 1950 topographical map. The latter also had Surinam Quarters WLD. The only other *quarter* surviving on the 1950 map was Fat Hog Quarter, naming a small place rather than an extensive district. Craskell and Simpson's 1760 map showed only Middle Quarter River, the district name emerging some time after.

The large urban settlements of Jamaica, notably Kingston, came to be divided up into zones on directional principles, using the points of the compass, and these sometimes entered regional place names. Most popular and persistent is the distinction West/East. West Kingston came to define a specific area of poverty to the immediate west of the Coronation Market, and this was often carefully distinguished from the broader "western Kingston". East Kingston was always much more mixed in socioeconomic status. These terms were also applied to routes within the towns, as in East Queen Street and Upper and Lower King Street. North Kingston is an uncommon term, generally replaced by Lower St Andrew. *South* is also unusual, though it appeared in Southside in the 1980s, naming an informally defined downtown territory, stretching from the harbour north towards East Queen Street and flowing a little beyond King Street to the west and South Camp Road to the east.[29] More broadly, the distinction between North Coast and South Coast became attached to the settlements along them, particularly in the period of tourism, when towns, resorts and attractions melded into a continuum. West, and to a lesser extent East, also had some currency at the island level.

Within the overwhelming dominance of British place names transferred

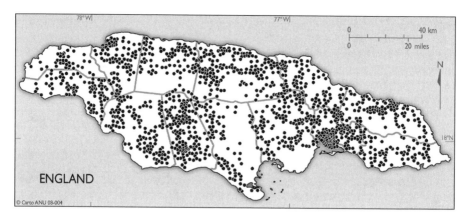

Figure 2.4 Jamaica: Transfer names from England

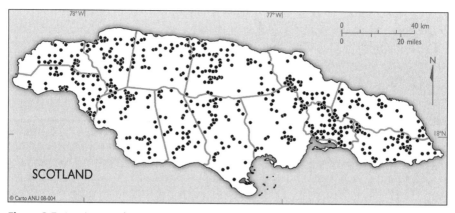

Figure 2.5 Jamaica: Transfer names from Scotland

to Jamaica, names derived specifically from England were also dominant but less dramatically so. "English" names accounted for 54 per cent of the overall total and 63 per cent of those transferred from "Britain". Next in importance was Scotland, the source of 26 per cent of the British names. Thus England and Scotland together supplied 89 per cent of all the place names drawn from Britain and Ireland, with just 8 per cent coming from Ireland and 3 per cent from Wales. British place names were broadly distributed across the Jamaican landscape with little evidence of clustering. Those from England spread like a blanket, thinning significantly only along

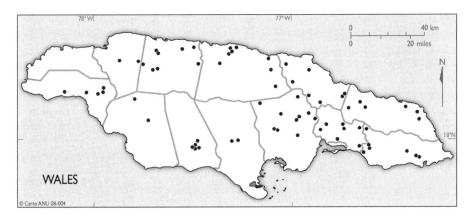

Figure 2.6 Jamaica: Transfer names from Wales

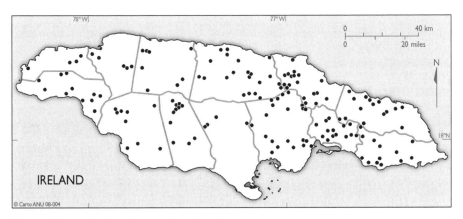

Figure 2.7 Jamaica: Transfer names from Ireland

the eastern borders of Clarendon (Figure 2.4). Much the same applied to the names transferred from Scotland, except for some clustering in northern St Elizabeth and along the margins of St Catherine and St Mary, and some relative sparseness in eastern St Elizabeth, southern Clarendon and northwestern St Catherine, where the English had been pioneers of the sugar industry (Figure 2.5). Names from Wales were more common in the eastern parishes than in the west, though with a minor clustering in southern Manchester that included Newport, Plinlimmon, Snowdon and Wales (Figure 2.6). Names from Ireland showed a similar eastern weighting, together with a striking absence from most of Clarendon (Figure 2.7).

Southern England was the most important source of Jamaica's transfer place-names, accounting for 40 per cent of the British Isles derivations, with a second clustering in the Midlands (Figure 2.8). There was a strong continuity in naming, at least from the late eighteenth century, and the distribution matches that for other plantation colonies of British America.[30] Within southern England it was the southeast that supplied the largest number of place names – around 30 per cent if London is included. The southwest was also significant, notably the region around the port of Bristol, which had developed in the early eighteenth century as a leading investor in West Indian commerce and the Atlantic slave trade. Here it is possible to discern some significant long-term change, the weight of the southeast declining from 25 per cent on Robertson's 1800 map to 18 per cent in the post-slavery cadastral series. London, on the other hand, gradually increased its proportion, as did southwest England.

Overall, England contributed a total of 923 names (taking account of extensions) and of these, 78 per cent were used for just one place in Jamaica, 12 per cent for two places, 5 per cent for three places, and the remaining 5 per cent duplicated in larger numbers up to a maximum of 15 appearances (Richmond Hill). The repetitions were significant but less so than the repetitions for other kinds of names, as discussed in the next chapter. The numbers increase for the transfer names if the various extensions are added together, though they still do not rival the leading sentiment names. In all its forms Richmond made thirty-four appearances: Richmond 3, Richmond Castle 1, Richmond Estate 2, Richmond Hill 15,

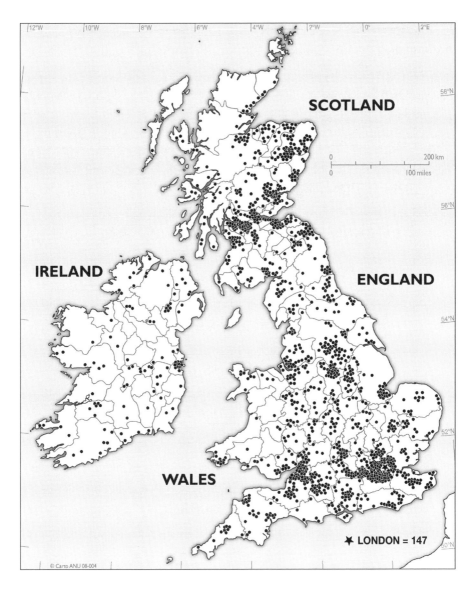

Figure 2.8 British Isles: Places named in Jamaica, cadastral series. Each dot indicates the presumed origin of a Jamaican place name, one dot for each occurrence in Jamaica. The county boundaries are those that existed prior to the 1972 Local Government Act.

Richmond Hill Plantation 1, Richmond Lodge 1, Richmond Mountain 1, Richmond Park 4, Richmond Pen 3, Richmond Plantation 1 and Richmond Vale 2. Windsor also made thirty-four appearances in different guises: Windsor 5, Windsor Castle 6, Windsor Castle Estate 3, Windsor Castle Mountain 1, Windsor Castle Pen 1, Windsor Estate 2, Windsor Farm 1, Windsor Forest 4, Windsor Forest Estate 1, Windsor Forest Pen 1, Windsor Lodge 4, Windsor Mountain 1, Windsor Park 1, Windsor Park Pen 1, Windsor Pen 1 and Windsor Plantation 1. After these came Clifton (24), Wakefield (15), Kensington (14), Claremont (12), Highgate (12), Oxford (11), Brighton (10), Cambridge (10) and Hampstead (10).

The leading English place names, Richmond and Windsor, are towns on the River Thames, to the west of London, both of them boasting royal residences. There is another English Richmond, in North Yorkshire, and this is the place after which the southern one, in the county of Surrey, was named. Richmond Castle, one of Britain's great Norman fortresses, still stands as an impressive ruin above Yorkshire's River Swale. Whether the "Lass of Richmond Hill", celebrated in song, was from Yorkshire or Surrey remains a matter of debate. The Surrey Richmond was called Sheen ("shelters") until 1500 when Henry VII renamed it after his earldom in Yorkshire, the original meaning "strong hill", derived from the Old French *riche* and *mont*. Richmond Hill was therefore something of a tautology. Windsor, in Berkshire, meaning "windlass-place on a river bank", has been the principal residence of English monarchs since William the Conqueror. Kensington was the home of yet another London royal palace. Highgate in north London was named for its tollgate, while Hampstead, a suburb to the northwest, was originally a spa but came to be favoured by artists and writers from Constable to Keats. The university towns Oxford and Cambridge lay west and north of London, respectively. Brighton, in Sussex, on the coast south of London, was a poor fishing village called Brighthelmstone at the beginning of the eighteenth century; it became popular as a resort only after 1800. Clifton, meaning "farm by a slope", is more common within England than either Richmond or Windsor, but the key example was the one on the fringes of Bristol. Claremont probably derives from Surrey, the country estate at Esher, within sight of Windsor Castle, famous for its eighteenth-century Palladian mansion and landscaped gardens and the property of the imperial adventurer Clive of India.

Jamaican place names from Scotland accounted for 22 per cent of the overall total of transferred names and 26 per cent of the names from Britain. These proportions placed Scotland second to England as a source, but Scotland is smaller in area and population. At the beginning of the nineteenth century, Scotland's population was only one-fifth that of England, so that, per capita, the Scottish supplied almost twice as many names to Jamaica as did England. This pattern contrasts with British North America, where Scottish names were relatively less frequently transferred than English names.[31] The strong showing of Scotland in Jamaica will not surprise the many Jamaicans who acknowledge Scottish ancestry, nor will it surprise historians, who have long stressed the role of the Scots in settling and managing the Jamaican economy in the eighteenth century.[32]

Scotland contributed 390 distinct place names to Jamaica, but the rate of duplication was greater than for the English names, with only 45 per cent of the names being used just once, probably because they drew on a smaller pool and a smaller geographical region. Further, most of the Scottish names came from the Lowlands, in the zone running from Glasgow to Edinburgh, and from the northeast, with little reference to the thinly populated northwestern Highlands (see Figure 2.8). The Lowlands have a relatively high proportion of anglicized Gaelic names – such as Glasgow from *Glaschu* – whereas the northwest is generally regarded as the site of the last stronghold of the Gaelic language.[33]

The most popular of the names from Scotland, in the 1880 cadastral series, was the problematic Hopewell (31 examples), followed by the general Caledonia (12), then Stirling Castle and Glasgow (10 each), Aberdeen and Southfield (8 each), Culloden and Dumfries (7 each), Blackness, Dee Side, Galloway, Inverness, Montrose and Roslin Castle (6 each), Albany, Argyle, Berrydale, Leith and Paisley (5 each), and Dumbarton, Dunbar, Dundee, Dunkeld, Dunrobin, Haddington, Keith Hall, Mount Vernon and Tulloch (4 each). Mount Vernon may alternatively have been applied as a tribute to Admiral Edward Vernon, in celebration of his naval service to the British in the Caribbean – notably his defeat of the Spanish at Porto Bello in 1739 – as part of a popular form of naming parallel to George Washington's application of Mount Vernon to his Virginia property. Next in order, with three examples each, came Armadale, Banff, Burnside, Clydesdale, Craig Head, Craigie, Dalvey, Dornock, Duff House, Elderslie, Ellerslie, Flower Hill, Glen Islay, Kilmarnock, Knapdale, Lennox, Moy Hall, Muirton, Nairn, Roxbro/Roxburgh, Ruthven, Stewarton and Ythanside, followed by Abbey Green, Alves, Arthurs Seat, Auchinbeddie, Bellwood, Benlomond, Burnside, Cathkin, Clydeside, Dumblane, Duplin, Eastwood, Edinburgh Castle, Eglinton, Elphinstowe, Flemington, Freefield, Glenmore, Gordon Castle, Greenock, Home Castle, Jocks Lodge, Kenmure, Killiekrankie, Kinloss, Marchmont, Maybole, Melrose, Minto, Mount Blow, Muirhead, Papine, Perth, Ravenswood, Scotland, Seafield, Stirling, Stonefield, Strathbogie, Strathdon and Waterton (2 each). All of these names were installed by 1900, but Scottish names were occasionally applied to new places. For example, a townhouse development of the 1990s, located on Montrose Road in Kingston, was named Aberdeen.[34]

Names transferred from Wales accounted for seventy place names in Jamaica, or slightly more than 3 per cent of the names derived from the British Isles.[35] Unlike the Scots, the Welsh never stood out as a distinct group within Jamaican culture and were generally rolled together with the English, as befitted their political status. The most common of the names from Wales were Pembroke (9 examples in Jamaica), Cardiff (5), Newport, Swansea and Wales (4 each), Denbigh, Milford and Monmouth (3 each), Chepstowe, Llandewey, Llandovery, Llangibby, Plinlimmon, Radnor and Snowdon (2 each).

Jamaican place names derived from Ireland accounted for 158, or 6 per cent of the overall total of transfers and 7 per cent of those that came from Great Britain. Most popular by far was Spring Garden, with nineteen examples in Jamaica, but the Irish origin of this name may be challenged by the possibility that it derived rather from the long-gone London pleasure ground of Spring Garden that had flourished in the seventeenth century. It was followed by Charlemont, Cherry Garden and Phoenix Park (each of these occurring six times in Jamaica), Clones and Hibernia (4 each), Donegal, Ireland, Kildare, Derry and Dublin Castle (3 each), Bryan

Castle, Cooper Hill, The Finn, Knockpatrick, Liffy Side, Limerick, Mount Eagle, Mount George, Recess and Riversdale (2 each). Single occurrences prominent in the Jamaican landscape included Altamont, Carrickfoyle, Clonmel, Irish Town and Newry. Several of these attributions are problematic – some because they may be eponymous (Bryan Castle, Cooper Hill), others because they are broadly generic (Riversdale, Cherry Garden) and still others because the naming of places within Ireland was in turn heavily influenced by English colonization.

France, Germany, Italy, Switzerland

Continental European transfer names totalled 157 in the 1880 cadastral series, including the 30 from Spain. As noted above, Spain was the not the major contributor, being outranked by France with 35, or almost one-quarter of the total, and equalled by Germany. In view of the absence of a French colonial population and the long wars fought between France and Britain, including much naval warfare in the Caribbean, this relatively high frequency may appear strange, but French forms of naming have proved influential and seductive in North America as well as the British Caribbean, with or without a demographic presence.[36] Alongside the cultural and political rivalry, the British admired aspects of French society and achievement, and the Grand Tour taken by many sons of the planter class in the eighteenth century exposed them to the visual delights of France as well as Italy.

The French place names were heavily dominated by variations of Montpelier and Mount Pelier, presumably derived from Montpellier, the picturesque principal town of Languedoc, located close to the Mediterranean coast and west of the port of Marseille, rather than from the Montpelier of Vermont. The French Montpellier was also a Huguenot centre and long known for its medical school. Montpelier accounted for twenty Jamaican places, more than half the total from France, the name diffusing within the island. Craskell and Simpson had four examples as early as 1760, two of them in the west, HAN JAS, and two in the east, AND THS.

There was also Languedoc MRY, suggesting an attraction to the region. The north of France supplied Ardenne AND, Chantilly WLD MAN, and Verdun ELZ MRY; and the east Bonneville ANN, Cluny CTH THS and Morvan PLD. From the environs of Paris came only Fontainbleau Plantation PLD, but Paris itself never named a Jamaican place.

Germany's strong role in the place names of Jamaica was only marginally the product of German immigration after 1835. More important was the British Crown's association through the House of Hanover (which gave its name to the western parish). By "Germany" we mean the nation within its borders of 2000. Over the previous five hundred years, fragmented concepts of territory and identity moved towards a troubled nationalism and political unification in 1865, but the English and colonial Jamaicans did understand the people as German. Many of the post-slavery immigrants came from the region of Westphalia, which came to name a place high in the mountains of St Andrew. The immigrants were settled at Seaford Town WLD, which came gradually to be known as German Town. Before and after 1838 there was also a sprinkling of individual planters and merchants of German heritage.

The most common German place names were Blenheim HAN MAN ANN, Charlottenburgh WLD MRY AND, Berlin ELZ TRL, Rhine JAS THS and Schwallenburgh ANN CTH. Blenheim marked the site of the battle between the English under Marlborough, who, together with the Austrians, defeated the French and the Bavarians in 1704. This was a turning point in the War of the Spanish Succession, commemorated in Blenheim Palace, built 1705–22 for the Duke of Marlborough, near Woodstock, Oxfordshire. Charlottenburgh was near Berlin, first so named in 1696 for the wife of the Elector Frederick. Schwallenburgh was a smaller place, south of the city of Hanover. Other German names with single uses included Bremen Valley PLD, Brunswick ANN, Carlsruhe AND, Frankfurt PLD, Halberstadt AND, Koningsberg MRY, Manheim THS, Mount Holstein PLD, Nassau ELZ, Potsdam ELZ, Saxony CLR, and Stettin TRL. Blenheim ANN and Charlottenburgh MRY appeared first on the 1760 map of Craskell and Simpson, and Blenheim HAN, Halberstadt AND and Rhine THS on Robertson's 1800 map, long before the arrival of the immigrant contingents.

Jamaican place names derived from Italy came next in importance after those from Germany, and generally referenced the high culture of Rome and Florence as experienced by the planter class on the Grand Tour and their general exposure to things classical.[37] Florence was the most common, contributing five of the seventeen Italian names, to which may be added Tuscany PLD, which referred to the larger region. The region around Rome supplied Latium JAS, Roman Hall CTH, Rome Pen HAN and Sabina Park AND. No names came from the region south of Rome except the classical Tarentum, and Sicily may have contributed Bronte WLD MAN as well as the name of a recent townhouse development in Kingston-St Andrew, The Palermo, on Upper Waterloo Road.[38] From the north of Italy, close to Switzerland, came the names Marengo Park AND, Piedmont TRL and Rivoli CTH. Cremona CTH derived from the northern city known for its cathedral and, from the sixteenth to the eighteenth century, its violin-makers. Switzerland provided Geneva HAN WLD ELZ, and probably The Alps TRL.

BELGIUM, THE NETHERLANDS, SCANDINAVIA, RUSSIA

The main Belgian contribution to Jamaica's place names is Waterloo JAS MAN CTH AND, celebrating the famous battle of 1815 and the triumph of Wellington over Napoleon. Only two other examples occur: Belgium THS and Brussels MAN. The Netherlands are represented in Holland WLD JAS ELZ TRL PLD THS, though a few of these places were named for the aristocratic planter-proprietors Lord and Lady Holland. An alternative source is the part of Lincolnshire, England, known as Holland. There is also Amsterdam HAN, Amby MAN, Leyden JAS and Riswick ANN. Leyden (Leiden) was famous for many things, notably its university, founded in 1575; Riswick (Ryswick/Rijswijk), for the treaty signed there in 1697 by England, France, Holland and Spain.

Scandinavia provided Norway ELZ MAN, Spitzbergen MAN, named for the archipelago to the north of Norway, and Lapland JAS, named for the territory stretching east from the north of Norway into Russia, most of it within the Arctic Circle. Siberia ANN referenced the icy wasteland further east, colonized by Russia in the seventeenth century. Long claimed in 1774 that the district was so called "from its being so little inhabited" but believed that "it is not in other respects deserving that appellation; for it is full of excellent timber, and furnishes a vast quantity of mahogany every year, the visitors of this part being chiefly cutters". Tobolski HAN ANN was the chief town of western Siberia. The Kremlin CLR pointed west to the more hospitable regions of Russia. Balaclava ELZ, an important station on the cross-island railway, took its name from the site of the famous 1854 charge of the Light Brigade and the Crimean War, in which Jamaica's Mary Seacole came to prominence.[39]

North America

As part of the same colonial system down to 1776, the mainland British colonies might seem likely places to have supplied names to Jamaica, but this occurred on only a limited scale. In the 1880 cadastral series, almost sixty Jamaican place names were unique transfers from North America, including Mexico, and fifty of these came from within the boundaries of the modern United States. Certainly Jamaica shared many names with North America – including Springfield – but most often these were drawn directly from Britain in each case rather than providing evidence of step-migration. The most numerous of the Jamaican names drawn from the territory of the United States drew on the names of southern colonies/states, though few of these are recorded earlier than 1800. Georgia was the earliest and most popular, with six examples, spread between Hanover, Trelawny, St Ann, St Mary and St Thomas. Three estates carried the name by 1800 and two as early as 1760. Maryland had six examples, in the parishes of Hanover, St Elizabeth, St Mary and St Andrew. There was also Louisiana WLD CTH MRY, New York ANN CTH, Virginia MAN, and Kentucky WLD. None of these was known before 1800. The names of few places smaller than colonies were transferred to Jamaica. Saratoga ELZ PLD derives originally from New York (the site of a British defeat in 1777) but had numerous transfers, and the same probably applies to Brooklyn MAN CTH, which is named for the Dutch town Breukelen. Salem HAN seems most likely to be of biblical origin or perhaps to be drawn from the name of an English or Welsh village. Flint River HAN MRY could derive from the stream in Georgia but probably was descriptive.

The other significant source of names from the modern United States was the War of Independence. Most popular was Bunkers Hill, derived from the Bunker Hill of Boston, Massachusetts, the site of a crucial battle between militia and British troops in 1775. The Battle of Bunker Hill was won by the British but seen as evidence that the colonial Americans were a match for them. Bunkers Hill Estate TRL was on the map by 1800, and another five were added in St James, Clarendon and St Catherine. Second in popularity was Concord ANN CTH THS, a name that might derive directly from the sentiment but may equally recognize the Massachusetts town that was the site of the first revolutionary skirmish of 1775 between Minutemen and British troops, which became a focus of American patriotism. Trenton MRY derived from the New Jersey town, first named in 1721, an important centre of the Revolution and the site of two American victories. Boundbrook PLD derived from the town in New Jersey where American troops were defeated by Cornwallis in 1777. These four towns provided a range of models that in the Jamaican context might be interpreted either as patriotic or as subversive of empire, reflecting the general ambivalence of the planter class to the ambiguous claims for liberty made by the American Revolution. Only Washington AND identifies a hero of the revolution, and the name might alternatively refer to the Washington in Durham, England, the home place of George Washington's ancestors.

Oberlin CTH may refer to the Ohio town famous as an early centre of antislavery activism and an important station on the Underground Railway. Niagara JAS ELZ no doubt refers to the falls, which were famous by the eighteenth century and were visited by Jamaican planters.[40] Niagara River was on the map by 1800 but the habitation names came later.

North of the United States border, the only places adopted by Jamaican name-givers were Quebec CTH, Quebec Estate MRY, Quebec Lodge AND and Montreal MRY, all from French Canada, with nothing at all from

English Canada. From even further north came Greenland MAN and Greenland Settlement HAN, apparently named ironically; though the original irony was the application of Greenland to the icy Arctic island. From south of the border came Mexico CTH, Mexico Estate ELZ and Mexico Mountain ELZ, the estate named as early as 1800 on Robertson's map.

CENTRAL AND SOUTH AMERICA

The nearness to Jamaica of Central and South America, and their interaction in settlement and trade, did not contribute much to the naming of Jamaican places. Indeed, as for several other regions (beyond Great Britain), it was exotic, fabled places further away that caught the attention of the namers rather than the places with which they might have had trade or of which they had direct knowledge. In spite of the vastness of South America and its prominence in the history of New World colonization, only two countries – Bolivia and Peru – contributed names to Jamaica. Further, although Peru and Bolivia contributed more than one-half of the twenty-one names derived from South and Central America, this relatively large proportion was made up of just three names: Lima JAS TRL, Peru TRL ELZ and Potosi HAN JAS TRL THS. The frequency of Lima and Peru seems to have depended on local diffusion and imitation, as in Peru Pen, Peru Mountain and Little Peru, whereas Potosi was somewhat more widespread within Jamaica. Potosi, sited high in the Bolivian Andes, owed its fame to the great wealth extracted from its silver mines in the sixteenth and seventeenth centuries. Lima, on the gently sloping plain at the foot of the Andes in Peru, was founded by Pizarro in 1535, ten years before Potosi, and was the chief city of colonial Spanish South America. It was the fame of these places that made them attractive names for the planters of Jamaica. Few if any of the colonists had visited them.

The smaller number of Jamaican place names drawn from Central America and the northern littoral of South America were associated with more easily accessible sites, and indeed some of them referred to sites of trade, conflict and skirmishes that directly engaged Jamaica. There were one or more names from each of Venezuela (Miranda Hill JAS), Panama (Porto Bello JAS), Nicaragua (Bluefields WLD ANN and Mosquito Cove HAN), and Guatemala PLD. Some of these names might appear sufficiently generic to have been reinvented in Jamaica rather than being transferred, and it is possible that the Bluefields of Jamaica was in fact the source of the Central American place name. The Mosquito Coast of Nicaragua took its name from the Miskito people who inhabited the region before the Spanish, rather than the insect, and this may be the source of the Jamaican name. The reference to Surinam found in Surinam Quarters WLD was to the English settlers who had left what was the English colony of Surinam when it was surrendered to the Dutch in exchange for New Amsterdam (New York). Thus Long in 1774 said of Westmoreland that "In the East part of the parish, near Scot's Cave [now Cove], were settled the Surinam planters in 1675, and in 1699 the remnant of the Scotch Darien colony, who may now be traced by the names of several settlements hereabouts, as Culloden, Auchindown, &c.".[41] It is striking that almost all of the Central and South American names were attached to places in the western end of Jamaica, that part of the island nearest to the isthmus.

CARIBBEAN

Naming a Jamaican place after some other place in the Caribbean was never popular. In the 1880 cadastral series only single examples were drawn from each of Barbados (Hillaby HAN) and St Kitts (St Kitts WLD), and only one each from the non-British islands Guadeloupe (Belcour Lodge AND), Martinique (Martinique PLD), Haiti (Leogan JAS) and Cuba (Cuba Mount AND). By comparison, there were three places named for the Atlantic island Bermuda (Bermuda PLD, New Bermuda PLD and Bermuda Mount AND) and one for St Helena (St Helena MAN). Barbadoes Valley Cockpits ELZ appeared on Craskell and Simpson's 1760 map but then disappeared. Only at the time of federation was there any enthusiasm for the English-speaking Caribbean, and then it spread little beyond streets in new developments.

AFRICA

Few Jamaican place names were transferred from Africa, and those that were had little to do with the places where most of Jamaica's people were taken from. Of the fifty-five "African" names in the cadastral series, twenty-four derived from Egypt, three from Algeria (Oran MRY, Gran Oran MRY and Oran Plantation PLD), two from Morocco (Tangier TRL and Upper Mount Atlas AND), and three were variations on the Barbary Coast (Barbary Hill ANN, Barbary Hill Wharf HAN and Barbary Hall ELZ). A fabulous, though real, place was Timbuctoo MAN. Several of the popular Egyptian names are generic, as in Egypt WLD ANN, Egypt Pen MRY and Mount Egypt PLD, and some, such as Alexandria, Tripoli and Goshen (discussed below), derived from classical or biblical sources.[42] Only four African place names appeared on Robertson's 1800 map, all of them the names of sugar estates and three of them drawn from this last classical/biblical Egyptian variety: Alexandria, Tripoli and Goshen. Aboukir ANN, close by Alexandria ANN, was named soon after 1800, for the bay near Alexandria where Nelson defeated the French in 1798 in the "Battle of the Nile". Also close by in Jamaica was Rosetta ANN, the site of yet another famous battle, east of Alexandria at the mouth of the Nile. Other Egyptian names were Cairo WLD, Grand Cairo ANN, and The Niles ELZ.

Of the regions associated with the Atlantic slave trade, eight names came from what is the modern state of Nigeria: Benin ANN, Calabar TRL, Ida MAN, variations of Mocho CLR, and Naggo Head CTH. The last of these referred to a Yoruba-speaking people, the Nago, but the *DJE* provides examples from the middle of the twentieth century of the use of *Naggo* to mean "a very black, ugly, or stupid" person. By the end of the century the interpretation was reported that "the Naggo people were displaced plantation labourers who were moved to the area from the original homes after slavery was abolished, protesting loudly, 'Wi nah go!' " Smaller numbers of Jamaican place names come from Angola (Jamba Spring TRL and Luana Pen ELZ), Ghana (Annamaboe TRL) and Benin (Whydah, Whydaw or Wydah PLD). Whydah was the only habitation name drawn from the West African coast on Robertson's 1800 map, though he also identified nearby

Whydah Bay (now known as Margarets Bay). By the beginning of the eighteenth century Whydah was the most important slave-trading port of West Africa, with ships coming from Britain, Portugal, Holland and Brazil, and the location of a small population of Europeans connected with West Indian planters through the process of Atlantic circulation. It was then the second most important town of the Dahomey kingdom, but is now located in the Republic of Benin (formerly Dahomey) and known as Ouidah. Its prominence was reflected in the application of the name in various ways during the time of the slave trade, used to identify the now famous ship *Whydah*, wrecked off the coast of Cape Cod in 1717, as well as to name a bird and a Haitian god. Robin Law has noticed that "there is a village called 'Widah' in Jamaica, originally a sugar plantation, presumably so named through being settled with slaves imported from Ouidah", but it seems equally possible that the name was chosen because of its general notoriety, just as it was thought a suitable name for a ship.[43]

Benin ANN appeared by 1832, taking its name from the Bight of Benin and the empire that flourished in the southern region of Nigeria. Calabar, to the east, on the Bight of Biafra, emerged in the seventeenth century as a major slave-trading port, at the centre of what was known as the Slave Coast. Annamaboe, now generally called Anomabu, played a similar role on the coast of Ghana. These few place names represented some of the major forts and ports through which the people of Jamaica were forced to leave Africa, but they were just a sample. Congo sounds like the African place but may have been eponymous, and named relatively minor places: Congo Bottom TRL, Congo Bridge JAS, Congo Mountain HAN and Congo Piece MRY.

ASIA AND THE PACIFIC

Although Jamaica received substantial numbers of immigrants from India, only a handful of places took their names from the subcontinent. Bengal dominated, with Bengal PLD and Bengal Estate TRL ANN, perhaps marking the firm establishment of British rule in the province under Warren Hastings in 1772. The only others are Bangalore ANN, Bombay MAN, and

Madras Plantation ANN. Porus MAN may take its name from the classical Greek or perhaps from the Porras brothers, who rebelled against Columbus in 1504, but is probably the Parvtaka or Parvatesha noted in Indian sources as a kingly opponent of Alexander the Great. Manchester parish also had a generic Asia. None of these names is found on Robertson's 1800 map, so the place names arrived with the immigrant population, even though the name-givers were typically planters.

If the Indian contribution seems tiny, explained by the cultural marginality of the people before the twentieth century, the complete absence of place names drawn from China is equally striking. Besides being few in number and politically inactive before the later twentieth century, the general absence of the Chinese from the agrarian scene and concentration in commerce reduced the chances of their naming places. The only other place name drawn from Asia is Java MAN. Australia supplied Botany Bay THS, referring either to the late eighteenth-century voyages of James Cook or to the British convict colony.

MIDDLE EAST

Migration from the Middle East to Jamaica was never substantial, in comparison with the shiploads that came from India and China, but the region supplied many more names. As was the case for Africa, continental Europe and South America, the majority of the "Middle East" names were drawn not so much from the region itself as from classical and biblical references. As many as thirty names came from within the modern borders of Lebanon and Israel, and an additional eleven from Syria and Jordan. Of these names, *Lebanon* stood out. The Lebanese did form a small but influential immigrant group (often mistakenly called Syrians), but none of them reached Jamaica before the late nineteenth century, long after the place names had become part of the landscape. Most of these names seem in fact to be drawn directly from the Bible. There are five examples of the simple Lebanon, spread from Hanover to St Thomas, as well as six cases of the biblical Mount Lebanon, three of Mount Lebanus and one of Mount Libanus, scattered widely across the island. Lebanon also supplied three cases of Mount Hermon WLD TRL ANN.

From within the borders of modern Israel came three cases of Bethany ELZ ANN and three of Jerusalem HAN WLD ELZ, as well as New Bethany ELZ, New Jerusalem CLR, and two cases of Bethlehem JAS ELZ and Mount Carmel WLD ANN. There was also Mount Moriah HAN, Bethel MAN, Mount Bethel CTH MRY and the larger Bethel Town WLD. All of these were concentrated in the western end of the island. This distribution is difficult to account for. It is possible that the names were given originally by Sephardic Jews, who came to Jamaica from Spain and Portugal in the sixteenth century and were joined by Ashkenazi after the American Revolution, but there is little to suggest that they had a demographic focus in the western parishes.

Jordan supplied Jericho HAN JAS CTH and Mount Nebo ANN, both places mentioned frequently in the Bible. Another strong biblical reference, found in Mesopotamia WLD and Mesopotamia Mountain WLD, had its origins outside the core biblical sites. The Bible knew Arabia, but the Jamaican Arabia Felix ANN drew on Ptolemaic Greek geography. In contrast, none of the names derived from within the borders of modern Syria appeared in the Bible, though they had a prominent place in the classical world: Palmyra ELZ CLR, Palmyra Estate JAS and Palmyra Pen CLR, as well as Baalbec ELZ MAN, the Heliopolis of the ancient world, and Aleppo Estate MRY. Although the concentration west of Spanish Town was not as marked for these names as it was for Lebanon and Israel, the regional pattern remained strong.

By the 1960s, Kingston in its modern industrial transformation came to be called Babylon by the poor and unemployed, though "Babylon" might also mean the larger social-political system, its values and its tools of repressive government, notably the police. Prime Minister Hugh Shearer was sometimes called "Pharaoh", reviving the link to the Egyptian captivity.[44] In the 1990s, Kingston localities included Tel Aviv, immediately to the north of Southside, along with Dunkirk, further east. In St James in 2002 the informal community Norwood contained a section known as Gulf, presumably a reference to the Gulf War of 1991.[45]

CLASSICAL

Greek and Roman history and mythology supplied a number of Jamaican place names, but nothing near the proportion found in the United States. Jamaica followed a different path. Wilbur Zelinsky argues that, after the War of Independence ended in 1783, there emerged a unique vision of the American as "the reincarnated Athenian or Roman" and of the new Republic as a New Athens or a New Rome, building on the older, colonial idea of America as the New Zion.[46]

In Jamaica more than one hundred place names drew on the Greek and Roman classical tradition, though sometimes indirectly. The most popular of all was Caledonia (twelve widely scattered examples), the name applied by Roman writers to the Scottish Highlands or northern Britain, and probably most often a regional Scottish transfer rather than a classical reference. Similarly, Albion (eight examples, mostly in the eastern end of the island) also had classical roots, first recorded by the Romans but derived from a Celtic or pre-Celtic name for Britain. (*Albion* was soon replaced by *Britannia*, but this name seems never to have named a Jamaican place.) Another name of this sort was Hibernia (four examples), the Greek name for Ireland. These three – Caledonia, Albion and Hibernia – were classical in the sense that they were ancient names, preferred over more modern forms.

Troy TRL MAN CLR MRY and, in its ancient form, Troja CTH MRY, derived from the famous Homeric city, now in Turkey. Hectors River THS references the most heroic of the Trojans in Homer's *Iliad*. Homer's Mountain ANN honours the poet himself. Colchis TRL refers to a region on the Black Sea, now in Georgia, famous in Greek mythology as the home of Medea and the destination of the Argonauts. Tyre TRL refers to the important Phoenician city. As noted in the discussion of names drawn from Africa, Alexandria (seven widespread examples) and Tripoli ANN had classical roots. Palmyra, Baalbec and Aleppo, located now in Syria and mentioned above, were also prominent in the classical world.

Some Jamaican names were drawn from places within the more immediate territory of classical Greece and Rome. Among these, the Greek mountains proved particularly popular. The most important of these names in Jamaica was Arcadia TRL MAN AND THS, specifically a mountainous pastoral area of central Greece but extended to mean a simple, rustic, contented place. Arcadia was one of the few classical names to be applied in recent naming of city housing developments, as in Gardens of Arcadia.[47] Parnassus occurred as Mount Parnassus JAS, Parnassus Estate CLR and Parnassus TRL PLD, referring to the massive, sacred limestone mountain in the Pindus Range. Mount Olympus PLD is the highest of the mountains of the Greek peninsula and is central to mythology and religion. Mount Ossa AND refers to the large mountain close to Olympus. Helicon ANN derives from yet another large Greek mountain, the sanctuary of the Muses. Tarentum CLR ANN CTH is the modern Taranto of southern Italy, famous as a Greek colonial city-state. Mount Augusta CTH has several potential ancient sources.

Of the Jamaican place names derived from classical mythology, the most popular was Phoenix, including Phoenix Park, with eight examples. Although several mythological figures bore the name Phoenix, the reference as used in Jamaica is most likely the fabulous bird restored to life through fire and death, which had appeal in the context of Christian theology and equally in the context of capitalist entrepreneurship, and hence the plantocracy. An alternative origin may be sought in Phoenix Park, Dublin, but this large enclosed city park was not opened until 1747. Mount Atlas AND draws on Atlas, the Titan who held up the sky. Bacchus Run MAN derived from a name for Dionysus, a god of vegetation but in modern times more often associated with wine. Pans Lodge MAN had a more direct association, Pan being the mythological herdsman of Arcadia. Tellus MAN refers to the ancient Roman earth-goddess, and Juno Pen MRY to another very old and important classical Roman goddess. Concordia JAS recognized the personification of agreement within the Roman world but probably was a more broadly sentimental reference. Other classical names of less specific attribution include Minimus CTH, Eureka AND, Mount Salus AND, Elysium JAS PLD, Lethe JAS, Dignum Mountain CTH, Dulce Domum AND THS, Aurora HAN ANN, Adelphi JAS, Aeolus Valley THS, Iter Boreale MRY and Saxetum JAS.

BIBLICAL

The importance of Lebanon and Mount Lebanon has already been noted in discussing names transferred to Jamaica from the Middle East. There are numerous references to these names in the Bible, but all of them occur in the Old Testament, beginning with Moses, who asked God to let him "go over, and see that good land that is beyond Jordan, that goodly mountain, and Lebanon" (Deuteronomy 3:25). Mount Hermon also appears only in the Old Testament, sometimes elided with Mount Zion, but is thought to be the place of the Transfiguration of Jesus, when Moses appeared to the disciples (Matthew 17:1–3). Of the places located in modern Israel, Jerusalem and Bethlehem appear throughout the Bible, whereas Mount Carmel and Bethel are found only in the Old Testament, and New Jerusalem occurs only in Revelation and Bethany in the Gospels. Mount Moriah was the site of the temple in Jerusalem. Although the biblical place names of Jamaica were heavily weighted to the Old Testament, there is no reason to believe that they were therefore given by Jewish planters. Place names derived specifically from Old Testament references were equally appealing to Christian planters and colonists.[48]

Of the names derived from modern Jordan, the city of Jericho is mentioned throughout the Bible, but Mount Nebo is confined to the Old Testament. References to Mesopotamia are scattered from Genesis to Acts. Less certain in its original location is Eden, occurring broadly across Jamaica at twelve places, in Eden CLR, Eden Estate JAS MRY PLD – all three estates named by 1800, Eden Hill MRY, Eden Mount MAN, Eden Mountain JAS, Eden Vale PLD, Eden Park TRL and Eden Wood PLD. New Eden ELZ was named after 1838.

An important source of names is the biblical account of the enslavement of the ancient Israelites and their exodus from Egypt. The first of these is Goshen, represented in the broadly scattered Goshen CLR, Goshen Estate MRY, Goshen Estate and Pen ANN, and Goshen Pen ELZ CTH. Because the biblical Goshen was the place of the Egyptian captivity, it might seem that there was a symbolic connection with the slavery of Africans in Jamaica. The parallel experience of the Israelites and the people of Jamaica was indeed frequently noticed, beginning around the time of emancipation. Three of the five places named Goshen were, however, established during the period of slavery, two of them appearing on Craskell and Simpson's map of 1760, so it was a name that appealed to planter-slaveowners. Elim, where the children of Israel first found water and rested after their escape from Egypt, gave its name to Elim Estate and Elim Mountain ELZ. Although Moravians came to Elim in the 1750s to Christianize the enslaved people, the property was given its name earlier, by the planter who brought the missionaries to the estate. Meribah ELZ, apparently named after the abolition of slavery in Jamaica, was the next stopping place of the Israelites, where Moses smote the rock with his rod at Horeb and brought forth water. The name Meribah means "My God is an help" (Exodus 17:7). More easily understood as a name appealing to the planter class was Canaan, the "promised land" of the Israelites, the ancient Palestine between the Mediterranean shore and the River Jordan and the Dead Sea. Jamaican representatives were Canaan Estate WLD JAS, these two named by 1760, as well as Canaan Valley CLR and Canaan TRL. Even New Canaan JAS was known by 1760. Beulah Park ANN, named after emancipation, drew its name from Isaiah's prophetic hope that the Lord's people of Jerusalem should "no more be termed Forsaken; neither shall thy land any more be termed Desolate: but thou shalt be called Hephzibah, and thy land Beulah" (Isaiah 62:4).

Pisgah, of the Penateuch, named a plantation by 1760, in St Elizabeth. Mount Olive CTH appeared on maps by 1760, but another seven scattered examples appeared after 1838, along with Mount Olivet ELZ ANN. Similarly, Mount Sinai THS was mapped by 1800, and another three appeared after 1838. There were twelve instances of Mount Sion or Mount Zion and one of Zion Hill, all emerging after 1838. Other Old Testament names applied to Jamaica included Mount Ephraim Pen THS, named before 1838, and Mount Gilead WLD, named after 1838. New Testament names given after emancipation included Emmaus ELZ AND and Gethsemane AND. Places named for biblical persons included Pharaoh CTH, Belthazar CTH, Ebenezer MAN ANN and Mount Moses CLR AND. Other vaguely biblical place names include Holy Mount Plantation CTH, Jubilee Pen PLD, Mount Manna HAN,

Pilgrim Plantation ANN, Purgatory ELZ TRL, Pilgrimage Plantation PLD and Tabernacle ANN.

Paradise has strong biblical associations, though the word itself appears in the scriptures only three times, all of them in the New Testament. The presence of the place name within slave society sometimes struck outside white observers as ironic, though often with a selfish twist. Thus Thistlewood, just two years in Westmoreland and having taken off his first – unsuccessful – sugar crop as overseer at Egypt, moved on to Richard Bowen's property exclaiming that it was "named Paradise!" The irony for Thistlewood was not so much the fact of slavery and the oppressive system he vigorously managed but rather his own condition and situation.[49] Describing a visit to an estate in 1802, on the road to Derry in St Elizabeth, Maria Nugent wrote: "Nothing could well be more frightful than the road – hills and precipices continually, . . . The views were beautiful between the openings of the mountains; fine vales, covered with sugar estates, penns, &c. One place that we passed was called Paradise, and a Mr. Angel was the inhabitant."[50] Like Thistlewood, Nugent had in mind the personal discomfort of her journey as counterpoint to the appropriateness of an improbable naming. Presumably, the givers of such names sought to express in them an ironic, even playful, perception of Jamaican places in the long harsh period of sugar and slavery. In this vision, Paradise was not so much the eschatological abode of God and his angels and the future home of the redeemed – the Christian heaven – as the Garden of Eden and its park-like descendants, which offered places of great beauty and delight, suffused with bliss and happiness.

By the time of Robertson's surveys, at the end of the eighteenth century, he was able to record Paradise HAN CLR PLD, as well as New Paradise HAN, proving the popularity of the name during slavery. In the cadastral series thirteen instances of Paradise occurred, now with a strong concentration in the western end of the island; the proportions named before and after abolition were roughly equal. The 1950 map has six examples of Paradise, all without extension and concentrated in Hanover, Westmoreland, St Elizabeth, Clarendon and St Mary. There is also Paradise Bridge CTH. The more modern version of Thistlewood's Paradise became Paradise

Park WLD, strongly emphasizing the Edenic landscape idea. Jamaica – the island – has in modern times occasionally been called Paradise, both for its tourist image and for its social relations.

Saints and angels, traditional inhabitants of Paradise, also provided popular names for Jamaican places. In 1950 *Saint* was popular, with eighteen occurrences, naming the saints Ann, Christopher, D'Acre, Faith, Helen, Jago, John, Leonard, Margaret, Mary, Paul, Peter, Toolis and Vincent. Spanish versions survived in Santa Cruz ELZ and Santa Maria CTH. Another long-term survivor was Angels CTH, presumably derived from the Spanish *Los Angeles*.

One more term, *providence*, might seem to qualify as broadly biblical, but the word is found only once in the Bible, in Acts, and the concept has secular as well as religious interpretations.[51] Providence occurs much more frequently as a Jamaican place name than any of the biblical references discussed here, and its pattern of distribution belongs therefore to the subject of the next chapter, which is concerned with the most common of Jamaica's place names.

CHAPTER THREE

Common Names

TWO PRINCIPAL TYPES OF PLACE NAMES dominate the Jamaican landscape: the names of physical features and the names of human settlements. In the early phases of British colonization, many of the latter derived directly from the name of a settler or planter-proprietor. Personal names were used initially as a simple record of the location of a particular person's landholding or, less certainly, of his (and sometimes her) place of residence, as discussed in chapter 1. These were not true place names, but over time a proportion of them did become established in reference and inscribed on the map. Similarly, some of the names used on early maps for physical features and habitations were generic, identifying only a river or savanna, a pen or a plantation, and these did not constitute place names. Just as for the personal names, these generics could become place names in time – as, for example, Cascade or Constant Spring – but their high frequency (as generics labelling types, as opposed to the individuality of personal names) made this less likely.

The broad pattern of change, from the 1680 map of Bochart and Knollis to the 1950 topographical map, is set out in Table 3.1. Overall, it is striking that the total number of names recorded on these maps doubled between 1680 and 1760 and again between 1760 and 1800, and that the numbers in 1800 and 1950 were almost exactly the same. This pattern reflects changes in the practice of recording personal names. On the first three maps, down to 1800, personal names always made up slightly more than half the total.

Table 3.1: Types of Names on Maps, 1680–1950

Map date	Personal (%)	Habitation (%)	Physical (%)	Total names
1680	51.6	13.7	34.7	1,139
1760	53.6	27.7	18.7	2,276
1800	52.2	16.3	31.5	4,595
1950	0.4	74.0	25.6	4,586

Source: See chapter 1, pp. 13–18.

The 1950 map included few names that might have identified the location of a living person or their landholding, such as John Robinson MAN, Butlers ELZ and Fyffe and Rankin JAS. It did, however, record a good number of eponymous place names derived from individuals known to be long or recently dead, such as Juan de Bolas CTH and the less obvious May Pen CLR. Over time, the personal names were largely absorbed by the habitation names, the two together counting for a consistent three-quarters of the total since the end of the seventeenth century. As noted in the previous chapter, the cadastral series of circa 1880 fitted neatly into the long-term trend, with the proportion of personal names slipping below the halfway mark to 42 per cent.

In spite of the long-lasting persistence of the eponymous place names and the broad dominance of transfer names among the habitation names, outlined in the previous chapter, most of these names were not individually frequent. The truly common place names of Jamaica, the ones that are scattered far and wide and happily duplicated, and that give the Jamaican settlement pattern a particular character, are of quite a different style. Rather than being derived from personal names or transferred from other places, the most common names are associated with sentiment.

CONTENT

Of Jamaica's habitation place names, the most common is Content. The 1950 topographical map identified twenty-eight cases, including twenty-three simple examples of Content and another five extended names such as Content Gap AND, Content Village CLR and Sherwood Content TRL, making up almost 1 per cent of the total (Table 3.2). In the 1880 cadastral series, excluding all personal names, Content contributed more than 1 per cent of all habitation names (Table 3.3). The dominance of the name Content was noted at least as early as the 1840s, when the British naturalist Philip Henry Gosse, based in Westmoreland, rode from Bluefields to "a little cottage, most singularly and romantically perched on a mass of bare rock on the steep mountain-side. The coffee property on which it stands is called by

Table 3.2: Top Ten Settlement Place Names, Including Extensions: 1950 Topographic Map

Name	Simple	Extended	Total	Percentage of all settlement names
Content	23	5	28	0.85
Friendship	15	7	22	0.66
Mount Pleasant	14	1	15	0.45
Belmont	12	–	12	0.36
Retirement	12	–	12	0.36
Williamsfield	12	–	12	0.36
Hopewell	10	2	12	0.36
Hermitage	10	–	10	0.30
Springfield	9	–	9	0.27
Spring Garden	9	–	9	0.27
Prospect	8	1	9	0.27

Source: See chapter 1, pp. 13–18.

Table 3.3: Top Ten Habitation Place Names, Including Extensions: Cadastral Database

Name	Simple	Extended	Total	Percentage of all habitation names
Content	46	19	65	1.19
Friendship	20	29	49	0.90
Prospect	16	26	42	0.77
Retreat	21	19	40	0.73
Mount Pleasant	27	7	34	0.62
Retirement	23	11	34	0.62
Hopewell	14	19	33	0.61
Springfield	17	6	23	0.42
Providence	13	7	20	0.36
Hermitage	12	8	20	0.36

Source: See chapter 1, pp. 13–18.

the favourite appellation (in Jamaica) of 'Content'."[1] Not only is Content more common and ubiquitous than any other place name, by a good stretch; its frequency in Jamaica is matched by its rarity in comparable countries.

Content is spread widely across the island. It has a pan-Jamaican character rather than reflecting simply the whim of a region or select group of name-givers. It is clear from Figure 3.1 that propinquity was no barrier to the repetition of the name, as only the three cases in St Andrew in 1950 took extensions to distinguish themselves. The name was even more common in the cadastral series, with sixty-five occurrences. Of these, forty-six were called simply Content, and an additional nineteen had extensions: Content Estate, Content Garden, Content Mountain, Content Pen, Content Plantation and Content Settlement, occurring in multiples.

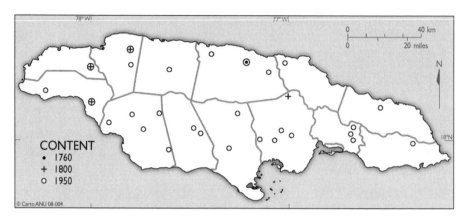

Figure 3.1 Jamaica: *Content*, habitation and settlement names, 1760, 1800 and 1950

It is equally striking that most of the Contents were named before 1838, only ten of the sixty-five examples in the cadastral series coming after the abolition of slavery. The peak period of naming can be narrowed even further, to the final decades of slavery. Using the 1834 claims for compensation, a precisely specified map can be drawn distinguishing the different varieties of Content (Figure 3.2). A small proportion of these fifty-eight cases may represent separate slave-holdings at the same place, but a minimum forty-three were distinctly named. The latter used generic labels, as shown on Figure 3.2, or prefixed Content with descriptives such as Pleasant Happy Content CTH, Hall Green Content AND and Labour Content ELZ, or with eponymous possessives such as Ross's Content CTH. Most of these Contents were small properties with small numbers of slaves. There were only two *estates* among them and two *pens*. Because of the relatively small scale of most of the properties and places, it is difficult to establish when these names were first used. Robertson's 1800 map named only four Contents, the three in the west identified as estates, with a single cattle mill each, while the lone Content in the east was a pen or a plantation. Craskell and Simpson's 1760 map had shown just one Content – a pen or plantation, not an estate – in the hills behind St Anns Bay, which did not appear on Robertson's map but resurfaced in later cartography (see Figure 3.1).

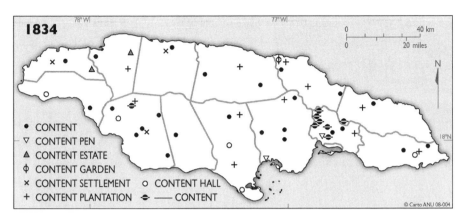

Figure 3.2 Jamaica: *Content,* habitation names, 1834

Although a few Contents were added to the landscape during the Apprenticeship and a few more after 1838, the sentiment was not broadly associated with freedom or the ending of slavery but rather represented the state of mind of the free smallholding class near the end of slavery. This pattern suggests a match with the idea of *content* as meaning not simply pleasure or delight but rather the state of being satisfied with one's lot, an acceptance of what one has though it is less than might have been wished. In this sense the meaning of *content* as "bounded" or "limited" fitted well the ambitions of the free white people of Jamaica during slavery, who dreamed of becoming wealthy sugar planters and the owners of large numbers of enslaved people, but – most certainly after the abolition of the transatlantic trade in 1807 – acknowledged that their hopes were unlikely to be realized. These people had to be content with what they had, to rest satisfied. In the same way, planters of greater wealth came to hope that the people they owned as slaves were "content" with their conditions of life, rather than rebellious, but this was not translated into place-naming.[2] In the long term, in very different social and economic contexts, Content resonated with the other sentimental names that dominated the landscape and lost associations it might have had with the feelings and perhaps unfulfilled desires of the pro-slavery class.

By the end of the nineteenth century, Content was disconnected from this particular history and freely used by the black smallholding class to name their homes and freeholds, with Happy Content sitting comfortably alongside Friendship, New Providence, Poor Man's Corner, Primrose Cottage and Comfort Castle. In the immediate post-slavery years, homes were named Content, Content my Own, and Liberty Content.[3] What is certain is that once Content had been raised to the top of the list as the most popular Jamaican place name, it was never dislodged or demoted.

Closely related to the concept of *content* are *comfort* and *rest*. In 1950 there was one place simply called Comfort, in Manchester parish, as well as Comfort Castle PLD, Comfort Village CLR and the more popular Comfort Hall JAS MAN TRL. On the 1950 map, Rest named three places, the most expressive example being Rest and Be Thankful TRL. This last may not be a Jamaican construction, since it matches the name of a place in the Highlands of Scotland, marked in 1753 by a stone bearing these words. Later, the Rest and Be Thankful Inn was established there and became well known through being frequented by famous visitors such as James Boswell, Dr Johnson, and the poet Wordsworth. If Rest and Be Thankful is indeed an import, it matches well the character of Jamaican naming of this sort. In 1869, exploring the high mountains of Port Royal parish, Sawkins came to "Easy-mind", a place that seems never to have made it onto maps or to have persisted. He put quotation marks around this name, suggesting its newness or localness, but then he did the same with nearby "Hall's Delight", a name that has survived successfully.[4]

These may be contrasted with Little Ease, the name of a place in St Elizabeth inhabited by smallholders during the Apprenticeship: Elizabeth Alexander claimed compensation for four slaves located there, and Benjamin Allen claimed for one. It survived to the 1950 map but appeared then inland of Rose Hall JAS. Immediately after the Apprenticeship, a free coloured man, James Sloss, purchased a few acres from Bluefields Mountain and named his freehold Little Ease, reflecting probably both the scale of his venture and the need to keep ahead of nature.[5]

Besides Content, eight more of the top ten place names in the cadastral database express "sentiment", or feelings, though sometimes ambiguously:

Friendship, Prospect, Retreat, Mount Pleasant, Retirement, Hopewell, Providence and Hermitage (see Table 3.3). Together, these nine sentiment place names account for 6.2 per cent of all Jamaica's habitation names. With Springfield, the top ten make up 6.6 per cent of the total in the cadastral series, and in this series 25 per cent of (non-personal) property names contain sentiment terms. These are high concentrations. A similar pattern is found in the habitation names on the 1950 topographic map, though Retreat slipped to twelfth place and Providence to thirtieth, being replaced by Belmont, Williamsfield and Spring Garden (see Table 3.2). The top ten now made up only 4.6 per cent of the habitation names; the decline was largely a result of the relative growth of eponymous place names.

FRIENDSHIP

The second most common name in both 1950 and the cadastral series, *Friendship* was also widely distributed across Jamaica but, compared with Content, a larger proportion of the places named Friendship in the cadastral list were named after 1838 (Figure 3.3). Friendship was more often extended than Content, these extensions including Cross, Mountain, Valley, Gap, Estate, Farm, Pen, Hall and Plantation. In 1950 there were thirteen distinct cases of the simple Friendship, as well as Friendship Valley THS, Friendship Gap MRY, Friendship Pen ANN, and the three neighbouring places Friendship Cross WLD, Friendship Farm WLD and Friendship Mountain WLD. The name established itself early. Although Bochart and Knollis had no examples, Craskell and Simpson's 1760 map had five, in Westmoreland, St James, Clarendon, St Mary and St Thomas.

The closely related idea of *fellowship*, meaning friendliness or the association of friends, named eleven places in the cadastral series, the majority extended to Fellowship Hall or Fellowship Hall Pen and scattered widely, but Robertson in 1800 had recorded only Fellowship Hall MRY, and earlier mapmakers, none. The sentiment persisted strongly, with five examples on the 1950 map: Fellowship ELZ PLD and three examples of Fellowship Hall CTH MRY. The related concept of *amity* has an even stronger history of per-

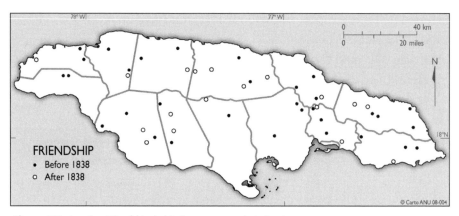

Figure 3.3 Jamaica: *Friendship*, habitation names, cadastral series

sistence, with a similar association with *hall*. Craskell and Simpson had Amity Hall JAS THS, and Robertson included on his map Amity WLD and Amity Hall JAS CLR THS. The cadastral series added to these Amity Hall ANN CTH, for a total of eleven occurrences that included Amity Hall Pen and Amity Mountain WLD. In 1950 there were six widely spread cases of Amity Hall (three of them in Clarendon, the others in St James, St Elizabeth and St Andrew), and one of Amity Cross WLD.

Harmony, suggesting a peaceable community of views, maintained the association with *hall* but was a relative latecomer, with two examples of Harmony Hall TRL CLR in 1800 and twelve by the 1880s, including Harmony Hall Mountain TRL and Harmony Hall Pen CLR. The cadastral series also had four examples of Harmony Hill TRL ANN CTH THS, Harmony Pen CTH, Harmony Plantation PLD and Harmony Vale Settlement ANN. Harmony Farm Pen AND is known from 1838 when it was subdivided "to form a village", but it is certain that the notion of *harmony* as an appropriate sentiment to associate with an enterprise was not restricted to the period after slavery.[6] In 1950 there was Harmony Hall TRL MRY, Harmony Hill ANN and Harmony Vale ANN.

Unity, signifying oneness and the harmony of persons and actions, provided the name for three places in its simple form on the 1950 map, in St

Elizabeth, St Mary and St Thomas. There were also in 1950 Unity House MRY, Unity Hall JAS and two cases of Unity Valley ANN THS. The 1880 cadastral series had a larger number of examples, eighteen, and added to the range Mount Unity ELZ, Unity Grove AND and Unity Pen ANN CLR. As early as 1760, Craskell and Simpson had Unity HAN JAS ANN MRY and Unity Valley THS. Robertson identified five estates so named: Unity TRL MRY, Unity Hall HAN JAS and Unity Valley PLD. *Union*, which has much the same meaning, named two estates in 1800 and seventeen places in the cadastral series, including Brothers Union JAS, Union Hill ANN MRY AND THS, Union Lodge CTH, Union Mountain ELZ, Union Pen ANN CTH, Union Plantation PLD and Union Run MRY. The 1950 map showed two cases of the simple form Union ELZ MRY, as well as Union Hill ANN MRY THS and Union Pen ANN.

Welcome, the spirit of friendliness and good feelings to strangers, named three places in 1950 in its simple form, in Hanover, Westmoreland and St Ann, as well as the extension Welcome Hall JAS. The Hanover example went back to the eighteenth century, whereas those in St James and St Ann appeared first in the cadastral series.

Envy, the apparent opposite of friendliness, was rare in place names. Although signifying jealousy, hostility and rivalry, as a place name Envy seems most likely to suggest that the occupiers saw it as a place to be envied and therefore intended a positive evaluation of the place itself. It was rare, not emerging until the cadastral series, in Mount Envy PLD and Envy Valley Pen CTH, and only the latter survives on the 1950 topographic map. In the early 1840s, however, Phillippo included Envy Not in his list of house names adopted by the emerging peasantry.[7]

PROSPECT

Although *Prospect* was the third most common name on the cadastral list, it slipped to tenth place on the 1950 map. It is included among the sentiments but may also indicate the view from an elevated site, looking into the landscape rather than into the future. The latter interpretation is com-

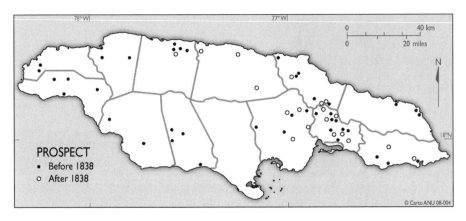

Figure 3.4 Jamaica: *Prospect*, habitation names, cadastral series

pelling, because the name is relatively localized in its distribution, with most of the examples concentrated in the high mountains of the eastern end of the island and along the north coast where there are views out to sea (Figure 3.4). Prospect was also unusual in that the simple version, Prospect, was less common than its extensions, notably Prospect Hill. On the other hand, Prospect became popular at an early stage of settlement and colonization, when the proprietor had still to prove the productivity of the land and his ability to create wealth; there are six examples on Craskell and Simpson's 1760 map, spread widely from one end of the island to the other. Few of the sites possessed any substantial elevation, supporting the view that *prospect* was more to do with the hopes and fears of planter prosperity. Robertson had only five examples, and by 1950 there was only one Prospect with an extension, and the name barely scraped into the top ten.

After generations had passed, names like Prospect often seemed less appropriate if the proprietors had in fact succeeded – or failed – in amassing fortunes. This may account for the relative decline of the name by the later twentieth century. Closely related is *hope*, which counterbalanced *content*, the latter more often suggesting a failure to succeed as fully as might have been hoped, an acceptance of one's situation as opposed to expectations of greater fortune. As noted earlier, care is essential in the

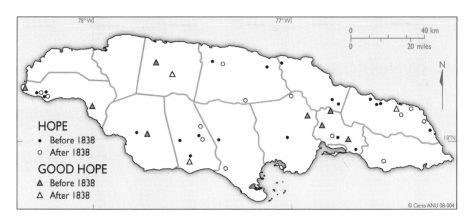

Figure 3.5 Jamaica: *Hope* and *Good Hope*, habitation names, cadastral series

interpretation of *hope* because of the founding role of the surname Hope. Major Roger Hope was a member of the English army that took Jamaica from the Spanish in 1655, and he was granted an extensive stretch of land in the parish of St Andrew. This was gradually reduced to smaller proportions to make up Hope Estate, but the extent of the original title lent the surname to Hope River, Hope Road, Old Hope Road and the Hope Aqueduct, built in the 1750s by the then proprietor, Thomas Hope Elletson. Contraction of the estate after 1850 went together with the creation of Hope (Botanical) Gardens in the 1880s and, later, Hope Zoo and the suburb Hope Pastures with its central artery, Hope Boulevard. By the middle of the twentieth century most people had probably forgotten the eponymous Hopes and thought of Hope in its sentimental sense. The prophet Bedward transformed Hope River into the "healing stream", and that it was "better to live in Hope than die in Constant Spring" became a popular expression. The other places that used *hope* in their names were probably expressing sentiment rather than recording personal connections.

In 1680 Bochart and Knollis identified both the Hope River AND and HopefullVally CTH, but Craskell and Simpson in 1760 had only Hope AND. At the end of the eighteenth century, Robertson recorded Hope AND PLD THS and Good Hope TRL AND, all but one of these in the eastern end of the island, close enough to the source of the original eponymous Hopes. In the 1880 cadastral series, Hope named twenty-five places and Good Hope twelve, then broadly distributed (Figure 3.5). On the 1950 map there were just two places called simply Hope MAN CLR, and a Hope Bay MRY. Compound versions included one Hopefield PLD, three of Hopeton WLD JAS ELZ and the much more common Hopewell, with twelve widely spread examples. Placed seventh in the cadastral series, Hopewell is complicated by the existence of places so named in Scotland and colonial North America. However, although the name may not derive from any notion of wellness, common usage came to transform Hopewell in the same way as the eponymous Hopes of Jamaica. More directly, in 1950 there were Good Hope TRL ELZ and Good Hope Mountain AND, which expressed positive expectations in the same spirit as Good Intent MAN and Goodwill JAS.

MOUNT PLEASANT

Placed fifth on the cadastral list and third in 1950, Mount Pleasant is a common place name in Britain and North America. Much like *hope* and *prospect*, and the related place names Bellevue and Belvedere, Mount Pleasant blends physical and sentiment characteristics (Figure 3.6). Its synonym Belmont, meaning fine or beautiful hill, which placed fourth in 1950, is also common in Britain and the United States but used only for relatively small places, and sometimes − in England − actually replacing Mount Pleasant.[8] Variations of *bel* and *belle* prefix nearly one hundred Jamaican place names, including eleven cases of Belmont.

Bellevue derived from the French *belle vue* for "beautiful or lovely view", whereas the Italian *belvedere* can mean either a turret or tower located on the top of a house, designed for the better viewing of the surrounding scene, or a summerhouse that similarly affords a "beautiful view". Bellevue was popular in 1950, with seven cases, though the best-known was probably the mental hospital in Kingston. In 1950 there were only four disconnected examples of Belvedere. Variants of *belle* in 1950 were Belle Air ANN, Belle Castle THS, Belle Clare THS, Belle Plain CLR, Bellefield MAN, Belleisle

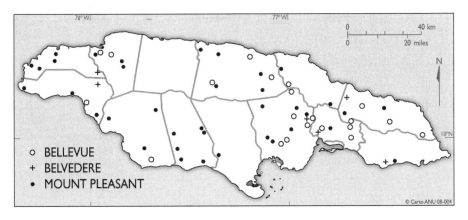

Figure 3.6 Jamaica: *Bellevue*, *Belvedere* and *Mount Pleasant*, habitation names, cadastral series

WLD and Fontabelle WLD TRL MRY. Less common related names included Bonavista JAS ELZ and Bon Hill THS. Boon Hall AND could be a related name, though both Bon and Boon might also be eponymous. In the cadastral series twenty-two places used Bellevue in their names, most of these located in the eastern end of the island outside the karst zones, and most of them named before 1838 (see Figure 3.6). Some of these might have been transferred from French Caribbean colonies where they were popular as plantation names.[9] Belvidere appeared much earlier than Bellevue, with one example by 1680 and two by 1760, in St Mary and St Thomas.

PROVIDENCE

There are two distinct meanings of *providence*, one pointing to the secular practice of thrift and frugality, applying foresight to the management of resources, and the other indicating the divine control or direction of human life in which individuals must accept the lot assigned them by God. The second of these meanings connects with the idea of chance suggested in *lucky* and *lottery* but with the addition of the notions of design and divine wisdom. Probably the secular version dominated in Jamaica in the period of sugar and slavery, whereas the theological ruled after 1838.

To be lucky is to have good fortune or success not so much as the result of one's own efforts but rather through being favoured by chance. The luck of the draw also underpins the notion of life as a lottery, a concept sometimes used by eighteenth-century planters to suggest that their fortunes depended on chance rather than good management. Probably the first Lucky Valley was the plantation of the Long family in upper Clarendon, to which Robertson added Lucky Valley AND. In 1950 there were three cases of Lucky Valley CLR CTH AND, two of Lucky Hill MRY CTH and Lucky Hill Pen MRY. Robertson indicated Lottery TRL, and the cadastral series added Lottery Pen JAS and Lottery Mountain TRL. These persisted on the 1950 topographic map.

The theological concept of *providence* was occasionally brought to the fore during slavery, when cataclysm was interpreted as punishment of the sinful. Thus Judgement Cliff THS, a great raw scar created by the 1692 earthquake, was a sign of particular retribution, paralleling the general striking down of the ungodly at Port Royal. Stone and earth fell from the mountainside on to a plantation owned by "an atrociously wicked Dutchman, who overtopped the licentious wickedness of the times by procreating with his own children".[10]

Providence ranked ninth in the cadastral series but sank to forty-fifth in 1950. Robertson found only three examples of Providence, in Westmoreland, St James and St Thomas, but in the cadastral series twenty-three property names included Providence, widely scattered though maintaining the western concentration. The closely related *resource* appeared eight times in the cadastral series and four times, always without extension, on the 1950 map in the parishes Manchester, St Ann, St Catherine and St Andrew. The word referred to the idea of possessing a reserve of capabilities, a means of supplying a need, whether the gift of God or the secular necessity of good management. There were no examples from the early period of English settlement.

Counterpoints to *providence* and *resource* were the common terms *endeavour* and *industry*. Endeavour was as common as Providence in the cadastral series and by the 1950 map had a marginal lead. It points to the idea of striving towards an objective, putting effort into an enterprise, rather than depending on a beneficent power. Robertson had examples of Endeavour only in Hanover and Westmoreland, but in the longer term the name was concentrated in St Ann. A related, more risky, name was Bold Attempt, found by 1800 in Trelawny, then establishing itself in St Ann and persisting into the twentieth century. The idea of *industry* was similar to that of *endeavour*, suggesting an assiduous application to labour, the well-directed work of an enterprise. Industry WLD existed by 1760, and three estates had the name by 1800, in Hanover, St James and St Ann. It was popular in the cadastral series with twenty-five instances, most of them named in the period of slavery and with a broad geographical distribution. The fact that both Endeavour and Industry were used most often during slavery and were therefore chosen directly by planters and slaveowners might seem to signal their hopes for the hard labour of enslaved people on these proper-ties, but it is more likely that they thought of themselves as industrious and virtuous, fully committed to their endeavours to create fortunes for them-selves, whatever the cost to others.

RETREAT, RETIREMENT, HERMITAGE

A number of very popular Jamaican place names point to the idea of seclu-sion and the desire for privacy. *Retreat* suggests the search for and finding of a place of refuge or safety in the face of danger (as in warfare), a withdrawal from the heat of battle to a more secure situation. *Retirement* has much the same meaning. *Hermitage* suggests even more strongly than Retreat and Retirement the notion of a secluded or solitary place. These three names were placed fourth, sixth and tenth, respectively, in the cadastral series.

Retreat, next in rank after Prospect on the cadastral list (with fifty-one instances) and pipped by it in 1950, was almost equally divided between its simple and compound versions. As expected, there was a strong concentra-tion away from the coast but also an eastern weighting (Figure 3.7). The term was used more often during the period of slavery than after. The first

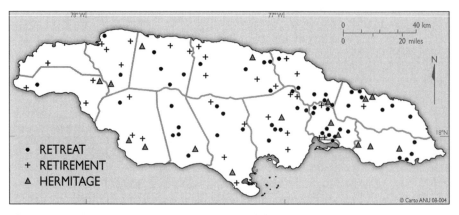

Figure 3.7 Jamaica: *Retreat, Retirement* and *Hermitage*, habitation names, cadastral series

examples appeared on maps in 1760, in Westmoreland, St James, Clarendon and St Thomas. Robertson had eight cases, widely spread. Retreat appeared six times on the 1950 map, in its simple form, in the parishes Hanover, Clarendon, St Ann, St Mary, St Thomas and Portland, while The Retreat sat beside Retreat Pen ANN.

Retirement ranked sixth on the cadastral list (thirty-four instances) and fifth in 1950, but was weighted more towards the western end of the island (see Figure 3.7). On the 1950 map it appeared exclusively in its simple form, in twelve places, with two examples in each of Hanover, St James, St Elizabeth and St Ann, and one in each of Westmoreland, Trelawny and St Andrew. Craskell and Simpson had Retirement JAS, and Robertson found no more. Hermitage appeared much earlier, the first example in 1680 in St Mary, with later additions in Westmoreland, St Ann and Portland. It named twenty distinct places in the cadastral series and ten on the 1950 map, all of the latter without extension, with one exception, Hermitage Reservoir AND.

Notions of refuge and isolation contained in *retirement* and *retreat* were not confined to large or small landholders with legal tenure but were equally desired by those who resisted the system of plantation slavery and fought to establish themselves in places outside its ambit. The words they used to name such places of refuge and retreat were different but expressed similar sentiments. For example, in 1825 there was published an account of attacks on a Maroon settlement in the interior of Trelawny, together with a "Diagram, or plan of the town, inhabited by the runaway and rebellious Negroes, called by them, 'We No Sen', You No Come' ". The *Cornwall Gazette* was cited, referring to "the now famous town, called by its refined and polished inhabitants, 'me no sen, you no come' ".[11] It is this last form that has survived intact into the present, only occasionally corrupted to "Me no call you no come".

THE DOMINANCE OF SENTIMENT NAMES

Why did such a high proportion of Jamaica's common habitation names relate to sentiment and why were these terms so enthusiastically duplicated? The system of place-naming need not have developed this way. Why are there no names in the top-ten lists reflecting topographical or environmental features or the plantation economy, and why no eponyms? The absence of eponyms is easy enough to explain, because although they were numerous they were also often unique, and they were undermined by their potential transience.

Only one of the top ten place names – Springfield – is a transfer-name derived from an existing place in some other country, being common in both England and English colonial North America. It was joined in 1950 by Spring Garden. This might be a local growth but seems more likely to derive from the Spring Garden of London, a seventeenth-century pleasure garden famous for its fountain, and may perhaps echo the spread of the name across the United States, where the original derived from a small estate near Philadelphia.[12] Springfield and Spring Garden are in turn complicated by the commonness of *spring* as an element in the Jamaican naming system, giving a physical-environmental twist. The other new top-ten name of 1950 was Williamsfield, neither a sentiment name nor a name obviously derived from some other place. It paralleled Springfield as one of the many Jamaican names with the *-field* suffix, Williams being a common surname in the island and William a common given name.

The dominance of sentiment names is confirmed by looking beyond the top ten names to the full cadastral set, in which almost five hundred different words and phrases expressing sentiment are identified, far more than any other category of naming (Table 3.4). The most common of the sentiment names occurred more frequently than the most common of the transfer names in spite of the apparent strong presence of British names within the Jamaican landscape.

Table 3.4: Habitation Place Names, Not Counting Extensions in Combination, Frequency Five or More: Cadastral Database

No. of cases	Habitation place names
46	Content
27	Mount Pleasant
23	Retirement
21	Retreat
20	Friendship
17	Springfield
16	Prospect
15	Richmond Hill
14	Hopewell
13	Endeavour, Providence
12	Belmont, Hermitage
11	Gibraltar, Rose Hill, Wakefield, Woodlands
10	Harmony Hall, Industry, Pleasant Hill
9	Claremont, Spring Garden, Shooters Hill, Top Hill
8	Brighton, Caledonia, Clifton, Golden Grove, Kensington, Orange Hill, Orange Valley, Retreat Pen, Stirling Castle

Table continues

Table 3.1 continued

No. of cases	Habitation place names
7	Bellevue, Cocoa Walk, Friendship Pen, Good Hope, Look Out, Mount Olive, Ramble, Rose Hall, Spring Garden Estate, The Cottage
6	Aberdeen, Amity Hall, Belle Vue, Brandon Hill, Clifton Hill, Content Plantation, Coolshade, Farm Pen, Friendship Mountain, Green Vale, Hampstead, Happy Grove, Highgate, Hopewell Pen, Lucky Valley, Montrose, Mount Lebanon, Mount Sion, Mount Zion, Mountain Spring, Petersfield, Prospect Hill, Ramble Pen, Resource, Southfield, Unity, Windsor Castle, Woodstock
5	Arcadia, Blue Hole, Bushy Park, Cambridge, Cedar Valley, Chesterfield, Clifton Pen, Cold Spring, Comfort Hall, Cottage Pen, Dee Side, Enfield, Fellowship Hall, Folly Pen, Glasgow, Good Intent, Green Hill, Greenfield, Hillside, Lancaster, Lebanon, Mount Alta, New Castle, Orange Grove, Paradise Pen, Prospect Pen, Rest Pen, Retirement Pen, Retrieve, River Head, Rock Hall, Rock Spring, Rosemount, Round Hill, Silent Hill, Somerset, Spring Estate, Spring Hill, Trafalgar, Tweedside, Twickenham, White Hall, Windsor

Source: See chapter 1, pp. 13–18.

It is equally striking that the sentiments expressed tend to be positive, with an emphasis on feelings of satisfaction, present or future, as well as on warm human relationships and the comfort of refuge. The dominance of the name Content expresses these feelings clearly, and it is the Jamaicanness of this name that sets it apart from the others. Of the sentiment names in the cadastral series, 28 per cent can be classified as signifying satisfaction in the present and another 10 per cent, satisfaction in the future. Names suggesting dissatisfaction in the present accounted for only 3 per cent, and only a handful risked referencing a pessimistic outlook. The next most substantial class of names had to do with ideas of refuge and retreat, contributing 17 per cent of the total sentiment names. After these, names including value terms (such as liberty, equity) made up another 10 per cent, human-association concepts (friendship, harmony) 8 per cent, virtues (goodwill, plenty) 6 per cent, chance (luck, folly) 5 per cent, enterprise (perseverance, industry) 4 per cent, and domesticity (rest, welcome) 1 per cent, with other terms making up the remaining 8 per cent.

Whereas names associated with status (estate, castle and the like) commonly identified the achievements of proprietors and the wealth and honour they already had in hand, sentiment names more often pointed modestly to a state of satisfaction with the way things were or might become. Thus the most common of all Jamaican place names, Content, could be applied generally without necessarily making great claims. Other names suggested related positive sentiments or emphasized hopes and aspirations. Of the leading place names, ambiguity was most apparent in Retirement, Retreat and Hermitage, which express a desire for a peaceful existence far from the worries of the world, but might also mean a more simple remoteness and inaccessibility. Irony was often present, explicit or implied, and perhaps not always easily detected. Although some of the sentiment place names may have had other sources or derived from a combination of ideas, the strong impression remains of a system dominated by sentiment.

Interesting nuances emerge when comparison is made between the different types of economic enterprise, particularly the fact that neither sugar planters nor small farmers ever used terms of dissatisfaction (present or future), and that negative sentiments were associated exclusively with the non–sugar plantation sector and, more often, with the penkeepers. Perhaps proprietors of the latter classes felt they had fallen short of their ambitions, having failed to match the fortunes of the sugar planters. The apparent satisfaction of the small farmers, by contrast, was a measure of their more modest expectations and their successful upward mobility from field labourer to planter. The values and virtues, and the notions of chance and enterprise, were, however, broadly shared across all sectors.

The supposed high frequency of name repetition in Jamaica, particularly sentiment names, sometimes led commentators to wonder at a supposed failure of imagination. Thus Frank Cundall thought that "the number of Bellevues, Belvideres, Contents, Richmonds, speaks little for the inventive faculties of those who named them".[13] Variations of *bel* and *belle* prefixed nearly one hundred Jamaican place names. It is, however, important not to be transfixed by these examples of repetition. After the top ten habitation place names came the great mass of infrequent and singular constructions. Indeed, 53 per cent of the names on the cadastral list were used just once, for a single place. Those used twice accounted for 18 per cent, and those applied three or four times for another 12 per cent of the total list of place names. Thus the most common of the habitation place names, with five or more occurrences each, accounted for only 17 per cent of the total. This pattern makes clear how unusual the high frequency of the simple Content looks within the larger context. Most namers came up with unique constructions, but when a name became popular it was taken on with enthusiasm.

A similar result comes from the "fully updated" Jamaica road map of 2000 that lists 1,113 places, only one-fifth the number in the cadastral database, but with Content the most popular name at seven cases, or 0.6 per cent of the total. Content was followed by Friendship and Springfield, as before, and, as in 1950, Williamsfield, together with a new entrant, Freetown (Table 3.5). Overall, 19.4 per cent of names were duplicated on the 2000 map, roughly the same proportion as in the cadastral database. Content was also the leading habitation name on the 1960 Jamaica Automobile Society map (five cases, making up 0.8 per cent of the total), with 21 per cent of the place names duplicated and a total of 795 places listed.

The way in which Jamaica's most common habitation place names became established and proliferated is harder to trace. In their 1680 map Bochart and Knollis showed not one Content, and habitation names of any sort, independent of a personal name, were rare. They did, however, have Hermitage MRY, Bellamount THS, and Spring Garden CTH and Spring Gardins THS. Craskell and Simpson's 1760 map, the most complete source for the eighteenth century, recorded only one Content. On this map the

Table 3.5: Settlement Place Names, Not Counting Extensions in Combination, Frequency Five or More: 1950 Topographic Map

No. of cases	Settlement place names
23	Content
15	Friendship
14	Mount Pleasant
12	Belmont, Retirement, Williamsfield
10	Hermitage, Hopewell
9	Spring Garden, Springfield
8	Prospect
7	Albion, Farm, Retreat, Top Hill, Windsor
6	Amity Hall, Bellevue, Belvedere, Caledonia, Clifton, Endeavour, Forest Hut, Golden Grove, Goshen, Green Hill, Look Out, Orange Hill, Paradise, Richmond Hill, Rose Hill, Wakefield, White Hall
5	Blue Hole, Cambridge, Cedar Valley, Cottage, Freetown, Glasgow, Huntley, Kensington, Mocho, Montpelier, Oxford, Providence, Ramble, Richmond, Richmond Hill, Round Hill, Somerset, Winchester, Woodlands

Source: See chapter 1, pp. 13–18.

eleven most common habitation names were Prospect (8), Friendship (6), Unity, Hopewell, Mount Pleasant, Retreat, Montpelier, Golden Grove, Windsor, Williamsfield and Spring Garden (4 each). Robertson in 1800 recorded only four examples of Content, but in that year the name shared twelfth place with Amity Hall, Providence and Wakefield. In 1800 the most common name was Friendship (8 examples, including extensions), followed by Hopewell, Retreat and Spring Garden (7 each), Bog and Golden Grove (6), and Oxford, Prospect, Spring, White Hall and Windsor (5 each). The proliferation of Contents in Jamaica came after 1800 but was completed by 1840. It follows that the great mass of Contents were named in the last decades of slavery, though some of them may have existed in local parlance without finding their way onto maps. The dominance of sentiment names was firmly established by the early nineteenth century. Over the long term, the great stayers were Friendship, Prospect, Hopewell and Retreat.

Thus far, it is the role of descriptive terms that has been emphasized, whether in personal names, transfer names or sentiment names, and their frequency of occurrence. In many cases, however, the identification of a particular place depended on an extension or generic label. Thus Content Pen and Content Estate are different places, though these complex versions were themselves duplicated. Adding a proprietor's name could also help, so Dawkins Caymanas was distinguished from Taylors Caymanas. Another solution was to add the parish name, but this was to give two place names rather than to combine the parts into a unitary whole – like a postal address, as in Dundee, Trelawny. Once the number of descriptives and generics combined in a single place name became numerous, the naming system began to seem clumsy. For example, Georges Plain Estate Mountain, with its four words, was no doubt a mouthful that began to stretch the limits, but at the same time it functioned efficiently in the way it provided precise information about the character of the place it named.

In the Jamaican naming system, the enthusiasm for and duplication of certain particular descriptive terms could have proved a recipe for confusion. Why did this not worry the namers? In part, the reason is that, when the names were given, movement through the regions of Jamaica was limited and controlled, and life was highly localized. Where populations move through the landscape as a matter of course, as in the case of nomads, the necessity to avoid repetition of place names is much greater.[14] By contrast, the generic elements of Jamaica's place names were designed for repetition and functioned best when few in number. They were meant to be common. It was these classificatory hierarchies that contributed many of the strikingly unique features of the island's place names. Whereas the descriptive elements or terms drew from a fairly standard English vocabulary, the generics often attached new meanings to words or even created new words. These are the subject of the following chapters, taking up first the generic terms applied to physical features and next those attached to settlement or habitation sites. The frequency and duplication of the common names considered in this chapter must be placed within this alternative perspective.

CHAPTER FOUR

Topographical Names

JAMAICA IS A RELATIVELY SMALL PLACE, but local variations in elevation, slope, soil and rainfall provide the foundations for a richly textured topography and system of named places. The whole of the landscape, from shore to shore, has been shaped by the interaction of water and rock – hydrology and geology. Simple distinctions between those landforms in which the geology or earth is dominant and those in which water is regarded as the defining variable are not always easily made. In spite of this apparent difficulty, the present chapter is concerned particularly with places named for their relative elevation or geological morphology, while the next two chapters cover names based on hydrological features and names applied to coastal landforms, respectively.

Topographical names were applied both to "natural" features and to habitation and settlement sites. It is a good question which came first, the names for the natural topographic features or the names of the habitations and settlements. In practice, some physical features were sufficiently prominent to be named early and gave their names to later settlements, whereas others were simply recognized generically and named as unique places only after settlement. Thus early maps of Jamaica identified many springs simply by the word *spring*, and only over time did such labelling retreat, as these gained compound names as in Cotton Tree Spring CLR or Cuffee Spring CLR. More important, it is certain that early cartographers and namers paid much more attention to the presence and volume of streams than they did to the overall relief of the land. This difference had to do with the value of water as a resource but also reflected the difficulty of identifying a mountain compared with observing a stream. The result was that elevation features were hardly ever named in generic terms, whereas such naming of streams was widespread. Early maps contained many *springs* and *rivers* but hardly any *mountains* or *hills*.

Only a handful of physical features were named without the attachment of generic labels. Most often, these names marked known stopping points or stages on important routes in locations that lacked permanent habitations. In the shadow of the Main Ridge of the Blue Mountains, for example, the 1950 map shows to the north Abraham, and to the south Dinner Time, Half-a-Bottle, Macca Sucker and Gossamer. Big Level PLD gives an idea of the landscape immediately west of the John Crow Mountains. Devils Race Course CTH identifies the hazardous descent from Guys Hill into St Thomas in the Vale. All of these allusive names have picturesque qualities but fail to satisfy the classificatory capacity of naming by generic labels.

Before looking at the different kinds of names applied to topographic features, it is useful to notice that although these features can be said to belong to the natural world – mountains, rivers and plains – the identification as well as the naming of them depends on human perception and systems of classification. Whereas habitation sites are often demarcated by precise legal boundaries which can be drawn on the ground and on maps, indicating the limits of a place and its name, the topographic features discussed in this chapter are usually less easily defined and bounded. Identification and naming are often the same thing and are essential to the finding of individual features in the continuum of surface variation and the essential vagueness of transitions.[1]

MOUNTAIN, MOUNT, PEAK, RIDGE

What is a *mountain*? For Jamaicans, the term not only refers to a steep-sided, very high mass of land but also can be used for a particular type of agricultural land settlement. Although the latter definition is now essentially historical, it had currency from the eighteenth century to the middle of the twentieth century. Over this long period *mountain* was applied more commonly to places of the latter type than to places known and named purely for their relative elevation and prominence. *Mountain* as settlement name is a Jamaicanism, dealt with in chapter 7. The more common English version of *mountain* – the strictly topographic variety – is the type discussed here, but the difficulty of distinguishing it from the settlement type makes mapping problematic. Beyond this linguistic difficulty in the particular case of Jamaica, there is the broader difficulty of deciding when a landform deserves the term *mountain* and how it might be distinguished from a *hill*, or when indeed the *mountain* might be better understood as simply one side of its alter ego, a *valley*, as clearly expressed in the name of the sugar estate Mountain Valley HAN.

The highest point in Jamaica is Blue Mountain Peak, 2,254 metres above sea level, located in the eastern end of the island, where the distance from north to south coast is just forty kilometres. It is now commonly referred to simply as The Peak. In spite of its prominence, however, Blue Mountain Peak appeared only slowly as a name on maps. Bochart and Knollis in 1680 provided no names at all in the zone of the eastern mountain ridge, simply filling the space with perspective drawings of lumpy hills. Craskell and Simpson in 1760 identified only The Blue Mountains, using a long sweep of large letters. Similarly, Long in his 1774 *History of Jamaica* referred to "the majestic Blue Mountains, rising above one another in gradation, till they seem to touch the clouds" and, from a Kingston perspective, saw the Liguanea Mountains seeming "to increase in magnitude and elevation, till we arrive at the highest of all, called the Blue Mountain Ridges". Long reported recent trigonometric measurements putting Blue Mountain summit at 7,553 feet (2,303 metres).[2] James Robertson's 1800 map ignored the peaks, naming only "The Grand Ridge of the Blue Mountains", running this title along the border between the parishes of Portland and St Thomas. This absence is not as surprising as it might seem. In Robertson's time, and indeed until the end of the nineteenth century, the measurement of elevations remained difficult and the use of contour lines to indicate points of equal elevation was virtually unknown.

References to the highest points in the Blue Mountains as *peaks* began to emerge only in the early nineteenth century. In 1848 James Maxwell could talk about Jamaica "from the water's edge to the Blue Mountain peak". By the 1860s a larger number of readings were available, and Sawkins could refer both to "Blue Mountain peak" and to St Catherine's Peak, the latter demoted in the twentieth century to the less saintly Catherine's Peak.[3]

Although the Grand Ridge of the Blue Mountains was by far the most impressive ridge in Jamaica, it was not the only one recognized by mapmakers. Craskell and Simpson had Chocolata Ridge ELZ and Mammee Ridge ANN, and Robertson referred to Portland Ridge CLR. Sawkins found in the parish of Portland a ridge bearing "the local names of Main Ridge, Blue Mountain, Cold Ridge, Cuni Cuni, &c.".[4] The 1950 map ignored those shown on Craskell and Simpson, but added Main Ridge CLR, Calabash Ridge CTH, Cocoa Ridge CTH, Ginger Ridge CTH, Queensbury Ridge THS, Kenmure Ridge THS and Cowards Ridge THS. Several of these places were close neighbours, suggesting a degree of imitative naming, in appropriate locations.

The 1950 topographical map included a larger number of *peaks*, all of them found in the Blue Mountains but not always associated with the term *mountain*: Silver Hill Peak AND, John Crow Peak THS, Mossmans Peak THS, Stoddarts Peak THS, Candlefly Peak THS, Sir Johns Peak PLD, High Peak PLD, Two Claw Peak PLD and Sugar Loaf Peak PLD. The term *sugarloaf*, used effectively as a generic label, has considerable currency in the Americas and elsewhere. It identifies a high, conical hill, taking as its model the characteristic shape of crystallized sugar formed in a pottery mould that drained syrup through its tip when inverted. Once removed from the mould, the metre-tall sugarloaf was stood on its flat base, making the shape of a hill or mountain. Such sugarloaves were prominent in markets by the sixteenth century.[5]

Craskell and Simpson rarely used the label *mountain* in naming a physical feature, though they did have, for example, Black Spring Mountain ELZ and The Long Mountain AND. Leslie, in 1739, had called the latter simply "the long Mountain".[6] Although Long Mountain is sometimes said to take its name from the Long planter family, the longevity of the name suggests a simple association with its elongated shape, as indicated in the early sources. Craskell and Simpson in 1760 had eleven examples of the plural *mountains* as physical features, in addition to the Blue Mountains. Apart from Carpenters Mountains CLR and New Savana Mountains HAN, all of these were found in St Elizabeth: Burnt Savanna Mountains, Don Figuerero's Mountains, Edmund's Valley Mountains, Essex Valley Mountains, Luana Mountains, May Day Mountains, Montes de las Uves, Nassau Mountains, Santa Cruz Mountains and Wild Slip or Lacovia Mountains. This concentration suggests imitative naming rather than real topographic variation.

Robertson in 1800 gave only two places the label *mountain*: Lacovia Mountain ELZ, to the north of the present town of Lacovia, and Don Figuerero's Mountain MAN, stretching north along the ridge from Spur Tree. In addition to these two, Robertson included on his map the plural Mocho Mountains CLR, Nassau Mountains ELZ, Santa Cruz Mountains ELZ and Carpenter Mountains MAN, all far away from the Blue Mountains. Mocho Mountains might appear to be a misnomer, since Spanish meanings of *mocho* point to shortness and truncation or, in Mexico, to a stream that has no apparent outlet but disappears into the ground. In Jamaica *mocho* has come to mean a remote, uncivilized place.[7] Robertson also used *mountain* as a qualifier for streams, as in Mountain Spring WLD and Mountain River CTH.

The 1950 topographic map showed nine examples of *mountain* and twelve of *mountains* as physical features. Robertson's singulars were pluralized as Lacovia Mountains and Don Figuerero Mountains, as they had been on Craskell and Simpson's earlier map. New examples introduced in 1950 were Geneva Mountain WLD, Mosquito Cove Mountain HAN, Quasheba Mountain HAN, Mile Gully Mountain MAN, Bull Head Mountain CLR, Crofts Mountain CLR, Dallas Mountain AND and Good Hope Mountain AND. New plurals were Dry Harbour Mountains ANN, Brazilletto Mountains CLR, Osborne Mountains MRY and John Crow Mountains PLD. John Crow is a Jamaicanism for the carrion crow, first recorded in the 1820s, but applied to the mountains at some later, unknown, date. According to Sibley, Governor Sir Henry Blake decreed in 1890 that the John Crow Mountains PLD should be renamed Blake Mountains, supposedly to commemorate the crossing of this hostile range by the intrepid police officer Herbert Thomas. The American botantist Forrest Shreve referred in 1914 to "the Blake, or John Crow, range" but John Crow easily overpowered Blake in the long run.[8] Dallas Mountain gained its name from Dallas Castle plantation and its owners, the Dallas family, whose members included the author of the *History of the Maroons* (1803) and the founder of Dallas, Texas.

As well as appearing among the names of particular landforms, *mountain* and indeed many other topographic terms had a greater presence and longevity in the names of settlements. Whether the term already existed independent of local settlement or whether the term was applied only when a settlement was established is often hard to determine, but the use and long-term survival of a topographic term within a habitation name makes possible a much broader analysis of the application and acceptance of such terms. On the 1950 topographical map, seventy-five habitation names carried the *mountain* label, many more instances than for the physical features, but their distribution was quite different and seemingly unrelated to variations in relief. The *mountain* habitation places of 1950 matched much more closely the unique Jamaican usage that made a mountain a specific type of agricultural unit, as discussed in chapter 7, and provided no real clue to the reality or perception of the island's topography (Figure 4.1).

In Britain, *mount* is used to identify a conical hill of moderate height rising from a plain, but there as well as in Jamaica the term has become effectively obsolete in everyday speech and survives only in place names.[9] Bochart and Knollis in 1680 had only Mount Maria CTH as a physical feature, and Craskell and Simpson only Mount Misery ANN. Robertson in 1800 listed no mountainous natural features with names beginning with *mount*, though he implied their existence, as in Mount de las Uvas River ELZ and Mount Diabolo River CTH. He also included on his map ten sugar estates the names of which began with *mount*, and the small settlement Mount Ida THS, located close to the estate Mount Libanus. The 1950 map had only Mount Cromwell WLD, Mount Diablo CTH, Mount Telegraph

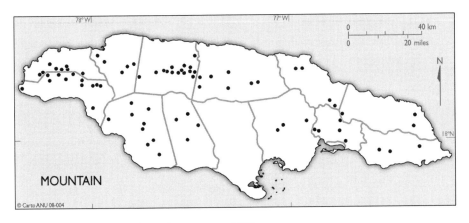

Figure 4.1 Jamaica: *Mountain*, settlement names, 1950

MRY and Mount Horeb AND as physical features, but had 109 instances of *mount* in settlement names, almost all of them using the term as their first word. Few of these referred to physical characteristics, and generally the references were vague, as in Mount Airy WLD MAN AND, Marlie Mount CLR and Spring Mount JAS. Most popular overall on the 1950 map was Mount Pleasant (perhaps derived directly from the British places so named), and a significant proportion of the names referred to biblical and classical places, from Mount Ararat to Mount Zion.

HILL, BUMP, HUMMOCK

The height and mass qualifications for hills have always been less demanding than those applied to mountains, so that in general more examples should exist in the topography, with many appropriate land shapes available for naming. On the other hand, because hills lacked the visibility and prominence of mountains they might more easily be overlooked. Bochart and Knollis had only Round Hill CLR, Negril Hills WLD and Sand Hills CTH. Craskell and Simpson ignored the last two and added only Camps Hill CLR, Plowden Hill MAN, Cudjoe Hill CTH, Long Hill ANN, Salt Pond Hill

CTH, Tims Hill ELZ, Sand Hills ELZ and Red Hill THS as physical features, fewer than the number of mountains they had identified. A *hill* might also help to identify a stretch of road, such as the long, steep climbs needed to get to the top of Long Hill JAS, Spur Tree Hill MAN and Melrose Hill MAN.

Similarly, Robertson was no more generous in his application of *hill* than he was with *mountain*. He had May Day Hill in southern Manchester and nearby Plowden Hill CLR. More interestingly, Robertson identified in St James "Cut Through Hill", suggesting perhaps some elaborate road works. The latter interpretation is not borne out by the modern contour map, however, on which the place is called Cut Throat Hill, so it may be that Robertson or his engraver misunderstood what they heard or saw. In any case, these three were the only natural features identified by Robertson with the singular *hill*, and he never used the plural *hills*. *Hill* did occur, however, as an element in the names of estates, plantations and pens, as discussed in chapter 7, but it is unknown how many of these settlement names drew from existing names for natural features.

Hill was much more commonly used to name physical features on the 1950 map, with thirty discrete examples. Probably one-half of these compound names were eponymous. Other names referred to vegetation: Mahogany Hill HAN, Mammee Hill ANN, Spur Tree [prickly cotton tree] Hill MAN, Grass Piece Hill CTH and Pumpkin Hill PLD. Animals were incorporated in Goat Hill MRY, John Crow Hill PLD and Hog House Hill PLD. John Crow Hill had been recognized in literature, at least by 1850, as a "gigantic summit".[10] Haycock Hill PLD, like *sugarloaf*, drew on the conical shape, although haystacks were virtually unknown in Jamaica. There was also Bogue Hill MAN, possibly referring to boggy land. Hellshire Hills CTH marked a desiccated limestone region with knife-edge ridges that made movement difficult through the equally unfriendly prickle bush and cacti. It had been known by the name for two centuries. Long, in 1774, referred to a range of hills "called Healthshire, corruptly Hellshire", but his and later attempts to make Healthshire stick were unsuccessful.[11]

Although *hill* was common on the 1950 map as a physical feature, it appeared many times more often in the names of settlements. In contrast to the pattern for *mount* habitation names, almost all of the *hill* examples used

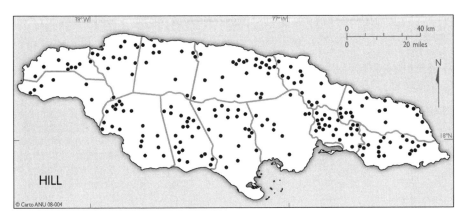

Figure 4.2 Jamaica: *Hill*, settlement names, 1950

the term as their second word, making it much more obviously a generic label. *Hill* habitation names on the 1950 map totalled 232, more than double the number of *mount* names, ranging from Albion Hill to Zion Hill, and were spread widely across the island, with significant absences only in the eastern mountains and the western interior uplands (some regions of which lacked settlements of any sort) and, less surprisingly, in the lowland plains (Figure 4.2). Not all of the *hill* habitation names identified striking eminences. Several were on quite level country – for example, Gravel Hill CLR – but hills often enough owed their visibility to the relative flatness of the surrounding country. Some of them stood out by occupying places perched above the narrow northern coastal plain with a view to the sea. The most popular hill names were Top Hill with seven instances, Orange Hill with six, Green Hill with five and Rose Hill with four, all of these widely scattered across the island. Eponymous names such as Jacks Hill, James Hill and Kemps Hill were, perhaps surprisingly, much less common for the habitation type than for *hill* as physical feature. Interestingly, *hill* habitation names sometimes refer to physical characteristics, as in Breezy Hill ANN, Chalky Hill ANN, Dry Hill HAN CLR, Marlie Hill MAN CTH, Stony Hill AND PLD, Rocky Hill ELZ and Sandy Hill CTH, and to flora and fauna, as in Ginger Hill ELZ and Jackass Hill MAN.

The *DJE* has *bump* as a Jamaicanism meaning the crest of a hill or the road that goes over it, sometimes the site of a village square. The 1950 map had Hog Grass Bump PLD and Hand Dog Bump PLD as physical features. In English generally, *hummock* designates a marginally elevated place, often well wooded and perhaps standing above marshy ground. The only Jamaican example on the 1950 map was Hellshire Hummock CTH, as a physical feature.

HEAD

As an inland landform, the term *head* appears rarely. The most significant example is Dolphin Head HAN which can be seen from the sea at a considerable distance from land. Its profile appeared on navigational maps from the 1780s. There is also Bull Head Mountain CLR, but this was sometimes called Bull Dead. In each of these cases resemblances may have been seen with the shape of the animal's head, but these mountains are particularly prominent, marking two of the highest points in the less mountainous western regions of the island.[12] The separate hydrological use of *head* to indicate the source of a river or spring is discussed in the next chapter.

GAP, PASS

The term *gap* identifies a breach or opening in a range of mountains, equivalent to a pass or gorge. It is used commonly in the United States but rarely in Britain. In Jamaica, *gap* appeared first on the 1950 map, all five examples found in the eastern high mountains: Hardwar Gap AND, Morces Gap PLD, Main Ridge Gap PLD, Portland Gap THS and Corn Puss Gap THS. The last of these is said to refer to the catching and corning of a feral cat by hungry travellers in the mountains. Sibley says Hardwar Gap was named after John Hardwar, the island's auditor-general in 1782; others claim it comes from the well-known Hindu holy place of pilgrimage in India, at the high headwaters of the Ganges, more commonly spelled Haridwar.

Morces Gap is apparently named after John Morce, acting postmaster, who died in 1834. New Haven Gap, between Morces Gap and Sir John Peak, was referred to around 1900 but rarely appeared on maps.[13]

The *DJE* identifies a Jamaican version of *pass* to mean a path or road or perhaps a river fording, matching an obsolete usage recorded in the *OED* to mean "a course, route, or road; a way into or out of somewhere", including a passage through mountains. In Jamaica, *pass* is even less common than *gap*, and like it appeared only on the 1950 map: Develders Pass ELZ and Cuna Cuna Pass THS. The latter matches the Cuni Cuni mentioned by Sawkins in the 1860s, though he did not attach *pass*, and the Cunhacunha Pass identified by Shreve in 1914.[14]

VALLEY, VALE

As a term to describe a physical feature, *valley* is one of those that became less rather than more popular over time. Bochart and Knollis, who consistently spelled *valley* as *vally*, found ten examples. Most of these were eponymous, the others being Manatee Vally MAN, Anchovy Vally CTH, Waters Vally MRY and Hopefull Vally CTH. Craskell and Simpson named only six physical features *valley*: Cabbage Vally ELZ, Cedar Valley ANN, Essex Valley ELZ, Jacksons Valley WLD, Lambs Valley HAN and Maiden Valley JAS. Matching his unwillingness to name mountains and hills, Robertson had just one *valley* as a natural feature: Pedro Valley ANN. He did, however, record the use of *valley* in the names of estates and plantations, as discussed in chapter 7. At least some of these seem unlikely to have taken their names from existing names for topographic features. Lucky Valley CLR, for example, seems most likely to have come complete as Lucky Valley Estate; the earliest known reference is from 1683, when it was referred to as "a plantation on Pindar's River, commonly called Lucky Valley".[15]

The 1950 map showed only six examples of *valley* as a physical feature: Webbers Valley WLD, Nassau Valley ELZ, Queen of Spains Valley TRL, Essex Valley ELZ, Ballards Valley ELZ and Blue Mountain Valley THS. Only one of these, Essex, had appeared on earlier maps. Like *mountain* and *hill*, habita-

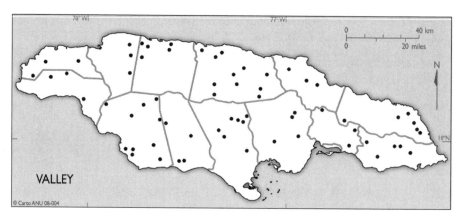

Figure 4.3 Jamaica: *Valley*, settlement names, 1950

tion names were more likely to include *valley* as an extension than were the recorded names of physical features. The 1950 map had seventy instances of *valley* habitation names, widely distributed but roughly matching what might be expected from the physiography (Figure 4.3). In some cases, *valley* and *hill* shared extensions, so that, for example, Breadnut Hill overlooked Breadnut Valley ELZ and Lucky Hill shadowed Lucky Valley CTH, but generally *hill* and *valley* were independently named. The most popular of the *valley* habitation names were Cedar Valley with five instances, Georges Valley with four and Water Valley with four, all of these widely distributed. None of these places had matching *hill* names.

Although closely associated with the contours of a valley, *vale* has a more particular use in Jamaica, applied sparingly. Bochart and Knollis had Ballards Vale MAN and Spring Vale CTH, Craskell and Simpson only Lynchs Vale ELZ. Robertson recorded just one topographic feature identified as a vale: Luidas Vale CTH. This vale is the most marked example of what geomorphologists came later to term a *polje*, meaning a large-scale depression formed by the collapse and solution of limestone, with a relatively flat alluvial floor.[16] The 1950 topographical map had this as Lluidas Vale, apparently following a directive from the Place Names Committee, the double *l* giving the name a Welsh feel rather than its purported Spanish original. It also added nearby Guanaboa Vale. This map found twenty-one settlement place names with *vale* as their final word, making it serve as a generic label. Almost all of these fell within the karst zones. The geomorphologist Marjorie Sweeting referred in 1972 to "poljes (or interior valleys as they are known in Jamaica)", the largest being the Queen of Spain's Valley TRL, ten kilometres by thirteen kilometres in extent, but partially drained by the Martha Brae River and therefore an "open polje". She thought Lluidas Vale fitted the definition better.[17]

BOTTOM

In North America, *bottom*, *hollow* and *valley* are typically used as synonyms, with *bottom* the least common, used to refer to low-lying land, an alluvial depression or dell. *Bottom* is also used to identify the bed beneath a body of water, as in the Jamaican *river bottom*.[18] More broadly, *bottom* can be used to describe any relatively flat tract of land, distinguished from its surrounding hills and mountains. Thus Patrick Browne, writing in the 1750s, divided Jamaica, "as it naturally is, into the mountainous, the hilly, and the bottom lands", meaning clearly that *bottom* was a suitable term for all types of level land which he also called "the lower parts of the island".[19]

Bochart and Knollis had only Calibash Bottom MRY. Craskell and Simpson never used the term as a physical feature. Neither did Robertson. The 1950 map had only one *bottom* as a physical feature, Hog Meat Bottom PLD, but it recorded the term more often in habitation names, with eleven instances. Some of these referred to physical features: Big Bottom JAS, Cave Bottom THS, Level Bottom TRL and Pretty Bottom CTH. Others associated them with large trees: Anchovy Bottom JAS, Breadnut Bottom CLR and Cabbage [Palm] Bottom THS. There was also Barbecue Bottom TRL, on the edge of the Cockpit Country, and Cooks Bottom ELZ, and the remainder were more certainly eponymous, Danbottom JAS and Hudsons Bottom MAN.

CAVE

The western two-thirds of Jamaica, the limestone region, is full of caves of one sort or another. In some cases it is possible to walk into a large cave mouth, but most often the caves are deep underground, the product of solution, with only small openings on the surface of the land. Sometimes these two types are combined in a single system. Some cave systems are dry, but many serve as the sources of springs or their sites of return underground. The place name *cave* may refer to any of these types and overlaps the hydrological terms *spring head*, *sink* and *sinkhole*.

Cave was one of the words frequently included on Robertson's 1804 map without any qualifier or extension. Thus it must be regarded as essentially descriptive – saying simply that there is a cave here – rather than naming that feature. Naming could, of course, easily follow, or alternatively the feature could be lost from maps and local naming vocabularies. Robertson simply declared *cave* in nine places and in one place identified "a cave". Occasionally he said a lot more. In the hills north of Worthy Park CTH, Robertson indicated a relatively large opening and declared, "This cave leads to a sunken area surrounded by perpendicular rocks." Immediately south of this cave he indicated a smaller opening that fed a rivulet and stated, "Pedro River is supposed to rise in this cave." To the west, he showed a small opening feeding into the Pindars River and identified this with more confidence as the "Cave where the river rises". Another five caves he named more fully. Two were distinguished by their scale: Great Cave ANN and Grand Cave CTH. There was also Peru Cave ELZ, Portland Cave CLR and, deep in the interior on the border between St Ann and Clarendon, Don Christopher's Cave. Further emphasizing the hydrological connection, Robertson recorded two cases of Cave River CLR MRY and a Cave Valley River HAN.

A modern register of Jamaican caves lists 1,272 named places, some of them having more than one name and some of them called sinks, holes, sinkholes and pits rather than caves. Many of these names derive from existing place names, as in Ipswich Cave ELZ and Worthy Park Cave CTH. Some relate to local people, such as Miss Miller's Cave PLD and Mistress

Bell Cave CLR. Others derive from the experience of cavers, as in Ed's Lost Rack Pit in the Me No Sen area of Trelawny, named for the fact that the explorer of 1985 – Ed – had rappelled through a narrow entrance shaft but later realized he had left his rappel rack at the bottom.[20] Few of these individual cave names appear on maps.

Related to cave features was the *light hole*, meaning a gap in the roof of a cave through which light might enter. *Light hole* is identified in the literature of karst geomorphology as a Jamaican term, though it is absent from the *DJE*. Sawkins, in the 1860s, explained the formation of light holes by "unequal denudation" or collapse, whereas modern geomorphologists emphasize the role of solution working downwards and the role of floodwaters passing through the underground drainage system.[21] The term was never popular as a place name, largely because of the feature's relative invisibility above ground. Robertson's map of 1800 included Light Hole ANN, and a Light Hole Cave, near Alderton ANN, is known, but most later maps ignore the term.

COCKPIT

The term *cockpit* is a Jamaicanism, first used as a landscape term in the 1680s. It derived from the cup shape of an arena for fighting cocks. In his *History of the Maroons* published in 1803, Dallas equated the cockpit with a glen. He declared:

> The grand object of a Maroon chief in war was to take a station in some glen, or, as it is called in the West Indies, Cockpit, enclosed by rocks and mountains nearly perpendicular, and to which the only practicable entrance is by a very narrow defile. From the first Cockpit there is a succession of them, running from east to west, on a line in which they are passable from one to the other, though with more or less difficulty. There are also parallel lines of Cockpits, but as their sides are often perpendicular, from fifty to eighty feet, a passage from one line to another is scarcely to be found practicable to any but a Maroon. The northern aspect is commonly the steepest and often a solid perpendicular rock, so that if the opposite ascent were practicable, to descend into the parallel line would be impossible. This is the general character of these recesses, though they may in some degree differ in

their direction. They have probably been formed along the large mountains of the island by violent earthquakes. On the difficult ascents there are either no trees, or such as have not strong roots: there are trees in the glens, and the entrance of the defiles is woody. In some, water is found near the passages on either end, but not in the centre.[22]

The *OED* definition of *cockpit* includes a "West Indies" meaning that simply recites the words of Dallas. The more general English meaning is simply a pit or enclosed space constructed to confine a contest but, in more modern times, suggesting also a centre of action, as in a ship or an aeroplane.

In the geomorphology of tropical humid karst, *cockpit* has become a technical term for depressions of this kind set among steep residual hills. As Sweeting observed, "the irregular depressions in tropical areas are now often known as cockpits, after the name given to them in Jamaica".[23] Jamaica has also provided the "type locality" for cockpit karst – *Cockpit Country* – discussed as a district term in chapter 2. In Cockpit Country, the conical hills occupy more of the land space than do the depressions and the hills are more closely interconnected, leaving the depressions relatively isolated. Thus the general pattern has sometimes been compared to that of an egg-box.[24] It is the hills that stand out most clearly in aerial photographs and topographic maps (Figure 4.4).

When was the term *Cockpit Country* first used? Dallas included in his book of 1803 "a map of the interior part of Jamaica, called the Cock-pits", drawn by James Robertson, with crude hachures indicating the character of the landform.[25] Robertson's map of Jamaica, published the following year, left the entire district blank and applied no general name to it. Robertson recorded Cockpit River Head CLR, but he otherwise made no use of the term. Before Robertson, in the late seventeenth century, few of the English had any realistic idea of the landscape of the Cockpit Country, and Bochart and Knollis merely continued through the district the generalized lines of hills/mountains that they applied indiscriminately across most of the interior. They identified only Pedros Cockpits CTH. Similarly, Craskell and Simpson showed Barbadoes Valley Cockpitts ELZ but left the Cockpit Country a blank.

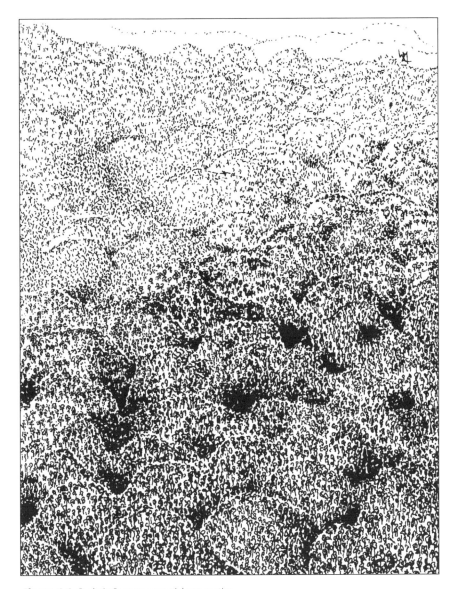

Figure 4.4 Cockpit Country, an aerial perspective

In the 1860s Sawkins referred several times to "the Cockpit country" but this merely defined a geographical type or region. He described the geology of southern Trelawny this way: "It is here [Windsor Pen] the Cockpit country commences; and from the difficulties presented by the uneven surface, the loose fragmentary limestone, the steepness of the declivities and acclivities, the absence of soil or water render this portion of the parish undeserving of attention either for agricultural or pastoral purposes, consequently it remains under the shadows of the virgin forests a terra incognita."[26]

It required a second capital *C* and the dropping of the definite article to become a place name. The earliest known use occurred in *The New Jamaica,* a book published in 1890 and written to encourage investment and tourism following the spread of the railway and hotels. The authors, Edgar Mayhew Bacon and Eugene Murray Aaron, declared: "The unsettled Cockpit Country and Black Lands in St. James and Trelawney Parishes are full of interest and well worth exploration. The mystery of lost rivers, of cavernous hills, of wild, weird forest tangles, of mystery sink holes and sudden cliffs, lure one to adventure."[27] They did not explain the meaning of *cockpit.* Within a few years, the Jamaican popular press had translated this to The Cockpit Country and installed it as a fully capitalized place name that began to appear on maps, though without a clear-cut boundary line.[28] The definite article gradually disappeared and the region became known simply as Cockpit Country. In the twentieth century, roads were built through the edges of Cockpit Country, eventually evolving into a "ring road" that helped to delimit and define it as a region.[29]

PLAIN

It is striking that, in Jamaica and elsewhere, lowland landscapes are much less likely to be named than upland features. In part this is simply because level areas are considered homogeneous and lacking in the differentiation required to make naming viable, and flatness equates in many minds to featurelessness. The pattern is also partly explained by the fact that fluvial features are often taken to be sufficient to name an area, so that the name of a river can be applied more broadly to its plain. This works well in Jamaica, where floodplains are generally constrained and small-scale. *Valley, vale* and *bottom* have the same function.[30]

Craskell and Simpson, and Robertson, used *plain* only for the extensive Pedro Plains ELZ. The 1950 map added just one occurrence as a physical feature: Liguanea Plain AND, the long sloping background to Kingston Harbour, known to the Spanish as *Hato de Liguanea*, cultivated by the English in sugar plantations and pens, and overspread by urban development in the later twentieth century. In habitation names there were also Belle Plain CLR and Spring Plain CLR. The small settlement Georges Plain WLD appeared on twentieth-century maps but the more extensive plain of which it was part did not, though it is commonly referred to as the Westmoreland Plain.

SAVANNA

In Jamaica, as in North America, vegetational landscapes have provided few generic terms for the names of physical features.[31] The *DJE* finds a unique Jamaican meaning for *morass*, defined as "a moist or swampy piece of land covered with vegetation", but the emphasis is on the water rather than the flora, so *morass* is discussed in chapter 5. *Pasture* and *meadow* have become common but generally only in the names of modern housing developments, discussed in chapter 8.

Place names including references to flora overwhelmingly identify trees, whereas grass is only occasionally noted, in much the same way that hills and mountains are more likely to be noticed than level plains. The biggest trees are the most visible in the landscape, though not the most common types. Thus studies of vegetation place names often seek to determine how far the names match the distribution of trees at the time of settlement, using the names as a means of reconstructing the actual vegetation. One approach to this question depends on the extent to which the place names differentiate vegetation types, referring to species such as logwood and mahogany rather than lumping them together in broad categories, such as *grove* or *forest*.[32] Another is to map densities and collocations. Here it is useful to study early maps and documents in comparison with later ones because over time true generic names, derived directly from existing stands, tend to be outnumbered by indirect or false generic terms that derive from other names rather than from the vegetation itself. For example, Santa Maria Savanna might indicate the existence of an original grassy savanna shaded by Santa Maria trees, whereas Savanna la Mar is a town, which borrows its *savanna* from an existing name.[33]

The word *savanna* entered Jamaican English through the Spanish, but its origin was in the Amerindian *çabana*, *zabana* or *sabána*, meaning a treeless plain, particularly an extensive one.[34] This was confused with the Spanish *sábana* or *sávana*, a tablecloth or sheet, as suggesting a similarly featureless, flat landscape. The rule that a *savanna* should be treeless and featureless was of course not honoured in practice, with varieties of large trees often giving their names to such places. Within Jamaica, a number of plants, most of them low-growing, were associated with the word *savanna*, giving them unique terminology. The *DJE* lists savanna grass or carpet grass, savanna weed, savanna purslane, savanna mustard, the more shrubby savanna broomweed and savanna flower (*Echites jamaicensis*, a slender climber growing to 6 metres).

In 1672 Richard Blome declared that Jamaica had "many Savanas which are intermixed with the Hills and Woods". He reported the understanding that these had been formerly planted in corn by the Tainos and converted to pasture by the Spanish but, by his time, "these Savanas are the most barren, as being so long made use of without tillage; yet doth they produce such a great plenty of grass". Similarly, Leslie in 1739 declared that the "savannahs or large plains" had been planted in maize by the Tainos and grazed by the cattle of the Spanish but were "now quite bare and barren". By the 1840s, Joseph John Gurney could argue that in Jamaican parlance a "savannah" was simply a flat plain. The *DJE* does not list *savanna* as a Jamaicanism, but in Florida, according to McMullen, "a savanna is commonly understood to be any grassland possessing some degree of saturation", sometimes flooded but sometimes so dry that fire might sweep across it.[35]

The 1680 map of Bochart and Knollis used the Spanish spelling *savaña* to name thirty-three places identified as physical features rather than settlement sites. This was a substantially larger number than on any later maps, indicating the long-term transformation of these land types into plantations and pens (Figure 4.5). The 1680 map provided drawings that give a clue to the character of these places and the way in which the savanna might be transformed into a pen (Figure 4.6). All but two of the savannas identified by Bochart and Knollis had compound names. Several of these names referred to flora: Samphir Savana JAS, Lime Savana ANN, Sancta Maria Savana CLR and Palmeto Savana CLR. Some related to nearby streams. Others pointed to physical dimensions, as in Round Savana WLD and Long Savana WLD. There were two places named Burnt Savana WLD ELZ, and a Roastmeat Hall Savana WLD. Perhaps six of the names retained strong Spanish elements but very few were eponymous. Bochart and Knollis also had Old Womans Savana CLR. Edward Long called this "a savannah, or plain" and believed it had got its name "from an elderly Spanish lady, who took up her abode here after the island was surrendered to the English, and resided here many years in a hut".[36]

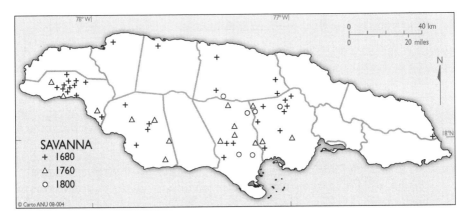

Figure 4.5 Jamaica: *Savanna* names, 1680, 1760 and 1800

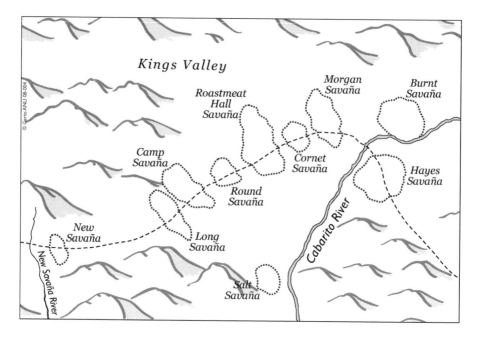

Figure 4.6 *Savañas*, redrawn from Bochart and Knollis, 1680

Craskell and Simpson in 1760 applied the term *savanna* to thirteen places, many fewer than the thirty-three of 1680, all of them now compound names (see Figure 4.5). Not surprisingly, in light of the overall reduction, most of the names on Craskell and Simpson's map repeated those used by Bochart and Knollis. New coinages included Bull Savanna ELZ and Horse Savanna ELZ, and the discouraging Tick Savanna CLR and Labour in Vain Savanna ELZ. The latter, said Long in 1774, was "a name perfectly descriptive of its nature".[37] Robertson's 1800 map identified no generic *savanna* but recorded ten with compound names, all natural features, not settlements. Few of these names were new. Robertson identified Savanna River CLR and Old Womans Savanna River CLR, both of these close to Old Womans Savanna, and Savanna Spring CTH. Only two of the savannas identified as natural features were eponymous: Harris's Savanna CLR and Hays Savanna CLR. The Tick Savanna of Craskell and Simpson became Teak Savanna on Robertson's map.

Long said that the northwest part of Sixteen Mile Walk or St Thomas in the Vale formed "a tract of savannah" near the foot of Monte Diablo called The Maggoti. He discussed the name at length, saying, "The name of this savannah gave rise to a story, that, whenever it rains here, the drops which fall upon any person's cloaths become maggots in half an hour." He believed this story had been concocted "probably at first by way of joke to some credulous inquirer", but had gained currency through repetition. He thought the savanna's name more probably derived from the Spanish, "compounded of Maga (an enchantress), and Oteo (watching on a high place); alluding probably to the pinnacle of *Monte Diablo*, over which the thunderclouds so frequently break, as, together with its horrid aspect, to make it seem a proper residence for a witch, under patronage of the Devil, to whom the mountain was dedicated".[38] Alternative explanations suggest an origin in the Spanish term *mogote*, identifying a low, flat-topped hill or an isolated conical knoll, a term that – as with *cockpit* – has found its way into modern geomorphology.

The long-term reduction in the number of places labelled *savanna* continued into the twentieth century. The 1950 topographic map named a mere eight as physical features, but *savanna* appeared also in the names of districts and settlements. None of the names were new. Survivors from the 1680s were Burnt Savanna ELZ, Old Womans Savanna CLR and Santa Maria Savanna CLR; from the 1760s, Bull Savanna ELZ and Horse Savanna ELZ; and from 1800, Vera Ma Hollis Savanna CLR, Harris Savanna CLR and Hayes (with an *e*) Savanna CLR. Most of these were matched on the map by habitation or settlement names, the only additions being New Savanna WLD, Salt Savanna CLR and Yates Savanna CLR.

GROVE, WOOD

An immensely popular habitation place name element in Jamaica is *grove*, the term often associated with a specific plant. Although this form is most common for habitation sites, the naming pattern is strongly suggestive of the existence of significant clumps or concentrations of particular trees,

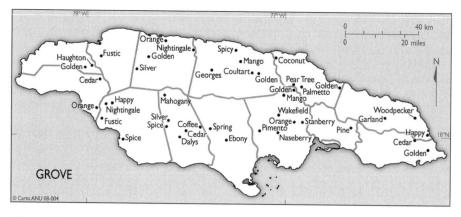

Figure 4.7 Jamaica: *Grove*, settlement names, 1950

often natural rather than the result of active planting. The 1950 map had forty examples in total, half of them including a tree (Figure 4.7). Most popular of these was Cedar Grove WLD MAN THS. Others referred to coconut, coffee, ebony, fustic, mahogany, mango, naseberry, orange, palmetto, pimento, pine and (avocado) pear tree. The last of these has been given visibility in Erna Brobder's history of the village, *Woodside, Pear Tree Grove P.O.*, in which she charts the rocky journey of the name itself, perched on the parochial boundary.[39] More general in their reference to vegetation were Garland Grove PLD, Spice Grove ELZ MAN and Spicy Grove ANN. Most popular overall was Golden Grove, with six widely spread occurrences in 1950, and this was joined by Silver Grove, Spring Grove and Happy Grove. Just occasionally they were named after birds, as in Nightingale Grove ELZ TRL and Woodpecker Grove PLD. Variants of *grove*, such as *copse* and *orchard*, are rare, though Copse HAN has survived as a settlement name, and the cadastral series included Orchard Estate HAN and Orchard Plantation JAS AND.

Wood is also popular, with fifty occurrences in 1950, but it was most often applied as a suffix, as in Blackwood CTH or Cotterwood ELZ, and often actually or potentially eponymous, as in Walkerswood ANN and Barkerswood MRY. Some of these are transfers, as in Birnamwood PLD.

Broadly descriptive were Big Woods WLD ELZ, and perhaps Longwood ELZ CLR and Shortwood JAS AND. Only a handful were associated with particular trees or shrubs, as in Jointwood ELZ, named for the pepper elder *Piper amalgo*, Lancewood ELZ, for *Xylopia muricata*, the straight-trunked, smooth-barked tree that grew in the limestone woodlands of the central parishes, and Logwood HAN MAN, for the gnarled *Haematoxylum campechianum* that long served as a common dyewood and formed many fences.

CHAPTER FIVE

Hydrological Names

JAMAICA HAS BEEN CALLED THE "land of wood and water" and the "land of springs", so it is not surprising to find that hydrological features have played a prominent role in the naming of the island's landscape.[1] Water resources – for sustenance of plants and animals, for motive power and for navigation – were always vital, but particularly in the early colonization of the land. Tainos, Spanish and English all approached Jamaica by sea and observed the inlets and river mouths that provided potential entries to the interior and evidence of fruitful vales. Streams were therefore among the first physical features to be identified and named, and they initially formed a large proportion of all named physical features. On the 1680 Bochart and Knollis map, streams made up more than 80 per cent of all physical features with compound names; on the 1760 Craskell and Simpson map, 73 per cent; on Robertson's 1800 map, 50 per cent; and on the 1950 topographic map, restored to the high of 80 per cent.

The changing relative importance of stream names mirrored the growing proportion of physical features among the named places generally, as noted in chapter 3. At the same time, the number of hydrological features with compound names reached almost 600 on Robertson's map, compared with 530 on the 1950 map. This reduction was partly a product of changed hydrology and rainfall patterns and water capture for human use, and partly a result of the engrossing of these features into habitation and settlement names. The climate of Jamaica in the later eighteenth century was cooler and wetter than in the late twentieth century, with heavier dry season rainfall. Deforestation, particularly after 1950, contributed to reduced surface runoff and underground water and to the loss of perennial flow in many rivers.[2]

The hydrology of Jamaica is shaped by two major factors. These are the shape of the island and its geological structure. With a long coastline encircling a compressed oval landmass and a central ridge, Jamaica was predestined to have a large number of short streams running quickly to the sea. In the rainy highlands at the eastern end of the island, where impermeable metamorphic, igneous and sedimentary rocks predominate, there are numerous surface streams. Their torrential flows down the steep gradients have carved deep valleys with precipitous sides. The typically dendritic drainage systems that have developed on each side of the mountain spine can be seen clearly on the map. In contrast, the lower, drier western two-thirds of the island is characterized by extensive areas of permeable limestone, a type of rock that is slowly soluble in rainwater. Here much of the drainage is below the surface. Streams often start as springs only to disappear underground before again emerging at the surface. Consequently, the map shows a multiplicity of short streams seemingly unrelated to any larger surface or subsurface network in a landscape that displays a range of physical features typical of karst topography.

In nature, fluvial landforms are part of a continuum, and the application of generic place names depends on an agreed classification of types that ultimately requires arbitrary decisions about the proper designation of each stream.[3] In Jamaica, the hydrological system created the potential for a high density of names, including the multiple naming of what was in fact a single stream as it appeared and disappeared in a series of superficially unrelated incarnations.

RIVER

From the beginning of English colonization and place-naming in Jamaica, the most common hydrological feature was the river. *River* was a common

English word, used for many centuries, meaning a substantial stream of water flowing in a channel and generally entering the sea or another, larger stream. This seems straightforward enough, but technical and legal definitions sometimes stumble on the "stream of water" requirement and the question of whether a bona fide river must always have perennial flow or whether intermittent, seasonal or ephemeral streamflow is sufficient.[4] Thus Charles Leslie, referring to Jamaica's rivers in 1739, declared that "An exact catalogue of them no man can pretend to give, for severals [*sic*] disappear after a storm, or alter their course, and lose their names".[5] Similar issues apply to the qualifications required of a waterfall or cascade. These questions applied to Jamaica as much as any other place but, with the island's generally abundant rainfall, early mapmakers had no difficulty in identifying large numbers of streams deserving of the appellation *river*.

Of all the hydrological features named by Bochart and Knollis in 1684, *river* accounted for 85 per cent, and this high proportion persisted strongly, down to the 1950 topographic map when it was 78 per cent. Bochart and Knollis named sixty-nine *rivers* on land and another forty-three on the sea, beyond the mapped shoreline, at their mouths. The only term to come close to their use of *river* was its Spanish equivalent, *rio*. Bochart and Knollis had eight of these: Rio Hoa ANN, Rio de Cobre CTH, Rio Nuevo MRY, Rio Sambre CTH, Rio de Flora CTH, Rio de Pedro CTH and Rio Grande PLD. Craskell and Simpson in 1760 identified 105 streams as *rivers*, named on the land, together with an additional twenty-three named on the sea. This slight increase over Bochart and Knollis was balanced by fewer examples of *rio* – just six. Overall, 78 per cent of the hydrologic names identified by Craskell and Simpson were supplied by *river/rio*.

In his *History of the Maroons*, published in 1803, Dallas argued that Jamaica could "boast of one hundred rivers, although none of them are deep enough for navigation".[6] Perhaps Dallas had counted them from the map of Craskell and Simpson. Robertson's map, published the year after, found many more, recording 383 cases of the term *river*, widely spread across the island but with strong concentrations in the eastern end away from the limestone belts, in the interior-central region and, even more dramatic, in empty areas in the central zone (Figure 5.1). Robertson tripled

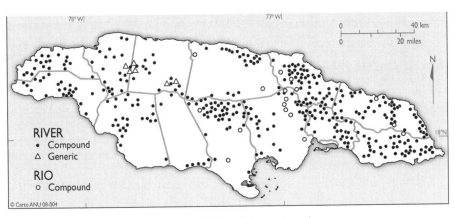

Figure 5.1 Jamaica: *River* and *rio* names, 1800 (as on Robertson's map)

the number of rivers named by Bochart and Knollis and by Craskell and Simpson, though *river/rio* accounted for a smaller proportion of the hydrologic names on Robertson's 1800 map, at 70 per cent. Only six of Robertson's river names were strictly generic or descriptive – appearing simply as *river* – all the others were compound names, with extensions or qualifiers of one sort or another. Robertson identified a further 50 streams simply as *rivulet*, never adding an extension, so making these ineligible as place names; Dallas similarly referred to the many "delicious rivulets" that were common in parts of the island. Similar in meaning is *brook*, a term used by the English for a small stream or rivulet and applied very commonly in the northeastern United States but relatively rarely elsewhere.[7] Robertson named just one *brook* and this only as an alternative: Luidas River or Murmuring Brook CTH.

Few of the extensions were shared with the most popular settlement names. On Robertson's map there was no Content River or Friendship River, for example, and the sentiments were uncommon overall. Retirement River JAS was unusual in this respect. Hope River AND was an eponym. Golden River CTH was also positive, but the other possible sentiment names were less optimistic: Devils River CTH THS, River Styx ELZ, Styx River THS and Ugly River MRY. The contrast with settlement names was strong.

Many of the qualifiers and extensions added to *river* names represented physical characteristics of the streams themselves, such as Swift River, Roaring River and Black River, or related them to local physical features, as in Cave River and Buff Bay River. Of the river names on Robertson's 1800 map, some referred simply to scale and volume, such as Little River (8 examples), Short River (1), Great River (2) and Broad River (2). Others were named for their shape. Crooked River JAS entered the Tangle River, which in turn disappeared down a sinkhole. There was also Serpentine River CLR. Overall, physical characteristics accounted for 22 per cent of the river names on Robertson's map, and 11 per cent referred to the place of the river in the overall stream network. Vegetation was used to name 14 per cent of the rivers and animals another 7 per cent. Also important were eponymous names (17 per cent) and names transferred from other places, most of these local rather than foreign, as in the coves or bays into which the rivers flowed (9 per cent).

Some river names indicate the role of the stream in the larger system. This can be understood in terms of the ordering of streams as a branching system, the rankings of the channels generally matching the relative volumes of water they carried. The Little Rivers rarely had tributaries but flowed a short distance before disappearing down a sinkhole, or alternatively were second- or third-order streams, meaning that they flowed into one or two other named streams which ultimately flowed into the sea. Similarly, Back River (eight cases) was always represented by Robertson as a second- or third-order stream. In upper Clarendon, two separate Back Rivers were tributaries of the Juan de Bolas River, which in turn flowed into the Rio Minho. But a Back River might have tributaries – thus the Back River that entered the Rio Grande in Portland had its own Main Branch, East Branch and West Branch (Figure 5.2). The Back River remained part of Maroon topography, as *Baka Ribba*, lying beneath the lookout pinnacle Watch Hill or Pumpkin Hill (so named for a timely crop that saved the ancestors from starvation). Robertson in some cases simply identified "a branch" without extension, but when he recorded an East Branch, West Branch, Left Branch, Right Branch or Main Branch, these were always related to named rivers. Generally the branches were balanced

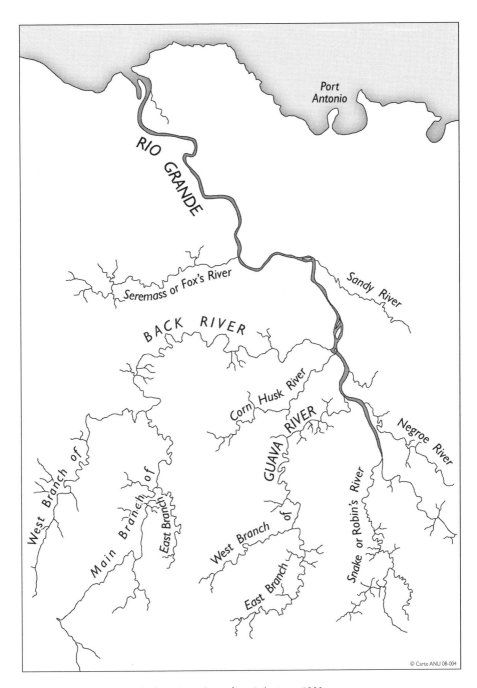

Figure 5.2 Rio Grande and tributaries, redrawn from Robertson, 1800

Port
Antonio

RIO GRANDE

Seremass or Fox's River

Sandy River

BACK RIVER

Corn Husk River

GUAVA RIVER

Negroe River

West Branch of

Main Branch of

East Branch

West Branch of

Snake or Robin's River

East Branch

© Carto ANU 08-004

pairs, so that the Forked River MRY had both East Branch and West Branch, but the Stony River MRY had Main Branch, North Branch and South Branch, as did the Guava River PLD. The Morant River THS had Left Arm and Right Arm on Robertson's map, but *arm* was less common than *branch*, indicating the far more useful image offered by a branching tree than that offered by the human body. On the 1950 map the only surviving examples were West Branch MRY and East Branch PLD. The use of *branch* as a true generic term to mean an independent small stream, common in parts of the United States, had no currency in Jamaica.[8]

Roaring River was another popular name, referring to the mighty sound of the stream in full flow over cascades and rapids, standing out in what in the eighteenth century was a relatively quiet world. Then, nature was sometimes more noisy than any sounds associated with human activity and industry. There were nine examples on Robertson's map, some of them very short streams, as in the Roaring River of interior Trelawny, which Robertson noted on his map "gushes out of the cleft of a rock with a loud noise" before quickly going underground again down a sink. The Roaring River TRL, which enters the Martha Brae River, first passes over a series of falls and, on Robertson's 1800 map, powered three watermills along the

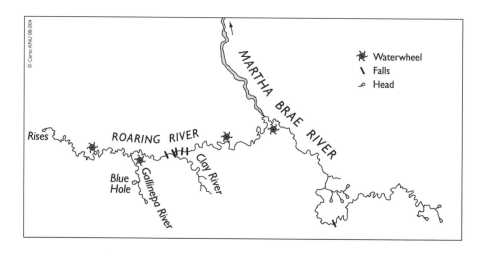

Figure 5.3 Roaring River and tributaries, redrawn from Robertson, 1800

way (Figure 5.3). The popular White River (twelve cases on Robertson's map) probably also refers to the cascading nature of the streams, as may Niagara River JAS and Brave River MRY, in contrast to more sluggish Black River (five cases on Robertson). Some river names refer to their rising and sinking, as in Cistern River ANN. A few are remarkable for their paucity of water rather than the usual abundance, as for example Dry River ELZ MRY PLD.

Geological features were elements of some river names on Robertson's map, as in Broad Stone River MRY, Chalky River AND, Clay River TRL, Flint River HAN MRY, Iron River AND, Sulphur River ELZ, Paved River MRY, Rock River CTH, Rocky River MRY, Stony River CLR ANN MRY and the more common Salt River WLD CLR CTH MRY AND and Sandy River CLR CTH MRY PLD. Some rivers were named after the vegetation that grew along their banks. Robertson identified forty-nine cases, 13 per cent of all the named rivers on his map. Fruit trees were represented in Anchovy River THS and Anchovy Valley River JAS, Banana River PLD THS, Calabash Bottom River MRY, Guava River PLD, Lime Bush River THS, Mammee River AND, Orange River HAN JAS ELZ CLR MRY, Pepper Bush River PLD, Plantain River CTH AND, Plantain Garden River THS, Plantain Walk River HAN MRY, and Pumpkin House River PLD. The anchovy pear was known in the eighteenth century as the West Indian mango and was described by Edward Long as "a beautiful tree . . . frequent in the mountains, as well as in low moist bottoms".[9] Others referred to sources of eighteenth-century building materials: Palmetto River THS and Thatch River CLR. There was also Cabbage River MRY, named for the cabbage tree palm and the source of hearts of palm, and Calabash Bottom River MRY. Food or provision-crop plants occurring in river names on Robertson's map included Cassava River CTH, Coco River TRL, Corn Husk River PLD and Ginger River CTH AND. Grasses gave names to Cane River ANN AND, Wild Cane River THS, Cutting Grass Spots River WLD and Grass River ELZ, while a vine gave its name to Cacoon River HAN.

Some of the rivers on Robertson's map were named for animals that swam in them: Alligator Hole River MAN, Alligator Pond River MAN, Eel River ELZ, Fish River HAN, Long Fish River JAS, Turtle River THS and

Turtle Crawle River PLD. The numbers of some of these creatures, notably the turtles, were greatly reduced by heavy exploitation into the twentieth century, so their roles in river names declined. The mobility of land animals made associations transient, even compared to the floral names. Feral pigs were prominent among these examples, as in Boar River AND, Hog River HAN, Hog Hole River AND and Fat Hog Quarter River HAN. Montego River JAS may have taken its name from the lard (Spanish *manteca*) boiled down from hogs and exported through Montego Bay in the sixteenth century, or directly from the bay settlement. Barbecue River AND perhaps recorded some momentous feast of feral meat. Directly or indirectly, cattle gave names to Bull Bay River AND and Bull Head River CLR, and horses to Horse Savanna River ELZ THS. Cabaritta River HAN adapted the Spanish for *goat*. A few rivers were named for the troublesome insects that no doubt concentrated around the stream edges. These included the Gallinepa River TRL recorded on Robertson's map, named for the gallinipper of the *DJE*, a large mosquito or other stinging insect, and the Mosquito River CLR.

On Robertson's 1800 map a number of rivers betrayed their Spanish origins, some of them the largest in the island. These included the Rio Bueno (forming part of the parish border between Trelawny and St Ann), Rio Grande PLD, Rio Hoe ANN (the name derived from the Spanish Rio Hoja), Rio Minho CLR, Rio Novo MRY and Rio Sambre MRY. The Rio Magno, Rio Pedro and Rio d'Ora, as well as its tributary the Rio d'Oro, all flow into the Rio Cobre CTH. At one point in its course, however, the Rio Minho was identified by Robertson as the "Rio Minho or Dry River". There was also the Great Spanish River MRY. Long referred to "the Rio Montando, or Mountain river" in the old parish of St John, but this does not appear on any of the maps.[10]

In his 1869 report on the geology of Jamaica, Sawkins said, "Upwards of 114 rivers or streams are known to find their way to the sea from the interior of the island, exclusive of the numerous tributaries which issue from every ravine of the mountain districts, or from the lakes and lagoons which overflow during the rainy season; this abundance of water justifies the appellation of 'island of springs,' which was applied to Jamaica by the Spanish discoverers." Although he counted a smaller number of rivers than

Robertson, Sawkins paid close attention to his map and noted that in several cases he had "laid down streams not noted in Robertson's map; and their magnitude justified my doing so, being larger than some of those represented on that map".[11] One reason for the numerous named rivers was that, particularly in the western limestone formation, as noted earlier, many went underground and gained new names when they re-emerged even though they were a continuous stream. For example, said Sawkins,

> the main branch of the Rio Cobre, rising in the north-western part of Clarendon, is first known as the Yankee river; after a course of some miles it sinks below the surface at Cave valley, and re-issues to form the great morass, from which, flowing south-east, it is termed the Pedro river, and divides the parishes of St. Ann and Clarendon, again sinking to re-appear in the parish of St. John, at Luidas Vale. After traversing this parish it again disappears below the limestone on the eastern side to finally re-appear at River Head, in St. Thomas-in-the- Vale, as the Black river, which unites at the Bog Walk with the Rio d'Oro and Rio Pedro streams to form the Rio Cobre, which flows through St. Catherine, entering the sea in the western part of the harbour of Kingston.[12]

Modern water tracing has positively identified many long-distance underground flows, to a maximum of twenty-seven kilometres from sink to rising.[13]

In spite of its many sheets, the 1950 topographic map of Jamaica had just 397 named rivers, only fourteen more than Robertson, and exactly the same number of examples of *rio* (eleven). Among the latter, the suite of names changed little, gaining only Rio Bronte MAN and losing Rio Magno CTH, which was degraded to the seasonal Rio Magno Gully. Of the rivers, Robertson had sixty-nine distinct names that did not appear in 1950, whereas the 1950 map had eighty names not found on Robertson. Some of this difference came from the corruption and modification of names and the modernization of spelling, so that, for example, Cashmans River CLR became Cushmans River, Hoddars River CLR became Hooders River, Mattee River THS became Mattys River, Moho River CLR became Mahoe River, Low River ANN became Lowe River and Yanky River ANN became Yankee River. These examples show that changes in orthography could shift meaning from a physical quality (low) to a possible surname (Lowe) or from a possible personal name (Moho/Mojo) to a tree (Mahoe). English versions of Spanish names also became more dominant. For example, the 1950 map recognized only Wag Water River, which Robertson had called Agua Alta or Wag Water River, as derived by the Spanish, supposedly, from the Arawak *Guayguata*. In 1890 Bacon and Aaron referred to "the Wag Water: the *Agua Alta*, – the Loud River".[14] The Spanish Crawle River MRY and Spanish Lookout River ANN of Robertson's map disappeared, though the 1950 map created a new Spanish River MRY.

Almost one-half of the sixty-nine river names lost from Robertson's map were eponymous, suggesting that the people for whom the rivers had been named had moved on, out of sight and out of memory. Nearly all of these losses were balanced by fresh eponymous names that appeared on the 1950 topographic map. This was not generally a simple exchange, however; the rivers that lost their old eponymous names were not always renamed for new people. Blake River ELZ on the 1950 map might appear to have been named for Governor Sir Henry Blake, who had an enthusiasm for giving his own name to Jamaican places, but this stream had been called Black River by Robertson, so the new form may simply indicate corruption. In other cases a general descriptive term was transformed into a folk character, as in the changing of Robertson's Roaring River WLD to Bragging Tom River, the sound of the stream retained and humanized.

Names relating to physical characteristics that disappeared from Robertson's map included: Broad Stone River MRY, Cistern River ANN, Clay River TRL, Lagoon River TRL, Morass River CTH and the more generic Long River CLR and Short River ANN. The 1950 map added few of this sort: Broadmouth River AND and Copper River THS. Names relating to flora that disappeared from Robertson's map included Anchovy River THS, Anchovy Valley River JAS, Cabbage River MRY, Cacoon River HAN, Pepper Bush River PLD, Plantain Walk River HAN MRY, Thatch River CLR and Water Cress River THS. Ruinate River AND, on the margin of the floral names, also disappeared. The 1950 map added Cashoo River ELZ, Cocoa River PLD THS, Coffee River THS and Mahoe River MRY. As expected, a smaller number of names relating to fauna disappeared from Robertson's map: Eel River ELZ and Gallinepa River TRL. The 1950 map added a perhaps surprisingly large number: Alligator Hole River MAN, Alligator Pond River ELZ, Bird River PLD, Bossue River PLD (for the small edible snail *busu*), Bugaboo River THS (for insects, termites or, possibly, a duppy/spirit – a Duppy River appeared nearby), Cony River THS, Crab River THS and Jackass River WLD. Other new names of 1950 were Rotten Gut River MAN, Sambo Bottom River THS and Savanna River CLR.

SPRING

Springs played an important role in Jamaican life before piped water and public reservoirs. Whereas rivers suffered variable flows – from flood to drought – and tended to occupy low-lying channels, springs were relatively reliable and often burst from the ground in elevated sites, managed by the underground hydrology of the island in its extensive limestone zones. As Dallas noted in 1803, "Jamaica indeed, as its name imports, abounds in springs that descend on both sides of the eminences that divide the island."[15]

Early maps of Jamaica identified surprisingly few physical features as springs. Bochart and Knollis had only one: Kettle Spring CLR. Craskell and Simpson identified just two: Launceswood Spring CLR and Plantain Spring CLR. *Spring* was more common on Robertson's map but still much less frequent than *river* and less likely to carry a compound name (Figure 5.4). Robertson had ninety-nine cases of *spring* and four of *springs*, as natural features, but sixty-eight of these were simple generic descriptions. For these, Robertson sometimes showed only a small round hole, known by contemporaries as a *cistern* or natural reservoir, the source from which the spring emerged from the ground. Similar was the short gash where Robertson identified "a constant spring, at the foot of a precipice". In other cases the cisterns were associated with short streams, often called *rivulets* (Figure 5.5). Sometimes a series of springs with compound names was shown by Robertson entering a river without the springs having clearly defined heads or cisterns: for example, Dawkins Spring, Pattons Spring, Try See Spring, Pump Spring, Cuffee Spring and Jew Spring all entered St

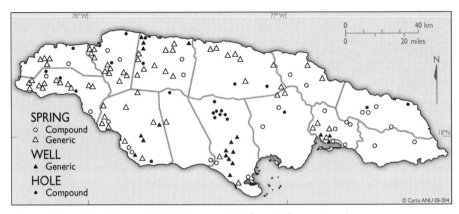

Figure 5.4 Jamaica: *Spring, well* and *hole* names, 1800 (as on Robertson's map)

Thomas's River CLR in this fashion, whereas Kenco Spring had a clearly defined spring head.

Several of the compound spring names on Robertson's map seem no more than simply descriptive in a generic fashion, as in Salt Spring CLR and Hot Salt Spring CLR, the latter feeding The Bath at Milk River, and Sulphur Hot Spring THS, which fed the Bath of St Thomas the Apostle. The mineral qualities of some of the springs was indicated in Mineral Spring CLR, Mineral Springs AND and Petrifying Springs MRY, and perhaps Hot Spring HAN PLD. Some referred to other characteristics of the water, as in Cold Spring AND, Dirty Spring AND, flowing into Kingston Harbour, Black Spring ELZ and the nearby Fresh Water Spring ELZ. Others, like rivers, mentioned physical characteristics of the streams themselves, as in Crooked Spring JAS and Five Fall Spring MRY. A few referred to vegetation, as in Cotton Tree Spring CLR, Mammee Spring AND and Savanna Spring CTH. Only Craw Fish Spring THS mentioned fauna. Eleven of the compound names were eponymous. Although most of Jamaica's springs were regarded generically and rarely retained the label *spring* once they became substantial, when they were usually named *rivers*, they had a significant impact on habitation and settlement names because of their economic importance in supplying regular water – a constant spring – as well as power.

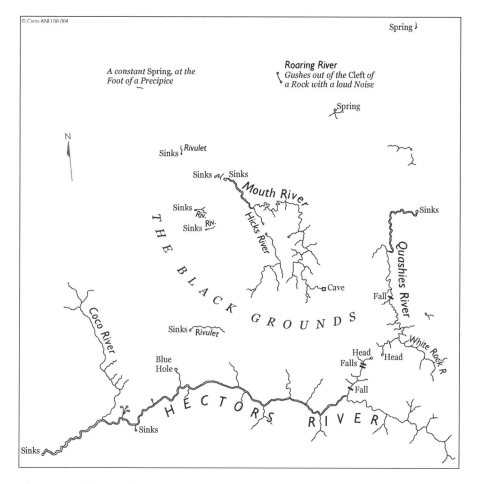

Figure 5.5 *Black Grounds* district, 1800, redrawn from Robertson's map

The 1950 map gave much less prominence to springs. It had no simple generic springs and only eighteen compound examples. The simple descriptives, such as the salt and mineral springs, disappeared, though the healing potential remained in Bath Spring PLD and perhaps Yaws Spring MRY. Probably eleven of the eighteen were eponymous. Crawfish Spring survived from Robertson's map and was joined by Fowl House Spring THS. In addition to these physical features, *spring* formed the second word in thirty-four settlement names on the 1950 map, thus preserving the reference. Some of these place names similarly preserved the physical details, such as Salt Spring HAN JAS ELZ AND, Mountain Spring WLD and Rock Spring HAN TRL.

HEAD, WELL, HOLE

The term *head* appeared frequently on Robertson's map, to indicate the source of a river or spring. Occasionally it occurred as the compound Spring Head (seven cases) or River Head (eleven cases), and in a few cases this might be appropriated to a specific river, as in Salt River Head AND and Cockpit River Head CLR. River-head or Riverhead had become firmly installed as a specific place name rather than a generic by the end of the eighteenth century.[16] Most often, Robertson used *head* (sixty-nine cases) or *heads* (ten cases) without extension, all of these occurring west of Spanish Town. He rarely added information, though in the case of the Rio Bueno he identified the "Head where an immense body of water rises up from the foot of a semicircular perpendicular rock". This place is now known as Dornoch Head.

Robertson used *rises* (twelve cases) to indicate the origin of a stream, most often a river rather than a spring, effectively with the same meaning as *head*. Only once did he specify Spring Rises, and he never used River Rises. He used *sinks* much more often (seventy-six cases), usually to identify the place where a spring disappeared into the earth but occasionally also to show where a river went underground. A *sink* might also mean simply a low-lying basin or area where ponds or marshes form, without being clearly identified as the place of underground disappearance.[17] In some cases, Robertson applied *rises* and *sinks* to the two ends of an unnamed stream, and in others he used *head* and *sinks* in the same way. Adding all his *rises* to his *heads* gives a total of 119 cases, significantly more than his 79 *sinks*, but the two terms were not meant to balance, and he thought it more useful to pinpoint appearances than disappearances. The map of 1950 contained only two cases of *rises* and one of *sinks*.

Most of the *wells* shown on Robertson's map (nineteen examples, as physical features) were simple generic identifiers (see Figure 5.4). These may be regarded as roughly equivalent to springs with cisterns, pools fed by springs. Although some of the wells, most obviously those located close to crossroads, had been dug to provide artificial access to water supplies, others emerged in unlikely places and had small stream-like lines drawn out of them. Old English usage applied *well* to a spring of water rising or "boiling" (bubbling vigorously) to the surface, there forming a small pool before flowing into a stream. Some of Jamaica's boiling springs have impressive flow: Fontabelle Spring near Windsor TRL discharges three cubic metres per second.[18]

The regional concentrations of *well* within Jamaica suggest local imitation rather than variation in physical structure. *Well* also appeared in compound names. It was combined with *hope* in the common case Hopewell, which in Old English might suggest the site of a spring, but came to be included among the sentiments.[19] Hopewell might equally have been named for an overseas place, as also might Hollywell. The mountain location of Jamaica's Holywell AND (sometimes spelled Hollywell), however, suggests an unlikely association with *holy well* as a healing stream. Wellspring, meaning the head of a stream or spring, had no currency in Jamaica as a place name. The 1950 map had Sea Well MRY as a coastal feature.

Robertson's understanding of a sink or cistern associated it directly with *sinkhole* – the common modern term – but he used this only once. However, he recorded ten cases of Blue Hole, and this came to name places and districts. A blue hole is characterized by the intense clarity of its water and purported great depth. Robertson also had Mannattee Hole TRL. The only terrestrial Blue Hole on the 1950 map was in St James, though there were several well-known coastal examples, as discussed in the next chapter. Jamaica's blue holes are relatively quiescent, compared to the island's "boiling springs", upwelling through deep natural pipes. Sweeting described blue holes as "among the most impressive karst phenomena in the world" and observed that in those of Jamaica "water rising in the blue holes is of a blue-green colour, possibly due to the presence of calcareous algae". Sawkins in 1869 illustrated Devils Hole THS as an example of the white limestone formation in which a very thick, compact, uncrystallized limestone overlay laminated limestones, characterized by horizontal bedding and layers of flint and clay.[20]

GULLY

Gully is identified in the *DJE* as a Jamaicanism when used to mean a small stream. This usage distinguishes it from the usual *OED* definition of *gully* as "a channel or ravine worn in the earth by the action of water, esp. in a mountain or hill side". The earliest *OED* citation for this more common meaning comes, interestingly, from Richard Ligon's 1657 account of Barbados, and many other of the early references are from North America, where gullies came to be considered an extreme form of soil erosion, closely associated with plantation agriculture and the South. Robert Baird, a Scottish traveller in Jamaica in 1849, declared: "The mountains of Port Royal and the Blue Mountains, . . . are intersected in every direction by deep fissures, glens, and 'gullies,' formed by the convulsions of nature during some one or other of the many earthquakes from which Jamaica has suffered, or by the washings of the impetuous torrents (which sweep down the mountain sides, carrying everything before them) during the frequent hurricanes by which the island has been devastated." Another traveller, Mrs Henry Lynch, remarked on the Jamaican usage of *gulley* in 1856, saying they formed watercourses in storms, and that when these torrents formed, the locals would say "Gulley come down".[21]

The etymology of *gully* stretches back into the sixteenth century, when it was derived from the model of the throat as "gullet, gullye or gargle", linking the flow of liquid to its channelling as in the specific Jamaican usage. There is no doubt, however, that although Jamaican uses of *gully* refer to a stream, the flow of many of such streams is seasonal, intermittent or discontinuous, though dramatic during the extreme flooding that is the major force shaping them. In karst or limestone landscapes, valleys of all sorts take on special characteristics, with gorge-like systems created by chemical solution and collapse, river action and caves, resulting in natural bridges, blind valleys and dry valleys. In few cases are the gullies of Jamaica true dry valleys – fossil features created in times of higher rainfall – of the sort common in Barbados.[22] This dual usage can complicate the analysis of place-name meanings.

Bochart and Knollis identified just two examples of *gully* as a physical feature: Mount Diablo Gully CTH and Town Gully CTH. Craskell and Simpson had as physical features twenty-two examples of *gully*, 13 per cent of the hydrological features named on their map. They showed *The Town Gully* as a large stream running all the way from Spanish Town south to the sea but did not name Mount Diablo Gully. On Craskell and Simpson's map, several of the names referenced flora: Anchovy Gully JAS, Breadnut Gully CLR, Crab Lanthorn Gully MRY, Palmeto Gully CLR, Santa Maria Gully CLR, Sleepy Tree Gully ANN and Trumpet Tree Gully AND. There was a Sandy Gully in Clarendon and another in St Andrew, as well as Stoney Gully CTH and Swampey Gully CTH. Another six were eponymous.

Robertson's use of *gully* seems always to follow the Jamaican usage, identifying streams rather than dry ravines. His gullies work like his rivulets and springs, flowing into rivers or having their own heads and sinks. This was true whether the gully was identified generically or in a compound name. Robertson recorded a total of eighty-four gullies, slightly fewer than his springs, but whereas a majority of his springs were generic most of his gullies had compound names. Robertson used the simple *gully* in nine cases, *a gully* in six, and *gullies* in three cases, for a total of only 22 per cent. The compound versions made up 13 per cent of the hydrological features named by Robertson, the same proportion as for Craskell and Simpson. These types were widely distributed (Figure 5.6).

Why should the gullies of Robertson's map more often have compound names than the highly valued springs? Was it that the uniqueness of the Jamaican usage of *gully* – compared to *river* or *spring* – associated the term with local knowledge and local ideas? Of the gullies with compound names, the pattern was similar to that for rivers, except that a gully was more likely to have an eponymous extension (25 per cent) or be named for vegetation (22 per cent). Only one – Snake Gully AND – was named for an animal. Few gully names on Robertson's map were transferred from other places, not one of them from overseas. The sentiments were a little more evident than in river names but still rare: Too Good Gully CLR, Cut Throat

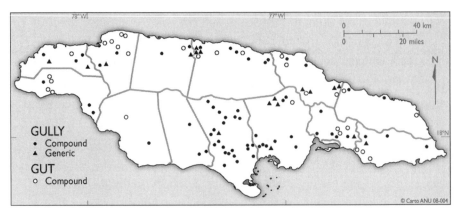

Figure 5.6 Jamaica: *Gully* and *gut* names, 1800 (as on Robertson's map)

Gully CTH and Worlds End Gully CTH, which may be read as a warning. Cocrocoe Gully THS has a Jamaican sound (and is spelled Cocorocoe on later maps) but its meaning is unknown. The same applies to Waa Wee Gully PLD.

Vegetation names applied to gullies on Robertson's map included Anchovy and Mammee (three cases each), Breadnut, Cedar, Manchineel, Palmetto, Plantain Walk, Santa Maria and Scotch Grass. Physical features occurred in Deep Gully PLD and Round Hill Gully HAN, and geological ones in Limestone Gully AND, Rocky Gully CLR, Salt Gully CLR and the more common Sandy Gully (four) and Stony Gully (two). Some of these persisted as place names; others were simply Robertson's cartographic descriptive labels, lacking any contemporary currency. Few gullies were given a place in the hydrological network or hierarchy in the way rivers were ordered. Cistern Gully CTH suggests assimilation to a spring, while Main Gully TRL had no named subsidiary streams and fed into the Martha Brae River, and Main Gully TRL similarly fed the Rio Bueno. In some areas, imitation seems to have affected labelling. For example, the Milk River CLR was fed by Figurary Gully, Santa Maria Gully, St Ann's Gully, Salt Gully and Baldwin's River or Main Savanna Gully, and by Sandy Gully, as well as by other types of streams.

Some of the gullies identified by Robertson gave their names to districts or retained a strong presence in the landscape even when their origins seem simply descriptive. The best examples are Mile Gully MAN, shown by Robertson as a short stream emerging from two springs, Sandy Gully CLR and the more extensive Sandy Gully AND. The modern Cuffy Gully MRY did not appear on Robertson, and the eponymous gully names on his map betray fewer African naming influences than either springs or rivers.

Perhaps the best-known gully of modern Jamaica is Fern Gully ANN, which serves as the starting point of the main route across the island from the tourist mecca of Ocho Rios to Kingston, the road rising rapidly and winding through its steep, fern-bedecked gorge. When the name was first applied is uncertain. On maps, it is hard to find before the 1950 topographical series, when Fern Gully appears as the name of a district rather than a stream or ravine. Robertson applied the name Ocho Rios Gully to the route followed by the road, only the northern section of which followed the same path as the stream, which he called Moncrieff's Gully.

Overall, the 1950 map named a smaller number of gullies than did Robertson, just fifty-three with compound names, or 10 per cent of the hydrological features in total. Most of the names persisted from the early nineteenth century, and about 40 per cent were eponymous. New names appearing in 1950 included some related to flora, as in Calabash Gully CLR and Cotton Tree Gully CLR, and fauna, as in Goat Gully WLD and Yerry Yerry Gully CLR, named for the tiny fish that swam in its waters. There were also the newly named Pot Gully ELZ, Glory Gully CTH and Hungry Gully THS. African words were relatively uncommon in gully names (though *yerry-yerry* may derive from Yoruba), and colloquial Jamaican English was only somewhat more prominent. Names that did not make it onto the map were more likely to be of this type, as in Chocho Gully WLD and its better-known cousin Callaloo Gutters WLD.

Gut, gutter

Unlike *gully*, the related term *gut* has no unique Jamaican usage. The two words are closely associated in etymology, but *gut* indicates a short gorge rather than the more extended stream of a Jamaican gully. Anatomically, *gut* is the extension of the throat or gullet into the alimentary canal, stomach and intestines. Outside Jamaica, *gullet* is occasionally used as a topographic term, though apparently never in place names. In topographic terms it refers to a narrow channel of water or a branch of a stream, this meaning traced to sixteenth-century English. *Gut* is also said to derive from the Dutch *gat*, meaning generally opening or gap, or arse, and more specifically pothole or wash-out, but the English form seems adequate to explain colonial usage in North America as well as Jamaica.[23]

Bochart and Knollis had just one *gut*: St Anns Gut CLR, which became Manchineel Gully on Robertson's 1800 chart. Craskell and Simpson found Lacovia Gutt ELZ, close by Jenny's Gutt, and farther away Spring Gut THS. As expected, Robertson identified many more, recording twenty-nine examples. Every one of these had a compound name, and Robertson never applied *gut* in the simple descriptive generic fashion he used for *spring*, *gully* and *river* (see Figure 5.6). Robertson's guts were dominated by names referring to physical characteristics: Boggy Gut JAS, Crooked Gut PLD, Dry Gut ANN THS, Morass Gut WLD, Running Gut JAS, Salt Gut MRY, Salt Water Gut WLD, Slippery Gut JAS, Spring Gut THS and Stony Gut JAS CTH AND. Stony Gut CTH, a stream flowing into the Rio d'Oro, was the site of the Sandy Gully sugar works, with a cattle mill rather than a waterwheel. Vegetation names were Palmetto Gut AND, Pear Tree Gut ANN and Trumpet Tree Gut AND. On Robertson's map, none of the guts were named for fauna (except that Wivel Gut WLD may have meant an insect) or stream network hierarchies. The proportion of eponymous names was similar to that for *gully* but there was one probable transfer from overseas, Cambridge Gut THS.

Few of the guts on Robertson's 1800 map survived in the long term. The 1950 topographical map used *gut* only in settlement names and recorded just three instances: Running Gut JAS, Salt Gut MRY and Stony Gut THS. The last of these was the best known, the Stony Gut that provided the harsh environment for Paul Bogle's chapel and the beginnings of the Morant Bay Rebellion of 1865. On Robertson's map this Stony Gut was named, but only as the name of a sugar plantation with a cattle mill, lacking a stream flowing through its centre. In Bogle's time Stony Gut was a village, whose small farmers sometimes worked on neighbouring – better watered – sugar estates.[24]

Although *gutter* has a particular Jamaican meaning, it rarely appears in the island's place names. As a Jamaicanism, *gutter* is used to identify spaces or channels in cultivated fields, as between yam hills, and also for the furrow or depression that runs down the human body's spine or backbone. Interestingly, an alternative Jamaicanism for the spinal furrow is *back-gully*, thus continuing the use of bodily referents. *Gutter*, like the term *canal*, was used widely in Jamaica to indicate a regular channel, dug in the ground or built of masonry, to carry water to sugar or coffee mills. Perhaps it was this usage that made *gutter* less viable as a place name or generic label for a physical feature. The word was used more often in colonial North America, particularly for slow-flowing, steep-sided streams in lowland marshy locations, running into the sea. In Jamaica, these characteristics were typically named *gut* rather than *gutter*, and in North America *gut* largely disappeared (considered even less attractive than *gutter*), whereas *gut* survived strongly in Jamaica. Thus *gutter* began life in North America as a euphemism for *gut*, and *gutter* was in turn euphemized to *brook*. As already noted, *brook* was not commonly applied to watercourses in Jamaica and rarely appeared on maps of the island (except in compound names such as Bybrook and Boundbrook), while *gut* persisted alongside *gully*. The Running Gutter of Massachusetts is the polite form of Running Gut.[25]

Wild patches of callaloo, and sometimes deliberate plantings, cultivated in micro-landscapes crisscrossed by channels or *gutters*, provided fertile ground for the term, though mostly on an informal, local basis. The best-known example is Callaloo Gutters WLD. The name was first encountered in print in the 1920s, when it was described as "the river known as Calalue Gutter leading into the district of Bleauwearie". By 1933 it was called "Calaloo Gutter" and the following year "Calalu Gutter".[26] The name remains firmly established within the community. On the other hand, the well-known Gutters MAN, at the foot of Spur Tree Hill, names a small settlement rather than a physical feature. Sibley believed Gutters was "well named, because after heavy rain, water flows from three directions, making it almost impassable", but the 1950 topographic map shows no streams of any sort. In other examples, as at Gutters Pen CTH, *gutters* is collocated with the surname Gutterez, and it is probable that the original was an eponym rather than representing a physical feature.

MORASS

Cassidy and Le Page include *morass* in the *DJE*, giving it a particular Jamaican meaning. Their entry begins by citing the *OED*, which declared, "the word is now confined to literary use, exc. in some parts of the West Indies". Recent editions of the *OED* in turn cite the *DJE* on *morass* as an abbreviation of *morass weed*. The simple use of *morass* is defined by the *OED* as meaning "a wet or swampy tract, a bog; an area of very wet or muddy ground"; and by the *DJE* as "a moist or swampy piece of land covered with vegetation". In Florida, according to McMullen, *morass* is distinguished from *marsh*, where "a morass is spongy like a bog".[27] Thus the difference lies chiefly in the fact that Jamaican usage emphasizes the role of vegetation. As with *gully*, both meanings were used separately and elided.

Bochart and Knollis used *morass* as a generic in three places, all of them in Hanover and Westmoreland, and as a compound name only in The Black Morass WLD. Craskell and Simpson applied *morass* to eleven physical features but most of these indicated the simple existence of a morass, and the compound examples extended no further than Great Morass or Black Morass. Craskell and Simpson similarly used the rare term *swamp*, identifying Salt Swamp JAS and a generic Swamp WLD, both close to the coast. The Swamp CLR was a settlement.

Robertson is less helpful with *morass* than with *gully*, and in any case he hardly ever recorded compound names for *morass*, even fewer than he did for *spring*. On his 1800 map the generic *morass* occurred twenty-six times and Great Morass seven times. He also indicated an area of Salina (saline marsh) and Morass CLR; a Salina on the edge of the Morass by Old Harbour Bay CTH, fed by the Salt River; and a Salina on the edge of Hunt's Bay CTH, within a morass through which flowed the Salt River and the Fresh River and which was bounded by the Lagoon River. The most

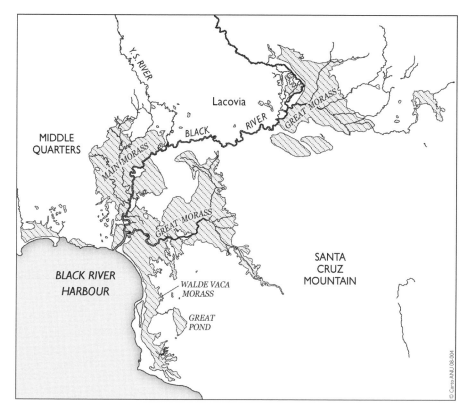

Figure 5.7 Black River *morasses*, redrawn from Robertson, 1800

extensive morass, known in modern times simply as the Great Morass, behind Black River in St Elizabeth, was broken up by Robertson into separate elements: Main Morass, Great Morass and the uniquely extended Walde-Vaca Morass towards the shoreline, and further inland another Great Morass and three smaller morasses (Figure 5.7). These morasses were crossed by streams, some navigable; one of them, the Grass River, indicated in its name the strong role of vegetation in naming. Some of the streams were fed by springs rising at the very edge of the morass. Towards the south, Robertson named Pass Water, a convenient place to ford the tip of the morass. The 1950 map had only two examples of The Great Morass HAN ELZ.

ISLAND

Islands as physical features could be physically isolated in various ways, without necessarily being coastal features. Bochart and Knollis in 1684 named just one: Boar Isle ELZ, in the Black River Morass. Craskell and Simpson retained this name and added Frenchmans Island and Rinchin Island, also within the Black River Morass, and Breadnutt Island WLD. On Robertson's map, Boar Island ELZ was located in the Main Morass, with the Black River on one side and the smaller Frenchmans River on the other; Breadnut Island WLD was bounded by the sea to the south and a large morass to the north, with the New Savanna River completing its eastern boundary; Caves Island TRL was completely surrounded by morass, joined by road to Falmouth. *Island* persisted as an element in a small number of settlement names. On the 1950 map the best-known examples at interior sites were Paul Island WLD and Serge Island THS. Offshore islands are discussed in the next chapter.

LAKE

Jamaica has no claim to extensive lakes. The only *lake* mentioned on any of the maps studied occurs on the 1950 topographic and notes merely "site of Moneague Lake", which is an intermittent phenomenon, filling with water sufficiently deep to cover bravely built houses every few decades, then gradually disappearing again. It is a product of complex underground hydraulics in the limestone strata, not simply a rise in the water table. Other places in Jamaica, notably Newmarket WLD and Coldspring HAN, experience similar erratic lake-formation processes, though generally only after extreme rainfall events. Equally alarming in their way are the red mud lakes, created in recent decades to store the waste of bauxite/alumina processing. These fill large storages and dominate local landscapes, but seem not to have named places as *lakes*.

POND

Ponds are more common than lakes and are generally found along the coastal fringes of the island rather than inland. Bochart and Knollis had Luaetree Pond ELZ, Pedro Pond ELZ, Modifords Salt Pond CTH, Flemingo Pond TRL and two examples of the generic Pond JAS ANN. Craskell and Simpson had Flamingo Pond JAS (close to the sea but more enclosed by firm land than the nearby Salta Marsh), Mountain Pond WLD, Spanish Pond ELZ, Pedro Pond ELZ and two examples of Green Pond JAS ELZ. They also had the plurals Saint Jago Ponds CLR and Turtle Ponds ANN. More obviously generic were Salt Pond ANN THS, Great Salt Pond CTH, Pondside HAN and the simplex Pond ELZ.

On Robertson's 1800 map, to the west of the Walde-Vaca Morass, between it and the sea, he showed a Salt Pond, and to the east a Great Pond of Fresh Water, the latter filled from a Spring Head and flowing into the morass whereas the salt pond was not connected. Overall, Robertson recorded fourteen examples of the simple generic *pond* and three *ponds*. Another twenty-five cases had compound names, placing *pond* alongside *gully* in its frequency of compound-naming. As well as the Salt Pond already noted, there were Salt Island Pond CTH and the well-known The Salt Ponds on the coast of St Thomas, east of Yallahs. Equally well known in the eighteenth century was the Great Salt Pond CTH, near Fort Clarence and shown by Robertson to be backed by a morass which began to be encroached on by the urban sprawl of Greater Kingston in the late twentieth century.

Other pond names identified by Robertson pointed to the role of vegetation: Grassy Pond AND, Sedge Pond CLR and Rush Ponds CLR. There was also Alligator Pond MRY, far away from the place known in modern times as Alligator Pond ELZ, where Robertson identified only Alligator Pond Bay and Alligator Pond River. Six of the pond names were eponymous, including Quaws Pond TRL. In the interior of Clarendon, near Chapelton, Robertson showed a relatively small pond playfully named The Great Sea.

The 1950 topographic map had only The Salt Ponds THS as a coastal feature, but thirteen settlement place names included *pond* as an element,
always their last word and hence serving as a generic label. Some of the
names referred to shape or scale, as in Great Pond ANN, Great Salt Ponds
CTH, Wallywash Great Pond ELZ and Long Pond TRL MRY. The Trelawny
Long Pond gave its name to a major sugar mill and district. Sedge Pond,
the two Green Ponds and Alligator Pond persisted, and these were joined
in 1950 by Bamboo Pond TRL.

LAGOON

Bochart and Knollis applied the word *lagune* to two places, as a generic.
Robertson labelled seven places *lagoon*, almost all of them close to the sea
but occasionally lying behind a morass, the lagoon being water-filled and
the morass vegetated. The exceptional inland lagoons were near Rio Hoe
ANN and Spring Vale CTH. The latter lagoon fed ultimately into the Rio
Cobre, but so did a pond. Why Robertson termed one a *lagoon* and the
other a *pond* is a mystery, though the etymology of both of these words, as
well as that of *pool*, can all be traced to the Latin *lacuna*. Similarly,
Robertson distinguished an apparently continuous surface between *lagoon*
and *bog*, beside Bog Estate CTH; here the lagoon element was fed from a
spring that became the Spring Garden River. This was the only physical
feature that Robertson named as a *bog*.

FALL, CASCADE

A large number of *falls* were shown on Robertson's map but he never
added extensions to them to make them unique place names, except that
he did identify Fall River AND. He had twelve simple cases of *fall*, even
when multiples occurred along a single stream, as well as eleven plural *falls*
and one case of Two Falls. He also had six cases of Great Fall, one Three
Great Falls, one High Fall, a 60 Feet Fall and a 120 Feet Fall. These were of
economic importance for the water power they offered to planters in the
eighteenth century, and aesthetically important for their visual spectacle

and the roaring sound they contributed to the soundscape. Before 1900 *fall* was used to indicate not only the falling of a stream down a steep slope, as in a cascade, cataract or waterfall, but also to mean the very sound they produced.[28]

Robertson treated *cascade* much as he treated *fall*. His Cascade River AND joined the Fall River as a tributary to the Yallahs River. Robertson had nine cases of *cascade* along the course of streams, four of Great Cascade and one of Grand Cascade. The last of these, the Grand Cascade, was on the White River that formed the boundary between St Ann and St Mary. Long included "A View of the White River Cascade" in his 1774 *History of Jamaica*. He attributed it to St Ann, saying the parish had two "remarkable cascades", the other being on the Roaring River immediately west of Dunn's River. Robertson identified the one on the Roaring River simply with the word *cascade*, and indicated no *fall* at the now popular attraction Dunn's River Falls. Long devoted some of his most picturesque prose to these two falls, identifying the one on White River as a "great cascade, more properly a cataract" that "precipitates in a fall of about three hundred feet or more, obliquely measured, with such a hoarse and thundering noise, as to be heard at a great distance". It was, said Long, "grand and sublime" inspiring "reverential wonder". The White River Cascade, said Long, was "said to exceed in grandeur that of Tivoli, or any other in Europe, though much inferior to that of Niagara".[29] *Cascade* named significant settlements in Hanover and St Ann.

CHAPTER SIX

Coastal Names

NAMING AND MAPPING THE PHYSICAL FEATURES that marked the coastline of Jamaica was a priority for its colonizing people, all of whom approached by sea. Detailed sea charts were vital to safe navigation, both to identify where along the coast a voyager had sighted land and to pinpoint hazards hidden beneath the surface reefs and bars. In the eastern end of the island the mountains towered above the sea, while in the west the land seemed much flatter viewed from a boat, but everywhere the coastline had its particular characteristics and difficulties, demanding the sailor's close attention. Once on shore, it was the resources of the coastal zone that were first exploited and that provided sites for early settlement. In the longer term, the coastal zone was not only the focus of Jamaica's maritime economy but also the prime location of urban settlement. The outcome was a high but declining ratio of named coastal places.

The 1680 map of Bochart and Knollis named 235 physical features along the coast, more than on the land. This ratio was turned around on the 1760 Craskell and Simpson map. On Robertson's 1800 map, inland names were more than three times as numerous as coastal ones, but they were only twice as common on the 1950 map. The reasons for this general reversal were the growing English knowledge and settlement of the inland regions of the island, the finite landscape offered by the coast and the development of specialized maps for marine navigation. Another reason was that early mapmakers often named rivers only at their mouths, where they were most

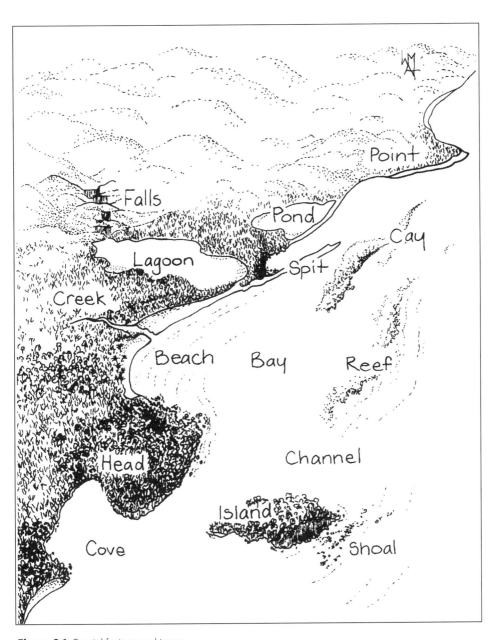

Figure 6.1 Coastal features and terms

obviously part of the coastal landscape, placing the lettering on the sea itself. This practice became less common over time and had virtually disappeared by 1950, making rivers definitively part of the terrestrial topography. Craskell and Simpson named 192 physical features along the coast in 1760, Robertson 337 in 1800, and the 1950 topographic map, 340. Deducting the names of rivers written along the coast to identify their mouths, the numbers drop to, respectively, 151, 283 and 338. Taking all kinds of names, the share taken by coastal physical features fell from 21 per cent in 1680 to 8 per cent in 1760, and to 7 per cent in both 1800 and 1950.

Some coastal places share landforms with terrestrial sites, as in lagoons and cliffs, but the streams that enter the sea change their character at the coast, becoming creeks, inlets or estuaries and merging with the ocean. Other coastal places combine water with distinct landforms, as in bays, coves and harbours (Figure 6.1).

BAY

On all of the maps studied, from 1680 to 1950, the most common named coastal feature is the *bay*, an English landform term of long standing meaning a wide-mouthed indentation of the sea into land. It was equally dominant in non-map documentary texts.[1] The dominance of *bay* suggests the importance of identification for navigation and trade. Further, from the beginning, the bays were almost all given compound names; simply noting the existence of a bay or, worse, a long series of bays, was insufficient for the sailor. It was important to distinguish and identify each bay clearly to define location precisely and navigate along the coast. Even maps not designed for navigational purposes represented the same pattern. Further, bays increased their dominance over time, rising steadily from 29 per cent of all coastal physical names in 1680 to 39 per cent in 1950.

Bochart and Knollis marked sixty-eight bays, every one of them having a compound name. Some of these names were simply descriptive of the physical characteristics of the landform and hence numerous.[2] Only some stuck in the long term. These included the popular Long Bay HAN JAS MAN

140

CLR MRY AND PLD, as well as Sandy Bay HAN THS, Rocky Bay CTH, Little Sand Bay THS, Platform Bay TRL, Flint Bay CLR and White Cliff Bay PLD. Vegetation names on Bochart and Knollis included Orange Bay HAN PLD, Lymetree Bay HAN, Coquar Plumb Bay MAN, Plumtree Bay PLD, Savana Bay THS, Mangrove Bay ELZ and Sedgy Bay ELZ. Fauna accounted for Manatee Bay CTH, Manatte Bay TRL, Pig Bay CLR, Hogghole Bay MRY, Cow Bay THS, Bull Bay THS and perhaps Craul Bay THS. Apart from Canoe Bay THS and Fishermans Bay THS, few of the names pointed to the functions of the bays as shipping points. The meaning of Starvegutt Bay ELZ is not certain, though the name was persistent. In North America, a Starvegoat Island lies in Narragansett Bay, Rhode Island. Runaway Bay ANN is generally said to be named for the last Spanish governor of Jamaica, Don Cristóbal Arnaldo de Ysassi, who fled the island in 1660 after years of resistance to English occupation. Ysassi's precise point of embarkation is uncertain, and it has been argued that the bay's name is a reference to "runaway" slaves.[3] The remainder of the names on Bochart and Knollis were either eponymous or took their names from nearby physical features or settlements.

The number of bays reached a minimum on Craskell and Simpson's 1760 map, falling to fifty-eight, all with compound names. The number of Long Bays was reduced from eight to five, and the Sandy Bays and Rocky Bays disappeared altogether. Half Moon Bay HAN, pointing to the open shape of the indentation, was named for the first time. New vegetation names were Callabash Bay MAN, Anotta Bay MRY, Figtree Bay MRY, Mammee Bay ANN and Cocoa Bay CTH, though this last might be an ironic *cocobay*, meaning a kind of leprosy. The new fauna names were Alligator Pond Bay ELZ, Carrion Crow Bay JAS and, most importantly, Montego [*manteca*, lard] Bay JAS. Craskell and Simpson also added to the number of names indicating function or maritime event, as in Ballast Bay HAN, Boatmans Bay ELZ and Wreck Bay CTH.

After the low point on Craskell and Simpson's 1760 map, the number of named bays increased again, and substantially. Robertson marked eighty-seven, every one of them a compound name. These bays were strung around Jamaica like a chain of pearls, with significant gaps found only

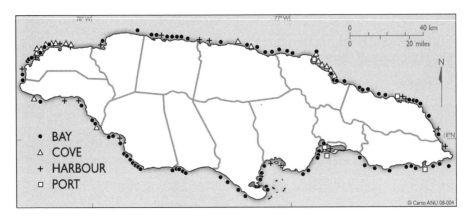

Figure 6.2 Jamaica: *Bay, cove, harbour* and *port*, 1800 (as on Robertson's map)

along sections of Hanover/St James and Westmoreland (Figure 6.2). Some
of them had streams running into them; others did not. Almost one-half of
the bays on Robertson's 1804 map were either eponymous or took their
names from nearby physical features or settlements. Nine described the
morphology of the bay itself. The Long Bays were reduced further to four,
but two new Half Moon Bays TRL CTH were added. Vegetation was even
more common, appearing in eleven names, adding to those of Craskell and
Simpson: Chocolata Bay ELZ, Mahoe Bay ELZ and additional examples of
Mammee Bay HAN and Calabash Bay ELZ. Cocoa Bay CTH became Coquar
Bay. Fauna accounted for six of the bays on Robertson, the only new one
being Crab Hole Bay MRY. Robertson added no new names related to
function.

The 1950 topographic map named 132 bays, almost double the number
on the 1680 map of Bochart and Knollis, and again all had compound
names. As expected, many of the names had persisted over the long term.
The Long Bays returned to five, as in 1760, and the Half Moons were three,
in Hanover, Trelawny and St Catherine. New names referring to landforms
included Sugar Loaf Bay HAN THS, Rocky Point Bay THS and Shell Bay
THS. Flora and fauna remained important, as did contiguous landforms
such as springs and ponds. Bloody Bay HAN emerged, supposedly referring

to a historic battle or perhaps the killing of whales, but only as an alternative to Negril Harbour, and distinguishing it from the Long Bay zone to the south of the harbour. Other new names included Old Man Bay PLD, Lime Kiln Bay PLD, Swimmers Bay THS, Folly Bay THS, Louzy Bay CTH and Succabus Bay MRY, the last presumably for a succubus – a demon, evil spirit or strumpet.

COVE

A *cove* is a small bay, usually with a narrow mouth, creating a recess or inlet in a coast where ships can hide or shelter from the storm. The more extreme versions are gourd- or bottle-shaped, whereas others are more open and bay-like. A section of the Hanover coast, as drawn on Robertson's 1800 map, shows these differences but also demonstrates that size was not the only factor determining the hierarchy of terms (Figure 6.3).

Bochart and Knollis showed thirteen *coves*, fewer than one-fifth the number of bays on their map. As with the bays, all of the cove names were compound. The pattern of naming was different, however, with none of the cove names referring directly to flora or fauna. A Long Cove would have been contrary to the definition, but there were Rocky Cove MRY, Flatt Cove MRY and Little Cove HAN. One referred to function: Canoa Cove ELZ. About half of the names were eponymous, including the persistent Scots Cove WLD and Don Christopher's Cove ANN MRY. Craskell and Simpson showed sixteen coves, largely repeating those named by Bochart and Knollis. Additions included the persistent Cousins's Cove, Davis's Cove, Musquito Cove, Magotty Cove and Orange Cove, all in Hanover.

There were eighteen coves on Robertson's 1800 map, less than one-quarter as numerous as the bays and none of them particularly important for Jamaica's shipping (see Figure 6.2). The coves were much less widespread than the bays, with only two on the south coast: Homers Cove WLD and Scotts Cove WLD. There were two zones of concentration on the north coast. The first, in St Mary, dominated a stretch of coast, but in the second, in Hanover, coves were interspersed between bays and harbours. In spite of

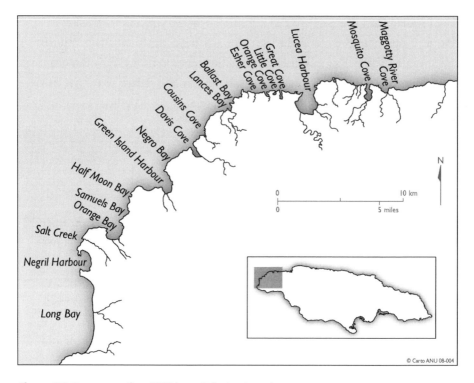

Figure 6.3 Hanover coastline, 1800 (as on Robertson's map)

their relative unimportance, Robertson identified only one with the simple generic *cove*; the others all had compound names. The coves were overwhelmingly named for people or nearby land features and sites. The 1950 topographic map made no significant change to the number of coves, naming nineteen, or 6 per cent of the coastal names. Scots Cove became Scotts or Seals Cove WLD.

HOLE

As a coastal feature, *hole* identified a cove or small harbour. This usage is generally considered American rather than British, but it was common only on the earliest Jamaican maps. Bochart and Knollis had seven: Bull Hole HAN, Mallard Hole PLD, Hobbys Hole THS, Michaels Hole CLR, Devils Hole THS, Hudsons Hole ELZ and Chocolata Hole ELZ. Craskell and Simpson had no coastal holes. Robertson used *hole* for both coastal and inland physical features, with Blue Hole occurring in both kinds of sites, and holes appearing also within bays. The 1950 topographic map named seven holes, still fewer than on Bochart and Knollis, but with a completely new set of names: Dunns Hole JAS, Manatee Hole JAS, Jacks Hole ELZ, Codrington Hole PLD, Goat Pen Hole PLD and Hales Hole PLD, the last three clustered near Manchioneal, and Blue Hole or Blue Lagoon PLD, which became a well-known tourist attraction.

CREEK, MOAT

Jamaican usage followed the English system in applying *creek* to a narrow saltwater coastal inlet or tidal estuary. North American terminology, which applied *creek* to a freshwater inland stream, was unknown in Jamaica, along with *run* and *gulch*, which were equally unheard of.[4] Thus in 1672 Blome said Jamaica had good fish in its "rivers, bayes, roads, and creeks".[5] However, no creeks occurred on the maps of Bochart and Knollis or Craskell and Simpson. Robertson's map identified seven creeks along the coastline. In Portland, near Manchioneal, Peters Creek, Patricks Creek and Coddringtons Creek all consisted of small inlets without associated streams, but Salt Creek, near Cold Harbour, had a distinct short stream feeding it. Other creeks were associated with estuarine morasses and generally lacked evidence of a stream-course. Salt Creek HAN came out of the Great Morass at Negril (see Figure 6.3), while Stanhopes Creek CTH and an unnamed generic *creek* formed small inlets in the morass at Hunts Bay. Robertson named only one creek on land: Salt Creek WLD, at the southern extremity of Bluefields Bay. Philip Gosse, the British naturalist, based in Westmoreland in the 1840s, described this as a "small stream" that ran through a morass and crossed the road at Belmont Beach, close to Bluefields, known locally as a "creek".[6] Few of these survived in the long term, and the 1950 topographic map merely repeated Salt Creek HAN and added Salt Creek PLD, suggesting the major role played by saltwater.

Apparently similar in meaning to *creek* was the term *moat*, used just twice by Robertson and close together, near Hope Bay in Portland – Salters Moat and Stringers Moat – suggesting a broad stretch of water making progress along the coast road difficult. Stringers Moat had appeared earlier, on Craskell and Simpson's 1760 map, and survived to the 1950 map, along with Bellers Moat PLD, in the same localized zone.

HARBOUR

Unlike the common terms discussed thus far, *harbour* serves not only to identify a particular kind of coastal landform but also to define the function of providing a place of safety from winds, waves and currents. Indeed, *harbour* can be used to describe any place of shelter or refuge – a safe harbour – offering various forms of physical and psychological protection. As coastal landforms, the harbours of Jamaica were generally distinguished from the bays and coves of the island by their greater scale (see Figure 6.3). A harbour is not always as securely enclosed as a bay or cove, however, and it was the places that shared both scale and protective enclosure that became most important, as most obviously in the case of Kingston Harbour.

On their 1680 map Bochart and Knollis showed ten harbours: Negrill Harbour HAN, St Lucys Harbour HAN (Lucea), Cove Harbour HAN (Mosquito Cove), Dry Harbour ANN, St Anns Harbour ANN, Cold Harbour PLD, Manchanil Harbour THS, Port Royall Harbour AND, Old Harbour CTH and West Harbour CLR. A few years later, John Taylor in 1687 similarly found ten "cheife harbours" but identified them as "Port Royal Harbour, Old Harbour, or Spanish Harbour, Founts, Lainuna, Sivila, Palmero, Alestro, Old North Harbour, Saint Ann's and Morrant Harbour".[7] Craskell and Simpson named only six harbours and added just one to the list: Green Island Harbour HAN. All of these survived on Robertson's 1800 map with the exception of West Harbour. That map named seventeen harbours, fairly evenly spaced along both north and south coasts (see Figure 6.2). All of them had compound names. Some of these harbours effectively duplicated bays, as in Close Harbour JAS in the northern section of Montego Bay, on Robertson's map. Others were not effectual in offering the sheltered haven expected of a safe harbour but merely indicated places where ships might lie at anchor out to sea, as at Savanna la Mar Harbour WLD, in the *road*, somewhat protected by shoals.

Kingston Harbour did everything expected of a harbour, with its long curving spit providing protection for vessels that entered through its narrow passage. Robertson called it Kingston Harbour, but Bochart and Knollis in 1680 – before the earthquake – thought Port Royall Harbour more appropriate. Craskell and Simpson left it unnamed. Some of the harbours were at river mouths, such as Black River Harbour ELZ and Plantain Garden River Harbour THS. These offered limited possibilities of inland navigation. Another, Martha Brea Harbour TRL, unlike the other river mouths mentioned, was relatively well protected and was making the transition to the name Falmouth Harbour by the time of Robertson's map. Most of the harbours on his map had names derived from persons or nearby physical and settlement features, but Close Harbour did hint at the security offered to shipping, and Galleon Harbour CLR and Turtle Crawle Harbour PLD suggested function. The 1950 topographic map named twelve harbours, matching closely the pattern on the earlier maps in terms of proportion and geographic location.

PORT

Whereas a coastal inlet capable of providing a safe and convenient anchorage for ships can be termed a *harbour*, unless its location makes it useful for commercial or naval purposes it may not develop into a *port*. A *port* is where vessels come and go for the purposes of trade, taking on or discharging cargo, passengers and crew, refuelling, obtaining repairs and carrying out related activities. Where there is sufficient economic or strategic reason, a port may develop where no natural harbour exists.[8]

Bochart and Knollis showed seven ports: Brid Port in Old Harbour CTH, Olim Port Maria MRY and the nearby New Port, Port Antonio PLD and Port St Frances in the eastern sector of the same harbour, Port St Thomas THS (Port Morant), and Port Royall AND.[9] Craskell and Simpson had only one port: Port Antonio. Robertson named five, all compound names with *port* the first word, all in the eastern end of the island and varied in shape and scale: Port Maria MRY, Port Antonio PLD, Port Morant THS, Port Henderson CTH and Port Royal AND. None of these names refer to physical features. Port Maria, Port Antonio and Port Morant were named by the Spanish, Port Royal was named by the English for Charles II and Port Henderson reputedly recognized John Henderson, colonel of the militia in the eighteenth century. The 1950 map named only Port Antonio and Port Morant as physical features (and repeated the names for the settlements), whereas Port Henderson and Port Royal appeared only as settlements, and Port Maria as a settlement located on Port Maria Bay.

Later additions were products of the bauxite/alumina industry that flourished after World War II: Port Kaiser ELZ, Port Rhodes ANN and Port Esquivel CLR. New ways of doing business created Montego Freeport JAS. Newport East and Newport West constituted the modern container port of Kingston Harbour, and Portmore, the urban development across the causeway over Kingston Harbour at Hunts Bay, was created in the same post-independence period. In this last group of new names, *port* was incorporated in Newport and Portmore rather than being used as a generic label.

POINT, SPIT, PALISADE

Typically separating sea inlets, *points* are peninsulas of various kinds, some of them high headlands formed by marine erosion and others low-lying projections like *spits*, which are products of deposition. In Jamaica, all of these are typically called *points*. On Bochart and Knollis's 1680 map, *point* was the second most common coastal physical feature, after *bay*. The points were the natural corollaries of the bays and coves, jutting out between them but also designating places where inlets were not identified. Bochart and Knollis showed thirty-three points, all of them bearing compound names. Their physical features were emphasized in some of the names: Long Point HAN, Rocky Point CLR, Stony Point ELZ and Blowin Point MRY (which became Blowing Point on Craskell and Simpson's map). Vegetation was more common: Palmeto Point WLD (where it had the alias Luglatchet) and MRY, Savana Point PLD, Plumb Point AND and Mangrove Point AND. Birds named Pelican Point CTH and Fowle Point THS; goats, Cabarita Point CTH and Cabarito Point WLD; and pigs, Mantica Point JAS. Musquito Point CTH (as well as Mosquito Bay HAN) may be an association with the insect but may equally be transfers from the Miskito people of Nicaragua. Very few point names were eponymous. More were related to associated physical features, like Starvegutt Point ELZ which took its name from the bay.

The 1760 map of Craskell and Simpson identified thirty-two points, all of them with compound names, including The Point JAS. Some referred to their own physical characteristics, such as Cockpit Point CTH and Flat Point ANN, and the popular Rocky Point CLR THS. Craskell and Simpson also had the more complete High Land of Pedro Point ELZ. By this time, *point* had gained an additional meaning in English, referring to the peak of a hill or mountain, as in Point Hill Plantation CTH. More of the names were eponymous than on Bochart and Knollis's earlier map. Craskell and Simpson had fewer point names associated with flora and fauna, though they introduced alligator and crab.

As in the case of the earlier mapmakers, *point* was the second most important coastal feature named by Robertson, after *bay*. He named fifty-three points, all of them with compound names, useful in navigation, though few were simple extensions of the names of bays, like Montego Bay Point JAS or Cow Bay Point THS. Robertson added mangrove and bush to the vegetation names, as well as Forges Point MRY, Free Point MRY, and the more allusive Welch Womans Point PLD, Old Womans Point MAN and Cuckolds Point MAN. Hanover had both Point Estate and Point Pen. Threatening names included Gallows Point CTH and Gun Point WLD. A Hellshire Point was known by the time of Robertson's map but did not appear on it.[10]

The 1950 topographic map continued the pattern, with *point* the second most common named coastal feature at 29 per cent and applied to ninety-eight places. *Point* increased its share of the coastal names dramatically, tripling the numbers on the earliest maps rather than merely doubling as in the case of *bay*. All of the points had compound names. Part of the increase in the proportion of points came from a finer differentiation, as in North Negril Point HAN (which Robertson had charted but called merely North Negril), South Negril Point WLD and West Point WLD (marking the westernmost point of the island, which Robertson had designated, more broadly, West End). The 1950 map had also North West or Pedro Point HAN and South West Point WLD. Welch Womans Point became Welsh Womans Point. Other styles of new names in 1950 included Friars Cap Point WLD, Nose Point PLD, Sharpnose Point THS, Umbrella Point JAS and Shorthaul Point ELZ. Folly Point PLD did not match the newly named Folly Bay, nor did Lousy Point JAS relate to Louzy Bay. Gallows Point and Gun Point remained current, joined by Burial Ground Point CLR. A few new probable eponymous names were applied, as in Merrimans Point ELZ, Pegg Point PLD and the seemingly anachronistic Quaco Point THS, which perhaps codified an existing popular name. Overall, eponymous naming was never common for this landform.

Much less common than *point* is the term *spit*, the depositional form. Robertson named three spits: Pelican Spit CTH, Greek Pond Spit AND and the combined Rocky Point and Spit CLR. Otherwise, spit is effectively unknown in Jamaican speech and cartography. Robertson applied the terms The Palisades and Palisades to the great long spit that encloses Kingston Harbour, but Craskell and Simpson had come closer to the modern spelling, with Pallisadoes. Bochart and Knollis left it blank. Other early maps occasionally called it Long Point or distinguished its parts as Pelican Point and Mangrove Point, and the first non-map text references appear to come from 1716. Sawkins in 1869 called this "the 'Pallisades'" and the 1950 map The Palisadoes. The origin of the name lies in a *palisade*, or protective fence, constructed on the eastern side of Port Royal, across the peninsula.[11] More broadly, the term *palisade* may seem appropriate for a long, curving spit which forms a protective enclosing barrier around the waters.

ISLAND

Like peninsulas, islands can be formed by erosion, deposition or both, and they can be equally diverse in form. Bochart and Knollis named four offshore *isles* (Green Isle HAN, Perexil Isle MRY, Goat Isle CLR and Merry Isle PLD) and three *islands* (Dorrels Island CLR, Pidgeon Island CLR and Lynch Island PLD). Craskell and Simpson named eight offshore *islands*, few of the names overlapping. Craskell and Simpson had two pairs: Great Salt Island and Little Salt Island CLR, and Great Goat Island and Little Goat Island CTH. Goats also appeared in Cabarita Island MRY, and there was Pidgeon Island CTH. The others were Long Island CLR and Navy Island PLD.

Islands were the most common offshore physical feature on Robertson's map. He gave sixteen of them compound names and two others the simple generic *island*. Some were named for features on land, but a proportion were identified by their fauna – the goats, as well as Dolphin Island CLR and Pigeon Island CLR. Vegetation marked Santa Maria Island MRY, Woods Island PLD and Green Island HAN. Ship Island PLD and Navy Island PLD pointed directly to function. Robertson's map also named Pellew Island PLD and Christmas Island THS, and the Bog Islands west of Montego Bay.

The 1950 topographic map named a similar number of islands, fourteen, and added few new names. Tower Isle MRY and Emerald Island THS were new, while Careening Island CLR had been identified as a *cay* on earlier maps. Robertson's Bog Islands became Bogue Islands JAS, which raises questions of origin. The name Bog may have come from the swampy conditions of the area, with island-formation active in the shallow waters, or perhaps from the nearby Bog Estate. *Bogue*, however, as well as being an old Scots surname and the name of a Scottish village, is a word with several meanings. Some of them relate to water features – *bayou* or *waterway*, for example – while another is a nautical term associated with the navigation of sailing vessels. Dictionary definitions include "to fall from the wind" and "to edge away from leeward". Any or all of these might apply to Bogue Islands. In the late twentieth century, some of these islands were linked together and joined to the mainland by a reclamation scheme which created the site of Montego Freeport.

CAY, KEY, KAY

A common coastal term is *cay*, designating a small, low-lying offshore island or islet, often rocky, generally of coral formation, or sandy. Sand cays are common on the coral reefs and submerged shoals that surround Jamaica and naturally form part of a continuum from solid island to isle, islet, sand island or cay, with mangrove wetland gradually giving way to submerged or semi-submerged flat reef (see Figure 6.1). These processes of evolution complicate the use of generic terms as classifiers. Port Royal, for example, began life as a cay, hence its instability in the face of earthquake, and it has been argued that the Palisadoes linked a series of earlier cays. The Palisadoes has from time to time broken up into a discontinuous feature, the combination of spit and cays known technically as a *tombolo*.[12]

The word *cay* is derived from the Taino and was adapted by the Spanish as *cayo*. The pronunciation *key* came later, but Jamaican orthography has largely persisted with *cay*. Bochart and Knollis showed eleven cays, more than their *isles* and *islands*, and all with compound names.[13] Some of the names referred to physical characteristics: Rocky Cay ANN and Sandy Cay CTH. Vegetation was sparse, as in One Bush Cay CTH and Three Bush Cay AND. Others pointed to function, as in Gunne Cay CTH, Burying Cay CTH and Carining Coi CLR. Craskell and Simpson used the spelling *kay*, naming nine, all of them compound. Barebush Kay CLR pointed to a paucity of vegetation, and the name remained appropriate into the twentieth century, when Barebush Cay was covered only by grass, creeping plants and small shrubs.[14] Other names referred to fauna: Booby Kay HAN, Great Pelican Kay and Little Pelican Kay CTH, and by propinquity Alligator Pond Kay MAN. Others had a functional flavour, as in Careening Kay CLR and Man of War Kays CLR. Paralleling terms used to describe bays, there was a Half Moon Kay CLR and Long Kay AND. Robertson in turn used the spelling *key*, duplicating all nine of the named *cays* on Craskell and Simpson and adding another eight. All of Robertson's had compound names. Some of the new names referred to vegetation: Bush Key TRL and perhaps Lime Key AND. Gun Key CTH had a strong naval flavour, as did, perhaps, Drunkenmans Key CTH. Most of the other new cay names on Robertson were eponymous.

The number of cays on the 1950 map was fifteen, two fewer than on Robertson. New names were Refuge Cay AND, One Bush Cay TRL and the (punning?) Tern Cay CTH. Robertson's Half Moon Key CLR became Little Half Moon Cay and Big Half Moon Cay, reflecting long-term land-form change. Off the map to the south were the Morant and Pedro Cays, annexed as part of Jamaican territory in 1882 and frequented by itinerant Jamaican fishermen. By 1950 Jamaica's cays had been studied in some detail, particularly by the British geographer J.A. Steers, who used the established names but included among them the Bogue Islands, which cartographers had never called *cays*, distinguishing within the group *islets* and *pseudo-atolls*. Salt Island he considered half island, half cay, with some immature islets (in the southwest corner). Steers also applied a more comprehensive name to the Port Royal Cays.[15]

SHOAL, REEF, BANK, CHANNEL

Some cays are little more than half-submerged shoals, reefs or banks, marine features that pose severe navigational hazards. Lurking beneath the waves, these threats to the sailor were not always marked on maps. Bochart and Knollis named only Ripleys Shoals CTH, and Craskell and Simpson ignored the term completely. Robertson indicated twelve *shoals*, all but one of them given a compound name. Most of the names were physically descriptive, such as Breaker Shoal CTH, Dry Shoal CTH and Three Head Shoals CTH, to make them more easily recognizable. Shoals named for people were rare, though one said to have been discovered in 1798 was called Robertson's Shoal CLR, and here Robertson may have applied his own name – perhaps after grounding on it. The 1950 map had only West Middle Shoal CTH.

Bochart and Knollis named no reefs, and Craskell and Simpson showed only two: Moore's Reef WLD and Roaring Reef WLD. Robertson had four: Bucknors Reef HAN, Moors Reef WLD, Wreck Reef CTH and One Bush Reef CTH. The 1950 map had only the last two of these. Banks were even less commonly named. Robertson noted two: Green Bay Bank CTH and the nearby Three Fathom Bank CTH. Bochart and Knollis had only Sandy Bank CLR, and Craskell and Simpson, none. The 1950 map included the appropriately nautical Ship Rock PLD, Sail Rock THS and Shanty Rock MRY, and the eponymous Lilys Rock JAS and Johns Rock ELZ. The Rockfort of Kingston harbour began its life, in the late seventeenth century, simply as "the Rock", renowned as a pure source of water.[16]

Passages through the shoals, reefs and banks that surround Jamaica are best found through the channels that provide relatively safe entries to bays and harbours. Some of these were named, but almost always these names were simply descriptive. On Robertson's map, Feriagua Channel ELZ defied the rule, but the dominant form was Middle Channel CTH or Main Channel ELZ. Craskell and Simpson followed the same principle, but Bochart and Knollis had Savana Chanel THS, and the 1950 map, Ram Goat Channel CLR.

B EACH

One modern image of Jamaica is a tourist paradise, a place to lie on a sandy beach and be pampered in a beachside hotel that often has *beach* in its name. It is surprising that the term *beach* entered the place names of the island relatively late. None of the pre-twentieth-century maps named beaches, and, indeed, before 1900 the beach was most often a place to go fishing or join a boat rather than a site of solar indulgence. By 1950, however, the topographic map could identify five: two examples of Palm Beach ANN AND, Boston Beach PLD, Dunns River Falls and Beach ANN and Farquhars Beach CLR, which remains an isolated fishing village. The famous Doctors Cave Beach JAS was indicated simply as Doctors Cave. Modern tourist maps identify thirty or more beaches.

CHAPTER SEVEN

Enterprise Names

MOST OF THE JAMAICAN PLACES NAMED for economic activities or functions were associated with the agricultural pursuits that dominated the island throughout its modern history. A close reading of the names of rural places provides an entry into the pattern of production and agrarian structure, though often this analysis must be undertaken indirectly. In some cases the names of agricultural enterprises identified the plants cultivated and animals reared, but these were relatively few and in themselves incapable of telling much about the history of the island's land-use patterns. The dominant export plantation crops – sugar, coffee, bananas – were rarely mentioned in place names, and basic food crops such as yam and plantain were similarly uncommon.

In spite of this apparent inadequacy, Jamaica's place names can in fact be used to create quite a complete picture of the history of land use within the island. This is possible because the major enterprise place names were constructed according to strict rules, the most important of which was that specific generic labels were to be used consistently and systematically as shorthand for more complex descriptions of activity, in the same way as a spring was different from a river. Further, generic labels of this sort were almost always added to other words rather than being used by themselves. A word used as a generic label was hardly ever allowed to stand by itself as a complete place name. Strict application of the rules made reference to specific crops and animals redundant. Thus the descriptive terms used in place names of this type are less important than the generics. Significantly, several of the generic labels used in the island are strict Jamaicanisms, developed to cope with the subtleties of the island's economic structure and organization.

The plantation economy of Jamaica was highly differentiated and integrated, and this economic system was closely reflected in the hierarchies and varieties of generic labels applied to agricultural properties. Thus the specificity of usage enables a reconstruction of land use. None of the words used were new coinages, but they were given new meanings or used in more limited ways. Most of these new meanings were established during the great period of place-naming between 1670 and 1770, when the system of sugar and slavery spread rapidly across the island's fertile lowlands and stretched into interior pockets of rich soil. The construction of the hierarchical system of enterprise types was effectively complete by the end of the eighteenth century. By the time of the abolition of the British Atlantic slave trade in 1807, the plantation economy had reached its limits and was already beginning to retreat in regions such as coastal Portland. In 1805 Jamaica was the world's largest exporter of sugar and in 1810 it was the leader in coffee. These two crops were produced on large-scale properties with large populations, creating viable bases for the names of districts even when the plantations themselves diminished or were totally abandoned after the abolition of slavery in 1838.

ESTATE

The agricultural enterprise at the top of the hierarchy for most of modern Jamaica's history was the *estate*. The Jamaican meaning of *estate* was very specific, identifying a large landholding producing sugar, with its own fields, factory, village, workforce and managers. This usage was not unique to the island, but elsewhere in the English-speaking Caribbean *estate* was often replaced by *sugar plantation* or simply *plantation*, and an estate could produce crops other than sugar, giving rise to *cocoa-estate* and *coconut-estate*, for example, which had no currency in Jamaica. Any Jamaican place name with the label *estate* could be assumed to be an active or former large-scale producer of sugar. The high status of the estate was founded directly upon the profits of sugar-making, which easily outstripped the fortunes that could be made from other crops in the seventeenth and eighteenth centuries. It was a status built on slavery.

The specificity of Jamaican usage, applying *estate* strictly to sugar, has not always been recognized by the makers of dictionaries. The *OED* defines the relevant meaning of *estate* as "A landed property; usually, one of considerable extent. (Now the commonest sense [of estate].) spec. a property on which a crop, as rubber, tea, etc., is cultivated; also a vineyard. Freq. preceded by a defining word." The *DJE* acknowledges that Jamaican usage is not strictly unique but is shared with other territories of the English-speaking Caribbean, and the *DCEU* simply defines *estate* as "A plantation (sugar-, cocoa-, coconut-, etc) including the fields, factory, and all living quarters". The evidence of the place names suggests, however, that such loose definition was relatively uncommon in Jamaica.

The word *estate* was common in Jamaican place names but never stood by itself. There is no place called simply Estate, and *estate* is never the first word of a compound place name; it always comes later, typically at the end. As well, to name a place Such-and-Such Sugar Estate was effectively a tautology, so "sugar" and "cane" were never included. This usage and placement enables *estate* to serve efficiently its role as a generic label of high specificity. Because of the strictness of usage, a map of places with the label *estate* closely matches a map of the distribution of sugar production at the maximum extent of the system around 1800 (Figure 7.1).[1] This labelling rarely appeared on contemporary maps, however, and most of the evidence for the use of the generic *estate* comes from other documentary sources. For example, a place listed in plantation documents as Mint Estate might appear on maps simply as Mint, associated with an identifying mill symbol.

The cadastral series of Jamaican place names, based on the parish maps of circa 1880, includes 495 places with the label *estate*. The vast majority of these were named in the period of slavery, when sugar dominated the landscape. Of the total, 19 per cent of estate names are eponymous. Of the 403

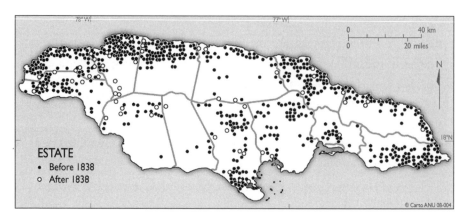

Figure 7.1 Jamaica: *Estate*, habitation names, cadastral series

estates not derived from personal names, 49 per cent were transferred from other places (83 per cent of these drawn from Great Britain and Ireland), 27 per cent referred to physical features, 19 per cent referred to sentiments, 12 per cent added a status element and 10 per cent were floral.[2]

Of the physical features used to name estates, the most common were Hill (15), Spring (14), Valley (10), River (9), Bog (6), Mount (4), Vale (3), Grand Vale (2), Island (2), Bay (2), Hillside (2), Hole (2) and Cove (2). Combining the types, references to water sources were dominant at forty-two cases overall, compared with twenty-seven for elevated topography and twenty for valley sites. Only four estate names referred explicitly to flat or level sites, and the terms were in some cases ambiguous, as, for example, Low Ground CLR, which was called in 1831 a "mountain estate".[3] Low Ground sits in a narrow pocket of relatively level land on the Rio Minho, near Chapelton, surrounded by hills. Only three estates derived their names from geological or soil characteristics, and two of these were indirect: Flint River Estate HAN, Salt Spring Estate JAS and Sod Hall Estate HAN.

The emphasis on water is striking, demonstrating the significance of that resource both for the culture of the sugar cane and for the powering of mills. The watermill was preferred over animal and wind power in the eighteenth century before the invention of the steam engine. The priority of *spring* further reflects the reliability afforded by such a source, compared to the relative inconstancy of many streams. Constant Spring Estate AND has a more fruitful ring to it than Rock River Estate CLR. On the other hand, the frequent reference to elevated landforms is surprising, in that level land and rich soil were always preferred for the cultivation of cane. In the great period of estate naming, down to about 1800, the emphasis on slope was less prominent than it was to become in the twentieth century, when the mechanization of field operations placed a premium on large-scale flatness. Hilly or mountainous landscapes, intersected by river valleys, always had greater aesthetic appeal than the homogeneity of extensive level lands. Of the twelve estate names that referenced aesthetic qualities, seven include Prospect and another two Belvedere. The name of an estate was meant not only to describe its site but also to give it character and status. The pattern parallels that found for physical features, particularly the emphasis on water and elevated landforms.

Vegetational references in the names of estates were dominated by the generalized Garden (7 cases), Grove (4) and Wood (4), together with Copse, Forest and Orchard. The more specific Orange (7) and Anchovy (2), with the single examples of Cinnamon, Olive and Mammee, similarly pointed to elements of the sites when first settled and before the establishment of sugar cultivation. The same might apply to the compounds Cherry Garden, Plantain Garden and even Rose Garden, but in every case the image was in seeming contrast to the actualities of life and culture on a sugar estate. Of the few faunal names, Fat Hog Quarter Estate HAN seems similarly to refer to the state of things before the establishment of sugar.

Another apparent paradox in the naming of estates can be found in the use of words to do with the sentiments, a highly popular form in Jamaica, as established in chapter 3. In contrast to the names of this variety applied to pens and plantations, discussed below, those applied to estates were almost uniformly optimistic or suggestive of satisfaction in the present or future. Only Hazard Estate MRY, hidden high in the inner recesses of the island, on the margins of profitability, suggested anything to the contrary, and this name could ultimately be eponymous. Perhaps this pattern reflects the extent to which the owners of sugar-producing properties felt confident of their fortunes in the early and mature periods of slavery, with prices high and the slave trade at full throttle. The most common names of this sort include Prospect (7), Hope (5), Unity (5) and Friendship (5). Some 5 per cent of estate names could be regarded as religious in character. These include Paradise Estate HAN PLD, New Paradise Estate HAN, Providence Estate JAS and Trinity Estate MRY.

Although *estate* speaks directly to the notion of status, as in a person of "high estate", a good proportion of Jamaican sugar planters were not satisfied with this and, in the cadastral series, fifty of them added elements to their names to further boost the extent of their supposed fortunes and rank. Most popular was *hall* (twenty-nine cases), followed by *castle, park, tower,* and single cases of *house, lodge, inn, court* and *chateau* (Figures 7.2 and 7.3). The dominance of *hall* in this class and in the overall ranking was established early. On Craskell and Simpson's 1760 map there were thirty-three places whose names ended in *hall,* followed at a distance by *castle* (11), *park* (7) and single instances of *lodge, court* and *inn.* Most of these status terms were borrowed directly from the British rural hierarchy, in which the country house played a large social and cultural role for both gentry and aristocracy. However, although the Jamaican plantocracy saw itself as a colonial equivalent to the British – particularly English – system in the

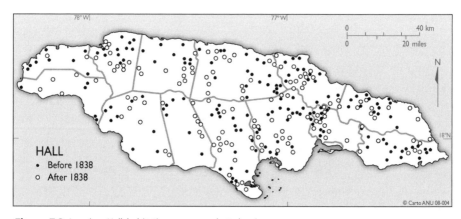

Figure 7.2 Jamaica: *Hall,* habitation names, cadastral series

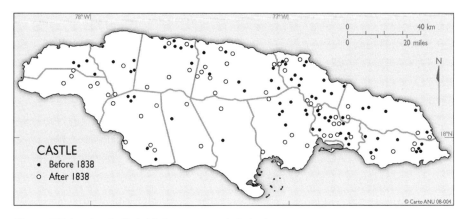

Figure 7.3 Jamaica: *Castle*, habitation names, cadastral series

seventeenth and eighteenth centuries, they rarely used *house*, *abbey* or *manor* in estate names in spite of their metropolitan popularity.[4]

Hall is redolent of the English country house, the seat of the landed gentry. In the English context *hall* meant at least a grand residence or mansion, with strong hints of royal court and palace, even temple. It stood out in Jamaica as by far the most popular and persistent status label and was not exclusively attached to *estate*. From the late seventeenth century to the present, *hall* has typically had three times as many examples as its nearest rival, *castle*. In the longer term, the proportion overall remained constant in spite of the decline of plantation and great house and the disappearance of a visible gentry and plantocracy. *Hall* suggests both the estate as landhold-ing and its great house. For example, in 1995 a new line of export furniture, made up of eighteenth-century reproductions reflective of "Jamaica's plan-tation house elegance", used "the names of Jamaican great houses" to iden-tify the several styles: Creighton Hall, Duckenfield Hall, Stokes Hall, Drax Hall, Halse Hall and Amity Hall.[5] All of these were originally estate names.

The roots of the significance of *hall* are found in the seventeenth cen-tury. Bochart and Knollis identified Heath Hall WLD and Wakefeild Hall CTH, both of which had sugar mills, and Thedford Hall CLR, which named a short-lived district north of Old Harbour Bay. They showed a sugar mill at "Drax" in St Ann, thus identifying only the surname of the original planter, William Drax. The plantation's impressive great house was probably built soon after his death in 1691 and made appropriate the addition of *hall* to the name.[6] Craskell and Simpson in 1760 showed two watermills and a windmill and called the place Drax Hall, but Robertson in 1800 showed a single watermill and contracted the name to "Draxhall". Robertson also reduced Wakefeild Hall to Wakefield. The Heath Hall of Bochart and Knollis became Black Heath, with a watermill, on Craskell and Simpson, and Blackheath on Robertson.

Castle, the second most common status term attached to the names of Jamaican estates, had originally been used fairly strictly in Britain, to mean a large building designed for defence, but came to have a more benign association with large mansions or country houses lacking functional fortifications. The great houses of early English Jamaica were often fortified. Typically built with thick defensive walls and arranged in towers, with gun slits at the corners, they provided defence from other European invaders and from attack by the enslaved people. Occasionally these were denominated *castles* but some, such as Stokes Hall THS, which was built to command a hill in full defensive style, were simply *halls*. In spite of the decline of this style of defensive architecture, there seems to have been no shift to either *hall* or *court* from the early practice of naming estate great houses *castles*.

In 1680 Bochart and Knollis had just one *castle*, Smart Castle CLR, a sugar plantation west of the Rio Minho and north of Alley, approximately where the Ashley family established what Robertson called Ashley Hall. Colbeck Castle CLR, established by Colonel John Colbeck of the army of 1655, appears on Robertson's map simply as Colbecks, and in the cadastral series as Colbecks Estate. In 1898 a writer in the *Gleaner* observed that a pretentious building had been commenced about one hundred years before but never completed and "known to this day as 'Colbeck Castle' ".[7] Not until 1950 did *Colbeck Castle*, appear on the map and then the label related strictly to the great house ruins, identified as an "antiquity". Stewart Castle TRL was also a later structure, built in the eighteenth century by James Stewart on the model of a fortress, but its designation as a *castle* emerged more rapidly than that of Colbeck. The site was indicated simply by the name Stewart on the 1760 map of Craskell and Simpson, but Robertson knew it as Stewart Castle.

Less common for estates were the status terms *court* and *lodge*. The English meaning of *court* derived from the general notion of an enclosed area or yard, and more particularly from the princely household occupying a palace or castle, featuring buildings set around a central courtyard or with a large building set within a courtyard. In England, *court* is a common element in the names of country houses. The term was applied only slowly in Jamaica, the first occurrences found on Robertson's 1800 map, naming three sugar estates: Haughton Court (Old Works and New Works) HAN and Hampton Court THS, the first eponymous and the second probably transferred from the English royal residence. In British usage a *lodge* is generally a modest dwelling place, often meant for temporary occupation, but royal hunting lodges were sometimes much more substantial. A *lodge* might also be the small house of a caretaker or keeper commanding the entrance to an estate. Although lodges of the second type existed in plantation Jamaica, most estate entrances had only simple shelters for their gatekeepers, and it seems probable that the label *lodge* attached to a plantation name derived from the temporary structures that preceded plantation development. The best-known long-term survivor is Bernard Lodge CTH and its resilient sugar factory.

From the French, *chateau* pointed simply to a castle or large mansion. Craskell and Simpson had only one case of *chateau*: Chatteau Morant CLR. This became simply Chatteau on Robertson's 1800 map, the site of an estate with a single watermill. The cadastral series had Chateau Estate CLR and Chateau WLD without extension.

A less likely association occurred in the application of *cottage* in the names of estates. In British usage *cottage* typically indicates a small, humble dwelling, and in Jamaican *cottage* was used often to describe the houses of enslaved people and of peasants and smallholders, contrasted to the great houses, halls and castles of the planter class. The meaning of the term did change in Britain, coming to define also a country residence of moderate scale and picturesque appearance, with the conveniences of modernity. This change did not occur until the 1840s, however, and seems unlikely to have had any great impact on Jamaica. The earliest maps had no instances of *cottage*, but Robertson in 1800 had Cottage PLD, an estate with a single cattle mill behind Port Antonio.

WORKS

The term *works* referred to the existence of buildings or other forms of construction used for the processing of materials. It was never used as a simplex name and was used most often in association with sugar-producing enterprises. In some cases, the term was applied early in the history of a plantation, indicating that a mill and factory had been established, and then disappeared later as the place became more firmly known as an *estate*. In other cases, the word was used to identify the establishment of a second set of works, most often at a new site on the large landholding of a planter or on a newly acquired adjacent piece of land. Craskell and Simpson in 1760 identified a Burnt Sugar Work CTH, two Dry Sugar Works CLR THS (meaning that they were powered by animals rather than a waterwheel) and a Lower Works ELZ.

The inclusion of the word *sugar* in these names was unusual, not matched by any other names on the Craskell and Simpson map and not followed by later mapmakers. Robertson in 1800 distinguished Enfield Old Works and Enfield New Works CTH, both using cattle mills; and Maggotty Estate Old Works and Maggotty Estate New Works HAN. A New Works was not always balanced by an Old Works, however, since the latter could use its simpler name, its priority taken for granted. For example, New Works CTH was implicitly part of Wallens Estate immediately to the north, both of them having only cattle mills. Robertson also identified New Works ANN, a watermill on the Stony River, without further labelling, leaving it unclear whether this was an independent venture or an offshoot of an existing nearby estate. In general, then, *works* was strictly functional, never attributed status by the addition of labels such as *hall* or *castle*.

PLANTATION

Historically, *plantation* was used not only for a particular type of agricultural unit or place but also to describe the act of planting seeds or crops and the establishment of colonies. Initially, for the English, the whole of Jamaica was a plantation, but the term was early replaced by *colony*. The *OED* makes the leap smoothly by defining the cadastral meaning of *plantation* as "An estate or large farm, esp. in a former British colony, on which crops such as cotton, sugar, and tobacco are grown (formerly with the aid of slave labour)". There was nothing unique about the Jamaican (or, indeed, English-speaking Caribbean) use of the term except the way it implicitly excluded sugar. In Jamaica *plantation* was used broadly to identify large landholdings producing crops for the export market but also, more specifically, to distinguish large units producing commodities other than sugar, the sugar-producing properties being known precisely as either sugar plantations or estates.

Like *estate*, *plantation* was common in Jamaican place names but was never used by itself. No place was named simply Plantation, and *plantation* was never the first word of a compound place name. Also like *estate*, the label rarely appeared on contemporary maps, though Craskell and Simpson in 1760 did identify Cabarita Plantation WLD and Seven Plantations CLR. Robertson had only Seven Plantations, which came to be known simply as Sevens. The word *planter*, however, originally identifying the owner of a plantation but sometimes merely pointing to a settler or white colonist, did occasionally appear by itself and did begin several place names, such as Planters Hall CLR MRY, Planters Retreat PLD and Planters View PLD. After the abolition of slavery, with the great growth of smallholdings, the owners of small units also came to be known, by themselves and others, as *planters*, but this seems not to have spilled over into place names.

Whereas the precise use of *estate* in place names enabled a matching with the geographical spread of sugar production, the more inclusive scope of *plantation* makes it less useful as a guide to past patterns of production for particular crops. Thus the distribution of *plantation* (Figure 7.4) does not match either coffee or pimento patterns but rather combines these crops

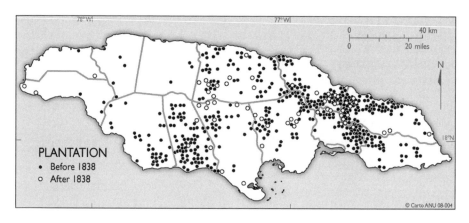

Figure 7.4 Jamaica: *Plantation*, habitation names, cadastral series

with small staples such as ginger, cotton, arrowroot and perhaps dyewoods. *Plantation* is surprisingly rare in place names of the western end of Jamaica. Much of this apparent gap is filled by places with the label *settlement*, discussed below, and to this extent it is possible to discern an equation of the two labels, *plantation* and *settlement*, which appropriately refers back to the originating concepts of colonization. In Jamaican place names, however, the equivalence is firmly rooted in common patterns of crop combination and scale of production.

The cadastral series contains 344 place names with the generic label *plantation*, 82 per cent of them known by 1838. Only 13 per cent had names derived from personal names. Of the remaining 300 plantation names, 51 per cent used elements transferred from the names of places outside Jamaica (86 per cent of these drawn from Great Britain and Ireland), 29 per cent included physical features, 25 per cent referred to sentiments, 13 per cent used vegetational elements and 8 per cent included "status" references. Compared with estates, the plantation names were less likely to be eponymous or to refer to status, and more likely to refer to features of the physical environment, though none of them referred to qualities of soil or to fauna.

In their relatively frequent references to the physical environment, the names of plantations used *hill* more often than any other word (28 cases), matching the ranking for estates but applying it more frequently. *hill* was followed by *mount* (15) and *valley* (6). Another nine plantation names included *hill* in compounds, as in, for example, Prospect Hill Plantation CTH AND, Three Hills Plantation MRY and Wind Hill Plantation THS. There was also Airy Mount Plantation CTH. Grouping all the variants, fifty-seven names referred to elevated landforms, more than twice the number for estates. In contrast, elements of the *valley* type (including also *glen* and *vale*) accounted for only fifteen plantation names, compared to twenty estate names. No plantation names included references to level land. The other strong contrast was that only eleven plantation names pointed to water resources, compared with forty-two estates. These differences are explained by the role of coffee in the definition of the plantation: the best crops always come from elevated sites. Other "plantation crops", as mentioned above, did not share this preference but similarly did not demand the level lands required for sugar cane. Water was used in the processing of coffee and sometimes also to power mills, but its supply was less of a preoccupation for the coffee planter than for the sugar planter. *Spring* occurred in only two plantation names – Cold Spring Plantation MRY and Spring Valley Plantation PLD – unlike the many occurrences for estates. Plantations did, however, sometimes include more spectacular water features than those found in estate names: Waterfall Plantation PLD and two examples of Cascade Plantation ANN MRY.

Unlike estates, plantations sometimes identified particular commercial plants, valued for their fruit or seed, including orange, coffee, pimento, strawberry, mango, mulberry, mammee and corn. There was also the ubiquitous rose and, from the late nineteenth century, cinchona. Some of these were combined in compound names with *grove* or *garden*: Orange Grove Plantation ANN CTH, Coffee Grove Plantation ANN, Pimento Grove Plantation CTH and Lime Tree Garden Plantation ANN. Grove and Orchard were also applied more generally and expanded to forms like Lovely Grove Plantation PLD. Commercial timber trees also featured, the most common being cedar and mahoe.

In aesthetic terms, the dominance of Prospect in estate names was matched in the names of plantations by Pleasant and variants of Bellevue. Similarly, the sentiments expressed were typically optimistic, most of them included in names during slavery. Content was most popular, with expectations often cast in a spiritual frame: Pilgrim Plantation ANN, Pilgrimage Plantation PLD and Holy Mount Plantation CTH. More risky was Hazard Plantation CTH, balanced by Lucky Hill Plantation MRY. The idea of refuge appeared in Retirement, Retreat, Happy Retreat and Far Enough, and the more obviously welcoming and Jamaican name Come See Plantation MRY.

The pattern of status elements employed in the names of plantations paralleled that followed for estates. Most common were *hall*, *castle* and *park*, but *hall* was less dominant than for estates while *castle* and *park* were relatively more common. A handful of plantations used *cottage*.

PEN

Jamaica is home to a number of generic agrarian terms that emphasized enclosure. Typically, the names of larger units emerged from the structure and function of smaller pioneer enclosures. The most common of these are *pen* and *crawl*, and these two words were also applied to larger human settlements. *Walk* and *run* were sometimes used in this way, as in *fowl-walk* and *fowl-run*, similarly indicating varieties of enclosure. The *OED* definition emphasizes the idea of *pen* as a small enclosure for cows, sheep, pigs, poultry or other animals, more or less equivalent with *fold*, *sty* and *coop*. The specifically Jamaican use of *pen* is said to have been used also in regions of the southern United States: "a large country estate, as a farm, plantation, etc.; a farmhouse set in such grounds; a country house". The *OED* takes its earliest examples (1695) from the *DJE* and its most recent (1988) from the Jamaican newspaper the *Gleaner*, and claims that the term used in this way is "now chiefly *Jamaican*". Allsopp's *Dictionary of Caribbean English Usage* (*DCEU*) of 1996 declares that the term is restricted to Jamaica and now effectively historical: "A large country estate of earlier times; the term survives today mainly in place names (May Pen, Slipe Pen Road, etc)."[8]

The word *pen* was used in Jamaica to identify two related yet distinct types of land use. The first was a rural property, often of considerable scale, that produced working livestock for sale to estates and plantations, and also fattened cattle for slaughter to supply the local meat markets. These highly specialized units were numerous both during the period of plantation prosperity and after the decline of the estates. The Jamaican pen of this sort was the property of a pen-keeper, whose status was second only to that of the sugar planter or estate owner.[9] Probably it was this superiority that made *pen* the most popular of the various terms derived from enclosure, with *crawl* and *yard* falling into disfavour fairly early.

The second type of pen was equally common down to the early twentieth century but was relatively limited in geographical scope. This property was less a productive unit than the setting for the residence of a wealthy merchant, shopkeeper or professional of the major towns, particularly Kingston. Knowing only the name of the property, the best clue to which type of pen one is dealing with is its location. Joseph John Gurney in 1840 related the Jamaican *penn* of this sort to a *park*, meaning an English country-house setting. Around Kingston, in the early eighteenth century, these units were called "pens or seats", and "At these pens or country-houses, and on the land adjoining, they breed plenty of hogs, sheep, goats, and poultry", as well as vegetables and fruit sent to market. The Kingston tax rolls identified twenty-six *penns* in 1776, and in 1832 found twenty-seven *pens* located outside the streets and lanes of the city.[10]

In the 1880 cadastral series, 746 places bear the label *pen*, slightly more than half of them known from the period before 1838. Like the labels *estate* and *plantation*, *pen* rarely appeared on earlier maps, but Craskell and Simpson in 1760 did identify six places with the term: Eden Pen MRY, which became Eden Estate; Government Pen CTH, used by governors as a retreat when the capital was Spanish Town; Mulatto Pen MAN; Old Cashue Pen ELZ, which became known as Cashew Pen; Slipe Pen ELZ, later called Slype Pen; and Swallowfield Pen AND, the only peri-urban example. Robertson's 1800 map identified only four pens, three of these given the label in order to distinguish them from their nearby estate "parents". This map did not use a particular symbol to identify pens, so whereas Hals (or

Halse) Hall was known to be an estate because the words were set beside the symbol for a cattle mill, it was necessary to write out fully Halse Hall Pen CLR to identify the function of that place. The same applied to Iter Boreale Pen MRY and the nearby Fort Stewart Pen. The exception was Nottingham Pen, high in the interior of Portland near Moore Town.

The pens were widely spread across the island, the pattern of new names given after 1838 following closely that laid out during the period of slavery.[11] Dense concentrations around Kingston and Spanish Town represented the peri-urban variety, but these pens blended indistinguishably into a belt running westward through southern St Catherine and into Clarendon, where the pens served to raise livestock for estates and plantations. Elsewhere, pens were relatively common in St Ann and St Elizabeth, the parishes best known for their cattle and horses. The St Elizabeth zone spread into eastern Westmoreland and Hanover, and the St Ann belt slipped across the borders into eastern Trelawny and western St Mary. These patterns had been firmly established by the end of the eighteenth century.

Pen was never sufficient in itself to name a place. Pen Hill Plantation AND was not a pen and was probably named after an English Pen Hill or Penhill. Of the 746 pens in the cadastral series, 31 per cent were eponymous, typically taking their names from a British landowner. These often began life in the possessive mode, as in May's Pen, but gradually creolized to become May Pen. Particularly in the modern urban context, the label became contentious and was considered disparaging, leading to further, more dramatic, changes, as discussed in chapter 8. Of the 524 pens that did not take their names from people, 44 per cent had names transferred from other places, almost all from Great Britain and Ireland, 29 per cent referred to sentiments, 22 per cent to physical features, 13 per cent to status and 10 per cent to vegetational elements. Thus the pattern for pens differed from that observed for estates and plantations, chiefly in making much greater use of personal names and of sentiments and less use of names transferred from places outside Jamaica. This difference may seem to be explained by the relatively high level of long-term owner-residency on the pens, compared with the substantial and ever-increasing absenteeism on estates, but this argument fails to account for the low level of eponymous names for plantations.

Among the 296 pen names which did not derive from personal names or the names of other places, 114 referred to their physical sites. Of these, the most common were *hill* (18), *mount* (9), *valley* (6), *bay* (6) and *spring* (6). References to soil or minerals were limited to salt (7), most often in the compound Salt Pond. Other topographic terms with more than one use included *bottom*, *ridge*, *bog* and *gully*, and the compounds Stony Hill, Spring Vale, Salt Spring and Sandy Gully. A handful referred to aesthetic properties, as in the common Prospect (5 cases), Pleasant (4) and Bellevue (3).

Pen names including vegetation words were common. Of fifty-four such names, the most frequent were the generalized Grove (6 cases), Forest (4), Garden (3) and Bushy (2), matched by the more specific Orange (4), Ebony (3), Cedar (2), Teak (2), Mammee (2) and Vineyard (2). There was also Cedar Grove Pen CTH, Fustic Grove Pen JAS, Lancewood Pen ELZ, Orange Grove Pen WLD, Tamarind Tree Grove Pen CTH and Lime Tree Garden Pen CTH. Others, with single occurrences, referred to bamboo, ginger, plum, cabbage, cashew, pepper, rose, berry, guinep, palmetto and thatch. Almost all of these names point to the kinds of products cultivated or harvested on the pens or thought to beautify their grounds.

Names mentioning the livestock that were the bread and butter of the pens were much less common, and references to the grass that fed them completely missing except for New Savanna Pen WLD. Only three pen names mentioned cattle: Bull Bay Pen AND, Bulls Pen JAS (which may be an eponym) and Cow Park Pen WLD. There was also Lambkin Hill Pen MRY, but horses were never included. More surprising were Dolphin Pen HAN (probably derived from the physical landmark Dolphin Head) and Nightingale Grove Pen AND.

Although pens were accorded an ambiguous status in the hierarchy of Jamaican agricultural enterprises, somewhere between the estates and plantations, sixty-six of the *pens* in the cadastral series made pretentious claims for themselves in their names. The ranking differed from that employed by both estates and plantations. For the pens, the most common status term was *park* (23 cases), which may be considered an essentially descriptive

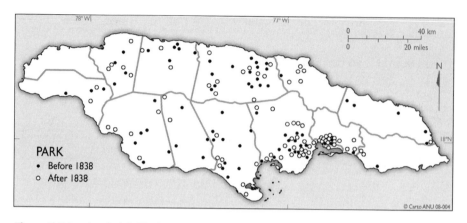

Figure 7.5 Jamaica: *Park*, habitation names, cadastral series

reference to the landscape of the pens (Figure 7.5). This was closely followed by *hall* (19) and *castle* (7). Less grandiose, and less common, were pen names including *lodge, house, cottage* and *inn*. The cadastral series had five instances of Cottage Pen WLD JAS ANN CTH. Pens also included *villa* and *hut* in their names, whereas estates and plantations never did.

The English use of *park* as an equivalent to *pen*, noted above, was not followed in Jamaica. Occasionally the two words occurred together in a single place name – as in Cow Park Pen WLD – showing that they were not understood as simple synonyms. Bochart and Knollis had Clarendon Parke CLR, Cow Park CTH and New Parke CTH. Craskell and Simpson in 1760 showed three times as many, keeping Clarendon Park and Cow Park and adding Green Park JAS, Greenwich Park HAN, Guava Park ANN, Longville Park CLR, Santa Cruz Park ELZ, Bushy Park CTH and Worthy Park CTH. Robertson had just one more example, for a total of ten, but dropped Cow Park, Greenwich Park, Guava Park, Longville Park and Santa Cruz Park, and introduced Dove Cote Park CTH, Linton Park TRL, Moor Park JAS, Olive Park CLR, Shaw Park ANN and Twickenham Park CTH, several of which have survived as well-known places. Some of these repeated the names of famous London parks: Bushy Park, Green Park, Greenwich Park and Twickenham Park.

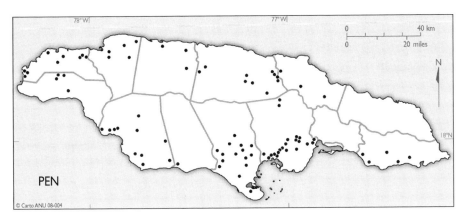

Figure 7.6 Jamaica: *Pen*, settlement names, 1950

A total 150 pen names employed terms that can be understood as representing sentiments, though a few of these (notably Prospect, Pleasant and
Bellevue) overlapped terms that might equally be defined as aesthetic.
Among the pens, the most common sentiment terms were Retreat (8
cases), Friendship (7), Ramble (6), Paradise (5), Retirement (5), Rest (5),
Folly (5), Union (4), Content (4), Hope (3) and Hermitage (3). A sense of
satisfaction, present or future, was four times more likely to be expressed
than a sense of dissatisfaction. There was only one each of Distress, Envy,
Lottery and the ambiguous Little Prospect.

Several of the sentiment names associated with pens were included
among the most common overall. *Ramble*, meaning the capacity to wander
at liberty through the landscape, to make one's own way in an unrestrained
manner, much as a plant – like a vine or a rambling rose – can spread in all
directions, was, however, more frequently applied to pens. There was only
one example by 1800, in Clarendon, but Ramble became increasingly popular after that date, in five places in its simple form on the 1950 map, in the
parishes Westmoreland, St Elizabeth, Manchester, St Ann and St Thomas,
and there were two cases of Ramble Pen JAS CLR.

The 1950 topographical map identified eighty-seven settlement names
with the label *pen* but omitted the urban and urban-fringe zones of

Kingston (Figure 7.6). The pattern is interesting, since it diverges strongly from the geographical distribution found in the cadastral series. The 1950 map showed the way in which *pen* had been incorporated into the names of small towns, villages and districts, derived from properties of the two sorts. Striking features of the distribution are a general absence of *pen* settlement names in the interior of the island and a strong concentration in lower St Catherine and Clarendon. In this way *pen* diverged significantly from the pattern for *estate* and *plantation*, which hardly ever entered settlement names on the 1950 map, though they remained viable as elements in enterprise place names.

Whether in country or town, it became extremely rare for a name-giver to choose *pen* as an appropriate label for their enterprise in the twentieth century, and the general tendency was for the term to decline in use. An exception was Tensing Pen, a Negril resort consisting of twelve cottages and a great house, developed in the 1970s. In 2001 it was said:

> The resort takes its unusual name from the pages of history. The original owners of the property had a faithful and beloved dog, Tensing, named after Tensing Norgay [Norkey Tenzing], the Nepalese guide who escorted Sir Edward Hilary [Edmund Hillary] on his historical [sic] climb of Mount Everest in the 1950s [1953]. The feisty dog then had a bark which convinced all who visited they were on his territory, with [sic] eventually led everyone to refer in jest to the property as Tensing's Pen.[12]

CRAWL, CRAWLE

Defining *crawl*, in the first edition of the *DJE*, published in 1967, Cassidy and Le Page quoted first the *OED*: "An enclosure, pen, or building for keeping hogs (in the West Indies)", noting that the usage was considered obsolete. The *OED* cited Hickeringill as the earliest known reference. He had in 1661 attributed the term and the practice to the Spanish: "Near some convenient place, in the wood, that is best stored with all sorts of fruit-bearing trees, as orange-trees, a sort of cabbage-trees, rag'd with berries, &c. they build two or three little houses, or more; by them called a Crawle, and in these, they first inclose these tame hogs, with which they begin their stock, and there feed them; that after (being let out) they will come to the haunt, at the sound of a horn." Sloane in 1707 had said much the same, comparing *crawls* to sties, and saying that they were "kept by some Whites, Indians or Blacks". Edward Long in 1774 shifted the spelling: "The word craal being commonly used in the West-Indies to signify a place where provisions are planted, and hogs bred."[13] An extension of the meaning applied *crawl* to indicate an offshore aquatic enclosure used to hold turtles, and such turtle crawls were common in Jamaica from the seventeenth century until the early twentieth century, used for holding live animals until sale or slaughter.

Crawl and *crawle* are generally considered relatives of the Spanish *corral*, the colonial Dutch and Afrikaans *kraal* and the Portuguese *curral*. In eighteenth-century Southern Africa a *kraal* was a village or group of huts surrounded by a fence, mud wall or palisade, generally with a secondary inner enclosure for cattle. Closer to the Jamaican usage, *kraal* was also applied in Southern Africa to an enclosure for sheep or cattle, equivalent to a stockade, cattle pen or sheepfold. *Kraal* is the form most closely reflecting modern Jamaican pronunciation of the word and it emerges occasionally in Jamaican place names, as best exemplified by Beckford Kraal CLR.[14]

In Jamaican usage, *crawl* is generally glossed as equivalent in meaning to *pen*. In some cases, however, there was repetition either for emphasis or as a means to attribute superior status, as in five examples of Crawle Pen JAS CLR ANN CTH MRY. There was also a Crawle Estate JAS, indicating a shift from pioneer land use to the prosperity of sugar planting. Most examples of *crawl* were, however, attributed to proprietorship, such as Angwins Crawle ANN and Williamsons Crawle CTH. Another numerous group linked crawls to estates, in much the same way pens were associated with sugar plantations, as in Halse Hall Crawle CLR, Longville Crawle CTH, Denbigh Crawle CLR and, less obviously, Two Mile Wood Crawle MAN. There were also associations with physical features, as in Crawle Pond MRY and Crawle River CLR. As indicated by these examples, places containing *crawle* were heavily concentrated in the central interior regions of Jamaica, suggesting both the

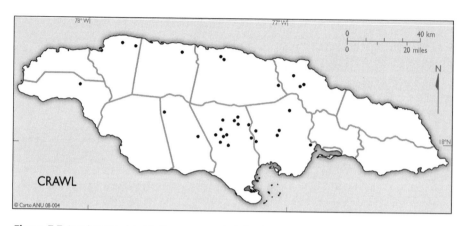

Figure 7.7 Jamaica: *Crawl*, habitation names, cadastral series

role of survivals related to early Spanish settlement patterns and the power of local imitation (Figure 7.7).

Crawl was unusual in serving as a simplex name, simply Crawle. The ability of the word to exist as a functional place name without embellishment can no doubt be traced to the early role of the crawl as an isolated unit, the one habitation feature in an otherwise empty economic landscape (see Figure 4.6). Once the term became uncommon, effectively displaced by *pen*, it was possible for a small number of places to retain Crawle as a name sufficiently distinctive in itself. Craskell and Simpson's map of 1760 showed only The Crawles CLR, but by the end of the nineteenth century this place had become simply Crawle, and there were by then also Crawle TRL and Crawle CTH. All of these were in central Jamaica but sufficiently distant from one another to avoid much confusion. Maps from the middle of the twentieth century showed only Crawle CTH, by then a point on the railway line known as Crawle Halt, and Crawle TRL, a substantial settlement near Duncans. No *crawl* seems ever to have had attached a status term such as *hall, castle* or *park*.

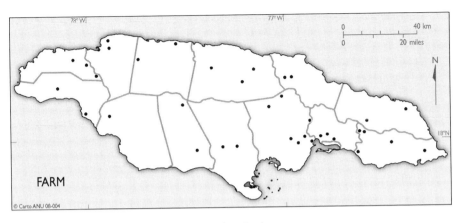

Figure 7.8 Jamaica: *Farm*, habitation names, cadastral series

FARM

In English usage a *farm* was understood from the sixteenth century to be a tract of land held on lease for cultivation, but in modern times the emphasis has shifted to the fact of cultivation or "farming" without regard to the form of land tenure. The former usage had no currency in Jamaica, and even the second was always uncommon in the island's place names. *Farm* was sometimes regarded as replaced by the Jamaicanism *pen*, a term sometimes defined by British commentators as a *grass-farm*.[15] About half of the examples of *farm* in Jamaica occur simply as Farm or occasionally The Farm. The other half applied *farm* as a generic label, most often added to a personal name, as in Dobsons Farm CTH and Gordons Farm HAN, and less frequently to an English place name, as in Cambridge Farm THS and Windsor Farm AND, or sentiment, as in Pleasant Farm CTH and Prospect Farm MRY. Modern examples include Nyerere Community Farm, established at Cacoon Castle HAN in the 1970s. In a few cases a personal name and a physical feature were combined with *farm*, as in Godfreys Spring Farm CTH and Dawkins Bog Farm CTH, the latter distinct from the nearby Dawkins Salt Pond Pen CTH.

The close association between *farm* and *pen* was made apparent in the six occurrences of Farm Pen in which *pen* was the generic label. This form paralleled the use Crawle Pen, found in St Catherine and St Mary. In other cases *farm* served as the original generic label and then became part of the individual element, with *pen* added as the generic label, as in the case of Rachaels Farm AND, which was transformed into Rachael's Farm Pen. In these examples *farm* is essentially redundant as a means of identifying the type of land use but suggests a transition from mixed cropping and livestock-raising to an emphasis on livestock. This association is confirmed by the naming of land units within pens as *farms*. In 1848, for example, Cumberland Pen CTH was mostly in pasture, grass and sorghum, but two units were called respectively Northern Provision Farm and Southern Provision Farm, indicating that they produced staple "food" crops such as tubers and plantains.[16] Other extensions were Farm Hill, Farm Mountain and Farm Plantation.

As expected, the geographical distribution of the word *farm* matches closely that of *pen*, though *farm* was less common in St Elizabeth and lacked the peri-urban type of pen, so that it was also rare in St Andrew (Figure 7.8).

SETTLEMENT

The word *settlement* was known in Jamaica as meaning the human occupation of specific sites at various scales and was used to identify grouped houses at a single site, as common throughout the English-speaking and particularly the colonial world, but it was also used with a peculiarly Jamaican meaning, not noted in the *DJE*. This was the notion of a *settlement* as a small-scale plantation, producing the dyewoods logwood and fustic, along with timber, livestock, provision crops, ginger, and limited quantities of coffee and pimento. In 1818 one writer referred to "coffee-settlements" and "provision settlements", the latter predecessors of the contemporary sugar-estate regime around Dry Harbour.[17]

In this way, *settlement* overlaps with the equally Jamaican usage *mountain*, as discussed below, though the geographical distribution of the two terms

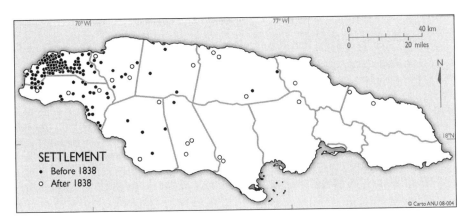

Figure 7.9 Jamaica: *Settlement*, habitation names, cadastral series

was very different (Figure 7.9). The most striking aspect of the distribution of *settlement* is its strongly western concentration, the vast majority of the examples occurring in Hanover and Westmoreland, with a primary hearth in western Hanover. This suggests naming by imitation with only limited diffusion. In this western region, some of the places known as settlements by the 1830s had been sugar mills on Robertson's 1800 map, and the term never appeared on his map. Why this should be the pattern for *settlement* in this part of the island is hard to say.

Settlement never named a place but was always preceded by a descriptive name. Further, most of the sixty-nine places that used *settlement* as a generic label had unique descriptive names. In the few cases where two or more settlements had the same name, they were always in different parishes, as in Content Settlement HAN ELZ ANN, Industry Settlement HAN WLD, Retirement Settlement WLD JAS and Thornhill Settlement HAN WLD. Unlike *mountain*, a settlement was not the satellite of an estate or plantation but rather an independent small-farming unit. Thus the *Amsterdam* in Amsterdam Settlement HAN did not occur in any other place name, nor did the *axe and adze* of Axe and Adze Settlement HAN.

Even where the name was a common one, like the *bellevue* of Bellevue Settlement WLD, there was no other Bellevue nearby that might have served as the original of the name. Cacoon Settlement HAN was distant from Cacoon Castle Pen though in the same parish. A few close connections did occur: Bonny Pen Settlement MRY was close by Bonny Pen; Lincoln Pen Settlement ANN near to Lincoln Pen; Hopewell Settlement JAS close by Hopewell Mountain; Industry Settlement HAN close by Industry Mountain; and Vale Royal Cottage Settlement TRL close by Vale Royal Mountain. It is also striking that only five of the settlement names were potentially eponymous, and only a few transferred names from places outside Jamaica (as in Amsterdam, Boston, Maryland or Tweedside). Only one, Ginger Hill Settlement HAN, hinted at the character of land use. Most used either physical descriptors or referred to sentiments. The status elements that helped define and elevate estates, plantations and pens were rarely used in the names of enterprises called *settlements*. The only two cases were Bower Hall Settlement and Cottage Settlement, both in Hanover in the core region of settlements. In modern Jamaica, none of these places has retained the *settlement* label, though a number have survived without it – for example, Axe and Adze.

WALK

The *walk* of Jamaica indicated an agricultural area or land unit planted in tall trees, generally set out in a geometrical pattern of lines and with a shady canopy. In this way usage moved away from the idea of mobility, as in walking through a wood or garden, to identify instead a tract of cultivated or planted land. The *OED* identifies this usage as uniquely "West Indian" in equating a *walk* with a *plantation*. According to Cassidy in his *Jamaica Talk* of 1961, "The word 'orchard' would seldom be heard in this island, and no more would 'grove'. What one hears for a group of trees planted or naturally growing together is *walk*, and one hears it in a great many combinations."[18] One early variety was the *plantain walk*. In 1672 Blome provided detailed directions on the planting of a "Cocao Walk". Others, in the early eighteenth century, referred to "Plantane and Bonana Walks" and "Cotton Walks".[19] When "planted with regularity and care", said Beckford in 1790,

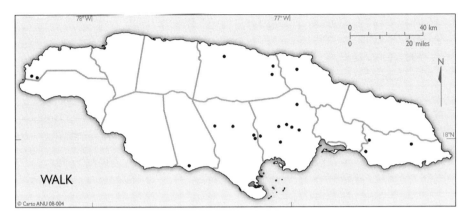

Figure 7.10 Jamaica: *Walk*, habitation names, cadastral series

and reaching maturity, "it is hardly possible to conceive a prospect more solemn, gloomy, and impressive, than is exhibited in the verdant aisles which the spreading glooms occasion, and which at a little distance appear to be a forest of shade, over which is beginning to descend the curtain of night". Here in this plantain walk, said Beckford, the "contemplative man" might "wander through the walks of nature improved by art".[20] In this way, Beckford brought the meaning of the *walk* back to its perambulatory origins, bringing together the planted land with movement through it.

Not all of these variations found a home in Jamaican place names. No place was named simply Walk in the way places became known as Crawle or Farm. Further, although such plantings were well known, no places were named Banana Walk or Pimento Walk.[21] Cocoa Walk survived best, naming eight widely distributed places. Most of the rest occur but once: Coconut Walk CTH, Coffee Walk ANN, Green Walk ANN, Ham Walk CTH, Lime Walk CTH, Thatch Walk ANN CLR, Murray's Plantain Walk THS and Seven Mile Walk CTH. In Kingston, Ackee Walk in the Smith Village area was well known by the 1930s.[22] Occasionally a place with *walk* in its name was given a further extension, as in Coffee Walk Mountain HAN, suggesting an associated property. Like *crawl*, the geographical distribution of *walk* is strongly concentrated in the central regions of Jamaica (Figure 7.10). It is less obvious why this should be so, since *walk*'s etymology seems to be purely English.

Walk was also used occasionally for an extensive stretch of country. Seven-Mile-Walk CTH, which was close to the head of Bog Walk, appeared on Craskell and Simpson's 1760 map. Sixteen-Mile-Walk CTH appeared on Robertson's map and was so named in documents from the seventeenth century. These walks were, however, understood as essentially natural features rather than habitation names, and the distances in the names – seven and sixteen miles – represented the length of the journey from Spanish Town rather than the extent of the feature. Leslie identified Sixteen-Mile Walk as early as 1739. He also mentioned "Major Needham's Walk".[23] The Scottish traveller Robert Baird, in Jamaica in the late 1840s, advised visitors to view the gorge "known by the extraordinary cognomen of the 'Bog Walk' ". Baird thought this ravine "might much more fittingly be denominated the Mountain Glen or the Dark Valley" but praised its "exceedingly picturesque beauty" created by the depth of the gorge, its stream and the vegetation clothing its walls.[24] Just as there is uncertainty about the word *bog* in several Jamaican place names, the term *walk*, as used here, is in some doubt. It is commonly claimed that Bog Walk is an English corruption of the Spanish Boca d'Agua, meaning Water's Mouth.

GARDEN

The term *garden* is common and widespread but difficult to interpret since, although it sometimes was used as a generic label, in other, probably most, cases it operated as a descriptive element (Figure 7.11). *Garden* never occurred as a simplex name, being just too generic to be functional, but the cadastral series included Garden Hall ANN, Garden Hill WLD ANN AND, Garden Hill Plantation CTH, Garden Valley Settlement HAN (which became the town of Dias) and New Garden AND PLD. "Botanic garden" indicated a particular kind of enterprise defined as a *garden*, hence Castleton Garden MRY and Spring Garden AND. It is a reasonable assumption that a name like Naseberry Garden CTH might suggest that naseberry trees were plentiful or

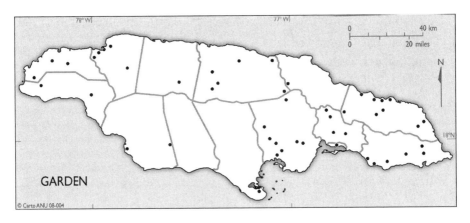

Figure 7.11 Jamaica: *Garden*, habitation names, cadastral series

perhaps cultivated there. A good proportion of the places including *garden* in their names refer also to plants. The most common of these is the broadly scattered Cherry Garden AND CTH MAN, plus Cherry Garden Estate THS and Cherry Garden Mountain CTH. Of trees, there were also Lime Tree Garden Pen CTH, Lime Tree Garden Plantation ANN and Mahoe Gardens CLR. Much more popular overall was *rose*, but in association with *garden* it appeared only in Rose Garden Estate THS and the nearby Rose Garden Mountain. Also close by was Plantain Garden River Estate.

In the cadastral series, *garden* names including botanical references were numerous and varied, but by far the most common association was with *spring*. There were nine examples of Spring Garden HAN JAS ELZ TRL ANN PLD THS, seven of Spring Garden Estate HAN WLD JAS PLD MRY THS and two of Spring Garden Pen JAS CLR. This popularity is not surprising, since Spring Garden was a popular name overall (see Table 3.2), matching the frequency of *spring* and parallel combinations like Springfield. Relating *spring* and *garden* pointed to popular concepts of fruitfulness and horticultural order, as well as reliable, constant supplies of life-giving water. The notion of spring as the season of bourgeoning plant life, leaving behind the inertia of winter, had little practical application in tropical Jamaica, though it might have appealed to some residue of British memory when placed within the paradise of the pullulating, blooming garden. The original

Spring Garden may have been transferred from the London place of that name, as may Covent Garden JAS, which probably referred appropriately to the London markets rather than the opera house. Bournemouth Gardens AND recalled the English seaside resort.

Garden names emerged early. Craskell and Simpson's 1760 map included three examples of Spring Garden WLD ELZ THS, two of Cherry Garden AND MRY, a Garden Hill CTH and Mahoe Garden CLR. This early enthusiasm suggests that *garden* might signify a natural grove as often as a carefully cultivated landscape.[25] By the twentieth century, *gardens* became an increasingly common label for new and redeveloped suburbs, particularly around Kingston.

GROUND

In Jamaica a *ground* came to identify a unit of cultivation, generally small in scale, located at some distance from the cultivator's residence. During slavery this was typically known as a *provision ground* or, less often, a *polink*. Where the ground was located within the boundaries of a plantation property, the name served as a field name rather than a place name with potential longevity. Thus *provision ground* and *polink* survived poorly in the cartographic record, though the more common term *Negro grounds* did anachronistically maintain some currency into the period after the abolition of slavery, appearing occasionally in forms such as Winchester Negro Grounds THS. In 1869 Sawkins recorded Banana Grounds in Portland, a small, level depression once cultivated by the Maroons.[26] In most cases the name survived because the provision ground had been established on a piece of land separated from the estate with which it was associated. Such names were common during slavery but rarely recorded on maps as part of the economic activity of the island, in spite of the vital role the grounds played in the internal marketing system and the feeding of the population.

Ground and *grounds* appeared in a number of types of place names. For example, Robertson identified The Black Grounds in a large semicircular sweep in southern Trelawny on the southeastern edge of the Cockpit

Country, as shown in Figure 5.5. Twentieth-century maps showed The Black Grounds stretching from Lorrimers through Wait-a-Bit to Albert Town. On Craskell and Simpson's map this district was an empty space. Only after abolition was it settled, and then densely, by small settlers. Sawkins in the 1860s said the Black Grounds differed from the white-limestone districts of Trelawny, being derived from shales and conglomerates, saying, "The name 'Black Grounds' implies a different soil from the rest; among the creoles it is more generally known as Abu or Bugádoo." The land is undulating, boggy alluvium.[27]

Mountain

In Jamaican English the word *mountain* developed a secondary meaning, disconnected from the fact of elevation and coming to identify a small plantation, farm or provision ground. The origin of this usage can be traced to the fact that such agricultural units were typically found in elevated sites, though generally not ruggedly mountainous, and in isolated heavily forested niches. The *OED* does not mention this Jamaican meaning but does refer to an Irish English and northern English regional use of *mountain* to mean a rough, unenclosed pasture or inferior wasteland, often on the slope of a hill. This seems to be a parallel rather than influential form. Cassidy and Le Page define the Jamaican meaning of *mountain* as "A small plantation in the mountains, esp[ecially] for crops that grow better at an altitude". Late-eighteenth-century usage sometimes also included the notion of a mountain as a retreat from the sultry heat of the lowlands and a refuge from the business of town, plantation and port. For example, Admiral's Pen, near Kingston, was matched by the "refreshing breezes" of Admiral's Mountain, the "hill-residence" of the commander-in-chief. *Mountain* has come to be used in much the same way in other mountainous Caribbean islands, as almost a synonym for *garden*.[28] In Jamaica, however, the topographic requirements were effectively abandoned, and the emphasis was placed strictly on the character of cultivation, resulting in such odd-sounding place names as Bunkers Hill Mountain TRL, Catherine

Mount Mountain JAS and Mount Pleasant Mountain HAN. Thus *mountain* demonstrates the way in which a topographical reference could be translated into an identifier of a particular variety of land use.

The origin of *mountain* as a small cultivated unit was firmly rooted in the typical site of the provision ground during slavery. The level land of the estates was devoted as far as possible to the cultivation of export crops to maximize the profits of the sugar planters, and the production of food crops for consumption by the enslaved people was allocated to steeper slopes, where the soil was often good for raising yams, cocos and plantains but not well suited to sugar cultivation. Particularly in the northwestern parishes, where the most complex *mountain* names were located, it became common in the later eighteenth century for planters to purchase separate blocks of land in the distant upland interior, and to allocate these as provision grounds to the enslaved. Eventually, the land that produced provision crops came to be known as a mountain, whether it was steep or level.

In his *Descriptive Account* of 1790 the planter William Beckford gave an account of the development of provision grounds by the enslaved, saying the people "generally make choice of such spots of land for their grounds as are encompassed by lofty mountains; and I think that they commonly prefer the sides of hills which are covered with loose stones, to the bottoms upon which they are not so abundant". On Sundays, said Beckford, they went to "the mountains" to harvest the fruits of their labour to sell in the local markets. In 1825 reference was made to "the Provision Mountain belonging to Pembroke Estate" in Trelawny.[29]

Some commentators did not confine the use of *mountain* to the provision grounds of the enslaved but included other non-sugar activities, and assimilated the term to the meaning of *settlement*. Thus Dallas, in his *History of the Maroons*, published in 1803, declared in a footnote that "The word mountain is applied to settlements on mountains, which are generally of coffee and ground provisions. Mr. Such-a-one's mountain, a coffee mountain, &c."[30] A mountain might also be mistaken for a pen. For example, in 1801 Maria Nugent noted that her husband, the governor, set off early one morning to walk from Government Pen, five kilometres southeast of Spanish Town, "to see a penn, or rather a mountain, belonging to Mr.

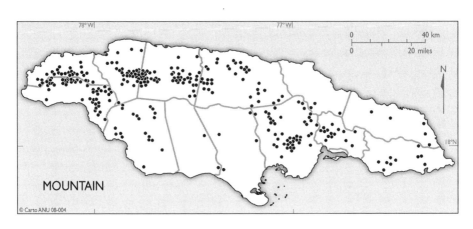

Figure 7.12 Jamaica: *Mountain*, habitation names, cadastral series

March, two miles off".[31] In 1830 an advertisement offered for sale a "mountain settlement" of thirty acres near Temple Hall in St Andrew, with a small house, barbecues and a store, growing yams, cocos, plantains, peas, corn, arrowroot, cassava, coffee and fruit trees. The same year, another advertisement read "Wanted, a steady black man who is capable of taking charge of a small mountain settlement, and who is not above working in the field". In 1839 Benjamin McMahon referred to Mr Gibs's "Coffee Mountain".[32] Other variations were Coffee Walk Mountain and Farm Mountain.

Only a few of these mountains entered the lists of named places during slavery. After 1838, however, there was a rapid proliferation of the use of the name. This proliferation reflected a catching up, with places known colloquially as mountains during slavery accepting the label as an element of a viable long-term place name and naming larger districts. The extensive geographical spread of the name in the interior uplands of the western parishes reflects this process (Figure 7.12). A secondary concentration, in the interior uplands of modern St Catherine, followed a similar pattern, though outside the central zones of sugar production the mountains were not all composed of the provision grounds of the enslaved. Not every mountain was linked to an estate or plantation, suggesting that in some cases naming may have had its roots in a field unit or been more directly eponymous, as in Congo Mountain HAN and Quasheba Mountain HAN, for example.

In the post-slavery period, the growth of the peasantry was often linked to a desire to acquire a small plot or generic mountain. This might be in the isolated upland interior but could equally be found in some wild or ruinate corner of an abandoned or partially abandoned sugar plantation. The currency of the term *mountain* seems, however, to have strongly followed the structural and spatial division established during slavery. Thus the great districts of peasant expansion after 1838, like northern Manchester, made no use of the term in naming newly settled places. On the other hand, where mountains had existed before 1838 as separated units, these were typically the lands the planters were most eager to sell after abolition, often subdivided and creating the basis for a named township or district. Few of these have survived. The most obvious example is the seeming misnomer Georges Plain Mountain HAN, formerly associated with Georges Plain Estate WLD. Most of the modern places with names ending in mountain are straightforwardly eponymous, as in Irons Mountain ANN and Johnson Mountain THS.

Land, run

The use of *land* as a generic label was intended to indicate tenure rather than an economic activity or land use. The most common usage was to identify a small area that had been divided from or attached to a larger property. Particularly when the area was not contiguous or absorbed into that larger property, it could gain a separate identity and achieve great longevity. For example, Running Gut Land JAS was a nearby but separate tract of Running Gut Estate, and Biddeford Pen Land ANN was just across the parish border from Biddeford TRL. Whereas most of the terms discussed thus far were applied to place names principally before the abolition of slavery, *land*, like *mountain*, is striking in its rarity before 1838 and in its widespread and common use after abolition (Figure 7.13). The separated

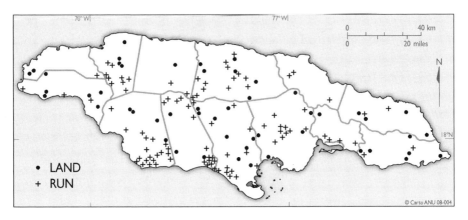

Figure 7.13 Jamaica: *Land* and *run*, habitation names, cadastral series

tracts purchased to be used as mountains in the eighteenth century seem never to have been called lands, because indicating tenure was less important than identifying land use. After 1838 issues of tenure came to the fore, with the subdivision and abandonment of estates and plantations, the establishment of free villages and the rapid growth of the peasantry by freehold and squatting. Thus the post-slavery place name Bank Mountain Land ANN indicated a topographic description rather than a repetition of land use. Remote and generally interior tracts were sometimes called back lands. Cambridge Back Lands PLD were towards the mountains from Cambridge Estate, and Muirton Back Land THS towards the mountains from Muirton Estate.

In other cases, the word *land* was used initially to identify ownership of a tract that remained undeveloped, and, again, these names sometimes stuck in the longer term – for example, Sanguinetti's Land MAN. Perhaps the best-known examples are the post-slavery Higgin Land ANN and Higgin Town, and, in Kingston, Fletchers Land (with Fletchers Lane), so named by the 1890s or even earlier.[33]

Place names of the type *-land* or *-lands* are harder to interpret, as they were often transported from places outside Jamaica and are not helpful in understanding local economic patterns. Thus Laughlands ANN may derive from a British surname: Laughlan or Lachlan. Lock Land WLD may be a corruption. Similarly, Longlands HAN ELZ may derive from the surname Longland, Langland or Langlands (meaning originally "dweller by the long piece of land") rather than describing the shape of the properties in Jamaica. Breadland Pen CLR is more likely to indicate cultivation but remains ambiguous. Place names of this sort were equally common before and after 1838, and hard to distinguish from the seemingly obvious transfer names such as Holland, Scotland, Old England, Sunderland and the like.

In much the same way as *land*, the word *run* was popular among Jamaican place names after 1838 but was rarely used in the period of slavery. In almost every case the form was simply a personal name followed by *run*, as in Carmichael's Run ANN and Mary Gales Run ELZ. Only in a handful of cases was *run* attached to an existing place name, as in Pomfret Run THS, St Anns Run WLD, Union Run MRY and Mason River Runs CLR. In all of these cases the meaning was simply a stretch or tract of land but, unlike *land*, the place names including *run* rarely matched the names of estates, plantations or pens. Rather, the runs had a separate existence. In 1854 Hampden Sugar Estate owned two separate "runs of mountain land" but these did not give rise to place names.[34]

Like *walk*, *run* has its origin in the idea of mobility, in this case the driving of livestock, particularly to pasture, and by extension the keeping of livestock on pasture. But none of the many Jamaican examples referred to livestock of any sort, with the possible exception of Hoggs Run ANN. Jamaicans use *run* to mean the chasing away of people and animals – to *run* a cow or a goat, for example – but the *runs* of the place names communicated this notion only tangentially. The distribution of places called *runs* did, however, reflect the geographical pattern of livestock-raising and pen-keeping (see Figure 7.13).

Piece, Pasture, Field

In Jamaican English *piece* replaced *field* as the most common word used to identify a subdivision of a larger property, particularly of an *estate*. Pieces were further specified by reference to the crops they were planted in, such as cane piece, yam piece, grass piece and potato piece. Most of these pieces had their own compound names, bestowed in order to facilitate management, but only occasionally did they come in turn to name a larger area or district.[35] As with the comparable term *pasture*, the places named *piece* fell mostly into a small area of concentration, in this case in the interior of St Mary: Belle Piece, Campbell Piece, Congo Piece, Crawle Piece, Gully Piece and Tucker Piece. As well as this concentration, there were Evans Piece ELZ and, nearby, Wild Pen Piece ELZ and the more isolated Owen Piece MAN. The comedian Ranny Williams did write a story in 1956 about the joys of Christmas festivities at "Callaloo Piece", somewhere past Bog Walk, but this was a fictional district.[36]

The naming of field units had a practical purpose. Thus Thistlewood, as overseer at Egypt Estate WLD, took action to label cane pieces that lacked names, something he saw as essential to the efficient management of the plantation. When the sugar crop was being taken off in January 1752, he recorded in his journal that the enslaved people were "Employed cutting canes towards Dunbar ground. Cut a little piece we call the corner piece, and began another we called the Dogwood tree piece, from dogwood tree growing on it. . . . I say called, because none of their cane pieces here have names, so that it is hard to distinguish one from another in discourse therefore gave them names."[37] Naming the pieces was useful not only for ease of reference in giving directions but also important to plantation record-keeping and the calculation of yields. Further references in his journal mentioned Breadnut Tree piece, Coffee Ground Pass piece, Potato piece, Marl Pit piece, Coffee Tree piece, Milkwood piece and Pimento Tree piece, suggesting a strong emphasis on dominant trees as the most obvious markers. In many contexts, field names proved efficient identifiers without using generic labels. For example, in the late 1940s, according to Patrick Leigh Fermor, Maroon names for fields and valleys on the fringes of Accompong included "Good Hope, Hill Middle, Saucy Train Cross-roads, New Lumber Road, and Old Mill".[38]

Eight place names take the label *pasture*. These seem all to have derived their names from tracts of estate or plantation land used to pasture livestock. What is most striking about this small group is that, with two exceptions, they all occur within a small district of Vere, suggesting imitation behaviour more than unique land use patterns. Even the exceptions, Browns Pasture CLR and Shickles Pasture CLR, are not far away from this concentration. Shickles Pasture was associated with Shickles Pen, as Suttons Pasture was linked with Suttons Estate. In most cases these places depended on personal names, including names which may have belonged to enslaved people, as in Quamina's Pasture and, less certainly, Dicks Pasture and Charles Pasture. There were also Church Pasture and Dry River Pasture. In St Andrew, the Hope Estate was broken up in the twentieth century, first naming Hope Gardens (which became officially the Royal Botanic Gardens, Hope, following a visit by Queen Elizabeth II in 1953), then the middle-class suburb Hope Pastures.

As with -*land*, a substantial number of Jamaican place names had the ending -*field*, including the popular Springfield and Williamsfield. These names are common and widespread but difficult to interpret. Some derived directly from surnames. Others attached -*field* as a suffix. Thus Scarlettfield WLD emerged where early maps showed simply Scarlett. Phillipsfield THS put together the name of the seventeenth-century English planter family Phillips and *field*. Other examples, such as Sheffield and Wakefield, transferred British place names fully formed. In the latter, *field* derived not from the idea of an enclosed unit of agricultural land but rather from the Old English *feld*, meaning "open country" or "open land", which came to be generally spelled *field*.[39] Rarely does -*field* seem to operate in the same way as *piece* or *pasture*, naming a place for what was originally a tract of plantation land.

MINE, PLANT

The varieties of enterprise considered so far were all essentially rural and agricultural. Few enterprises outside this agrarian stream developed generic labels that found a place in the system of place names before World War II. The manufacturing establishments of the twentieth century were almost all sited in towns or along major routes connecting towns, and typically bore the name of the entrepreneur or company they belonged to. A branch plant was identified by the nearest existing place name.

Plant did appear on some modern maps, generally to show the location of an alumina processing plant, but most of the great bauxite mines scattered across the landscape after 1950 took their names from pre-existing places, such as Lydford ANN and Nain ELZ. Exceptions include Kirkvine MAN, the works of ALCAN, built in the 1950s and by the 1960s the largest industrial plant in Jamaica, named for the president of the company, and Port Kaiser ELZ, west of Alligator Pond, built by the Kaiser Bauxite Company. Most of the bauxite has been extracted by open-cut mining, which created a temporary scar that was eventually replanted in grass or trees when the mine moved on, leaving little reason for long-term naming. In the 1960s Jamaica was, briefly, the world's largest exporter of bauxite.

Before bauxite, Jamaica was mined for copper in the eastern mountains, with adits creating more lasting, though isolated, landmarks. Here the name Mine THS became attached without further description, and there were two examples of The Mines ANN AND. Only one of these appeared on the 1950 map, as Mines, in the hills above Llandovery ANN. There was also Mine Pen MRY. In all of these cases, *mine* merely describes the location of an enterprise in generic terms, always without a descriptive prefix to make a compound place name.

HOTEL

The first hotels were constructed in the 1890s, encouraged by the Jamaica Hotels Law of 1890 and the International Exhibition planned for the following year. These developments took advantage of the railway that finally crossed the island from Kingston to Montego Bay and to Port Antonio, and the banana trade that brought the first large contingents of tourists. The hotels were initially equally distributed between the coast and the cooler – more healthy – interior uplands of the island. They quickly became large and imposing structures and soon were concentrated along the north coast and, later, at Negril in the west. Before the emergence of the hotel, with its substantial footprint and place-naming potential, travellers within Jamaica who could afford to pay for accommodation had sought temporary refuge in taverns, inns and lodging houses or depended on the hospitality of plantation great houses.[40]

As economic enterprises, hotels had a status in twentieth-century Jamaica somewhat similar to that of plantations before them, and in listing their names, the generic label was, similarly, often omitted. They offered temporary rather than permanent residence for most of their population but sat, uneasily, alongside other kinds of enterprise and habitation sites in much the same way plantations served as population foci in the eighteenth century. Some of the first commercial hotels of the twentieth century occupied great houses on former estates, making a concrete link with the past and the possibilities of retrospective naming. A notable example is Good Hope TRL, a beautifully preserved Georgian house that was converted into a hotel in 1933 and still serves that purpose.

A list produced by the Jamaica Tourist Board in 1992 named 111 hotels, with the largest concentrations in Montego Bay, Negril and Ocho Rios, but added the label *hotel* to fewer than one-half of them. Of the total, seven included *Jamaica* in their names: Jamaica Jamaica, Jamaica Pegasus, Jamaica Grande, Jamaica Inn, Jamaica Palace, Ambiance Jamaica and Holiday Inn Jamaica. Versions of *Caribbean* were also fairly common, as in Caribbean Isle and Sandals Royal Caribbean. Both *Jamaica* and *Caribbean* appeared in the older established zones, with none in Negril. *Beach*, a landscape term rarely applied to enterprise names before tourism, appeared widely and in varied locations, from Doctor's Cave Beach to Boscobel Beach, and was joined by versions of *sea* and *sand*, as in Seasplash Resort and Ocean Sands Resort, and *cliffs* and *reefs*, as in Coral Cliff and perhaps Swept Away Resorts. The simpler Sandals Inn and Sandals Negril extended the theme. The idea of the *garden* appeared in Enchanted Gardens and Hibiscus Lodge, for example, but no names introduced the unique flora and fauna of Jamaica. References to Jamaica's Taino past occurred in Ciboney Ocho Rios and Arawak Inn; to the Spanish in Casa Maria and Rio Blanco Village; and to the British in Mayfair and Bonnie View Plantation. Older styles of gracious living were found in The Courtleigh, Royal Court, Gloucestershire, Terra Nova, Sans Souci and Villa Bella. More modern versions of the hotel – the all-inclusive, self-indulgent variety – appeared boldly in Hedonism, Couples, Singles Negril, Fantasy Resort, La Mirage, Life Styles Resort and Thrills.

Of the establishments that did not use the *hotel* label, several applied *inn*, and smaller numbers *resort*, *country club*, *house*, *cabins* and *village*. Enterprises called *guest houses* also became common but, operating at a smaller scale, were less likely than the major hotels to serve as places of reference and less likely to give their names to larger territories. At the end of the twentieth century, many guest houses used labels equivalent to those applied by hotels but were more likely to call themselves *cottage*, *house* or *resort*, and less often *inn*, *chalet*, *spa* and *villa*.

CHAPTER EIGHT

Settlement Names

THE NAMING OF SETTLEMENTS AND THE routes that connect and inter-
sect them reflect the changing structure of Jamaican economy and society.
During the period of slavery, when the plantation system spread across the
island, the people typically lived and worked on rural holdings. Enslaved
people were allowed only limited movement. Because the estates, plantations and pens were large, the villages that grew up near the works buildings and great houses constituted population concentrations that easily
exceeded those of all but the largest towns. There were no independent
settlements termed *villages* anywhere in the interior, and very few called
towns. The dynamic internal marketing system, supplied from the provision
grounds of the enslaved, was broadly intermittent and ephemeral, sellers
setting up at intersections to maximize their exposure to purchasers for a
day, then clearing the site at evening time. The consequence was that,
during slavery, Jamaica had only a limited urban system, almost completely
dominated by port towns on their bays and harbours, as discussed in
chapter 6.

   The abolition of slavery in 1838 and the decline of the plantation led
rapidly to dramatic change. Villages were established to house the people
who spilled off the plantations, and small towns developed as rural service,
distribution and marketing centres based on the produce of the peasantry.
The parish and county capitals performed an expanded range of administrative roles. The populations of these new centres quickly came to rival

and exceed those of the old plantation settlements and sometimes coalesced with them. Although the twentieth century saw major growth in the largest of the urban centres, in structural and naming terms it was the watershed of 1838 that most significantly transformed the landscape of settlement.

VILLAGE, -VILLE

During slavery most people lived in villages, or settlements, composed of grouped houses and sometimes barracks, concentrated on a particular piece of land and surrounded by a fence or wall. These village sites were located within plantation boundaries and generally close to factories and great houses. In spite of their substantial populations, the villages had no separate identity and were therefore simply associated with the names of the plantations themselves, whereas bridges and fields within the plantation might be named. The early maps of Jamaica, down to the time of Robertson at the beginning of the nineteenth century, indicated not one village. Plantation plans typically identified the space occupied by a village with the designation "Negro houses", and occasionally the village was called a "Negro town".[1] The enslaved people who lived in these plantation villages may have had their own names for the sites and their internal divisions and routes, separate from those imposed by the planters, but, if so, these names are not known.

After the abolition of slavery, scores of independent "free villages" were established, either by the people themselves or by church and missionary groups. Although historians persist in referring to these settlements as *villages*, most of them were in fact called *towns*. They were named by their founders and were typically eponymous and honorific. Such names were promoted by the church founders and thought appropriate. Thus the British missionary James Mursell Phillippo in 1843 compared the harsh and immoral life of "negro villages" during slavery with that of the "new villages" established after abolition, which were neatly "laid out in regular order, being divided into lots more or less intersected by roads or streets".

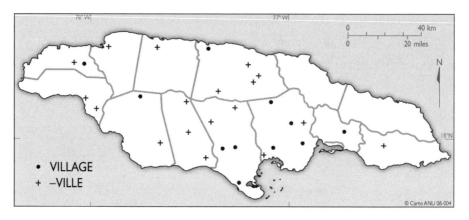

Figure 8.1 Jamaica: *Village* and *-ville*, settlement names, 1950

Phillippo thought there were between 150 and 200 villages in the island by about 1843 but listed only the following "appellations": Victoria, Normanby, Vale Lionel, Buxton, Gurney, Albert, Sligoville, Clarkson, Brougham, Sturge, Adelaide, Wilberforce, Macauley, Harvey and Thompson.[2] The cadastral series from the late nineteenth century noted twenty-three villages but only one of these − Liberty Valley Village ANN − suggested an association with abolition, and in this series the free villages were typically called *towns* or *townships*. Some of the names in the list soon dropped the *village* label, as in Santa Cruz Village ELZ, Whithorn Village WLD and Golden Grove Village THS.

The Place Names Committee set up in the Office of the Director of Surveys in the 1940s generally sought the removal of the label *village* from place names, preferring for example Alderton to Alderton Village. The 1950 topographical map identified only eleven settlements with the generic label *village*, broadly scattered across the island (Figure 8.1). The best known of these were Central Village CTH on the Spanish Town Road and Industry Village AND on the road out of Kingston leading to Newcastle. Others were Comfort Village CLR, Content Village CLR, Spring Village CLR, Maroon Village ELZ and some eponymous examples. Helicon Village ANN, in the hills above Discovery Bay, took its name from a small property apparently named in the late nineteenth century, referring in turn to the high mountain in Greece with its glen that was believed to serve as a sanctuary of the Muses. When tourism took over along this stretch of the north coast in the later twentieth century, *village* became a popular name for hotel developments drawing on a rustic, exotic image of Jamaican life – Jamaica Safari Village, Bay Vista Village – and further west Jack Tar Village. In 1992 a Freedom Village was constructed at Roaring River WLD, intended as a site for the development of craft industries with tourist potential.[3] The word was used occasionally for new shopping centres within Kingston, as in Village Plaza. It was also applied in fictional accounts of rural life, notably the radio serial of the 1970s *Life in Hopeful Village*.

Place names with the suffix *-ville* are a little more common than *village*, with eighteen cases on the 1950 map, but are fairly strongly concentrated in the central parishes (see Figure 8.1). The 1880 cadastral list had seven places with *ville* as a separate word, but only one of these survived in this form down to 1950, namely Trinity Ville THS, and the others disappeared rather than becoming *-ville* names. Some of the *-ville* settlements derived from abolitionism and the free village movement – as in Clarksonville ANN and Sligoville CTH – though their promoters commonly called them *townships*.[4] Overall the *-ville* places are difficult to interpret, more likely to be copies and heavily eponymous. Examples of this usage were established in the seventeenth century, as in Longville and Longville Park CLR, named for the Long family of planters. Mandeville MAN, the most prominent town with a name of this sort, emerged late, following the creation of Manchester parish in 1814, and became the site of the parish church and vestry. Manchester, the parish, was named for William, Duke of Manchester, who was governor of Jamaica for most of the years from 1808 to 1827. Mandeville, according to Clinton V. Black, derives from "the title of the heir to the dukedom of Manchester".[5] Thus the name is eponymous but the *-ville* suffix works well as the name of a settlement.

TOWN

By far the most common term for an urban settlement of any scale was *town*. This pattern was established by the early eighteenth century and persisted. The 1950 topographical map identified seventy-three places with this generic label, widely scattered but, like *village*, showing a strong concentration in the central parishes, with a band running across the island through Manchester and eastern Trelawny and another along the north coast to St Mary (Figure 8.2). The cadastral series, centred on the late nineteenth century, contained a surprisingly similar number: seventy-one *towns* and seven *townships*. The pattern of geographical distribution differed somewhat, with the cadastral maps lacking a geographical concentration, so the similarity of number implied only a broad continuity.

Overall, about two-thirds of the names of towns shown on the 1950 map were eponymous. The band of towns running through the central parishes included places that had begun life as free villages, such as Albert Town TRL, Clarks Town MAN, Sturge Town ANN and Victoria Town MAN. The naming of Clarkson Town, high in the hills of St Catherine, was proposed "in honour of the celebrated philanthropist of that name [Thomas Clarkson], to whose long and untiring efforts on behalf of the African race the great boon of emancipation was mainly to be attributed".[6] But the monarchs and humanitarians had many rivals. Browns Town ANN was founded by Hamilton Brown, rabid leader of the pro-slavery Colonial Church Union. Seaford Town WLD was named for the planter Lord Seaford, who gave the land for a settlement of German immigrants brought to Jamaica during the Apprenticeship period, with the intention of placing pressure on the former enslaved population. Occasion Town CLR is enigmatic, though Phillippo in 1843 had listed Occasion Call as the name of a house lot in an unidentified free village, saying, "On asking a good man who had given this designation to his freehold its meaning, he replied – 'If any person have business wid me, him can come in; but if him don't want me in pottickler, me no wants him company, and him no 'casion to come.'" Excellent Town ANN was formally renamed by the Place Names Committee in the 1940s, becoming simply Bamboo, a village.[7]

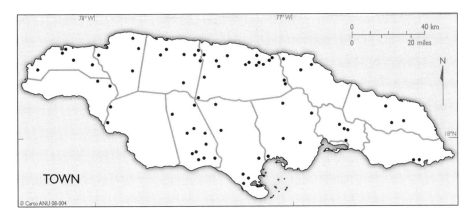

Figure 8.2 Jamaica: *Town*, settlement names, 1950

Of the other varieties of town naming, August Town AND no doubt celebrated the end of slavery, declared on 1 August, and was known by this
name at least by the 1860s.[8] The word *free* attached to *town* might seem
similarly to relate to the abolition of slavery, but the origins are more complex. The topographical map of 1950 identified five examples of Freetown:
two in Clarendon and one each in Manchester, St Catherine and
St Andrew. Four of these also appeared on the more selective 2000 road
map, only the Manchester Freetown being absent, indicating their relative
significance and staying power. The 2000 map also identified Freedom, a
settlement close to Freetown CTH. An association with the abolition of
slavery seems an obvious explanation, but Bochart and Knollis recorded
Free Towne on their map of 1680, at the site of what would become
Morant Bay, between the mouth of the Morant River and Freemans Bay,
named for the large landholder Freeman. By 1739 Charles Leslie referred
to this as a small settlement "called Free-Town" in the parish of St David
(now part of St Thomas).[9] In 1760 Craskell and Simpson clearly identified
the town as Morant Bay, and in 1774 Long called it simply the hamlet of
Morant. Craskell and Simpson identified a Free Point MRY at the eastern
cusp of Annotto Bay, which has retained its name to the present. A Free
Town existed in Vere at the time of abolition, probably the site of the mod-

ern place near Portland Ridge CLR, occupied by smallholder slaveowners who were probably free coloured people.

The association of *town* with settlements of free people was even more striking in the case of the Maroons. Thus Long in 1774 identified seventeen towns, six of which he termed "Negroe-towns", meaning that they were inhabited largely by Maroons and other freed people. In the county of Middlesex, Long listed St Jago de la Vega, "commonly called" Spanish Town, Old Harbour, Scots Hall Negro Town and St Anne (the modern St Ann's Bay), together with the hamlets Passage Fort, Old Harbour Market, Cross CLR and Chapel (Chapelton, identified on Craskell and Simpson's map as The Chappel), Carlisle Bay, Rio Nuevo, Port Maria, Saltgut, Laughlands and Runaway Bay. Passage Fort had earlier been called The Passage, where boats embarked for Port Royal, but by the 1770s its shallow-water port was losing ground to a new shipping point with a better depth of water established by "an enterprizing and spirited gentleman", Mr Henderson. Long said that place was rapidly becoming a town and was "called at present by the name of Port-Henderson". This eponymous name stuck firmly. In the county of "Surry", Long found Kingston, "the county-town", with the towns of Port Royal, Bath, Titchfield, "Moore, Negroe-town" and "Crawford, now Charlestown, Negroe-town". There were also the hamlets Half-way Tree, Yallahs, Morant and Manchineel. In Cornwall, Long located the towns Lacovia, "Accompong, Negroe- Town", "Savannah la Mar, the county-town", Lucea, Montego, "Furry's, Negroe Town" and "Trelawny, Negroe Town", along with the hamlets Black River, "Queen's Town, *alias* Beckford Town, *alias* the Savannah" and Marthabrae.[10]

In spite of their importance in eighteenth-century Jamaica, none of the settlements termed by Long "Negroe-towns" became major settlements in the modern urban system, and some struggled to survive in any form. On the other hand, several of the hamlets became large and important, such as Morant and Black River, mentioned above. Craskell and Simpson's earlier map of 1760 identified only ten towns, half of them associated with Maroons: Furrys Town JAS, Negroe Town MRY, Old Crawford Town PLD and New Crawford Town PLD , and "Old Nanny Town deserted". Negroe Town was beside Scotshall, and the latter became the dominant form soon after. Old Crawford Town was already "deserted" by 1760, having been burned, and its history is somewhat shadowy until its replacement by Charles Town at the end of the century. The general tendency was a shift from using the African names of Maroon leaders to a more English pattern, no doubt reflecting the influence of the treaties. Before 1750, the major settlements were Cudjoes (Trelawny) Town, Furrys Town, Goomers Town, Cuffees Town and Accompongs Town.[11]

A similar pattern occurred on Robertson's 1800 map. He used the label *town* for eleven places, at least seven of them identified with the Maroons, three associated with the leeward or western groups and four with the windward. These were, to leeward, Trelawney Town JAS and immediately to the south New Town JAS and Accompong-Town ELZ, and to windward, Scotts-Hall Town MRY, Charles Town PLD, "Old Nanny-Town deserted" PLD and Moore-Town PLD. Nanny Town, named for the Maroon leader Nanny, who became a national hero, had been established in the 1720s but was destroyed by the British in the early 1730s when it was referred to as "the great Negro Town". Both the leeward and windward Maroons signed treaties in 1739, but the windward group then divided between the followers of Quao and Nanny. Quao did not have a town named for him; rather, it was given to another leader, Edward or Ned Crawford, whose name was celebrated in Crawford Town. Nanny had also established two temporary outlying settlements in the John Crow Mountains for the protection of the Maroon women and children; these were known as Woman Town and Young Gal Town, the latter remembered in Young Gal Hill. Macungo Hill PLD, perhaps a Congo term for a lost town or cemetery – a "town of the dead" – probably marks the site of one of Nanny's Maroon settlements.[12]

The four towns recorded by Robertson which were not associated with the Maroons varied greatly in their significance and persistence. Spanish Town CTH was the island's capital at the time of Robertson's map. Queens-Town, or Cross-Path, had been the major settlement of Westmoreland until 1730, when it was overtaken by Savanna la Mar. Queens Town was to the north of the port, at a four-way intersection, and from the later nineteenth century became known as Banbury Cross, then was reduced to Banbury. Margaret Town PLD was a similarly small settlement, on the coast west of the mouth of the Rio Grande, at what is now known as St Margarets Bay but was identified by Robertson as Whydah Bay. Finally, Robertson named St Anns Bay as a bay and simply wrote "Town" beside his rendition of the occupied district to indicate its existence. Whereas the towns associated with the Maroons that appeared on Robertson's map retained their *town* appellations in the long run, only one of the other four survived, namely Spanish Town, and it in turn battled against the mouthful St Jago de la Vega. As happens in most places, of course, many Jamaican places deserving to be recognized as substantial urban settlements were never given a generic label to place them in a hierarchy, but retained terms like *bay* or were composed of a single word that gave no clues to rank.

Within Kingston, growth beyond the central core generally occurred in "towns". Thus in 1832 two new towns were identified for tax purposes, Raes Town, with twenty-eight taxpayers, and Browns Town, with just two.[13] Something similar happened in the major port towns: the 1861 census, for instance, included in Port Maria the settlements Mannings Town and Stennetts Town. The more recent pattern is discussed below, together with suburban pens and gardens.

-TON

The colonial use of -*ton* seems almost always to mean *town*. British examples derive from the Old English *tūn*, meaning a manor, estate or large farm. In its early Anglo-Saxon history the word also meant *village*, especially when used as a compound with a personal name, but by the time of the English settlement of Jamaica *estate* was the typical understanding. The common and widespread English place name *Kingston* means "king's manor" or "royal farm". The best known example, Kingston on Thames, dates from AD 838.[14] Another English example, Kingston upon Hull, is better known by the name of the river on which it stands: the Hull.

The origins of Jamaica's Kingston are shrouded in mystery. It might be a simple transfer from Kingston on Thames or some other English example. Kingston did not exist before the 1692 earthquake that destroyed Port

Royal, across the harbour, but within weeks the council called for the building of the "new town of Kingston". In 1693 the assembly passed an "Act for making Kingston a Parish", which defined its boundaries and declared that it was to be "called and known by the name of the town and parish of Kingston".[15] William of Orange was on the English throne, crowned in 1688. A Kingston already existed in the colony of New York, named by the British in 1667 (when Charles II was king, crowned 1661) and replacing the former Dutch settlement of Wiltwyck, on the banks of the Hudson River; this too may have served as a model. Although there were many large estates along the Hudson, it is improbable that the idea of a royal manor remained in mind. No such establishment existed in Jamaica from which Kingston could have derived its name, and it seems more likely to have been intended to honour the monarch. Sibley claims Kingston was in fact first spelled King's Town. This would have been a misreading of the council's intent, but the notion that what was being constructed was indeed a town led easily to this construction of the name, and the idea that -*ton* simply meant *town*. In the eastern Caribbean, the capital town of St Vincent was named Kingstown by the British in 1763, and Kingstown (now Dun Laoghaire), the port of Dublin, was named in 1821 in honour of a visit by George IV. Thus the idea that Kingston was the "king's town" probably existed from early times.

Other -*ton* names in Jamaica have the same difficulty of interpretation, but at least some of them are recognized as *town* settlements. The 1950 map had ninety-nine examples, many eponymous and apparently drawn from British places. Jamaica's several Islingtons and Kensingtons probably were transfers from London. Appleton sugar estate in St Elizabeth is believed to have got its name from an early planter family, who derived it through association with the place meaning "the estate or village where apple trees grow". Baillieston CLR and Bensonton ANN, located in the interior uplands and not yet settled in the time of slavery, seem more likely to be local compounds with personal names.

CITY

Rather than a term for the largest urban settlements, *city* was used for smaller units within greater Kingston, initially with irony. The best known is probably Independence City CTH, established as the first optimistic unit of what was to become Portmore. Within Kingston proper, Patrick City is one of a number of new suburbs built in its western borders in the 1960s for middle-income residents. Both of these were, however, preceded by Moonlight City, established as a squatter settlement in 1959, neighbouring Majesty Pen.[16] In some cases, squatting followed modernization. Thus the establishment of Riverton City in 1955, as part of a western Kingston industrial estate, was quickly followed by informal building along the lower Sandy Gully and within the subdivision itself, while it remained unoccupied by industry. In 1960 "beautiful" Harbour View was established as a "new residential city overlooking Kingston harbour", but the label *city* was never attached.[17]

TAVERN, SHOP, STORE, MARKET

In much the same way that an intersection of routes might give its name to a settlement that built upon the basis of transient, then permanent, commerce, settlements sometimes grew far beyond the scale of an originating establishment but retained the name. *Tavern* was common on early maps, a useful guide to white people travelling in an island lacking hotels and lodging houses. Robertson identified fourteen taverns as a simple generic, as well as the compound place-name Bog Walk Tavern CTH, which by the end of the nineteenth century became Bog Walk Village and then simply Bog Walk, with the gorge distinguished from the settlement as Bog Walk Gorge. Only one example of a compound name persisted on the 1950 map, namely Lawrence Tavern AND, but other smaller places remained, in common parlance, simply Tavern (Figure 8.3). Well known down to the middle of the nineteenth century was the Moneague Tavern, which later became the Moneague Hotel, but it did not name the place. Late-

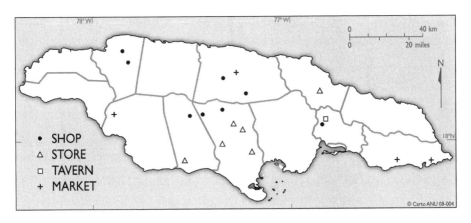

Figure 8.3 Jamaica: *Shop, store, tavern* and *market,* settlement names, 1950

nineteenth-century examples such as McMahons Tavern CLR, Crown Tavern HAN, Logwood Tavern CTH and Meagre Tavern MRY did not persist.

Shop survived more successfully. It seems never to have appeared on island maps as a simple generic, naming a place, but the 1950 map had eight compounds (see Figure 8.3). Black Shop JAS was close to Coolie Shop JAS, and the two may have named in contradistinction. There was also White Shop CLR, known from the later nineteenth century. This could have been eponymous, but it lacked the possessive (as did Black Shop), unlike Caines Shop MAN and Wilsons Shop ANN. Burnt Shop AND no doubt marked a well-known site. There were two examples of Corner Shop CLR ANN, marking intersections.

Store, like *shop*, was a feature of the post-slavery Jamaican landscape, and similarly successful as a survivor, perhaps because of its late appearance. The 1950 map had six examples. With the exception of Rest Store MAN, at a three-way intersection on the descent down Plowden Hill, and perhaps Ivy Store CLR, all of the stores were eponymous. The best known is Osborne Store CLR, standing on the main route across the southern plains, at a five-way intersection, between Four Paths and Toll Gate, with Milk River Bath to the south and Mocho to the north. The others are Gordons Store CLR, Lewis Store MRY and Rodons Store CLR. Osborne Store, Rest Store and Lewis Store all appear on the 2000 Jamaica road map.

Market is an ancient element but a poor survivor. Newmarket ELZ sat at an important junction and continues to be the site of an important small market town but is commonly assumed to have received its name from the well-known English town. New Market THS, on the 1950 map, is a better candidate, along with Chigoe [chigger or jigger] Foot Market THS, loudly declaring its poverty, and Dry Market CLR. Chigoe Foot Market, on the Morant River, was a village close to Stony Gut and was similarly involved in the rebellion of 1865.[18] Down to the early nineteenth century, Old Harbour Market required its full name to distinguish it from the initially more significant Old Harbour Bay (which Long in 1774 had called simply Old Harbour), but gradually the market became the more important settlement, with its clock tower and multiple intersections, and was in its turn reduced to Old Harbour, in spite of its inland location.

HALL, CASTLE, HUT

Although the association with the plantocracy and the great house was very strong, a good proportion of the *halls* and *castles* of Jamaica were named after 1838, and many of these developed into recognized settlements. Thus the distribution of *hall* and *castle* partly reflects the geographical pattern of the plantation system but also a continuing replication of naming, as shown by the cadastral series (see Figures 7.2 and 7.3). This persistence was less obvious in the twentieth century, and by the topographic map of 1950 the geographical distribution was somewhat different (Figure 8.4). The 1950 map had 125 places with the label *hall* compared to 45 with *castle*, a ratio of roughly 3:1 that was typical of all of the sources studied, back to the Bochart and Knollis 1680 map.

A significant proportion of *hall* place names were eponymous, of the Drax Hall type. This applied to about one-third of the cases on the 1950 map, several of them named for or by seventeenth-century planter families: Halse, Haughton and Stokes, for example. By the late twentieth century the most common example was the more recent Johns Hall that appeared in St James, Manchester and Clarendon. Some *hall* names were transfers

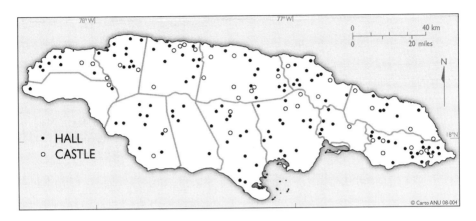

Figure 8.4 Jamaica: *Hall* and *castle*, settlement names, 1950

from other, usually British, places, such as Berkshire Hall CTH and Cardiff Hall ANN. About one-quarter of the *hall* names referred to sentiments, as in the well-known and widely distributed Amity Hall JAS ANN CLR CTH THS and Harmony Hall TRL MRY, and the less prominent but equally common Comfort Hall JAS MAN TRL and Fellowship Hall MRY CTH. Other *hall* names referred to flora and fauna, as in Orange Hall ANN and Trout Hall CLR. Less typical is Rock Hall PLD, so named on the 1950 map and called Rock Hall Plantation in the cadastral list, but located at the site identified by Robertson simply as Hall's. Rock Hall AND seems never to have had an extended name.

An important variety of *hall* was Liberty Hall. The concept of *liberty* was used in Jamaican history specifically to indicate freedom or release from bondage and slavery, and it was used in this sense from the time of abolition to the time of Marcus Garvey, who occupied Liberty Hall on King Street in Kingston and set up Liberty Halls wherever the United Negro Improvement Association had bases in North America. As a Jamaican place name, however, *liberty* also referred to a broader theological and political meaning, suggesting freedom from hindrance or restraint, and the ability to act independent of fate or necessity. The slaveowning planter class was vociferous in defending its political and economic liberties, but

Robertson's 1800 map had no examples of the use of liberty in a place name, indicating its strong association with abolition. In 1950 there was the simple Liberty ANN, as well as Liberty Hall TRL and Liberty Hill ANN. According to Sibley, Liberty Hall ANN was given its name when the "Liberty Tree" was planted there on 1 August 1838, Emancipation Day. The cadastral series, centred on the late nineteenth century, had four Liberty Halls TRL MRY CTH PLD, as well as Liberty Pen TRL, Liberty Castle MRY, Liberty Hill ANN and Liberty Valley Village ANN.

The pattern of distribution of *castle* differed quite strongly from that of *hall* (see Figure 8.4). On the 1950 map roughly one-half of the persistent *castle* names were transfers from other places. Scottish sources were popular, as in Douglas Castle ANN and Ness Castle THS, as were English borrowings such as Chester Castle HAN and York Castle MAN ANN. The high frequency of such borrowing suggests a transfer of whole place-names rather than the adding of *castle* as an extension, but the *castle* element must also have been appealing. Although *castle* showed considerable resilience, it was not applied to new settlement types in the later twentieth century with the same enthusiasm that was shown for *hall, court* and even *manor*.

The temporary and simple character suggested by *hut* made it an unlikely candidate for the long-term naming of places. Bochart and Knollis did have one in 1680, Palmers Hut CTH (in the vicinity of what became Bybrook), and they associated the name with a sugar mill, suggesting that a plantation had been established there and that the name of a pioneer structure was still the best way of identifying its location. Craskell and Simpson in 1760 retained this place name, though making it Palmers Hutt, and added Toneys Hutt ANN. The cadastral series added Chigury Hut ANN, Happy Hut PLD, Taylor Hut CLR and Salt Pond Hut Pen CTH. The 1950 map had six instances of Forest Hut but this was effectively generic, with almost all of them found in the Blue Mountains. It retained Taylors Hut and added only Jacob Hut CLR and Style Hut THS.

Robertson showed no *hut* on his 1800 map but did indicate the site of Three Finger Jacks Huts THS. Jack Mansong, alias Bristol, alias Three Finger Jack, had formed a small settlement of escaped slaves in the coastal hills of the old parish of St David, near a road that led to the east from Kingston.

He terrorized travellers for close to two years but was killed by Maroons in 1781. Remembered as a gentlemanly bandit and obeah man, he lives on as a folk hero. Maroon tradition associates him with another place, Three Finger Woman Tumble, on the Cuna Cuna trail or Cunu Cunu Wood, through the Blue Mountains, where his wife escaped by sliding down a rocky slope with her baby on her back.[19]

WHARF

In the period of the sailing ship, and even in that of the steamship, before rail and road transport came to dominate the movement of goods across the island, numerous wharves were scattered around the coastline. They ranged from the large to the small and frequently marked important transport nodes, places where roads and paths converged. They were named either for their immediate locations, as in Davis Cove Wharf HAN and Dry Harbour Wharf ANN, or for the estates and plantations to which they were directly linked and under whose ownership they fell, as in Montpelier Wharf JAS, attached to the inland Montpelier Estate. A few were located on rivers rather than on the coast, as in Bartons Wharf ELZ on the Black River, associated with the nearby Bartons Plantation. In the long term, *wharf* never came to name a substantial settlement, and the Jamaicanism *barquadier* seems never to have been applied in a place name.

SUBURBAN PEN, TOWN, YARD, MEWS, MEADOWS AND GARDEN

From the eighteenth century to the beginning of the twentieth, much of Kingston's periphery, extending into lower St Andrew, was occupied by *pens* of the secondary type, the small parkland homes of the wealthy. A few estates continued to operate on the fringes until World War I, but *pen* and *park* were then the most common and widespread generic labels attached to settlements, and sugar cultivation quickly collapsed (Figure 8.5). By the 1930s, many of the *pens* had ceased to serve as the genteel residences of the

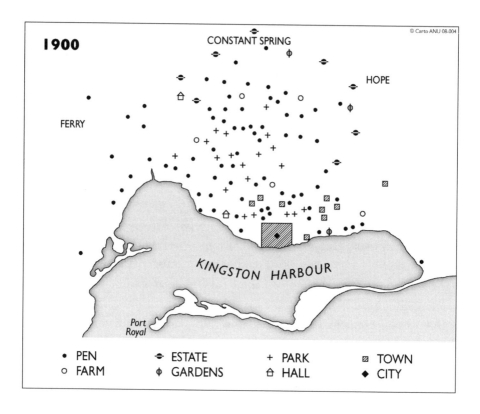

Figure 8.5 Kingston: *Pen, farm, estate, gardens, park, hall, town* and *city* names, 1900

moderately wealthy. The names persisted in downtown areas, but the functions changed dramatically. Rollington Pen, Johnson's Pen, Hannah's Pen, Trench Pen, Kingston Pen, Greenwich Pen and Majesty Pen were largely associated with the poor and the oppressed.

It was in the midst of the social and political turmoil of the 1930s that the urban pens began to be transformed into towns. There were already towns in some parts of Kingston and St Andrew, as, for example, the long-established Franklin Town, Passmore Town and Browns Town, originally on the eastern fringes of urban settlement, and the more recent Hannah Town, which bordered Hannahs Pen and eventually displaced it. A simple case of the transition from *pen* to *town* occurred in the renaming of Trench Pen to the now familiar Trench Town. The form *Trench Town* seems to have been first used in 1939, and by the following year the place was described as "a fine township", but the new name existed alongside Trench Pen throughout the early 1940s. Sometimes *pen* and *town* were used interchangeably.[20] In the same way, by the 1950s Greenwich Pen became Greenwich Town and Jones Pen became Jones Town.

Smith Village, adjoining Trench Pen and stretching as far west as May Pen Cemetery, was renamed Denham Town as part of the process of slum clearance and the building of "model housing". One section of Smith Village, Ackee Walk, was reputedly among the worst of the slum areas. In November 1939 the *Gleaner* observed, "The appellation Denham Town will serve to perpetuate the memory of a Governor who, throughout his close upon four years' connection with the Colony, was particularly interested in the welfare of the masses and middle class. The change from Smith Village to Denham Town is appropriate for more reasons than one." The slums of Kingston were "a social blot upon Christianity and civilization", said the *Gleaner*, and the process of demolition and reconstruction essential to the building of "self-respect".[21]

The term *town* maintained its long-established foundational role in informal as well as official naming. For example, in the 1980s a member of the Sistren Theatre Collective recalled that she "grew up in di area of King Avenue, di main road. On one side was Greenfield Town. On di odder side was Flowers Town. Further over behind Flowers Town was Rock City. I live in Rock City, Greenfield Town, in front of The People's Theatre and further up. Me also live near a standpipe beside di area dem call almshouse burying ground – later known as Ghost Town. I also live in Macca Land."[22] Other places mentioned by this woman included Tewan Crescent, Love Lane, Brown's Lane, Seaview Avenue, Spanish Town Road, Ashley Road, Harris Street, Bert Road, Palestine, Lebanon, all within the general context of Kingston.

Some urban pens developed distinct sections and internal subdivisions which had their own particular names. These names tended to be colloquial or local in flavour and generally, it would seem, were coined by the occupants themselves, many of whom were branded as squatters. Kingston

Pen came to be known as Back o'Wall in the 1920s, recognized as a district or "little settlement in the Smith Village area".[23] It was known for crime, and probably the name Back o'Wall came from the notion that it was a place beyond the pale, the site of shifty deals and skulduggery, rarely known or visited by politicians before 1938. Back o'Wall was cleared in 1966 and replaced by a government high-rise development named Tivoli Gardens, on the south side of Spanish Town Road.[24] Why this new modern development became known as Tivoli Gardens is uncertain, though the Danish fairground version was known in Jamaica. Jamaica Omnibus Services had a depot at "Tivoli" as early as 1960, and this simple form persisted in the long term.[25] The Danish version was in turn named after the Tivoli of Rome, a fashionable residence for emperors and nobles.

When the government moved on the squatted lands in 1961, it was said that the minister of agriculture was acting to "acquire lands known as Tivoli Gardens (or Kingston Pen) in Western Kingston" or "formerly called Kingston Pen".[26] Many of the residents were Rastafarians, and they called it instead "Egypt". In 1963, with the bulldozers poised to tear down the shacks, Operation Friendship, led by Reverend William Blake, declared pride in its achievements in the area, saying, "People now regard themselves as a community and the area was no longer just a collection of individual families living near each other. For instance, the name Tivoli Gardens has been adopted for the area to escape the stigma of Back o'Wall." Others persisted in referring to the area as Kingston Pen but said it was "to be known as Tivoli Gardens in the future".[27] Kingston Pen was no more regarded as a suitable alternative than Back o'Wall or Egypt.

In the period of slavery, the inner urban equivalent of the pen was the *yard*, meaning a compound or small group of houses or huts clustered in a single enclosure, generally surrounding a central cleared area of swept earth. The Kingston parish tax roll of 1776 recorded 108 yards, many of them housing about ten enslaved people, and many apparently occupied by free black and free coloured people. These yards, particularly those housing free people, were typically located towards the fringes of the city's built-up zone. At the time of abolition, around 1838, enslaved people themselves often referred to their house lots as *yards*.[28] In view of the modern popularity of the term as a reference to individual (*mi yard*) or group residence (*tenement yard* and *government yard*), and the recent use of *yard* to mean the island of Jamaica, it is perhaps surprising that *yard* never attached itself to a substantial place name. No cases appeared on the early maps, and the comprehensive cadastral list had only Summer Hill Yard JAS and Mason Yard MRY. Certainly *yard* carried connotations even more negative than *pen*, but it also had a vernacular status and was applied in other contexts, such as the Yard Theatre. Perhaps the yards were simply too small and too transient to attach descriptive elements to their names, whereas many of the pens were large enough to provide the space for an entire small suburb.

In the later nineteenth century, new suburbs, built on the edge of Kingston and pushing into the traditional pen areas of St Andrew were increasingly associated with a bucolic vision that preferred exotic labels such as *gardens* and *meadows*. One of the earliest, commenced in the 1870s, was Kingston Gardens, a suburb built to house elite families.[29] At about the same time, some of the barren urban landscapes of Kingston were redesigned and renamed. The most visible of these was the Parade, no longer the home of the militia, which by the end of the nineteenth century was landscaped with an enclosed central area, planted in trees, lawn and flower beds, and known as "Victoria Park (Parade Gardens)".[30]

In the great expansion of housing development that followed independence, the names of some new suburbs reflected the constitutional change, as most obviously in the satellite Independence City, inaugurated in 1968 as a "suburban haven" linked to the equally modern-sounding Newport West by a causeway.[31] But their new neighbours quickly turned to more comfortable "English" names, and the larger Portmore area filled up with places like Surrey Meadows, Portsmouth, Edgewater, Bridgeview and Bridgeport, along with a well-known New York county, Westchester. The richness of spoken Jamaican was almost entirely neglected. Even Garveymeade had an English ring to it. The later-settled Braeton came to contain a series of places named for international sporting venues such as Monza, Daytona, Sandown, Ascot, Aintree, Queen's Park, Kensington and the local Sabina and Chedwin. A few names survived from earlier eras in the midst of this new settlement, such as Cumberland, Gregory Park and Passage Fort.

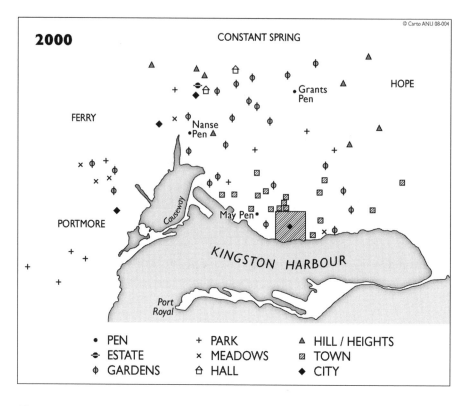

Figure 8.6 Kingston: *Pen, estate, gardens, park, meadows, hall, hill/heights, town* and *city* names, 2000

By the end of the twentieth century, it was hard to find a *pen* in Kingston (Figure 8.6). Tinson Pen, as airfield, retained its *pen*, as did the cemetery May Pen, and Nanse Pen was created in the 1970s as an industrial estate, but none of these were settlements occupied by living human beings. Only Grants Pen survived as a significant settlement, thought of as a not-particularly-salubrious territory increasingly surrounded by middle-class suburbs, with its conduit, Grants Pen Road. New applications of *pen* were very rare, and none of them seems to have occurred within Kingston. *Towns* dominated the downtown areas, along with a sprinkling of *gardens*, as in Arnett Gardens (also known as Concrete Jungle), Tivoli Gardens and Bournemouth Gardens.[32] Uptown, *gardens* were even more dominant by

2000, together with *park* and *meadows* and a growing ring of surrounding *heights*.

Suburban development around Spanish Town and on the western fringe of Kingston tells a similar story, with a proliferation of *gardens* and *meadows*. Even Callaloo Meadows mixed the local with the verdant English landscape. Parallel changes occurred in the country but less consistently than in Kingston. In Clarendon, York Pen was transformed into York Town by the early 1980s. A new residential subdivision near May Pen, Clarendon, was announced in 1971 as Weston Park.[33] On the other hand, some developments promoted in the 1950s and 1960s were constructed at places which already possessed names of the preferred varieties, as for example Cardiff Hall ANN, which included the favoured *hall*, and Waltham MAN, which simply had a good ring to it.

In English usage, *mews* originally defined a yard surrounded by stables but came to mean living quarters above the stables, or stables converted to residential use, and later to identify any type of housing set out in this manner or even to attached housing arranged in rows. It was used in this sense for middle-class apartment developments, particularly around Kingston, beginning in the late 1960s. Most took their names from the streets on which they were sited or other existing local place names, as in Birdsucker Mews, Liguanea Mews and Meadowbrook Mews, which were joined in the middle of the 1970s by Ivy Green Mews, Cunningham Mews, Hope Mews, Calabar Mews (derived from the nearby school and ultimately from Africa), Belgrave Mews, Hopeton Mews, Mona Mews and Kings Mews. By the end of the twentieth century, versions began to appear outside the metropolis, as in Old Harbour Mews CTH. The term was also used as a style of downtown gentrification. In 1998 Callaloo Mews was called "a noted inner-city area". Riverton Meadows or "Riverton City, now called Riverton Mews" was being transformed from a zinc-shack ghetto by the construction of pre-fabricated plan houses, though Shanty Town remained an entrenched place name.[34] *Meadows* was also found in other grass-roots housing developments, such as Manley Meadows, and in new-style middle-class townhouse schemes, as epitomized by Meadowbrook Mews.

Outside Kingston the naming of new developments, which were gener-ally constituted of free-standing houses, followed somewhat different lines in the period after 1990. *Manor, gardens* and *park* were not used, though *court* (Cornwall Court JAS), *meadows* (Gazeland Meadows ELZ) and *estate* (as in Cave Hill Estate, Hellshire Park North Estate CTH and Anchovy Estate JAS) did have currency. These were joined by *glades* (Old Harbour Glades CLR) and, more surprisingly, *pen* (George's Pen CLR, a National Housing Trust project) and *plantation* (Plantation Heights AND). *Heights* was prominent, as it was in Kingston. Jack's View Heights THS, first approved in 1972 but inac-tive until 1999, was a development of three- and four-bedroom houses on the St Thomas Road. The developers said, "This property was a farm, the former home of renowned Jack Mansong or Three fingers Jack. The ceno-taph of Jack will be the centre stage; it is already named 'Jack's Place' for a restaurant and gift shop."[35] Jack's *huts* disappeared.

By the end of the twentieth century, *park* was not particularly fashion-able, though it appeared in the townhouse development Seymour Park, on Old Hope Road in Kingston, in 1998, and in the larger Hellshire Park North CTH in 1996.[36] The 1950 map had fewer than sixty instances, includ-ing only a sprinkling of new varieties, such as Caymanas Park, naming the island's major racecourse, carved out of the Caymanas Estate lands. The term *lodge* also lost favour in the twentieth century, with only seven instances shown on the 1950 map, and was used as a new name only in the alternative tourism sector, as in Beanbird Lodge, a villa opened near Ocho Rios in about 1990.

TOWNHOUSE, VILLA

The emergence of new types of settlement and land use have often been associated with new names or patterns of naming. In post-independence Jamaica, development in the Kingston area was often accompanied by the construction of apartment blocks, townhouses and gated communities for the middle class, as well as housing schemes and informal settlements for the less affluent. The names of these developments have not been studied in detail, but the overwhelming impression is one of real or faux Englishness, though this may have been filtered through North American experience and models.[37] The naming of suburban subdivisions and townhouse developments in the United States exhibited a taste for generic elements such as *manor, court, village, meadow, park* and *gardens* that was shared by Jamaica, where the names were used for new suburbs. The adoption of such naming practices can be interpreted as a variety of promotional hype on the part of property developers. It harked back to the status pretensions of the planter class but introduced elements unknown to plantation-naming, such as *mews* and *meadows*, which had no place in the Jamaican rural landscape system. More significant, perhaps, is the fact that Jamaican naming of this sort largely denied any place to the unique elements of the island's natural or political history.[38]

The most common generic labels applied to the names of post-1990 townhouse and duplex developments within Kingston were *manor, court, gardens* and *park*. These labels closely match the pattern observed in the United States, except that in Jamaica *meadows* was rarely applied to townhouse developments despite its popularity as a suburb name. Only a few of these more recent terms have equivalents in the plantation society of the eighteenth century. Some Kingston developments combined elements, as in Crotona Court at Ziadie Gardens, Gardens of Arcadia and Manor Park Estates, at Waterworks, Upper St Andrew.[39] Other, less frequently used, generic labels included *mews* (as in Stilwell Mews at Manor Park) and *abbey* (Glen Abbey).[40] *Chalet*, which originated with the cabins and cottages of the Swiss mountains, in Jamaica was applied more broadly to small villas and rustic dwellings and was occasionally used in naming townhouse developments, beginning in the late 1960s with the Skyline Chalets on Jacks Hill above Kingston. These were followed in the late 1990s by The Chalets on Great House Close, Cherry Gardens, St Andrew. The notion of elevation was also important, as in The Summit at Stony Hill Heights, Hillcrest on Skyline Drive and Long Mountain Country Club.[41]

Although *manor* was not used by the plantocracy, the word did surface in the twentieth century. The earliest known use was in the name of the Manor House Hotel, opened in the 1920s in buildings which "began life as a Great House" on the lands of Constant Spring Estate AND. Here emerged Manor House Gully, Manor Park Road, Manor Park Close and Manor Park Plaza, followed by Manor Centre. Other versions of *manor* appeared in the 1990s in associated townhouse developments such as Manor Park Estates, and also began to appear further away, as in Upper Musgrave Manor in New Kingston.[42]

Abbey emerged earlier than *manor* but had little currency before the middle of the nineteenth century. It first appeared soon after 1800, in Abbeydale Pen and Abbey Court in St Andrew, and Abbeydale Road, which came off the newly named Trafalgar Road. There was also The Abbey or Abbey Farm, on the Yallahs River, and Abbey Green, a coffee plantation nestled in the slopes below Portland Gap, high in the mountains of St Thomas. Abbey Court AND kept its name when it was converted from pen house to apartment block, and was joined in 1996 by Glen Abbey on Norbrook Road.[43] Later there was Priory Court on Devon Road, suggesting a relationship to Abbey Court, as the priory was traditionally a dependency of an abbey. Other townhouse developments included the already mentioned Crotona Court at Ziadie Gardens and Ravinia Court on Ravinia Road in Liguanea.[44]

It is striking that *manor* and *abbey* almost always appeared as the first word of a place name, the only exceptions being the punning Courtleigh Manor hotel and the latecomer apartment complexes Upper Musgrave Manor and Glen Abbey. These two terms contrast strongly with the loose generic labels offered by *hall, castle, court, park* and *lodge*, and indeed they sometimes took one of these as a classifier, as in Manor Park and Abbey Court. Jamaica had no sugar plantation to match the St Nicholas Abbey of Barbados, or the Fonthill Abbey of the absentee planter William Beckford, in the English county of Wiltshire, though there were Font Hill Estate ELZ and two Font Hills ANN THS. The Jamaican pattern of use also contrasted with that of US real estate developments in the same period, where *manor* was popular but used as a generic label.[45] Thus *abbey* and *manor* gave status to Jamaican places in an unusual fashion.

Other common elements in the names of recent urban housing were drawn from places outside Jamaica, as in Aberdeen, The Palermo on Upper

Waterloo Road and Santa Fe, Barbican.[46] Although there are echoes of eighteenth-century Jamaica in some of these names – *court* and *park* had precedents in the names of estates from that time – references to things Jamaican in this post-independence era are hard to find. Labels popular with planters – *castle*, *hall* and *lodge* – gave way to *manor*, *mews* and *abbey*. Among the less affluent, however, there was sometimes a pragmatic mixing of the truly local with more pretentious generic labels. For example, the humble leafy green vegetable callaloo, previously noted in Callaloo Gutters WLD, might be dignified by *mews*, and a former public tip by *meadows*. These attributions enabled members of the Pentecostal Gospel Shower Church to hold a peace march in 2005 through "Riverton Meadows, Shanty Town and Callaloo Mews".[47]

In classical Greek and Roman times, *villa* indicated an elaborate country residence or mansion with farmland and associated farm buildings, sometimes taking on the character of a plantation. Elements of this meaning persisted, but in English the term came to be applied more generally to any better-class house or superior residence, especially in the nineteenth century. None of the early maps used the term, but it was common in the 1880 cadastral series: Clarence Villa AND, Goldsmiths Villa AND, Liguanea Villa AND, Up Park Villa AND, Villa Field MRY, four cases of Villa Pen WLD ANN CTH AND and three of The Villa JAS MAN CTH. The villa flourished with tourism, developed most actively after 1980, alongside the hotel sector, discussed in the previous chapter.

A list from 1990 named thirty-six villa developments, distributed between Montego Bay, Negril, Ocho Rios and Runaway Bay. Jamaican elements were rare, with plants and flowers dominant, as in Pimento Villa, Poinciana Place Villa, Pineapple Villa and the less seductive Bitterwood Villa. There were also Valdemosa Villa and Villa Caribe, but most references to other places were distant, as in Villa Carmel, Villa La Alba and Villa D'Este, the last of these probably named after the famous Renaissance palace and gardens at Tivoli, near Rome. Other villa names were generic, as in Rock Edge Bay Villas, Baypoint Villas, Crystal Waters Villas, Sea Chalet Villas, White Sands Villas, Hill Crest Villa and Castle Peak Villa. Others were romantically unreal, as in Dream Scape Villa and Moonrise Villas, or vaguely mythological, as in Valhalla Villa and Villa Harlequin. The idea of retreat occurred in Hideaway Villa and perhaps Sea Esta Villa, along with the more obviously eponymous Cindy Villa. Even in small-scale projects the names rarely rang Jamaican bells. Thus the four styles of villas offered at Llandovery Beach in 1995 were all named for foreign fruit: Pomegranate (the largest), Apricot, Kiwi and Sultana (the smallest).[48] Such villa developments housed occasionally significant populations, but they were by intent transient. They did little to contribute to the concept of settlement as a site of residence.

CHAPTER NINE

Route Names

THE NAMING OF ROUTES DEPENDS ON their density and complexity.
Many significant routes are never given names but are known simply as the
road or *railway* to a particular settlement, indicating that these are the most
direct and efficient routes to travel. In this way, a route can, over time, take
on the name of its destination in a descriptive fashion, the same route having different descriptions depending on the starting point. Thus, standing at
Cave Valley, one could identify the way north as the Alexandria road,
whereas the same route viewed from Alexandria could be called the Cave
Valley road. Signs naming the route itself are not useful in this case; all that
is needed by the traveller is a fingerpost pointing the way to the next settlement. The railway or railroad, which came to Jamaica early – with the
first line, from Kingston to Spanish Town, opened in 1845 – operated
somewhat differently. The names of places were written boldly on signs at
the stations where the train stopped, so that passengers would know where
to get off. Most railways were known simply by their endpoints, as in the
Chapelton to Frankfield line. A railway proposed in 1862 linking Kingston
and Stony Hill was to be called The People's Railway, but it was not built.[1]
Tramways, or tramroads, simply ran down the middle of existing roads and
gained no new names.

A few major routes did gradually take on names in their own right, the
name reflecting the relative significance of the places connected. Thus,
under the British, the main road from Spanish Town to Kingston was

known first as the Kingston Road, but when Kingston became the more important city and eventually the island's capital, it was named Spanish Town Road. Rural roads were sometimes numbered, as for example "road number thirty-six, in the parish of Hanover, from the Lucea bridge, over Riley's river, to the main road at Glasgow, in Westmoreland".[2] Within the towns, naming by destination did occur, as in Kingston's Half Way Tree Road, but the density of the network made other kinds of naming much more common than in the countryside, even when the urban settlements were relatively small in scale. Thus James Hakewill in his *Picturesque Tour* of 1820 illustrated route names only for Kingston, including signs in two distinct styles on the corners of buildings marking the intersection of King Street and Harbour Street.[3]

As well as bearing names themselves, routes sometimes provided names for settlements. Most often it was the intersections of routes that were used in this way, indicating the significance of such junctions for internal trade and movement, as in *cross, corner, turn, roads* (including *cross roads*) and *bridge*. These examples are discussed first, before turning to the names of streets, lanes and avenues within the major urban settlements, especially Kingston. In towns, the general term for a route (meaning a passage or path from one point to another) is commonly *street*, and in the country it is *road*. Here, *street* and *road* are restricted to more specific meanings, and the entire network is thought of as made up of routes, including their intersections.

CROSS, ROADS, PATH, MILE

The image of the cross is perhaps the most obvious example of a four-way intersection. Although an older English meaning of *cross* as a market had lost favour by the time of Jamaica's seventeenth-century colonization, the notion that the cross roads served as an ideal site for local commerce persisted. On the 1950 topographical map, four distinct settlements are shown with the name Cross Roads, the most prominent being an important Kingston centre and the others in the parishes of St Ann, Clarendon and St Catherine (Figure 9.1). The Cross CLR, near May Pen, known from the sev-

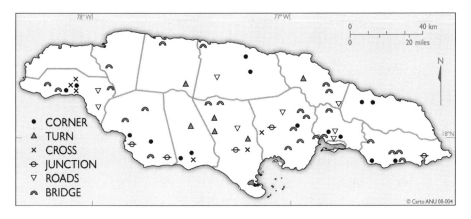

Figure 9.1 Jamaica: *Corner, turn, cross, junction, roads* and *bridge*, settlement names, 1950

enteenth century and listed by Long in 1774, was the only example of *cross* found on Robertson's 1800 map. It was later sometimes known as Palmers Cross, but most maps distinguish The Cross from the nearby separate place Palmers. Charing Cross CLR and Cross Keys MAN seem to derive directly from English places, but Whitehall Cross ELZ, with its unusual forked junction, took its name from a neighbouring plantation. There were also Amity Cross WLD, the nearby Friendship Cross WLD and Pedro Cross ELZ.

In 1950, there were two examples of Four Roads WLD AND and one each of Three Roads WLD and Two Roads MRY. *Path* worked in the same way, with two examples of Four Paths, the best known of these in Clarendon (together with the nearby Turners Four Paths) and the other in St Elizabeth. Two Paths was in Portland, very close to Two Roads. As elsewhere, the place names of Jamaica most likely to contain numbers relate to routes, along which the counting of corners or miles (not yet kilometres) serves as a practical navigational tool.[4] The 1950 map has Three Mile AND, Four Mile AND, Five Miles CTH, Seven Mile AND and two cases of Eleven Mile CTH THS. Most of these are concentrated around Kingston. Six Miles AND, three miles further along Spanish Town Road than Three Miles, later became the well-known junction with Washington Boulevard. Similar kinds of locational naming occurred in Central Village CTH and Halfway

Tree AND, though in these cases the external reference points have been frequently debated.

CORNER, TURN, ALLEY

Less obvious as an intersection is *corner*, sometimes merely marking an unusually sharp bend in a road, but the notion of intersection is very common, as in the meeting place of two edges or routes. *Corner* is rare in British place-naming but fairly common in New England (United States), where it is generally a habitation name, often including the personal names of people living there. The best-known examples within Kingston are Mary Browns Corner and Matildas Corner. Both are four-way intersections but made up of only three route names, the major road taking a sharp right-angle turn in each case (Constant Spring Road and Old Hope Road). Thus they equally represent a corner of that main road. The identities of Mary Brown and Matilda are not known, but it is possible they were coloured women, owners of lodging houses or shops at these sites. The earliest known reference to the former is from 1867, in the form "Mary Brown's Corner", and to the latter, "Matilda Corner" from 1876.[5] A British Army map based on surveys of the Kingston district made between 1904 and 1912 had these as Mary Brown Corner and Matilda Corner, and also found Papine Corner (now simply Papine) and Nigger House Corner on Mona Road, this last an unusually racist variety of place-naming.[6]

In rural Jamaica, the best-known example is Poor Mans Corner THS, near Yallahs, on the main road along the southern coast to the east, where a left-hand turn leads to Heartease and Norris. Another Poor Mans Corner existed before 1834, in upper Clarendon, a district on the Cave River occupied by a smallholder class of slaveowners. Eponymous corners were Whittakers Corner CLR, Graemes Corner CTH and Rabys Corner CTH. There was also Church Corner THS and Corner Pen TRL. Every one of these was named before the end of the nineteenth century, but none of them appeared on Robertson's 1800 map. The closest was Graemes Corner, on a great loop in the road, recorded by Robertson as "Grames's".

Bochart and Knollis, however, had Pye Corner CLR, running across the Rio Minho near its mouth, on their 1680 map.

Close to Pye Corner was the well-known crossroads settlement now referred to simply as Alley, but called The Alley on maps since Robertson's 1800 mapping. A 1760 plan of Suttons Pasture Estate CLR showed "Ally" in its southwestern corner, a triangle of three buildings at the intersection of "The Road from the Ally to Sympsons", heading north beside the Rio Minho, and "The Road from the Ally to Mrs Goulburnes". On the latter road, further to the east, the plan showed a "Church" and its "glebe land". At about the same time, Craskell and Simpson identified the larger district as Withy Wood but showed only the "Church", at a four-way intersection east of the river. It is the church that most strongly characterizes the place; established in 1671 as the parish church of Vere, it is said to be the oldest place of worship for Anglicans in Jamaica. But the place name probably derives from the meeting of routes or *alleys*, as suggested by Pye Corner and the 1760 plan.

New examples of *corner* that appeared on the 1950 map but not before were Churchill Corner PLD, Crane Corner ELZ, Dunbars Corner WLD, Pipers Corner WLD, Rowes Corner MAN, Rudds Corner MAN and School House Corner MRY (see Figure 9.1). There was also Corner Forty-Four ANN, marking a sharp bend on the road from St Anns Bay up the hills towards Lime Hall. Presumably it is the forty-fourth of its kind, counting from the coast. Further inland, beyond Claremont, Show Meself Corner ANN marked a simple four-way intersection. All of the nineteenth-century *corners* survived to 1950 except Graemes Corner, Whittaker Corner and Corner Pen. By the late twentieth century, Matildas Corner was becoming less current as the name of reference, often replaced by Liguanea, from the nearby Liguanea Villa (now lost beneath Sovereign Shopping Centre), Liguanea Avenue and Liguanea Plaza. Not appearing on maps, but well enough known to be used as a defining location in legislation, was Put Together Corner, near Mandeville, marking the place where higglers from the country paused to organize their wares before entering the market. Informally named *corners* emerged occasionally, such as Glock Corner – recognizing the rule of the gun, the popular Glock pistol – which was used to identify a stretch of land that connected Waltham Park Road and Maxfield Avenue.[7]

The best-known example of *turn* is Whitney Turn MAN, where the main road makes a deep loop and a smaller road comes off the lower side of the arc, leading to Whitney Estate. This name was well established by the end of the nineteenth century and persisted. Other examples from the 1950 map were Farm Turn MRY, which operated in much the same way, and the probably eponymous Tuckers Turn MAN and Tory Turn TRL. Soursop Turn CLR suggests the original existence of a tree or grove. Nine Turns CLR sounds like a match for Seven Corners ELZ and had its own intersection, but was located on the road through the high hills from Thompson Town to Frankfield at a particularly sinuous point.

JUNCTION

The best known use of *junction* is in Junction Road, the route that most directly connects Kingston with the north coast, reaching the sea a little west of Annotto Bay. The road was conceived in 1836 but advanced slowly until the 1850s. Although *junction* might derive from the notion of joining two points, north and south coasts in this case, an act of 1840 referred to the improvement of the route "from the junction road leading to the Plum-Tree tavern, and continued from thence, over Stoney-Hill eastward of the barracks, to Golden-Spring estate, and thence towards Annotto-Bay".[8] Probably it was this short initial section that gave its name to the whole of the Junction Road. The 1950 map did, however, record two examples of places simply called Junction (see Figure 9.1). The largest of these settlements was Junction ELZ, at the intersection of major roads leading to Southfield, Nain, Bull Savanna and Alligator Pond. The other, Junction CTH, was close to Point Hill, marked by a forked three-way intersection. Saltspring Junction ELZ, another three-way crossing, was just east of Crane Corner and Black River Bay, named for the neighbouring Salt Spring Pen. Arcadia Junction THS is similar, with a road leading off the main eastern route towards Arcadia Estate, though in 1950 there was also a light-railway crossing at the same point, serving Port Morant's banana trade. Logans Junction CLR marked only a three-way rail intersection near May Pen.

GATE, HALT

From the 1740s to the 1860s a system of turnpikes operated in Jamaica, with toll gates along them for the collection of payments. Independent of these, planters sometimes placed gates across roads passing through their lands, to secure property and monitor movement. The frequency of such gates is apparent from the number of settlement names containing *gate*, with seventeen occurrences on the 1950 map (Figure 9.2). In two cases the place name survives as Toll Gate. The best known of these is Toll Gate CLR, on the main road west between Four Paths and Porus, at an intersection with the road leading south to Milk River Bath. The other case is Toll Gate WLD, at a three-way intersection immediately north of Frome and just a kilometre from Truro Gate, another three-way intersection. Neither of these occurs in the cadastral series, but Truro Gate marks the location of Truro Pen and its former gate probably blocked the road at this point. Little Gate HAN was near Dias above Lucea; Glade Gate WLD guarded passage through Fort William Estate; Line Gate WLD marked a place near Ramble, on the main road from Savanna la Mar to Montego Bay. New toll roads with boom gates were opened in Jamaica in the 1990s, but these sites have not yet generated their own generic place names.

Several other *gate* place names suggest the locations of toll gates. King Gate JAS sat at the top of Long Hill, the beginning of the main western cross-island road that turned inland at Reading, beside a three-way intersection and the entry to a tunnel when the railway came. Another King Gate JAS was on the opposite, eastern, edge of the parish, at an unnamed three-way intersection on Robertson's 1800 map, back from the coast between Spot Valley and Scarlett Hall Estates. Cole Gate ANN, at the head of Fern Gully, had a hilltop situation similar to that of the first King Gate, marking another three-way junction. Cooks Gate CLR appeared on the

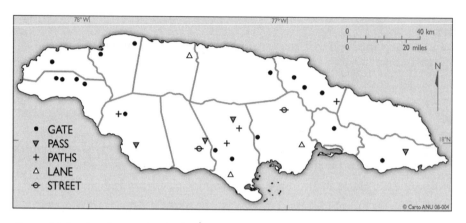

Figure 9.2 Jamaica: *Gate, pass, paths, lane* and *street*, settlement names, 1950

1950 map at a three-way intersection on level land near the Rio Minho, but on Robertson's 1800 map this was a five-way crossing on the boundary line between the old parishes of Vere and Clarendon, suggesting greater significance. Robertson provided no name for this place, and Cook's identity is unknown. Bonny Gate MRY marks a five-way intersection in the middle of Bagnolds District, apparently taking its name from Bonny Pen, the Bonny equally suggestive of an African or Scottish origin. Broadgate MRY on the Wag Water River road, inland from Chovey and the north coast, may have collected tolls. Redgate ELZ marks a three-way junction, the roads leading to YS, Four Paths and Ipswich. Scotland Gate THS in the hills above Yallahs may also have been a collection point. However, Happy Gate AND sounds an unlikely name for the payment of tolls, and its isolated location in the hills beyond Maryland indicates a road going nowhere. Bellas Gate CTH is in the high hills near Cocoa Ridge, and the name is apparently local. Highgate MRY, a large town with multiple intersections, probably copies English examples.

Common on the 1950 map was the term *halt*, always used along the railway line to mark a stopping point other than the major stations in towns (see Figure 9.1). There were twenty-four examples as compound names. Most simply referred to known, named places nearby, as in Grays Inn Halt MRY and Crawle Halt CTH. Michleton Halt CTH did the same but in this case replicated the eighteenth-century role of Mickleton Pen as a staging post for Worthy Park Estate.

FORD, BRIDGE

Travellers along Jamaica's roads typically remarked the numerous fordings through which they had to pass, these crossings reflecting the frequency of rivers and springs and the sinuous character of the routes. The 1950 topographic map marked sixty-seven stream crossings with the word *ford*, but this seems never to have become by itself a simplex place name, perhaps because of its ubiquity. Another six examples did develop into compound place names, generally eponymous: Coates Ford CLR, Derby Ford CLR, Jupiter Ford PLD, Scotts Ford CLR, Crawle Ford CTH and Deep Ford CLR. The Yallahs Ford is now the best known, a dangerous crossing where huge boulders are swept down by floodwaters and attempts to build bridges seem doomed. Elsewhere, engineering improvements, beginning in the later nineteenth century, removed a large proportion of the island's fords and replaced them with causeways and bridges that smoothed the way and removed remarkable landmarks.

As river crossings, bridges are generally superior to fords. There were twenty-two bridges with compound names on the 1950 map (see Figure 9.1). Some, such as Big Bridge WLD and Flat Bridge CTH, were merely descriptive. In spite of its simple name, Flat Bridge has been a well-known place for centuries. Essentially unimproved since the eighteenth century and still a single-lane crossing on a heavily travelled route joining the north and south coasts (to the west of the Junction Road), the structure has coped with the great floods that sweep over it when the Rio Cobre rushes through the Bog Walk Gorge. Other bridges are named for the streams they cross or places they link. But bridges offered one of the best chances for a colonial governor to attach his name to a place, as in Blake Bridge AND, Olivier Bridge THS and Stubbs Bridge CTH. Interestingly, no substantial urban settlement refers to a bridge in its name. Cambridge and Boroughbridge and the like are British transfer names.

Long before governors basked in the glory of having a bridge named in their honour, local names were applied to smaller structures. Few of these entered the larger stream of persistent place names. An exception is Bengal Bridge, which crosses the Rio Bueno and marks the boundary between St Ann and Trelawny. Its name has survived, perhaps because of its location on a major route and its unique architectural style. Built in the 1780s, the Bengal Bridge has a distinct incline, and its extended parapets terminate in boundary pillars. Where they were numerous, smaller bridges within properties were named. An interesting example dates from 1752, when Thistlewood worked as overseer at Egypt Estate, located in a low-lying area of Westmoreland. Egypt was in the process of being developed into a sugar plantation, and Thistlewood observed that much of the land was made up of water and morass, the dry land consisting effectively of islands in the midst of swamp, connected by bridges. He seems not to have personally named these bridges but noted, "Such bridges as that of ours going to the hogstyes are called Barbecue Bridges; as that going to Hill, Congo Bridges; those in the canepieces are Common Bridges."[9]

PASS

Morgans Pass CLR is sited at the confluence of the Orange and Stony rivers, tributaries of the Rio Minho, above Chapelton, with matching road intersections. It once had a railway station, suggesting its convenience as a way or *pass* through the surrounding steep hills of Morgans Valley. The Morgan in these place names is said by Sibley to be Henry, the pirate and governor of the 1670s, who acquired land. Scotts Pass CLR was in a similar situation, with a railway stop on the main road from Kingston leading up to Whitney Turn and Porus. Develders Pass ELZ identifies a physical feature more than a settlement on the 1950 map, though marking an intersection and crossing morass near Burnt Savanna and Mountainside (see Figure 9.2). Cross Pass THS suggests an intersection, but by 1950 there was just one route and no sign of habitation.

STREET, LANE, ROAD

The common generic route terms used to name Jamaican habitative and settlement sites, discussed above, were rarely used also to label routes within urban areas. The most significant exceptions are *cross roads* and *corner*, and these referred to points of intersection rather than the linear path of the route as a means of passage. Similarly, the generic terms used to classify routes within towns tend to be exclusive to that form of settlement. The few exceptions on the 1950 map came from the terms with the longest history in Jamaica, particularly *street* and *lane*. The use of the term *street* in the names of Jamaican village-type settlements, as in Ellen Street MAN and York Street CTH, mirrored Irish practice.[10] Water Lane CLR was close to a four-way crossing. Grange Lane CTH similarly marked an intersection, close to the railway and the Rio Cobre, east of Spanish Town (see Figure 9.2). In contrast, *road* in its singular form did not name settlements but was a common term for significant rural routes, particularly those that connected towns, such as Spanish Town Road. Occasionally, a rural route might be called a *lane*, the best example being Hampshire Lane TRL, a long straight piece of road leading to Clarks Town. Long Lane AND, now subsumed within greater Kingston, similarly led into the hills in a straight, steady rise before the road commenced its winding way. These were the exceptions. Most of Jamaica's *streets*, *lanes* and *roads* are to be found in urban settlements.

In Jamaica's old capital, Spanish Town, the pattern of streets laid out by the Spanish colonists survives, but the names they were given have been replaced by English ones. Red Church Street and White Church Street refer to religious buildings that existed in Spanish times, but most of the street names there are typically English, such as King Street, William Street, Adelaide Street, Wellington Street, Hanover Street, Manchester Street, Cumberland Road, Old Market Street and Waterloo Lane.[11] Montego Bay is another settlement originally established by the Spaniards where the street names suggest little or nothing of the first European colonists. Like other Jamaican towns, something of the history of Montego Bay is recorded in its street names, as, for example, in Strand Street, which indicates the original shoreline, and Harbour Street, which marks a stage in the reclamation of land from the sea that has continued to extend the site of the town into the bay.[12] Jamaican towns established by the English reflected those of their home country in many ways, including the names of their streets. Seventeenth-century Port Royal, for example, had the following thoroughfares: High Street, Thames Street, Lime Street, Fishers Row, Queen Street, New Street, York Street, Tower Street and Church Street.[13]

Although the Spaniards occupied the area now covered by Jamaica's modern capital and largest city, Kingston was a British foundation, established soon after the destruction of Port Royal by the 1692 earthquake.[14] The original planned town comprised a rectangular grid with a central square, a layout typical of colonial foundations since ancient Greece and Rome and commonly found throughout the former European colonies of the Americas. The generic term for Kingston's main routes was *street*, and the term *lane* was applied to many of the intervening parallel routes. Radiating from this urban centre were *roads* that connected it to other parts of Jamaica, such as the Windward Road leading to the eastern end of the island, which is exposed to the prevailing trade winds, and Spanish Town Road, connecting Kingston with the old capital. In the early years of Kingston's development, *street*, *lane* and *road* were by far the most common generic terms for the town's routes.

Downtown Kingston, that area comprising the original seventeenth-century grid and the extension made around 1750, is full of *streets* and *lanes*, rare exceptions being Ocean Boulevard and Nethersole Place, on part of the waterfront redevelopment of the 1960s. As Figure 9.3 shows, *streets* and *lanes* remain common in that area and in poor inner-city districts such as Trench Town and Greenwich Town, which extend westward along Spanish Town Road. Port Royal has a Dockyard Lane. Elsewhere, *lanes* crop up significantly in Trench Town and Liguanea and have come to be associated with zones of urban poverty. The *lanes* of the Liguanea area contrast markedly with adjacent middle- and upper-class residential districts, such as Hope Pastures and Beverly Hills, where *lanes* and *streets* are not to be found, and *roads*, apart from major arteries such as Old Hope Road, Barbican Road and Mona Road, are rare. The generic *road* is absent from

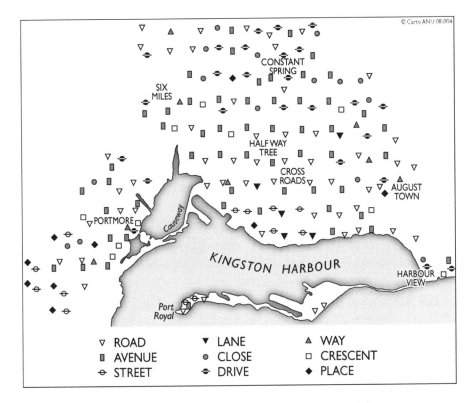

Figure 9.3 Kingston: *Road, avenue, street, lane, close, drive, way, crescent* and *place,* route names, 2000. The symbols indicate the two most common generic terms for each of the grid units of the Kingston map, as described on p. 17.

the old centre of Kingston but is found widely throughout the rest of the metropolitan area. It is the first or second most frequently occurring term over more than half of the area of Kingston (Figure 9.3). North of North Street, the northern edge of the original planned Kingston, *streets* and *lanes* persisted in the growth of the later nineteenth century but quickly lost ground to *road* and *avenue*. It is interesting to note, however, that the generic *street* found renewed favour in the post-1960s urban expansion of Portmore.

Within towns, the use of a generic label without associated descriptive terms was not viable. Generic labels were useful classifiers and modifiers but not practical as a means of navigation around the urban environment. In Kingston the descriptive words attached to the streets and lanes of the original urban core differed significantly from those associated with route names in the later-developed areas of the city. On the 2000 map, personal names were attached to 60 per cent of lanes and 40 per cent of streets. The lanes were also sometimes named for places within Jamaica and overseas but were hardly ever given the name of a plant or animal or a feature of the landscape. Lanes were even less likely to be given a number or a point of the compass (only 2 per cent were named this way), in strong contrast to the high proportion of streets (33 per cent) so named, the majority of the latter found in the new development areas of the late twentieth century where *street* had its resurgence.

Street names reflecting relative location in terms of the compass had early beginnings in Kingston, where North Street, East Street and West Street date from the town's seventeenth-century foundation. North, south, east and west are added to several street names to distinguish separate stretches of one continuous route or one route from another in the same area. Simple numerical names, such as First Street and Ninth Street, occur fairly widely, but it is in Greater Portmore that they are most dominant, from NW Seventh Street to SE Fifth Street.

In 1776 Kingston's streets were named as follows: King, Church, Blackmoor, Duke, Stanton, East, Hanover, Gold, Fleet, North, Sutton, East Queen, Lawes, Milk, Barry, Tower, Harbour, Port Royal, Little Port Royal, West, Orange, Knight, Princess, Mordant, Bernard, Heywood, Queen, Bourden and White. High Holbourn and Cornhill were listed without being given the generic *street*. By 1832 some of these had disappeared and new names had been added, such as Oxford, Regent, Water, Beckford, Charles, Wildman, James, Peck, Beeston, Lombard, Thames and Paradise.[15] Monarchs, together with metropolitan and local political figures, are prominent in these lists, as are British and local topographic references. It was a mix typical of British colonial naming practice.[16] *Paradise* stands out as the exception, a rare example of an urban route with a descriptive label rooted in sentiment, though even this could be a transfer name derived from an English city's streets.

The narrow lanes that intervened between the streets of downtown Kingston at the time of the American Revolution were named Love, Temple, Mark, Johns, Georges, Rum, Rosemary, Maiden, Foster, Water, Chancery, Peters, Matthews and Fetter. Lane name changes by the time of the abolition of slavery added Luke (to complete the gospel-writers), Broughton, Kingston, Chestnut, Park, Tulip, Percey, Gutters, Smiths, Ladds, Stephens and Charlotte. Once again, apart from the ambiguous Love Lane, there was little hint of sentiment. Love Lane may also be a transfer name – as were several other of the lane names – carried to Kingston from Port Royal and to Port Royal from London.[17]

The streets and lanes of the urban core of Kingston retained their names quite successfully, and the imperial and metropolitan stamp remained strong into the twentieth century. For example, in 1934 the streets of Smith Village (renamed Denham Town in 1939, in honour of the governor) were Albert, Dumfries, Elgin, Greenwich, King, Last, Market, Metcalf, Nelson, North, Nuttall, Percy, Regent, Upper Regent, Spanish Town, Victoria, Water and Wellington. It was in this period that lanes acquired an ugly reputation that seemed to accompany them to uptown locations. Park Lane and 100 Lane emerged early in 2002 as places many could not safely enter, notorious as the location of a series of vicious murders. Park Lane and 100 Lane both lead off Red Hills Road in White Hall Gardens, and became the site of a feud between rival gangs.[18] More persistent in the long term was Matthews Lane, which became known as a linear locality, not merely a route, celebrated in the folksong "Dog War a Mattuse Lane". By 1990 it was "commonly called 'Matches Lane' ", and its community needed defence: "Matthews Lane, in western Kingston, is no narrow, dark alley, as the name might imply."[19]

Imperial and metropolitan names also peppered the streets of post-slavery villages. Thus the main streets of Clarkson Town honoured the British monarch Victoria and her consort Albert. Here the naming was marked by ceremony and memorialization: "I name this street 'Victoria,' in honour of our beloved sovereign, by whose gracious will and pleasure the great boon of freedom was bestowed upon you and your children", followed by the singing of the national anthem.[20]

Because the *roads* of Kingston spread far beyond the urban core of streets and lanes, and because they were named over a longer period of historical change, the descriptive terms applied to them differed significantly. Roads did most often take the names of people (35 per cent of them), but they were four times more likely than streets to be named for a Jamaican place (22 per cent) and twice as likely to be named for a place outside the island (21 per cent). Landscape and natural-history references are rare, and roads were hardly ever named with numbers or compass points (3 per cent).

AVENUE, DRIVE, CLOSE, PLACE, CRESCENT, WAY, TERRACE

By the end of the twentieth century Kingston had 2,875 uniquely named routes. More than fifty generic terms were used in these names, and almost every route carried a specific generic. The most common was *avenue* (29 per cent of named routes), followed by *road* (18 per cent), *drive* (11 per cent), *street* (7 per cent), *close* (6 per cent), *place* (6 per cent), *crescent* (5 per cent), *lane* (4 per cent), *way* (4 per cent), *terrace* (3 per cent) and *boulevard* (1 per cent). The growing popularity of *avenue* and *drive* was a feature of the period after 1900 and of the increasingly rapid spread of suburban development across the Liguanea Plain.

To some extent, these changes mirror patterns in contemporary Britain, which remained the primary source of Jamaica's public name-givers in the colonial period. In urban Britain, however, *street* remained popular, and *terrace* – evoking rows of Regency mansions or humble workers' dwellings – was more common than in Jamaica. Fashion appeared to favour several alternative appellations, possibly suggestive of the living environments enjoyed by the nobility and gentry. *Avenues* and *drives* became common even where trees were absent and no elegant carriages conveyed residents and guests to fashionable homes. Many a *close* could now be found without a nearby cathedral, and roads of various alignments might be named *crescent*. Kingston's development history shows a similar trend.

It is interesting to compare the pattern of generics in Kingston with the contemporaneous frequencies found by John Algeo in London and New York.[21] Overall, Kingston reads rather more like London than New York. The range of generic terms is similar for Kingston and London, both of which employ more than New York, where the rigid grid is composed largely of very long avenues (north–south) and streets (east–west). In New York, according to Algeo's count, 64 per cent of routes have the generic *street*, and in London, 9 per cent, compared to the 7 per cent in Kingston. The prevalence of *avenue* in Kingston (29 per cent) far exceeds its popularity in both London (9 per cent) and New York (7 per cent), bearing in mind that in New York avenues account for a great length of the total route network while bearing few unique names. *Road* is the most common generic in London (37 per cent), whereas in Kingston *road* is second to *avenue*, only half as common as in London, but much more frequent than in New York, where fewer than 1 per cent of routes bear the generic *road*. In the case of *place*, Kingston falls between New York (9 per cent) and London (3 per cent). Of the most common Kingston generics, terms used in Kingston that are associated specifically with London include *drive, lane, crescent* and *way*, and with New York, *terrace* and *boulevard*.

In Kingston, *road* and *avenue* took over from *street* and *lane* as the preferred generic terms for routes within the broad band of suburban growth that developed after 1900 (see Figure 9.3). Even in tiny Port Royal, where much of the original pattern of streets survived the town's disastrous history, we can discern a trend that typifies the Kingston area as a whole – a rejection of *street* in favour of *road* and *avenue* in more recent developments. *Avenue* continued to be popular as Kingston spread towards and into the hills surrounding the Liguanea Plain, but competition from other terms became increasingly evident. *Drive* emerged among the top two generic terms in some areas, its popularity continuing to recent times and its areas of dominance extending to the expanding urban fringe. *Crescent* is one of the top two terms in a broad band north of Halfway Tree but does not maintain this level of relative popularity among the outer suburbs around Constant Spring and beyond. Here *close* assumes greater importance, continuing to be popular into the fringes of the urban sprawl, typically applied to short culs-de-sac. Another generic term associated with the outer sub-urbs is *way*, occasionally found in sparsely settled areas but also prominent in the dense networks of residential streets in developments such as Duhaney Park, Mona Heights and August Town. Rather than being applied to rows of townhouses in the British manner, *terrace* is used gener-ally in Kingston for streets of houses on individual lots.

Place is relatively common in the vicinity of the University of the West Indies at Mona, as in Payton Place, and occurs in particular concentrations in the Queensborough and Queensbury areas. In the latter two districts, the term has been given to short culs-de-sac in very dense small-lot devel-opments on either side of Constant Spring Gully. It is in the Portmore and Greater Portmore areas that *place* most commonly occurs as the first or sec-ond most frequent generic term (see Figure 9.3). Here again, the routes so named are recent small-lot developments of relatively low-cost housing. *Place* and *way* stand out as the only routes whose names were not domi-nated by personal names. This was most dramatic in the case of *place*, with 54 per cent of cases given a number or a number combined with a compass point and only 16 per cent taking a personal name. Plants and animals were the popular choice for a *way* (32 per cent), though barely outdoing the per-sonal names (31 per cent), with flowering plants dominating the *ways* of Mona Heights, for example – from Marigold to Petunia Way on the two sides of Garden Boulevard.

For all of *avenue, drive, crescent* and *terrace*, the second most popular name after a personal name was taken from an overseas site (23, 20, 24 and 24 per cent respectively), whereas for *close* it was a plant or animal (20 per cent). Looked at from a different perspective, the routes most likely to take per-sonal names were *lane* and *crescent*; to take a Jamaican place name, *road* and *drive*; an overseas place name, *crescent* and *terrace*; a plant or animal name, *way* and *close*; a landscape feature, *close* and *drive*; and a number or compass point name, *place* and *street*.

Taking all of the Kingston routes together, 27 per cent have been given names derived from surnames. Fewer than 2 per cent refer to specific peo-ple and just over 6 per cent are first names, almost equally divided between male and female. The relatively few named for identifiable individuals commemorate a wide range of people, from royalty, governors and their ladies, British war heroes and Jamaican national heroes to sportspersons and entertainers. Music-makers of all kinds are represented, from Beethoven, Mozart, Wagner and other classical composers in the upmarket Shortwood area to Bob Marley, the Wailers, Sonny Bradshaw and others in less fashionable Cooreville Gardens, and jazz notables like Basie, Ellington and Getz in Portmore. Literary figures, from Chaucer and Shakespeare to Selvon and Mais, are common on the *avenues* of Duhaney Park. About equal to the personal names are names of places, 31 per cent of the total. Many refer to places in and around the Kingston area, but even more appear to be named for places in England, accounting for over 9 per cent of Kingston route-name descriptives.

Other places represented include examples from various parts of Jamaica and elsewhere in the Caribbean, as well as from Britain and the United States. Among the other countries represented, places in the Commonwealth appear occasionally, as in the capital cities used to name Canberra Avenue, Wellington Drive, Ottawa Avenue, Karachi Avenue and Colombo Close, all of these clustered near Matildas Corner. The short-lived Federation of the West Indies, of which colonial Jamaica was a part from 1958 until 1962, had relatively little impact on the place names of the island, but New Kingston, laid out in 1958, recognized island partners in Grenada Crescent, Barbados Avenue, Trinidad Terrace, Tobago Avenue, St Lucia Avenue and Dominica Drive. Immediately north of New Kingston, on the other side of Trafalgar Road, are Caribbean Close and Caribbean Avenue. Other British West Indian islands, including Antigua and St Kitts, named streets leading off West Bay Farm Road in Balmagie, western Kingston.

An interesting minority of route names reflect the character of the locality, by referring to nearby landscape features, for example, or by celebrating the view. Riverside Drive and Martello Drive in Harbour View, a suburb at the mouth of the Hope River overlooked by a Martello tower (a small fort), are examples of the former, and the nearby Mountain View Avenue, of the latter style of reference. Just off this avenue, in Norman Gardens, are found Range Crescent, Target Street, Trigger Road and

Practise Street, which bespeak the rifle range that has been in the area since 1900.

What remains almost entirely absent from the route names of Kingston at the beginning of the twenty-first century is reference to the sentiments. In consequence, the most common place-names of the countryside rarely appear on the streets and avenues of Kingston. There is Content Avenue, off the Waltham Park Road; Friendship Lane, close by Retirement Crescent and the more significant Retirement Road; Friendship Park Road and Avenue, off Deanery Road; Retreat Avenue, off Old Hope Road; Retreat Lane, off Constant Spring Road; Hopewell Lane, off Spanish Town Road; Hermitage Road, approaching August Town; Belmont Road, off the Windward Road; and Belmont Heights, in Stony Hill. But there is no Prospect, no Mount Pleasant, no Spring Garden, no Springfield and no Providence. The optimistic tone of the rural landscape is missing.

BOULEVARD, HIGHWAY

Some of the terms applied to routes – notably *boulevard* and *road* – have a visibility in the landscape that is greater than their numerical frequency because they are much-travelled arteries that stretch across the map. *Boulevard* is the only term outside the top ten that accounts for over 1 per cent of Kingston's route names. Appropriately, this term is given to relatively important urban roads, ranging from Washington Boulevard, a major artery leading from the city and connecting with the main highway to the west and north of the island, to Hope Boulevard, a residential route that acts as a feeder road for the middle-class development of Hope Pastures. Hope Pastures and Hope Boulevard, adjacent to Hope Gardens, take their names from the former sugar estate owned by Richard Hope, one of the officers in the successful English invasion of Jamaica in 1655. Hope Boulevard, then, might be seen as an example of a route named for a person, but in this case it is more accurate to say that it is named for a place that was named for someone whose name survives in several local place names, such as Hope Gardens, Hope Road and Hope River. Overall, the boulevards of Kingston are more likely than any other type of route to have been named for a local or Jamaican place (34 per cent) and as likely as a road to be named for an individual (34 per cent).

In Jamaica, *highways* came to the island with the British, but the most important of these routes were known simply as the King's Highway, to distinguish them from parochial and private roads. Individually named highways were an invention of the later twentieth century. Spanish Town Road, west of the Six Miles junction, became the Mandela Highway in 1990 in honour of the South African freedom fighter Nelson Mandela, who visited Jamaica soon after his release from prison, while the main southern route leading west became Sir Alexander Bustamante Highway where it bypasses May Pen, honouring the former prime minister. A modern North Coast Highway was built, making its way slowly along the main tourist strip. Grand plans to throw a road across the island from Kingston to Montego Bay were at the centre of Highway 2000, a "Millennium Project" described in 2002 as "the largest construction project ever to be undertaken in Jamaica" and pushed ahead at great cost.[22]

ALLEY, WALK, CIRCLE . . . TRAIL, ROW, STRIP

As well as the terms discussed above, a rapidly growing string of relatively uncommon generic labels were attached to urban routes by the beginning of the twenty-first century. Some of these related directly to the idea of route as passage: *alley, walk, circle, circuit, loop, square, court, parade, chase, path, parkway, causeway, main, trail, row* and *strip*. Other terms are less readily recognized as having this function: *heights, rise, hill, view, aerie, slope, vale, ridge, flat, run, spring, gardens, park, green, glades, grove, dene* (a narrow wooded valley), *mead, meads, common, acres, plaza* and *mews*. In most cases these route terms appear to be applications of labels previously confined to rural habitation sites or small urban settlements and developments. As Algeo points out, some of these are associated more commonly with London (*court, green, hill, rise, view, vale, dene, mews, common, grove, gardens, mead, park, path, row* and *walk*) and others with New York (*alley, square, circle, parkway* and *plaza*).[23] In a good proportion of cases these newly popular terms provide strong reference to local physical geography and an elevated view of the landscape, an innovation tied closely to the rapid encroachment of building development on the hills ringing the city of Kingston.

It is also interesting to speculate that the adoption of new generic terms for routes may follow informal naming practice. Some names and terms flourished outside official cartography. For example, *alley* appears only twice on the Kingston road map of 2000, in Charlton Alley (a short route joining an *avenue* and a *drive* in Allerdyce Gardens) and Zebra Alley (a short route close by Tinson Pen Aerodrome). Roots versions occurred earlier, in "Calaloo Alley" branching off Slipe Road in 1917, the same path described in 1922 as "a roadway known as Calaloo Valley".[24] Perhaps it was this lane that confused a soldier giving evidence in an assault case in 1922, when he stated that he had been with his sweetheart near Torrington Bridge on Slipe Road and his assailant had run towards "Marescaux Road, Calalu Avenue". To the amusement of the court, the soldier was corrected by the judge, who said, "It is Connolly Avenue, not Calalu Avenue."[25]

Callaloo Alley was located close to the section of Smith Village known from the mid-1930s as Ackee Walk.[26] *Walk* occurred in habitation and settlement place names, in the spirit of Ackee Walk, as noted in chapter 7, but also named a few routes. The 2000 Kingston map has three examples. Banana Walk maintained the arboreal theme, found high in the hills along Long Lane in Orange Grove, and was joined there by Banana Walk Way. Also in the hills is Haven Walk, connecting Havendale Heights with Smokey Vale. Lower on the plain is White Wing Walk, in Cockburn Gardens, where it sits beside other birds, including Bald Pate Way and Grass Quit Glade.

Probably, some of the new and still uncommon generic labels will gradually increase their popularity over time and replace or outnumber existing terms, in the same way that *lane*, *alley* and *street* were overtaken by *avenue*, *drive*, *close*, *place* and *crescent*. Perhaps the sentiments will also become more common, bringing country to town and making the naming system more obviously Jamaican.

CHAPTER TEN

Conclusion

MODERN JAMAICANS RARELY REFER TO THEMSELVES as islanders. The fact of living "on" an island, let alone a small island, is rarely vocalized or problematized. The sea is not regularly in sight, and there are only rare opportunities for intervisibility with other islands, notably glimpses of Cuba from Blue Mountain Peak. Psychologically, Jamaica is continental. A peripatetic person may be referred to as temporarily "on the island" or "off the island", but for most Jamaica is simply *home, homeland, yard, the Rock, JA* or *Jamdown*. Jamaicans live "in" rather than "on" their earthly stage, unwanted and unsought though it might be. Although people may refer to "poor little" Jamaica and enthusiastically seek residence in other countries in hopes of a better life, Jamaicans have a strong sense of identity, of being Jamaican. When at home, it is the smaller places that provide references to the landscape's mosaic and matrix, with identity by parish, town or district, the unique image and character of each small place encapsulated in its name.

Massive billboards near the airports of Kingston and Montego Bay welcome arrivals to *Jamaica*. These are not designed to welcome home returning Jamaicans but intended rather to help inattentive visitors recall that it was the hotel strip of Jamaica they had briefly inhabited rather than the resorts of some competing destination. More modest signs alert travellers to the crossing of boundaries within the island, but not every place or border is identified by name. There are no signs to mark the lines of the counties, whereas the still-important parish boundaries are consistently marked by modest or more elaborate signs. Districts such as watersheds are also indicated, and sometimes the names of towns and villages. Fingerposts at country crossroads point travellers in the right direction. Streets and lanes are generally announced by road signs, and properties and hotels display their names at entrances. In recent times, some of these signs have been subsidized from private, corporate sources.

In the past, place names – painted on boards, cast in metal or carved in stone – were much less common in the landscape. The slower speed of travel and the greater embeddedness of routes within soil, rock and vegetation made signposts less necessary. During slavery, estates rarely had their names emblazoned on their gateposts, and estate buildings were more likely to have stones indicating their dates of erection than to declare names. Pillars within plantations sometimes marked boundaries. For example, in 1779 neighbouring planters in St Thomas in the East, in dispute over their boundary, agreed not only to mark the line on the ground but also to erect stone pillars engraved "Golden Grove" on their eastern faces and "Winchester" on the western. These were conspicuous, but many of the markers engraved in stone were hidden from the passer-by, designed as a permanent record, like a surveyor's mark, rather than as a public declamation of the name of the property. Aqueducts sometimes named the source of their water, as in the stone set discreetly into the gutter wall at Old Montpelier JAS that stated "1 Mile to Blue Hole 1746".[1] This and markers like it survived in place for hundreds of years.

The longevity and stability of Jamaica's place-name system, and the way in which the names of properties, districts, towns and parishes efficiently identify the characteristic features of settlement, have served to underpin their essential role in the appreciation of landscape and attachment to place. To understand the development and viability of the vocabulary of the system, it is necessary to ask how far it emerged in response to the physical and cultural environment of Jamaica, in appreciation of the landscape, and how far it was imposed on the land as an element of the imperial project. To what extent do the place names of Jamaica derive from outside, and to what extent may they be regarded as indigenous or creole creations? In attempting to answer this question, it is essential to give equal weight to the separate elements that make up the names, both the descriptive and the generic terms, and to compare the different kinds of features that were named.

It has sometimes been regarded as strange that so many of Jamaica's place names are drawn from places in the British Isles and other exotic overseas sources. This perception depends on a strict focus on the descriptive elements of the names. It has often been remarked by British people who find a lack of reference in the Jamaican landscape to the original sites from which the names were transferred. Thus, in 1831 John Roby introduced his antiquarian collection of the *Monuments of the Cathedral-Church and Parish of St. Catherine* by reflecting:

> I cannot recall to my memory, without a smile, the anomalous nomenclature of the island. Whilst confined within its limits, I drove through "Albion," "Hanover," "Holland," and "Savoy;" visited "Gibraltar" and "Seville;" called at "Frankfort," and *walked* upon "the Rhine." Without once beholding dear Wales, I saw "Anglesea," "Cardiff," "Llandovery," "Golden-Grove," "St. David's," and "Swansea." I even pursued my route to "Asia" as far as "Colchis" and "Bengal," whilst, in our own quarter of the Globe, I passed through "Quebec" and "Potosi." I travelled not only upon "Windsor's heights," and "Richmond hill," but also over "Mount Libanus" and "Parnassus;" staid a day in "Arcadia," nearly two days in "Eden," rested in the land of "Goshen," crossed the river "Styx," and passed through "Paradise." On my tour I saw "Black River" and "White Hall," "Buff Bay" and "Orange Cove," "Green Island" and "Blue Fields." On the other hand, though I drank of the hot springs of "Bath," I saw neither abbey nor crescent there. I beheld no observatory in "Greenwich Park," no cathedral in "Exeter," no castle in "Carlisle," and no Blenheim at "Woodstock." I observed no picturesque lakes in "Westmorland;" no Saxon antiquities in the "New Forest." "Falmouth" had no packet in port; "Whitney" produced no blanket, "Manchester" was without a cotton manufactory, and there was no college in "Oxford." Finally, "Kingston" in "Surrey," is not "upon Thames;" "Cornwall" yields neither tin nor copper; and in "Middlesex" I could not find London ...[2]

For Roby, such names represented colonial anomalies simply because they did not match the memories or visual images he associated with them. For the British as an imperial state, the place names of Jamaica represented the impress of empire, the power of the colonizers inscribed on the land. For people born in Jamaica, whether black or white, slave or free, such exotic names lacked the associations made by sojourners and the names came to attach themselves securely to Jamaican landscapes and sites in a direct and natural way.[3]

Whereas it is true that the descriptive terms used in Jamaican place names were often derivative, this occurred only in the cases in which a name-giver chose a transfer name. However, although transfer names account for a substantial proportion of the island's place names, they are balanced and indeed overwhelmed by names associated with sentiment. As noted in chapter 3, it is the role of sentiment that sets the place names of Jamaica apart, led by Content, Friendship, Prospect and Retreat, and supported strongly by further references to the hopes and fears of the name-givers, most often optimistic in spirit. Naming in this style had its origin in the names that planters applied to their properties during slavery, but persisted successfully in post-slavery communities and survived to the present in the names of settlements derived ultimately from plantation units. The result was that sentiment names covered much of the rural landscape of Jamaica, in a way they did not in any other British colonial context. These names were not borrowed from local physical features, which only occasionally used sentiment terms, but appear to have had a direct association with the purported objectives of the planter class.

In the towns, on the other hand, sentiment is almost completely lacking from the names of routes, and the same is true of the names given to parishes, counties and other administrative units. As noted in the previous chapter, the names of urban routes were much more likely to derive from personal names, particularly significant public figures, and from the monarchy. Thus King and Queen streets might prove central and long-lived routes in towns, whereas estates and plantations seeking status hardly ever looked in that direction. The difference between town and country can be explained in terms of the relative roles of government. The land occupied by urban routes was the property of the state rather than private individuals, so it was the agencies of government that had the power and responsibility to name them, often doing so through committees of various sorts and wishing above all to honour the great men of their time. Further, it was in the towns that the state established its presence and public buildings, most obviously in the Georgian square of Spanish Town with its monumental qualities. In the long period of Jamaican history in which the majority of the population lived in rural communities, the towns were strange places for most people and their inventory of names quite small. For most of Jamaica's history, and particularly the core period of name-giving that stretched from 1655 to 1800, agriculture dominated the economy, and most people lived in cultivated landscapes that were highly characteristic of the island. Thus the absence of sentiment names from the towns must have seemed appropriate and of no great significance when compared with the great sweep of rural place names.

An alternative perspective is obtained by considering generic labels rather than descriptive terms. Most of the words used in Jamaica as generic labels were derived from the English language, but several were used in new or modified ways to create a terminology and a classificatory system that suited the topographic, economic and cultural condition of the island.[4] Terms used in a uniquely Jamaican way to classify topographic features include *cockpit*, *gully* and *morass*. The creation of a system of naming specifically designed to describe the characteristic places of the island is particularly striking in the generic labels attached to units of settlement, both rural and urban. For the rural units, the most important of these terms are *estate*, *plantation*, *pen*, *crawl*, *settlement*, *mountain* and *walk*. All of these words are familiar to speakers of English, but their meanings in Jamaica diverged, subtly or dramatically, from those known uses. Further, the list of terms covers almost all of the generic labels in use for rural settlement types, the only significant exception being the broadly generalized *farm*.

Status terms used in Jamaican place names seem largely to have been drawn from British models rather than developing unique local creole qualities in the way that the habitation and settlement names had. *Hall* and *castle* might look like generic labels, but they did not operate as such. While a few great houses, notably Rose Hall, were impressively grand, most were modest compared to their British counterparts. Similarly, Jamaica's "castles" lacked the architectural qualities associated with British models. Even the most elaborate of them, such as Colbeck Castle, were not so named until the nineteenth century, when they acquired picturesque qualities. Whereas the enterprise terms served a practical function, status labels were simply affected and could be used with irony and wit in ways which were unacceptable for the names derived from the function or land use of the property.

Of the urban settlement terms, *town, village, market* and *city* were applied in Jamaica essentially unchanged from their English meaning. The functions of a Jamaican port town matched closely the functions of a British one and, during slavery, the towns contained a much larger concentration of British-born people than did the rural world. To apply new terms to the urban settlements of Jamaica was not necessary, whereas the classification of the island's distinctive agricultural units demanded a fresh system of generic labels. Although it is true that *pen* had an urban presence and that *walk* might have occasionally been used for a path in town, these terms were not unique to the urban environment but rather were carried over from the agrarian landscape. The place of *city* within the largest urban settlements, as in Riverton City, Moonlight City and Independence City, seems only a minor variation on the system. The same applies to the generic labels associated with routes: *street, road, lane* and so on. Equivalent terms of recent popularity, such as *meadows* or *gardens* and *drive* or *boulevard*, sound even more like imports rather than local growths.

The pattern of generic labelling reveals a strong tradition of local naming practice. Historically, the pattern observed in Jamaican place-name elements paralleled a similar redefining of English terms and words in other areas of life. For example, the supervisory hierarchy of the colonial plantation system in the eighteenth century ranged through *attorney, overseer, busha, bookkeeper* and *driver*, and these names were equally distinct in their usage in Jamaica, most notably in the case of *attorney* and *bookkeeper*. Similarly, the distinctive Jamaican use of *plantation* during slavery was matched by the post-slavery *planter*, who was more often a small-scale agriculturist than the owner of large acres.

Why did the British in Jamaica oversee the creation of a new system of generic terms to describe the types of enterprise in which they engaged?

Why were they not equally creative in the descriptives that they put in front of these generic labels? The best explanation for this strong divergence in practice can be found in the newness of the enterprise types and their evolving character within Jamaica. *Plantation* and *estate* could mean the same thing where a single crop – sugar – dominated the agrarian system, as in the case of Barbados, but the internal diversity of plantation-style production in Jamaica demanded a distinct term for the hierarchically superior sugar planter, and this was found in *estate*. The functions of the Jamaican livestock-farming enterprise also had unique characteristics, not found elsewhere in the British Caribbean, and unique origins in the post-Spanish agricultural pattern. Thus *pen* and, to a lesser extent, *crawl* proved more appropriate than the purported English equivalent *grass-farm*. Even more strongly rooted in the Jamaican experience of slavery and the development of the provision-ground system was *mountain*, its meaning derived locally from the convergence of topography and land-use pattern.

Not all of these generic terms have survived into the modern system of Jamaican place names. The once common *estate* has become a rarity, following the decline and structural transformation of the sugar industry, and the once regional frequency of *settlement* has disappeared. *Plantation* also became rare as a functional place name element. Relatively strong survivors in the modern system of everyday and official usage are *pen, mountain* and *walk*, understood as essentials in unitary place names that slide off the tongue, such as May Pen, Georges Plain Mountain and Pimento Walk, though the functions of these places no longer relate to the words that formerly served as defining generic labels.

The descriptive terms attached to generic labels functioned to identify particular sites of a type of enterprise. Thus Mona Estate and Papine Estate were different places – sharing boundaries and water resources – but both known by their *estate* labels to be sugar-producing landholdings. The choice of descriptive words was essentially arbitrary, because the descriptive labels were not required to follow closely specified classificatory rules in the way that generic labels were regulated by custom. The owner of a sugar estate would be thought foolish to call his place a *pen*, but he was entirely free to call it, for instance, Mona Estate, Retirement Estate or Lottery

Estate. Making up a completely new word only created difficulty, whereas taking a descriptive from an existing store of place names known to the colonial name-givers was an attractive possibility, as was reference to the sentiments. Although these descriptives were chosen arbitrarily, they have survived better in the system of place names than have the generic labels, partly because they serve as shorthand reference and partly because changes in the agrarian and social systems of settlement have altered the viability of the generics.

For modern Jamaicans – however well they understand that many place names have equivalents and perhaps origins outside the island – the validity and viability of the names as Jamaican names is undoubted. The place names have become creole versions, rooted in the land and the community. Thus Papine and May Pen seem equally natural units within the landscape, rarely considered candidates for change. They stand comfortably alongside the names thought to be more peculiarly or even quaintly Jamaican, the creole or colloquial types like Gimme-Me-Bit or Me No Sen You No Come, broadly appreciated as vital elements of culture.

The secure status of the Jamaican system of place-naming depends partly on its longevity. Although relatively few of the island's present place names were used earlier than 1655, a very large proportion date from the seventeenth and eighteenth centuries and have been known to many generations of inhabitants. The longevity and continuity of the place names match the longevity and continuity of British colonialism in Jamaica. Even within the Caribbean, relatively few islands remained the colonies of a single European state as long as the more than three hundred years during which Jamaica was subject to continuous British occupation and settlement. For more than half of those years, Jamaica was a slave society. The dominance of British government and culture, reinforced by the dominance of plantation slavery, placed the responsibility for naming places firmly in the hands of the planting class throughout the long era of founding the system. The place names did not reflect the demographic pattern of migration to Jamaica but derived specifically from the migrant origins of that dominant class.

The role of the planters in the great name-giving period of the seven-

teenth and eighteenth centuries overwhelmed all that came later. Not only
the poor and the powerless had difficulty in contributing to formal, public
naming. Even the considerable economic power of the Chinese in the
twentieth century came too late to name places. China was completely
ignored, even as an exotic choice. The Syrians and Lebanese might seem to
have fared better, but the relatively common naming of Jamaican places for
sites in the lands these people had left behind had less to do with their
commercial and political weight in the island than the appeal of biblical
geography to the planters of the eighteenth century. Similarly, most of the
European, African and Asian names given to Jamaican places were, in fact,
chosen by British planters. Some wanted, perhaps, to strike an exotic or
ironic note, but most sought to commemorate events associated with sites
of British imperial glory, particularly battles, or recalled places visited on
the Grand Tour or simply known through trade and commerce.

The dominance of planter-derived names, as well as the long-term continuity and stability of Jamaica's place names and their combination of
transferred and locally created terminology, can best be explained in terms
of the process of creolization. In linguistics, a creole language, such as that
spoken by Jamaicans since the eighteenth century, can be defined as a
restructured variety of the language that provided its vocabulary, a product
of contact between colonized and colonizing peoples. Thus creole languages vary according to the composition of the colonizing population
and, importantly, they are strongly influenced by a "founder principle" that
gives substantial weight to the vernacular spoken by the initial contingents
of colonists. Later arrivals might build on these foundations but had to
work within the existing lexical structure. The "founders" of the Jamaican
lexicon of place names were the English-speaking planter class, hence the
dominance of English in orthography and, to a lesser extent, speech.
Although the concept of creolization has been most strongly associated
with language and linguistics, historians have expanded its meaning to
encompass most areas of culture, following the influential example of
Kamau Brathwaite's classic study of Jamaica.[5]

English words were taken and reworked to name the landscape of
Jamaica, but the African languages of the majority of the population were

also influential. The fact that few Jamaican place names can be traced to specific places in Africa must be weighed against the role of African languages in the creation of Jamaican creole and hence the creole naming of places in Jamaica. Such naming is not always easily identified or thought of as African in origin or essence. For example, Cotterwood ELZ is a unique Jamaican place name, not found elsewhere, and likely derived from the Twi word *katá*, meaning to cover or conceal. Recorded first in the 1730s as Cotter-Wood, the name was originally applied to a place of concealment associated with the Maroons of Portland. Dallas later claimed that the St Elizabeth place name derived from a group of Maroons calling themselves "by the name of the Cottawoods; having, it is supposed, originally come from a place so called, near the present Maroon Charlestown". Recent versions of the Portland place name include Cotters Wood and Cattawood.[6]

Not all of the names applied to the land in early periods of settlement have survived. Some changed over time; others simply disappeared because they ceased to be functional. For example, the process of name-giving applied to the cane pieces of Egypt Estate in the middle of the eighteenth century, discussed in chapter 7, was by no means long-lasting. By the later twentieth century, the thirty-three cane pieces of the 1750s had themselves disappeared as units of production, "taking their names with them". Douglas Hall speculated that "The Negro provision ground at Hill, near the coast west of the mouth of the Cabaritta, was perhaps situated at a place now called 'Cookell', a name maybe derived from Hill, which became Cook's Hill (there was later a Mr Cook in that area), and so to Cookell". Even the plantation name became submerged. As Hall observed in the 1980s, "The name Egypt is today recognized only by local residents, who more affectionately call it 'Capture Land', that is, ruinate property settled by squatters long undisturbed in their possession."[7]

Over time, names once thought appropriate and functional came to seem offensive. In many cases, these fresh perceptions and attitudes resulted from changes in society and culture.[8] Words such as *Negro* and *coolie* were broadly recognized as disparaging and fundamentally racist by the end of the twentieth century and therefore inappropriate to use in new place names. Such words were not always removed from existing, long-lasting place names, however. Negro River, for example, and Coolie Shop remain in use. The Dungle, derived from the eighteenth-century *dung hill* or *dung'll* and used in the Jamaican form *dungle* (and occasionally the tautological Dungle Hill) from the beginning of the twentieth century, was bulldozed but persisted as a Kingston place name into the period of independence. In other cases, the modern offensive reading of place names resulted from a misunderstanding of the original meaning of a word or words or, more positively, from changed meanings, resulting in the creation of euphemisms. As noted in chapter 8, by the twentieth century the term *pen* came to seem offensive or problematic, or at least inferior to the more universal *town* or *village* when applied to an urban place. Pens' names were then changed to terminologies thought superior. By the end of the century, Philip Sherlock and Hazel Bennett could deplore the tendency, saying, "The names of the few surviving pens, such as Bamboo Pen, should be preserved and not forgotten as Admiral's Pen, Liguanea Pen, Rollington Pen have been. How wise and pleasing it would have been to have preserved two or three of the 'little grass penns with good houses on them' that were dispersed about Half Way Tree, 'and a small grass penn stocked with sheep and goats'. "[9]

Neither the short-lived Federation of the West Indies (for which the name Antillia was suggested but rejected) nor the formal independence of Jamaica in 1962 had any great impact on the formal or official place names of the island, except for the naming of routes and some minor settlement units.[10] Thoroughgoing replacement had occurred to an ill-defined extent following the Spanish displacement of the Taino and the English displacement of the Spanish, but not following independence. The continuity and stability of British colonial rule from 1655 to 1962, and the parallel processes of creolization and indigenization over three centuries, contributed to the persistence of the system of place names. Jamaica's transition to independence was not marked by war or revolution. The island got a new constitution and adopted national heroes and other national symbols, but the idea that Kingston or Spanish Town or any other substantial settlement should change its name seems not to have been taken seriously. Nor did symbols of independence, such as the national fruit (ackee), the national tree (mahoe) and the national flower (lignum vitae), play any substantial role in the new names of independent Jamaica. The name Jamaica demanded no change since it was already the ancient, original version. In the post-independence period, Jamaica maintained a stable democratic government, influenced by garrison electorates and political violence but without coups or assassinations.

Within the Caribbean, only the replacement of St Domingue by Haiti restored a Taino name on independence, and the ancient name was in any case applied only to the western half of the island that came to be known as Hispaniola.[11] Elsewhere, decolonization saw a renaming of countries that frequently consisted of restoring their names to those of ancient states or empires, as in, for example, the new African nations Ghana, Mali and Zimbabwe. In post-apartheid South Africa, the renaming of the state and its towns and streets became a matter of much debate, the names of colonialists frequently being displaced by those of freedom fighters. The restoration of ancient names in modern Israel represented a similar variety of nationalism.[12] The installation of ancient names in Hawai'i, on the other hand, has been interpreted as a stage in the colonization or "anti-conquest" of the islands.[13] Other countries of the world, notably revolutionary Russia and China, experienced very high rates of change in the twentieth century. In the USSR, one-half of its 700,000 populated places were given new names.[14]

In Jamaica, the names of streets and highways, and public parks and squares, were relatively easy to change and were given a political edge. Thus the declaration of Sam Sharpe as national hero in 1975, honouring his role as leader of the great slave rebellion of 1831–32, was marked in Montego Bay by the renaming of Charles Square as Sam Sharpe Square, the site of his public hanging. Throughout its history, Charles Square had been commonly known as Parade. Some claimed it was named for either Charles I or Charles II of England, but the more likely explanation is that its name came from Sir Charles Knowles, who was governor of Jamaica in the 1750s, the period of Montego Bay's early development. In 1975 the new name was welcomed: "Sam Sharpe Square is a befitting name in the sense that it will enhance, in a more modern context Montegonians desire to assert their traditional independence and freedom of thought and action in the same way as local national hero Sam Sharpe did in his own time."[15]

Of the original national heroes, Marcus Garvey (declared in 1964) is honoured in Garveymeade. Marcus Garvey Drive was named for him in 1956, marking the prominent new route formerly called the Foreshore Road, named for its littoral location. Marcus Garvey Avenue existed even earlier, but this "undistinguished roadway near the city dunghill" disappeared from the map.[16] Paul Bogle (declared in 1965) has only a small square fronting the Morant Bay courthouse. George William Gordon (also declared in 1965) has his name attached to the parliament building in Kingston, generally known as Gordon House. Alexander Bustamante (declared in 1969) is recalled in the Bustamante Highway. Norman Manley (declared in 1969) named Norman Manley Airport, formerly known as Palisadoes, and Manley Avenue. Not a national hero, the late Prime Minister Donald Sangster had his name given to the airport of Montego Bay. Nanny, declared in 1975 along with Sam Sharpe, is unusual in having had places named for her in her lifetime – Nanny Town and New Nanny Town, named in the eighteenth century – and she got a new name in Nannyville, on Mountain View Avenue, Kingston. The site of memorialization, National Heroes Park, was formerly called George VI Park, which was in turn an imperial relabelling of Kingston Racecourse.

Although independence saw an end to the naming of significant public places for imperial Britons, political fame remained important in the choosing of names from outside the island. Two high schools built in the 1970s, Jose Marti CTH and Garvey Maceo CLR, recognized Cuban revolutionaries of the late nineteenth century – both of them having taken refuge in Jamaica – rather than the contemporary revolutionaries who funded them. Julius Nyerere of Tanzania was honoured by Nyerere Farm in the 1970s, and Nelson Mandela of South Africa by Mandela Highway and Mandela Park in the 1990s. All of these names come from the political left, but they were carefully chosen.

The official naming of places was often paralleled by the use of alternatives, sometimes applied to subvert an established public version or simply to provide a familiar alias or playful pun. The simplest form of alternative naming derives from abbreviation, so that Savanna la Mar is reduced to "Sav" and Ocho Rios to "Ochie".[17] Montego Bay was long known to people in its hinterland simply as "the Bay" but modern Jamaicans abbreviate it to "Mo Bay" and tourists say "Montego". These forms are mutually comprehensible, but "The Republic" is more internal, pointing to the separate existence of Montego Bay, far from Kingston. Alternative naming was also common among followers of alternative cultures. In the 1950s, for example, newly inhabited camps of Rastafarians referred to Wareika Hill as "Warrior's Hill", and Back o' Wall was called "Egypt". A biblical geography drew in names from Africa and the Middle East, building on the precedents set by the planter class, and conflating Ethiopia and Zion.[18] In the 1990s Waltham Park Road was said to serve as "a 'Gaza Strip' for the thousands of nearby residents who seek the pleasures of its night life".[19] Lovenor Pen, off the Dyke Road, near Gregory Park, St Catherine, existed as a squatter community developed following hurricane Gilbert of 1988, but "known by most people as 'Lesser Portmore' " because it lacked the modern facilities and fabric of the better-resourced Greater Portmore.[20]

Very often, official names are used alongside local and informal names, the two combined into a system of reference that does not need to respect or recognize any difference in the validity of one or the other. For example, informal place names, not inscribed on any map, can easily find their way into the public record and as a consequence come to possess an "official" or legal status through their customary role in spatial reference. A similar pattern can be identified in the Maroon tradition of toponymy.[21] The coexistence of these layers of naming practice represents the variety of ways in which meaning has been given to the landscape, and further evidence of the creolization and creativity that has made Jamaican place names Jamaican.

Notes

Chapter 1

1. *Gleaner*, 10 June 1988, 15. Cf. Jean L. Goulbourne, "Same Names, Different Places", *Gleaner, Outlook*, 18 October 1998, 24.

2. James G. Sawkins, *Reports on the Geology of Jamaica; or, Part II of the West Indian Survey: Memoirs of the Geological Survey* (London: Longmans, Green and Co., 1869), 88n.

3. Philip Henry Gosse, *A Naturalist's Sojourn in Jamaica* (London: Longman, Brown, Green, and Longmans, 1851), 86.

4. Niclas Burenhult and Stephen C. Levinson, "Language and Landscape: A Cross-linguistic Perspective", *Language Sciences* 30 (2008): 137–38; Jeff Malpas, *Heidegger's Topology: Being, Place, World* (Cambridge, Mass.: MIT Press, 2006), 266; R.J. Nelson, *Naming and Reference: The Link of Word and Object* (London: Routledge, 1992); F.G. Cassidy, "The Etiology of Place Naming", *Names* 32 (1984): 402–6; George Redmonds, *Names and History: People, Places, and Things* (London: Hambledon and London, 2004). Valuable comparative studies include Kenneth Cameron, *English Place-Names* (London: B.T. Batsford, 1996 [1961]); George R. Stewart, *Names on the Globe* (New York: Oxford University Press, 1975); W.F.H. Nicolaisen, *Scottish Place-Names: Their Study and Significance* (London: B.T. Batsford, 1976); Margaret Gelling, *Signposts to the Past: Place-Names and the History of England* (Chichester: Phillimore and Co., 1997 [1978]); Margaret Gelling, *Place-Names in the Landscape* (London: J.M. Dent and Sons, 1984).

5. Erwin G. Gudde, "Naming Storms", *Names* 3 (1955): 34–37; Roger A. Pielke, *The Hurricane* (London: Routledge, 1990), 181; David DeCamp, "Cart Names in Jamaica", *Names* 8 (1960): 17.

6. Maria Nugent, *A Journal of a Voyage to, and Residence in, the Island of Jamaica, from 1801 to 1805, and of Subsequent Events in England from 1801 to 1811* (London, 1839), 2:73.

7. Cf. Riva Berleant-Schiller, "Hidden Places and Creole Forms: Naming the Barbudan Landscape", *Professional Geographer* 43 (1991): 98–99.

8. Joe Dillard, "Names or Slogans: Some Problems from the Cameroun, the Caribbean, Burundi, and the United States", *Caribbean Studies* 9 (1970): 104–10.

9. Nugent, *Journal,* 2:72.

10. Lorna Clarke, "My Favourite Jamaican Place Names", *Gleaner, Outlook,* 11 November 2001, 48. Cf. Lance Evans, "Interesting Jamaican Place Names", *Weekly Gleaner (N.A.),* 28 July–3 August 1995, 32.

11. Don L.F. Nilsen, "American Proper Noun Reference: The Humorous Naming of Persons, Places, and Things", *Names* 30 (1982): 171–82; Stanley Lieberson, *A Matter of Taste: How Names, Fashions, and Culture Change* (New Haven: Yale University Press, 2000).

12. E. Relph, *Place and Placelessness* (London: Pion, 1976), 29–30.

13. Cameron, *English Place-Names,* 27; Burenhult and Levinson, "Language and Landscape", 145–46.

14. George R. Stewart, "A Classification of Place Names", *Names* 2 (1954): 1–13; Vivian Zinkin, "The Syntax of Place-Names", *Names* 17 (1969): 181–98; Robert E. Ford, "Toponymic Generics, Environment, and Culture History in Pre-Independence Belize", *Names* 39 (1991): 5; Grant Smith, "Describing Types of Placename Information", *Names* 40 (1992): 299–306; Frank Nuessel, *The Study of Names: A Guide to the Principles and Topics* (Westport, Conn.: Greenwood Press, 1992), 47–50; Margaret Gelling, "Place-names and Landscape", in *The Uses of Place-Names,* ed. Simon Taylor, 75–100 (Edinburgh: Scottish Cultural Press, 1998); Robert Rennick, "How to Study Placenames", *Names* 53 (2005): 298–301.

15. Christian Jacob, *The Sovereign Map: Theoretical Approaches to Cartography throughout History* (Chicago: University of Chicago Press, 2006), 201; Mark Monmonier, *From Squaw Tit to Whorehouse Meadow: How Maps Name, Claim, and Inflame* (Chicago: University of Chicago Press, 2006), 8–9; Ivan Lind, "Geography and Place Names", in *Readings in Cultural Geography,* ed. Philip L. Wagner and Marvin W. Mikesell, 118–28 (Chicago: University of Chicago Press, 1962).

16. Hamill Kenny, "Place-Names from Surnames", *Names* 18 (1970): 137–54.

17. Ulrich Groenke, "Spurious Attribution of Meaning in Place-Name Translations", *Names* 15 (1967): 119–25; Nuessel, *Study of Names,* 54–58; Davide Buscaldi and Paulo Rosso, "A Conceptual Density-Based Approach to the Disambiguation of Toponyms", *International Journal of Geographical Information Science* 22 (2008): 301–13.

18. Patents, 1846, f. 154 (Jamaica Archives, Spanish Town).

19. G.W. Lasker, *Surnames and Genetic Structure* (Cambridge: Cambridge University Press, 1985); Redmonds, *Names and History,* 46–49.

20. Roger L. Payne, "Development and Implementation of the National Geographic Names Database", *Names* 43 (1995): 307–14; Monmonier, *From Squaw Tit*

to Whorehouse Meadow, 29–32; Carole Hough, "A Database for English Placenames", *Names* 43 (1995): 255–74.

21. Richard D.E. Burton, "Names and Naming in Afro-Caribbean Cultures", *New West Indian Guide* 73 (1999): 35–58; John Thornton, "Central African Names and African-American Naming Patterns", *William and Mary Quarterly* 50 (1993): 727–42; Jerome S. Handler and JoAnn Jacoby, "Slaves Names and Naming in Barbados, 1650–1830", *William and Mary Quarterly* 53 (1996): 685–728; Trevor G. Burnard, "Slave Naming Patterns: Onomastics and the Taxonomy of Race in Eighteenth-Century Jamaica", *Journal of Interdisciplinary History* 31 (2001): 325–46; Mark Sebba, *Spelling and Society: The Culture and Politics of Orthography Around the World* (Cambridge: Cambridge University Press, 2007), 118–26.

22. Donald J. Orth, "The US Board on Geographic Names: An Overview", *Names* 38 (1990): 165–72; United States Board on Geographic Names, *Directions for the Treatment of Geographical Names in Jamaica* (Washington, DC: Board on Geographic Names, 1947), 1–2.

23. *Gleaner*, 30 October 1969, 3; *Gleaner*, 16 December 1971, 31; Richard N. Hall, "Recent Progress in the International Standardization of Geographical Names", in *Proceedings of the Eighth International Congress of Onomastic Sciences*, ed. D.P. Blok (The Hague: Mouton and Co., 1966), 224–29; Richard R. Randall, "A Report and Summary of the Fourth United Nations Conference on the Standardization of Geographical Names, Geneva 1982", *Names* 32 (1984): 343–46; Richard R. Randall, "The US Board on Geographic Names and Its Work in Foreign Areas", *Names* 38 (1990): 173–82; Richard R. Randall, "The US Board on Geographic Names and International Programs", *Names* 39 (1991): 249–56.

24. Raven I. McDavid Jr, Raymond K. O'Cain, George T. Dorrill, and David Fischer, "Names *Not* on the Map", *Names* 33 (1985): 216–24; Audrey R. Duckert, "Place Nicknames", *Names* 21 (1973): 153–60; Lewis Heck, "Geographic Names in the US Coast and Geodetic Survey", *Names* 1 (1953): 109; Berleant-Schiller, "Hidden Places", 100.

25. Cf. Lucie Alida Möller, "Metadata for South African Geographic Names Databases", *Names* 47 (1999): 297–311; Ruth E. Richardson, "Using Field-Names", *Landscapes* 3 (2002): 70–83; Christopher Taylor, *Fields in the English Landscape* (Stroud, UK: Sutton Publishing, 2000 [1975]); J. Graham Cruickshank, "Field Names in Barbados", *Journal of the Barbados Museum and Historical Society* 2 (1935): 166.

26. For the history of Jamaica's maps, see B. W. Higman, *Jamaica Surveyed: Plantation Maps and Plans of the Eighteenth and Nineteenth Centuries* (Kingston: Institute of Jamaica Publications, 1988), 36–37; L. Alan Eyre, "James Robertson: Jamaica's Mapmaker Superlative", *Jamaica Journal* 17, no. 4 (1984–85): 57–63; Kit S. Kapp, *The Printed Maps of Jamaica up to 1825* (Kingston: Bolivar Press, 1968).

27. Higman, *Jamaica Surveyed*, 36–37; Eyre, "James Robertson".

28. Alistair Macdonald, *Mapping the World: A History of the Directorate of Overseas Surveys 1946–1985* (London: Her Majesty's Stationery Office, 1996), 49.

29. B. W. Higman, *Slave Population and Economy in Jamaica, 1807–1834* (Cambridge: Cambridge University Press, 1976), 9–10, 30–34, 46–51.

30. Jeremy W. Crampton, "Maps as Social Constructions: Power, Communication, and Visualization", *Progress in Human Geography* 25 (2001): 235–52; Charles W.J. Withers, "Authorizing Landscape: 'Authority', Naming, and the Ordnance Survey's Mapping of the Scottish Highlands in the Nineteenth Century", *Journal of Historical Geography* 26 (2000): 532–54.

31. George R. Stewart, *Names on the Land: A Historical Account of Placenaming in the United States* (San Francisco: Lexikos, 1982 [1945]), 444n3. Cf. Lewis Heck, "The Problem of a National Gazetteer", *Names* 1 (1953): 234; Monmonier, *From Squaw Tit to Whorehouse Meadow*, 21; Eugene Hunn, "Columbia Plateau Indian Place Names: What Can They Teach Us?" *Journal of Linguistic Anthropology* 6 (1996): 22.

32. Raven I. McDavid Jr, "Linguistic Geographic and Toponymic Research", *Names* 6 (1958): 65–73; W.F.H. Nicolaisen, "Scottish Place Names as Evidence for Language Change", *Names* 41 (1993): 306–13; Eric P. Hamp, "The Linguistic Evidence of Placenames for History", *Names* 43 (1995): 131–34; K.M. Laurence, "Continuity and Change in Trinidadian Toponyms", *New West Indian Guide* 50 (1975): 123–42.

Chapter 2

1. J.H. Elliott, *Empires of the Atlantic World: Britain and Spain in America 1492–1830* (New Haven: Yale University Press, 2006), 32–34; Stephen C. Levinson and David P. Wilkins, eds., *Grammars of Space: Explorations in Cognitive Diversity* (Cambridge: Cambridge University Press, 2006).

2. Cf. A.J. Christopher, *The British Empire at Its Zenith* (London: Croom Helm, 1988), 230–34.

3. Alan Rayburn, "The Transfer of Scottish Placenames to Canada", *Names* 47 (1999): 313; Leonard R.N. Ashley, "The Spanish Placenames of California: Proposition 1994", *Names* 44 (1996): 3–40; Harold E. Gulley, "British and Irish Toponyms in the South Atlantic States", *Names* 43 (1995): 86.

4. Laurence, "Continuity and Change in Trinidadian Toponyms", 124–30.

5. Marjorie Bingham Wesche, "Place Names as a Reflection of Cultural Change: An Example from the Lesser Antilles", *Caribbean Studies* 12 (1972): 95–96. See also Ford, "Toponymic Generics", 21–22.

6. Samuel Eliot Morison, *Admiral of the Ocean Sea: A Life of Christopher Columbus* (Boston: Northeastern University Press, 1983 [1942]), 450–51; Francisco Morales Padrón, *Spanish Jamaica*, trans. Patrick E. Bryan (Kingston: Ian Randle Publishers, 2003), 19, 23.

7. Nils M. Holmer, "Indian Place Names in South America and the Antilles II", *Names* 8 (1960): 219; Frederic G. Cassidy, "The Earliest Placenames in Jamaica", *Names* 36 (1988): 152; R.C. Dallas, *The History of the Maroons* (London: T. N. Longman and O. Rees, 1803), 1:xv; David Buisseret, ed., *Jamaica in 1687: The Taylor Manuscript in the National Library of Jamaica* (Kingston: University of the West Indies Press, 2008), 122.

8. Leonardo Olschki, "The Columbian Nomenclature of the Lesser Antilles", *Geographical Review* 33 (1943): 397; David Geggus, "The Naming of Haiti", *New West Indian Guide* 71 (1997): 43.

9. Cassidy, "Earliest Placenames in Jamaica", 154–55; Patrick Browne, *The Civil and Natural History of Jamaica* (New York: Arno, 1972 [1789]), 260.

10. Cassidy, "Earliest Placenames in Jamaica", 154–56.

11. Morison, *Admiral of the Ocean Sea*, 640–42; William Randel, "Survival of Pre-English Place Names in Jamaica", *Names* 8 (1960): 25; Morales Padrón, *Spanish Jamaica*, 9, 20.

12. Edward Long, *The History of Jamaica* (London: T. Lowndes, 1774), 2:139; Cassidy, "Earliest Placenames in Jamaica", 153–54; Morales Padrón, *Spanish Jamaica*, 26.

13. *West Indian Review*, January 1958, 20; Esther Chapman, ed., *Pleasure Island: The Book of Jamaica* (Kingston: Arawak, 1952 [1951]), 172; *Gleaner*, 22 October 1993, 45; Peter Abrahams, *Jamaica: An Island Mosaic* (London: Her Majesty's Stationery Office, 1957), xiv; Peter Abrahams, *The View from Coyaba* (London: Faber and Faber, 1985), 11.

14. Quoted in Cassidy, "Earliest Placenames", 151.

15. Charles Leslie, *A New and Exact Account of Jamaica* (Edinburgh: A. Kincaid, 1739), 55.

16. Morison, *Admiral of the Ocean Sea*, 451–53, 474–76; Morales Padrón, *Spanish Jamaica*, 2–3.

17. Cassidy, "Earliest Placenames in Jamaica", 155; Randel, "Survival of Pre-English Place Names in Jamaica", 24–25; Long, *History of Jamaica,* 1:347–49.

18. Long, *History of Jamaica,* 2:60; Frank Cundall, *Place-Names of Jamaica* (Kingston: Institute of Jamaica, 1939), 4; Cassidy, "Earliest Placenames in Jamaica", 156.

19. Long, *History of Jamaica,* 2:57, 72, 91.

20. Edgar Mayhew Bacon and Eugene Murray Aaron, *The New Jamaica* (New York: Walbridge and Co., 1890), 175.

21. Long, *History of Jamaica,* 2:186–88.

22. *Gleaner*, 18 February 1996, 12A.

23. Cf. Laurence, "Continuity and Change", 124.

24. Frank Cundall, *Historic Jamaica* (London: Institute of Jamaica, 1915), 42; Long, *History of Jamaica,* 2:1.

25. Wilma Williams, "Early Kingston", *Jamaica Journal* 6, nos. 2–3 (June–September 1971): 3.

26. Cundall, *Historic Jamaica*, 42–43; Long, *History of Jamaica,* 2:1, 102, 182.

27. *Gleaner*, 19 June 1984, 12; US Board on Geographic Names, *Treatment of Geographical Names in Jamaica*, 17; Returns to the House of Assembly under 1 Vic. Cap. 34 (Jamaica Archives, Spanish Town).

28. Mona Macmillan, *The Land of Look Behind: A Study of Jamaica* (London: Faber and Faber, 1957), 11.

29. *Gleaner*, 11 September 1996, 2A.

30. Trevor Burnard, "European Migration to Jamaica, 1655–1780", *William and Mary Quarterly* 53 (1996): 780–81; David Hackett Fischer, *Albion's Seed: Four British Folkways in America* (New York: Oxford University Press, 1989), 238–40, 442–45, 639–42. References in the text to the counties of the British Isles are to those that existed before the reforms of the 1970s. The 1972 (England and Wales) and 1973 (Scotland) Local Government Acts greatly altered county boundaries. Some counties disappeared while new ones were created. Before the reforms, the pattern of counties changed relatively little over many centuries, and it is these units that provided transfer-names for Jamaica.

31. Gulley, "British and Irish Toponyms in the South Atlantic States", 96; Rayburn, "Transfer of Scottish Placenames to Canada", 313; Ian A. Fraser, "Placenames of Scottish Origin in Nova Scotia", *Names* 34 (1986): 364–72.

32. Peter Marsden, *An Account of the Island of Jamaica* (Newcastle: the author, 1788), 7; Richard B. Sheridan, "The Role of the Scots in the Economy and Society of the West Indies", *Annals of the New York Academy of Sciences* 292 (1977): 94–106; Alan L. Karras, *Sojourners in the Sun: Scottish Migrants in Jamaica and the Chesapeake, 1740–1800* (Ithaca: Cornell University Press, 1992).

33. John G. Robb, "Toponymy in Lowland Scotland: Depictions of Linguistic Heritage", *Scottish Geographical Magazine* 112 (1996): 169, 175; Rayburn, "The Transfer of Scottish Placenames to Canada", 317.

34. Kathleen Wilson, "Empire, Trade, and Popular Politics in Mid-Hanoverian Britain: The Case of Admiral Vernon", *Past and Present* 121 (1988): 74–109; *Gleaner*, 18 February 1996, 12A.

35. Cf. Ruth L. Pearce, "Welsh Place-Names in Southeastern Pennsylvania", *Names* 11 (1963): 31–43.

36. Henriette Walter, *Honni soit qui mal y pense: L'incroyable histoire d'amour entre le français et l'anglais* (Paris: Robert Laffont, 2002), 203–16.

37. Betty Wood, ed., *The Letters of Simon Taylor of Jamaica to Chaloner Arcedekne, 1765–1775* (Cambridge: Cambridge University Press, 2002), 76, 107.

38. *Gleaner*, 18 February 1996, 12A.

39. Long, *History of Jamaica,* 2:91; Mary Seacole, *Wonderful Adventures of Mrs Seacole in Many Lands* (New York: Oxford University Press, 1988 [1857]).

40. Wood, *Letters of Simon Taylor*, 85.

41. Long, *History of Jamaica,* 2:203.

42. Cf. Grace Partridge Smith, "They Call It Egypt", *Names* 2 (1954): 51–54.

43. Chris Salewicz, quoted in David Howard, *Kingston: A Cultural and Literary History* (Kingston: Ian Randle Publishers, 2005), 231; Robin Law, *Ouidah: The Social History of a West African Slaving "Port" 1727–1892* (Oxford: James Currey, 2004), 2; K. G. Davies, *The Royal African Company* (London: Longman, 1957), 6, 121; Philip D. Curtin, *The Atlantic Slave Trade: A Census* (Madison: University of Wisconsin Press, 1969), 227.

44. Adam Kuper, *Changing Jamaica* (London: Routledge and Kegan Paul, 1976), 93.

45. *Gleaner*, 11 September 1996, 2A; *Gleaner*, 6 January 2002, 3A.

46. Wilbur Zelinsky, "Classical Town Names in the United States: The Historical Geography of an American Idea", *Geographical Review* 57 (1967): 464, 486; G. Thomas Fairclough, " 'New Light' on 'Old Zion' ", *Names* 8 (1960): 75–85.

47. *Gleaner*, 30 June 1994, 32.

48. Cf. Stanley D. Brunn and James O. Wheeler, "Notes on the Geography of Religious Town Names in the U.S.", *Names* 14 (1966): 197–202; John Leighley, "Biblical Place-Names in the United States", *Names* 27 (1979): 46–59; Kenneth A. Robb, "Names of Grants in Colonial Maryland", *Names* 17 (1969): 263–77.

49. Douglas Hall, *In Miserable Slavery: Thomas Thistlewood in Jamaica, 1750–86* (London: Macmillan, 1989), 48.

50. Nugent, *Journal,* 1:229.

51. Jacob Viner, *The Role of Providence in the Social Order: An Essay in Intellectual History* (Princeton: Princeton University Press, 1972).

Chapter 3

1. Gosse, *Naturalist's Sojourn in Jamaica,* 86.

2. Paul J. McCartney, *Henry De la Beche: Observations on an Observer* (Cardiff: Friends of the National Museum of Wales, 1977), 23.

3. Erna Brodber, *Woodside, Pear Tree Grove P.O.* (Kingston: University of the West

Indies Press, 2004), 126; James M. Phillippo, *Jamaica Its Past and Present State* (London: John Snow, 1843), 229.

4. Sawkins, *Reports on the Geology of Jamaica*, 92–94.

5. Swithin Wilmot, " 'A Stake in the Soil': Land and Creole Politics in Free Jamaica – the 1849 Elections", in *In the Shadow of the Plantation: Caribbean History and Legacy* , ed. Alvin O. Thompson (Kingston: Ian Randle Publishers, 2002), 321–22.

6. Higman, *Jamaica Surveyed*, 286.

7. Phillippo, *Jamaica Its Past and Present State*, 229.

8. John Field, *Place-Names of Great Britain and Ireland* (Newton Abbot, UK: David and Charles, 1980), 33.

9. Christian Schnakenbourg, *Histoire de l'industrie sucrière en Guadeloupe aux XIXe et XXe siècles: Tome I, La crise du système esclavagiste (1835–1847)* (Paris: L'Harmattan, 1980), 29.

10. James H. Stark, *Stark's Jamaica Guide (Illustrated)* (Boston: James H. Stark, 1898), 95–96.

11. [Alfred], *Account of a Shooting Excursion on the Mountains near Dromilly Estate, in the Parish of Trelawny, and Island of Jamaica, in the Month of October, 1824!!!* (London: Harvey and Darton, 1825), 7, 10.

12. George R. Stewart, *American Place-Names: A Concise and Selective Dictionary for the Continental United States of America* (New York: Oxford University Press, 1970), 457.

13. Cundall, *Place-Names of Jamaica*, 15. Cf. Henri Dorion, "L'homonymie et l'autore-production des noms de lieux", *Names* 47 (1999): 223–32; Schnakenbourg, *Histoire de l'industrie sucrière en Guadeloupe*, 27–30.

14. James Kari, "Some Principles of Alaskan Athabaskan Toponymic Knowledge", in *General and Amerindian Linguistics: In Remembrance of Stanley Newman*, ed. Mary Ritchie Key and Henry M. Hoenigswald (Berlin: Mouton de Gruyter, 1989), 135–36.

Chapter 4

1. Peter Fisher and Jo Wood, "What Is a Mountain? Or the Englishman Who Went Up a Boolean Geographical Concept but Realised It Was Fuzzy", *Geography* 83 (1998): 247–56; Peter Fisher, Jo Wood and Tao Cheng, "Where Is Helvellyn? Fuzziness of Multi-Scale Landscape Morphometry", *Transactions of the Institute of British Geographers* 29 (2004): 107.

2. Long, *History of Jamaica*, 2:124, 130.

3. Sawkins, *Reports on the Geology of Jamaica*, 42–43, 99. See also Robert Baird,

Impressions and Experiences of the West Indies and North America in 1849 (Philadelphia: Lea and Blanchard, 1850), 87; Forrest Shreve, *A Montane Rain-Forest: A Contribution to the Physiological Plant Geography of Jamaica* (Washington, DC: Publication No. 199, Carnegie Institution of Washington, 1914), 7.

4. James Maxwell, *Remarks on the Present State of Jamaica* (London: Smith, Elder and Co., 1848), 5; Sawkins, *Reports on the Geology of Jamaica*, 42–43.

5. Erwin G. Gudde, "Sugarloaf", *Names* 4 (1956): 241–43.

6. Leslie, *New and Exact Account of Jamaica*, 180.

7. Elisabeth K. Gudde, "Mocho Mountain", *Names* 5 (1957): 246–48.

8. Shreve, *Montane Rain-Forest*, 7; US Board on Geographic Names, *Treatment of Geographical Names in Jamaica*, 7.

9. Wilbur Zelinsky, "Some Problems in the Distribution of Generic Terms in the Place-Names of the Northeastern United States", *Annals of the Association of American Geographers* 45 (1955): 333.

10. Baird, *Impressions and Experiences*, 87.

11. Long, *History of Jamaica*, 2:43. Cf. US Board on Geographic Names, *Treatment of Geographical Names in Jamaica*, 11; Frank Fonda Taylor, "From Hellshire to Healthshire: The Genesis of the Tourist Industry in Jamaica", in *Trade, Government, and Society in Caribbean History 1700–1920: Essays Presented to Douglas Hall*, ed. B.W. Higman (Kingston: Heinemann Educational Books Caribbean, 1983), 139, 151; Howard, *Kingston*, 231.

12. Marjorie M. Sweeting, *Karst Landforms* (London: Macmillan, 1972), 128.

13. K.E. Ingram, *Sources of Jamaican History 1655–1838: A Bibliographical Survey with Particular Reference to Manuscript Sources* (Zug, Switzerland: Inter Documentation Company Ag, 1976), 1:287; Shreve, *Montane Rain-Forest*, 8.

14. Shreve, *Montane Rain-Forest*, 7.

15. Robert Mowbray Howard, ed., *Records and Letters of the Family of the Longs of Longville, Jamaica, and Hampton Lodge, Surrey* (London: Simpkin, Marshall, Hamilton, Kent and Co., 1925), 1:42.

16. Sweeting, *Karst Landforms*, 192; J.N. Jennings, *Karst Geomorphology* (Oxford: Basil Blackwell, 1985), 124–29; William B. White, *Geomorphology and Hydrology of Karst Terrains* (New York: Oxford University Press, 1988), 29, 41.

17. US Board on Geographic Names, *Treatment of Geographical Names in Jamaica*, 12; Sweeting, *Karst Landforms*, 202–3.

18. Celia Millward, "Place-Name Generics in Providence, R.I, 1636–1736", *Names* 19 (1971): 164–65; Edwin Wallace McMullen, Jr, *English Topographic Terms in Florida 1563–1874* (Gainesville: University of Florida Press, 1953), 76.

19. Browne, *Civil and Natural History of Jamaica*, 11.

20. Alan Fincham, *Jamaica Underground: The Caves, Sinkholes, and Underground Rivers of the Island* (Kingston: The Press, University of the West Indies, 1997), 167.

21. Sawkins, *Reports on the Geology of Jamaica*, 238; Fincham, *Jamaica Underground*, 228; Sweeting, *Karst Landforms*, 70–72.

22. Dallas, *History of the Maroons,* 1:39–40.

23. Sweeting, *Karst Landforms*, 69–73; Jennings, *Karst Geomorphology*, 120–21; White, *Geomorphology and Hydrology of Karst Terrains*, 29, 31–32, 108–11.

24. P. Lyew-Ayee, H.A. Viles, and G.E. Tucker, "The Use of GIS-based Digital Morphometric Techniques in the Study of Cockpit Karst", *Earth Surface Processes and Landforms* 32 (2007): 166, 177; Fincham, *Jamaica Underground*, 438.

25. Dallas, *The History of the Maroons,* 1:opp. 1.

26. Sawkins, *Reports on the Geology of Jamaica*, 216, 218.

27. Bacon and Aaron, *New Jamaica*, 210.

28. *Gleaner*, 30 August 1892, 4; *Gleaner*, 13 October 1894, 6; *Gleaner*, 15 October 1894, 4; Stark, *Stark's Jamaica Guide*, 117–18.

29. Lise Tole, "Measurement and Management of Human-Induced Patterns of Forest Fragmentation: A Case Study", *Environmental Management* 37 (2006): 790, 798.

30. Cf. Zelinsky, "Some Problems", 337.

31. Ibid., 337.

32. Clarence W. Minkel, "Names in the Mapping of Original Vegetation", *Names* 5 (1957): 157–61; Timothy S. Brothers and Lisa M. Kennedy, "The Changing Geography of Vegetation Placenames in the Indiana Prairie Border Region", *Names* 40 (1992): 18.

33. Brothers and Kennedy, "Changing Geography of Vegetation Placenames", 21.

34. Leo Waibel, "Place Names as an Aid in the Reconstruction of the Original Vegetation of Cuba", *Geographical Review* 33 (1943): 379.

35. Richard Blome, *A Description of the Island of Jamaica* (London: J. Williams, Jr, 1672), 3–5; Leslie, *New and Exact Account of Jamaica*, 25; Joseph John Gurney, *A Winter in the West Indies, Described in Familiar Letters to Henry Clay, of Kentucky* (London: John Murray, 1840), 161; McMullen, *English Topographic Terms in Florida*, 191.

36. Long, *History of Jamaica*, 2:62. Cf. Buisseret, *Jamaica in 1687*, 123.

37. Long, *History of Jamaica,* 2:189.

38. Ibid., 2:56.

39. Brodber, *Woodside, Pear Tree Grove*, 137–38.

Chapter 5

1. Dallas, *History of the Maroons,* 1:xv.

2. Michael Chenoweth, *The 18th Century Climate of Jamaica: Derived from the Journals of Thomas Thistlewood 1750–1786* (Philadelphia: American Philosophical Society, 2003), 75; Brian J. Hudson, *The Waterfalls of Jamaica: Sublime and Beautiful Objects* (Kingston: University of the West Indies Press, 2001), 69–70.

3. Cf. R.J. Eyles, "When Is a Stream Not a Stream?" *Malaysian Journal of Tropical Geography* 1 (1980): 7–8; Niclas Burenhult, "Streams of Words: Hydrological Lexicon in Jahai", *Language Sciences* 30 (2008): 182–99.

4. Mark Patrick Taylor and Robert Stokes, "When Is a River Not a River? Consideration of the Legal Definition of a River for Geomorphologists Practising in New South Wales, Australia", *Australian Geographer* 36 (2005): 183–200; Eyles, "When Is a Stream Not a Stream?"; Zelinsky, "Some Problems", 322.

5. Leslie, *New and Exact Account of Jamaica*, 19.

6. Dallas, *History of the Maroons,* 1:lxxiv.

7. Ibid., 1:lxxiv; Zelinsky, "Some Problems", 325; Jon C. Campbell, "Stream Generic Terms as Indicators of Historical Settlement Patterns", *Names* 39 (1991): 338.

8. Kenneth M. Bilby, *True-Born Maroons* (Kingston: Ian Randle Publishers, 2006), 259; Zelinsky, "Some Problems", 326; Campbell, "Stream Generic Terms", 337–38.

9. Long, *History of Jamaica,* 3:810.

10. Ibid., 2:50, 90.

11. Sawkins, *Reports on the Geology of Jamaica*, 17, 69.

12. Ibid., 18.

13. Fincham, *Jamaica Underground*, 39.

14. Bacon and Aaron, *New Jamaica*, 170.

15. Dallas, *History of the Maroons,* 1:lxxiv.

16. Long, *History of Jamaica,* 2:57.

17. Cf. McMullen, *English Topographic Terms in Florida*, 201.

18. Sweeting, *Karst Landforms*, 211.

19. Mattias Jacobsson, *Wells, Meres, and Pools: Hydronymic Terms in the Anglo-Saxon Landscape* (Uppsala, Sweden: Uppsala University Library, 1997), 34–35, 222–27; Cameron, *English Place-Names*, 169–70, 193.

20. Sweeting, *Karst Landforms*, 211; Sawkins, *Reports on the Geology of Jamaica*, 53.

21. Mrs Henry Lynch, *The Wonders of the West Indies* (London: Seeley, Jackson, and Halliday, 1856), 132–34; Baird, *Impressions and Experiences*, 86; Arthur Raper, "Gullies and What They Mean", *Social Forces* 16 (1937): 201.

22. Michael Day, "Limestone Valley Systems in North Central Jamaica", *Caribbean Geography* 2, no. 1 (November 1985): 20–22; Eyles, "When Is a Stream Not a Stream?", 8; Jennings, *Karst Geomorphology*, 88–106.

23. Millward, "Place-Name Generics in Providence, R.I.", 162; Meredith F. Burrill, "Toponymic Generics II", *Names* 4 (1956): 235; A.R. Dunlap, "Gat and Gut", *Names* 5 (1957): 248; McMullen, *English Topographic Terms in Florida*, 121.

24. Gad Heuman, *"The Killing Time": The Morant Bay Rebellion in Jamaica* (London: Macmillan Caribbean, 1994), 10.

25. Audrey R. Duckert, "Gutter: Its Rise and Fall", *Names* 4 (1956): 146–54; Millward, "Place-Name Generics in Providence, R.I.", 163.

26. *Gleaner*, 27 May 1929, 18; *Gleaner*, 16 June 1933, 20; *Gleaner*, 22 June 1934, 19.

27. McMullen, *English Topographic Terms in Florida*, 151–52.

28. Cf. ibid., 82, 106.

29. Long, *History of Jamaica,* 2:93–95.

Chapter 6

1. Leslie, *New and Exact Account of Jamaica*, 25.

2. Cf. Buisseret, *Jamaica in 1687*, 122.

3. Millward, "Place-Name Generics in Providence, R.I.", 158; Morales Padron, *Spanish Jamaica*, 206; Philip Wright and Paul F. White, *Exploring Jamaica: A Guide for Motorists* (London: Andre Deutsch, 1969), 63; Clinton V. Black, *The Story of Jamaica from Prehistory to the Present* (London: Collins, 1965 [1958]), 49.

4. Don W. Duckson Jr, "A Creek Is a Creek . . . or Is It?" *Names* 31 (1983): 51–61; Jon C. Campbell, "Stream Generic Terms", 337; Zelinsky, "Some Problems", 324–25. Cf. Ford, "Toponymic Generics", 12.

5. Blome, *Description of the Island of Jamaica*, 23.

6. Gosse, *Naturalist's Sojourn in Jamaica*, 50–51.

7. Buisseret, *Jamaica in 1687*, 122.

8. F.W. Morgan, *Ports and Harbours* (London: Hutchinson University Library, 1958 [1952]), 26, 54.

9. Cf. Buisseret, *Jamaica in 1687*, 121.

10. Ingram, *Sources of Jamaican History,* 1:286.

11. Sawkins, *Reports on the Geology of Jamaica*, 97; J.A. Steers, "The Cays and the Palisadoes, Port Royal, Jamaica", *Geographical Review* 30 (1940): 291; Michael Pawson and David Buisseret, *Port Royal, Jamaica* (Oxford: Clarendon Press, 1975), 13.

12. J.A. Steers, "The Coral Cays of Jamaica", *Geographical Journal* 95 (1940): 30; Steers,

"The Cays and the Palisadoes", 279–80. Cf. McMullen, *English Topographic Terms in Florida*, 83.

13. Cf. Buisseret, *Jamaica in 1687*, 123–26.

14. Steers, "The Coral Cays", 31.

15. Ibid., 32–37; J.A. Steers, "Sand Cays and Mangroves in Jamaica", *Geographical Journal* 96 (1940): 305; Steers, "The Cays and the Palisadoes", 281.

16. Buisseret, *Jamaica in 1687*, 53.

Chapter 7

1. Higman, *Slave Population and Economy*, 19, 32; Higman, *Jamaica Surveyed*, 12–15.

2. Cf. Jeffrey Alan Owens, "Naming the Plantation: An Analytical Survey from Tensas Parish, Louisiana", *Agricultural History* 68 (1994): 58–59.

3. "Report from the Select Committee on the Extinction of Slavery throughout the British Dominions", *British Parliamentary Papers* 20, no. 721 (1831–32), 434.

4. Mark Girouard, *Life in the English Country House: A Social and Architectural History* (New Haven: Yale University Press, 1978); Douglas Taylor, "Names on Dominica", *Names* 2 (1954): 37; Robb, "Names of Grants in Colonial Maryland", 265.

5. *Gleaner*, 11 July 1995, 3B; *Gleaner* 20 July 1995, 14A.

6. Douglas V. Armstrong, *The Old Village and the Great House: An Archaeological and Historical Examination of Drax Hall Plantation, St Ann's Bay, Jamaica* (Urbana: University of Illinois Press, 1990), 24.

7. *Gleaner*, 5 November 1898, 4.

8. Cf. Ford, "Toponymic Generics", 19.

9. William Beckford, *A Descriptive Account of the Island of Jamaica* (London: T. and J. Egerton, 1790), 2:169.

10. Gurney, *Winter in the West Indies*, 131; *The Importance of Jamaica to Great Britain, Consider'd* (London: A. Dodd, [1740]), 10; Marsden, *Account of the Island of Jamaica*, 10–11; Kingston Parish and Poll Tax Rolls, 1776, 1832 (Jamaica Archives).

11. For maps of the distribution of *pen* circa 1832 and 1880, see Higman, *Slave Population and Economy*, 33; Higman, *Jamaica Surveyed*, 15.

12. *Outlook, Gleaner*, 28 October 2001, 7.

13. Edmund Hickeringill, *Jamaica Viewed: With All the Ports, Harbours, and their Several Soundings, Town, and Settlements* (London: John Williams, 1661), 13; Hans Sloane, *A Voyage to the Islands Madera, Barbados, Nieves, S. Christophers, and Jamaica, with the Natural History of the Last of Those Islands* (London: 1707–25), 1:xvii; Long, *History of Jamaica*, 1:345.

14. Frederic G. Cassidy, *Jamaica Talk: Three Hundred Years of the English Language in Jamaica* (London: Macmillan, 1961), 95.

15. Beckford, *Descriptive Account* 2:167.

16. Higman, *Jamaica Surveyed*, 224.

17. Bernard Martin Senior, *Jamaica, As It Was, As It Is, and As It May Be* (London: T. Hurst, 1835), 39; *Royal Gazette*, 23 January and 6 March 1819; *St Jago de la Vega Gazette*, 29 September 1832; *Jamaica Quarterly Journal, and Literary Magazine* (Kingston) 2 (December 1818): 270, 275.

18. Cassidy, *Jamaica Talk*, 96. Cf. Ford, "Toponymic Generics", 19.

19. Blome, *Description of the Island of Jamaica*, 16; *Importance of Jamaica to Great Britain*, 8, 13.

20. Beckford, *Descriptive Account* 2:159–60.

21. *Jamaica Quarterly Journal* 2 (December 1818): 275.

22. *Gleaner*, 17 July 1933, 3.

23. Leslie, *New and Exact Account of Jamaica*, 180, 287.

24. Baird, *Impressions and Experiences*, 93.

25. McMullen, *English Topographic Terms in Florida*, 115.

26. Sawkins, *Reports on the Geology of Jamaica*, 67.

27. Ibid., 222.

28. Geraldine Mozley, ed., *Letters to Jane from Jamaica* (London: Institute of Jamaica, 1938), 20, 68; Hymie Rubenstein, " 'Bush', 'Garden', and 'Mountain' on the Leeward Coast of St Vincent and the Grenadines, 1719–1995", in *Islands, Forests, and Gardens in the Caribbean: Conservation and Conflict in Environmental History*, ed. Robert S. Anderson, Richard Grove, and Karis Hiebert (Oxford: Macmillan Caribbean, 2006), 194–95.

29. Beckford, *Descriptive Account*, 2:151–53; [Alfred], *Account of a Shooting Excursion*, 6.

30. Dallas, *History of the Maroons*, 1:245.

31. Nugent, *Journal*, 1:74.

32. *Watchman and Jamaica Free Press*, 29 May 1830, 6 November 1830; Benjamin McMahon, *Jamaica Plantership* (London: Effingham Wilson, 1839), 224.

33. *Gleaner*, 9 January 1892, 2.

34. *Falmouth Post*, 9 May 1854.

35. Ruth E. Richardson, "Using Field-Names", *Landscapes* 3 (2002): 70–83.

36. *Gleaner, Christmas Magazine*, 15 December 1956, 20.

37. Quoted in Hall, *In Miserable Slavery*, 40.

38. Patrick Leigh Fermor, *The Traveller's Tree: A Journey through the Caribbean Islands* (London: John Murray, 1950), 369.

39. Gelling, *Place-Names in the Landscape*, 235–45.

40. Taylor, *To Hell with Paradise*, 68–93.

Chapter 8

1. Hope Masterton Waddell, *Twenty-Nine Years in the West Indies and Central Africa* (London: T. Nelson and Sons, 1863), 147.

2. Phillippo, *Jamaica Its Past and Present State*, 216–29.

3. US Board on Geographic Names, *Treatment of Geographical Names in Jamaica*, 2–3; *Gleaner*, 8 December 1992, 27.

4. Phillippo, *Jamaica Its Past and Present State*, 221–22.

5. Black, *Story of Jamaica*, 122.

6. Phillippo, *Jamaica Its Past and Present State*, 223–25.

7. Ibid., 229; US Board on Geographic Names, *Treatment of Geographical Names in Jamaica*, 6.

8. Sawkins, *Reports on the Geology of Jamaica*, 103.

9. Leslie, *New and Exact Account of Jamaica*, 29.

10. Long, *History of Jamaica,* 2:1, 41–42, 102, 182.

11. Mavis C. Campbell, *The Maroons of Jamaica 1655–1796: A History of Resistance, Collaboration, and Betrayal* (Granby, Mass.: Begin and Garvey Publishers, 1988), 164–71; Bev Carey, *The Maroon Story: The Authentic and Original History of the Maroons in the History of Jamaica 1490–1880* (Gordon Town, Jamaica: Agouti Press, 1997), 386.

12. Campbell, *The Maroons of Jamaica*, 169, 179; Carey, *The Maroon Story*, 174, 387–88.

13. Kingston Parish and Poll Tax Rolls, 1832 (Jamaica Archives).

14. Cameron, *English Place-Names*, 133–34, 143–49.

15. Wilma Williams, "Early Kingston", *Jamaica Journal* 6, nos. 2–3 (June–September 1971): 3.

16. Colin Clarke, *Kingston, Jamaica: Urban Development and Social Change, 1692–2002* (Kingston: Ian Randle Publishers, 2006 [1975]), 178, 288; Kuper, *Changing Jamaica*, 93.

17. *Gleaner*, 9 February 1960, 15; *Gleaner*, 11 September 1996, 2A; Clarke, *Kingston*, 253.

18. Heuman, *"The Killing Time"*, 17–18.

19. William Earle, *Obi; or, the History of Three-Fingered Jack*, ed. Srinivas Aravamudan (Peterborough, Ont: Broadview Editions, 2005), 10–13; Bilby, *True-Born Maroons*, 308–12.

20. *Gleaner*, 30 November 1940, 7; *Gleaner*, 5 March 1948, 15.

21. *Gleaner*, 10 January 1935, 15; *Gleaner*, 10 September 1938, 12; *Gleaner*, 7 November 1938, 1; *Gleaner*, 29 November 1939, 16; *Gleaner*, 30 November 1940, 7; *Gleaner*, 5 December 1939, 9.

22. Sistren, *Lionheart Gal: Life Stories of Jamaican Women* (London: The Women's Press, 1986), 157.

23. *Gleaner*, 30 October 1931, 16; *Gleaner*, 27 December 1933, 3.

24. Colin Clarke, *Decolonizing the Colonial City: Urbanization and Stratification in Kingston, Jamaica* (Oxford: Oxford University Press, 2006), 61.

25. *Gleaner*, 29 September 1960, 3; *Gleaner*, 11 September 1996, 2A. Cf. Rob Rentenaar, "How Danish Is Tivoli?" *Names* 24 (1976): 24–29.

26. *Gleaner*, 31 October 1961, 1–2.

27. *Gleaner*, 26 May 1963, 10; *Gleaner*, 15 October 1963, 17.

28. Kingston Parish and Poll Tax Rolls, 1776, 1832 (Jamaica Archives); Waddell, *Twenty-Nine Years in the West Indies*, 147.

29. Clarke, *Kingston*, 75.

30. S. Lockett to Colonial Secretary, 17 September 1928: Public Gardens, Kingston – Improvement of Appearance, CSO 1B/5/77/1928/9 (Jamaica Archives).

31. *Gleaner*, 3 April 1968, 9–11.

32. *Gleaner*, 11 September 1996, 2A.

33. *Gleaner*, 31 May 1983, 12; *Gleaner*, 17 March 1958, 18; *Gleaner*, 30 April 1966, 20; *Gleaner*, 7 July 1971, 29.

34. Geof Brown, "The Truth about PRIDE", *Gleaner* 20 February 1998, 4A; *Gleaner* 12 June 2005, 3A.

35. *Gleaner*, 1 October 1995, 14A; *Gleaner*, 8 December 1996, 15F; *Gleaner*, 3 August 1997, 14A; *Gleaner*, 28 December 1997, 20B; *Gleaner*, 14 June 1998, 6C; *Gleaner*, 2 August 1998, 12B; *Gleaner*, 12 December 1999, 10C; *Gleaner*, 28 January 2001, 9F.

36. *Gleaner*, 8 August 1998, 6B; *Gleaner*, 8 December 1996, 15F.

37. Arthur Minton, "Names of Real-Estate Developments: I, II, and III", *Names* 7 (1959): 129–53, 233–55; 9 (1961): 8–36; Darrell A. Norris, "Unreal Estate: Words, Names, and Allusions in Suburban Home Advertising", *Names* 47 (1999): 365–80.

38. Cf. Gulley, "British and Irish Toponyms in the South Atlantic States", 97.

39. *Gleaner*, 26 June 1994, 28A; *Gleaner*, 30 June 1994, 32; *Gleaner*, 26 November 1995, 15E.

40. *Gleaner*, 24 September 1995, 8C; *Gleaner*, 17 January 1996, 6B; *Gleaner*, 19 February 1996, 11A.

41. *Gleaner*, 24 July 1994; *Gleaner*, 2 July 1995, 1E; *Gleaner*, 19 February 1996, 11A; *Gleaner*, 10 June 2001, 8B–9B.

42. *West Indian Review*, 12 February 1955, 15–16; *Gleaner*, 24 September 1995, 8C; *Gleaner*, 26 November 1995, 15E.

43. *Gleaner*, 17 January 1996, 6B.

44. *Gleaner*, 26 June 1994, 28A; *Gleaner*, 27 November 1994, 15C.

45. Minton, "Names of Real-Estate Developments: I", 141–43.

46. *Gleaner*, 18 February 1996, 12A; *Gleaner*, 18 February 1996, 12A; *Gleaner*, 18 February 1996, 12A.

47. *Gleaner*, 12 June 2005, 3A.

48. *Gleaner*, 18 June 1995, 8D–9D; Brochure in *Gleaner*, 15 March 1996; *Gleaner*, 23 June, 1996, 3F; *Gleaner*, 4 July 1996, 16A; *Gleaner*, 29 September 1996, 8E–9E.

Chapter 9

1. Laws of Jamaica, 1862, cap. 32, An act for making and maintaining a railway from Kingston to Stoney-Hill, and for other purposes.

2. Laws of Jamaica, 1865, cap. 30, An act to constitute the road number thirty-six, in the parish of Hanover, from the Lucea bridge, over Riley's river, to the main road at Glasgow, Westmoreland, a main road.

3. James Hakewill, *A Picturesque Tour of the Island of Jamaica* (London: 1825), 4.

4. Frank R. Hamlin, "Numbers in Placenames", *Names* 47 (1999): 233–42.

5. *Gleaner*, 28 October 1867, 3; *Gleaner*, 26 June 1876, 2.

6. War Office, Geographical Section, *Jamaica: Kingston District*, 1920 (C.O. 1047/516, National Archives, Kew, UK).

7. *Gleaner*, 11 September 1996, 2A.

8. Laws of Jamaica, 1840, cap. 49, An act to alter, explain, and amend an act, entitled "An act for making a new and easy carriage-road over Stoney-Hill, and for raising a toll or turnpike thereon".

9. Quoted in Hall, *In Miserable Slavery*, 26.

10. William J. Smyth, *Map-making, Landscapes, and Memory: A Geography of Colonial and Early Modern Ireland c.1530–1750* (Notre Dame, Ind.: University of Notre Dame Press, 2006), 293–94.

11. James Robertson, *Gone is the Ancient Glory: Spanish Town, Jamaica, 1534–2000* (Kingston: Ian Randle Publishers, 2005), 24–27, 159.

12. Brian J. Hudson, "Waterfront Development and Redevelopment in the West Indies", *Caribbean Geography* 2 (1989): 229–30.

13. Pawson and Buisseret, *Port Royal, Jamaica*, 82.

14. For the development of Kingston's plan, see Clarke, *Kingston*; Colin Clarke, *Decolonizing the Colonial City: Urbanization and Stratification in Kingston, Jamaica* (Oxford: Oxford University Press, 2006).

15. Kingston Parish and Poll Tax Rolls, 1776, 832 (Jamaica Archives).

16. Richard Pillsbury, "The Street Name Systems of Pennsylvania before 1820", *Names* 17 (1969): 219–21; Victor R. Savage and Brenda S. Yeoh, eds., *Toponymics: A Study of Singapore Street Names* (Singapore: Eastern Universities Press, 2004

[2003]), 9–11. Cf. Georges Augustins, "Naming, Dedicating: Street Names and Tradition", *History and Anthropology* 15 (2004): 289–99.

17. Kingston Parish and Poll Tax Rolls, 1776, 1832 (Jamaica Archives); James Robertson, "Stuart London and the Idea of a Royal Capital City", *Renaissance Studies* 15 (2001): 57.

18. *Gleaner*, 6 January 2002, 7A.

19. *Gleaner*, 14 November 1952, 9; *Gleaner*, 7 September 1990, 18; *Gleaner*, 11 September 1996, 2A.

20. Phillippo, *Jamaica Its Past and Present State*, 223–27.

21. John Algeo, "Trans-Atlantic Street Names", *Names* 47 (1999): 207–8. The samples used by Algeo for London (881) and New York (845) are both smaller than the count for Kingston (2,875).

22. *Gleaner, Highway 2000 Supplement*, 24 April 2002.

23. Algeo, "Trans-Atlantic Street Names", 208.

24. *Gleaner*, 5 May 1917, 16; *Gleaner*, 19 January 1922, 9.

25. *Gleaner*, 10 June 1922, 12.

26. *Gleaner*, 10 January 1935, 15; *Gleaner*, 10 September 1938, 12; *Gleaner*, 7 November 1938, 1.

Chapter 10

1. B.W. Higman, *Plantation Jamaica 1750–1850: Capital and Control in a Colonial Economy* (Kingston: University of the West Indies Press, 2005), 189; B.W. Higman, *Montpelier, Jamaica: A Plantation Community on Slavery and Freedom 1739–1912* (Kingston: The Press, University of the West Indies, 1998), 86.

2. John Roby, *Monuments of the Cathedral-Church and Parish of St. Catherine: Being Part I of Church Notes and Monumental Inscriptions of Jamaica* (Montego Bay: Alexander Holmes, 1831), 1–2. We thank James Robertson for this quotation.

3. Verna Lee Davis-Daly, "What's in a Name?" *Gleaner*, 5–7 August 1994, 20; Goulbourne, "Same Name, Different Places", 24. Cf. Wilbur Zelinsky, "Nationalism in the American Place-Name Cover", *Names* 31 (1983): 1–28; John Algeo, "The Australianness of Australian Placenames", *Names* 36 (1988): 173–85; Schnakenbourg, *Histoire de l'industrie sucrière en Guadeloupe*, 29.

4. Cf. Janet H. Gritzner, "Seventeenth-Century Generic Place-Names: Culture and Process on the Eastern Shore", *Names* 20 (1972): 238–39; Ford, "Toponymic Generics", 21–22.

5. Edward Brathwaite, *The Development of Creole Society in Jamaica, 1770–1820* (Oxford: Oxford University Press, 1971); Salikoko S. Mufwene, *The Ecology of*

Language Evolution (Cambridge: Cambridge University Press, 2001), 28–29; Pauline Christie, *Language in Jamaica* (Kingston: Arawak Publications, 2003), 8–10; Peter A. Roberts, *West Indians and Their Language* (Cambridge: Cambridge University Press, 1988), 13–14.

6. Dallas, *History of the Maroons,* 1:30.

7. Hall, *In Miserable Slavery*, 26–27.

8. Cf. Roland Dickison, "Onomastic Amelioration in California Place Names", *Names* 16 (1968): 13–18; Leonard R.N. Ashley, "The Spanish Placenames of California: Proposition 1994", *Names* 44 (1996): 3; Monmonier, *From Squaw Tit to Whorehouse Meadow.*

9. *Gleaner*, 7 May 1920, 4; *Gleaner*, 27 October 1938, 20; Philip Sherlock and Hazel Bennett, *The Story of the Jamaican People* (Kingston: Ian Randle Publishers, 1998), 163.

10. *Gleaner*, 20 December 1956, 12.

11. Geggus, "Naming of Haiti", 43.

12. Curtis Adler, "Name Changes in Israel", *Names* 2 (1954): 38–39; Saul B. Cohen and Nurit Kliot, "Israel's Place-Names as Reflection of Continuity and Change in Nation-Building", *Names* 29 (1981): 244; Saul B. Cohen and Nurit Kliot, "Place-Names in Israel's Ideological Struggle over the Administered Territories", *Annals of the Association of American Geographers* 82 (1992): 653–80; Maoz Azaryahu and Arnon Golan, "(Re)naming the Landscape: The Formation of the Hebrew Map of Israel 1949–1960", *Journal of Historical Geography* 27 (2001): 178–95; Maoz Azaryahu, "Street Names and Political Identity: The Case of East Berlin", *Journal of Contemporary History* 21 (1986): 581–604; Lawrence D. Berg and Robin A. Kearns, "Naming as Norming: 'Race', Gender, and the Identity Politics of Naming Places in Aotearoa/New Zealand", *Environment and Planning D: Space and Society* 14 (1996): 99–122.

13. R.D.K. Herman, "The Aloha State: Place Names and the Anti-Conquest of Hawai'i", *Annals of the Association of American Geographers* 89 (1999): 76–102.

14. Adrian Room, *Place-Name Changes since 1900: A World Gazetteer* (London: Routledge and Kegan Paul, 1980), v–vi.

15. *Gleaner, Sunday Magazine*, 26 October 1975, 10–11. Cf. Savage and Yeoh, *Toponymics*, 2–3.

16. *Gleaner*, 6 November 1956, 8.

17. Cf. Irving Lewis Allen, "Some Informal Neighborhood and Street Names in Manhattan: From *Alphabet City* to *The Dead End*", *Names* 41 (1993): 219–27.

18. John P. Homiak, "Dub History: Soundings on Rastafari Livity and Language", in *Rastafari and Other African-Caribbean Worldviews*, ed. Barry Chevannes (The Hague: Institute of Social Studies, 1998), 137; Barry Chevannes, "Rastafari:

Towards a New Approach", *New West Indian Guide* 64 (1990): 135; L. Alan Eyre, "Biblical Symbolism and the Role of Fantasy Geography among the Rastafarians of Jamaica", *Journal of Geography* 84 (1985): 144–48.

19. *Gleaner*, 30 September 1995, 8B.

20. *Gleaner*, 13 March 1995, 2A; *Gleaner*, 4 November 1972, 30; *Gleaner*, 6 February 1990, 1.

21. Sistren, *Lionheart Gal*, 157; Bilby, *True-Born Maroons*, 105–9 and *passim*.

Bibliography

MANUSCRIPTS

Jamaica Archives, Spanish Town

CSO: Colonial Secretary's Office.

Kingston, Parish and Poll Tax Rolls.

Patents/Deeds.

Returns of Registrations of Slaves.

Returns to the House of Assembly under 1 Vic. Cap. 34.

MAPS AND PLANS

Arrowsmith, John. *Map of Jamaica compiled chiefly from Manuscripts in the Colonial Office and Admiralty*. London, 1842. Maps 80710(2), British Library.

Bochart, Charles, and Humphrey Knollis. *A New and Exact Mapp of the Island of Jamaica*. London, [1684]. C.O. 700/JAMAICA 3, National Archives, Kew, UK.

Browne, Patrick. *A New Map of Jamaica . . . from Actual Surveys Made by Mr. Sheffield and Others, from the Year 1730 to 1749*. London, 1758. Maps: 80710 (35), British Library.

Campbell, Major General Archibald. *Survey of the South Coast of Jamaica* [1782]. King's Topographical Collection: Maps CXXIII/53-1, British Library.

Craskell, Thomas, and James Simpson. *A Map of the County of Cornwall [and Middlesex and Surrey] in the Island of Jamaica (surveyed 1756–61)*. London, 1762–63. C.O. 700/Jamaica 17, National Archives, Kew, UK.

De Mayne, Anthony. *The Island of Jamaica, from Observations taken on the Principal Headlands*. London, 1821. Maps: Sec. 8, 446, British Library.

Foster, G. *A New Map of the Island of Jamaica*. London, 1740. King's Topographical Collection: Maps CXXIII/49, British Library.

Harrison, Thomas. *Cadastral Survey of Jamaica, 1886–91*. National Library of Jamaica.

Jamaica Automobile Association. *Road Map of Jamaica*. Kingston: Jamaica Automobile Association, 1960.

Kapp, Capt. Kit S. *The Printed Maps of Jamaica up to 1825.* Kingston: Bolivar Press, 1968.

Lea, Philip. *A New Mapp of the Island of Jamaica.* London, 1685. Maps: 80710.17, British Library.

Liddell, Colin. *Map of Jamaica prepared from the best authorities.* Kingston, 1888.

Robertson, James. *Map of the County of Cornwall (and Middlesex and Surrey), in the island of Jamaica, constructed from actual surveys, under the authority of the Honb. House of Assembly.* London, 1804.

Shell. *Jamaica Road Map.* London: Macmillan Education, 1999.

Slaney, Edward. *Jamaica.* London: 1678. King's Topographical Collection: Maps CXXII/47, British Library.

Speed, John. *A Map of Jamaica.* London, 1666. Maps: C.7.e.6, British Library.

War Office, Intelligence Division. *Rough Sketch of Country round Kingston, Jamaica.* June 1891. C.O. 700/JAMAICA38, National Archives, Kew, UK.

War Office, Geographical Section. *Jamaica: Kingston District.* 1920. C.O. 1047/516, National Archives, Kew, UK.

Wyld, James. *The Island of Jamaica.* London, 1851. Maps: 80710(3), British Library.

DICTIONARIES, DIRECTORIES, GAZETTEERS AND ENCYCLOPEDIAS

Allsopp, Richard, ed. *Dictionary of Caribbean English Usage.* Oxford: Oxford University Press, 1996.

Barnhart, Clarence L., ed. *The New Century Cyclopedia of Names.* New York: Appleton-Century-Crofts, 1954.

Bartholomew, John. *The Survey Gazetteer of the British Isles.* Edinburgh: J. Bartholomew, [19—].

Cable and Wireless. *2006 Business Telephone Directory (Kingston and St Andrew, Jamaica).* Kingston: Cable and Wireless Jamaica Ltd, 2006.

———. *2006 Residential Telephone Directory (all Parishes).* Kingston: Cable and Wireless Jamaica, 2006.

Cassidy, F.G., and R.B. Le Page, eds. *Dictionary of Jamaican English.* Cambridge: Cambridge University Press, 1980 [1967].

Cruden, Alexander. *Cruden's Complete Concordance to the Old and New Testaments.* London: Lutterworth Press, 1930.

Crystal, David. *The Cambridge Encyclopedia of the English Language.* Cambridge: Cambridge University Press, 1995.

Dauzat, Albert, and Ch. Rostaing. *Dictionnaire etymologique des noms de lieux de France.* Paris: Larousse, 1963.

Division of National Mapping, Department of Minerals and Energy. *Australia 1:250,000 Map Series Gazetteer*. Canberra: Australian Government Publishing Service, 1975.

Field, John. *Place-Names of Great Britain and Ireland*. Newton Abbot, UK: David and Charles, 1980.

Gudde, Erwin G. *California Place Names: The Origin and Etymology of Current Geographical Names*. Berkeley: University of California Press, 1969 [1949].

Hammond, N.G.L., and H.H. Scullard, eds. *The Oxford Classical Dictionary*. Oxford: Clarendon Press, 1996 [1940].

Hobson, Archie, ed. *The Cambridge Gazetteer of the United States and Canada: A Dictionary of Places*. Cambridge: Cambridge University Press, 1995.

Knox, Alexander. *Glossary of Geographical and Topographical Terms and of Words of Frequent Occurrence in the Composition of Such Terms and of Place-Names*. London: Edward Stanford, 1904.

Mason, Oliver. *The Gazetteer of England: England's Cities, Towns, Villages, and Hamlets*. Newton Abbot, UK: David and Charles, 1972.

Mills, A.D. *A Dictionary of English Place Names*. Oxford: Oxford University Press, 1991.

Moore, W.G. *The Penguin Encyclopedia of Places*. Harmondsworth: Penguin Books, 1978 [1971].

Munro, David, ed. *Chambers World Gazetteer: An A–Z of Geographical Information*. Edinburgh: Chambers, 1988.

Oxford English Dictionary. http://dictionary.oed.com/

Reaney, P.H. *A Dictionary of British Surnames*. London: Routledge and Kegan Paul, 1958.

Room, Adrian. *A Dictionary of Irish Place-Names*. Belfast: Appletree Press, 1986.

———. *Place-Name Changes since 1900: A World Gazetteer*. London: Routledge and Kegan Paul, 1980.

Savage, Victor R., and Brenda S.A. Yeoh. *Toponymics: A Study of Singapore Street Names*. Singapore: Eastern Universities Press, 2004.

Schlebecker, John T. *The Many Names of Country People: An Historical Dictionary from the Twelfth Century Onward*. New York: Greenwood Press, 1989.

Seltzer, Leon E. *The Columbia Lippincott Gazetteer of the World*. New York: Columbia University Press, 1962.

Senior, Olive. *Encyclopedia of Jamaican Heritage*. Red Hills, Jamaica: Twin Guinep Publishers, 2003.

Sibley, Inez Knibb. *Dictionary of Place-Names in Jamaica*. Kingston: Institute of Jamaica, 1978.

Smith, A.H. *English Place-Name Elements*. Cambridge: Cambridge University Press, 1956.

Smith, William. *A Dictionary of Greek and Roman Geography.* New York: AMS Press, 1966 [1870].

Stewart, George R. *American Place-Names: A Concise and Selective Dictionary for the Continental United States of America.* New York: Oxford University Press, 1970.

The Times Index-Gazetteer of the World. London: The Times Publishing Co., 1965.

Watts, Victor, and John Insley, eds. *The Cambridge Dictionary of English Place-Names: Based on the Collections of the English Place-Name Society.* Cambridge: Cambridge University Press, 2004.

Webster's Geographical Dictionary. Springfield, Mass.: G. and C. Merriam [1966].

OFFICIAL PUBLICATIONS

British Parliamentary Papers, XX (721) 1831–32. "Report from the Select Committee on the Extinction of Slavery throughout the British Dominions".

Central Housing Advisory Board. *Memorandum dealing with Development of Trench Pen Township and Improvement of Smith Village and Surrounding Districts.* Kingston: Government Printer, 1936.

Claims for Compensation. Filed with the Assistant Commissioners for Jamaica [Spanish Town: 1834–38].

Jamaica Census. 1871, 1881, 1891, 1911.

Jamaica, House of Assembly, Journals.

Jamaica, House of Assembly, Votes.

The Jamaican Censuses of 1844 and 1861. Edited by B.W. Higman. Mona: Social History Project, 1980.

Laws of Jamaica.

NEWSPAPERS AND PERIODICALS

Falmouth Post.

Gleaner (Kingston).

Jamaica Quarterly Journal, and Literary Magazine (Kingston).

Royal Gazette (Spanish Town).

St Jago de la Vega Gazette (Spanish Town).

Watchman and Jamaica Free Press (Kingston).

Weekly Gleaner (Kingston).

West Indian Critic and Review (Kingston).

West Indian Review (Kingston).

Books and Articles

Abrahams, Peter. *Jamaica: An Island Mosaic*. London: Her Majesty's Stationery Office, 1957.

———. *The View from Coyaba*. London: Faber and Faber, 1985.

Adler, Curtis. "Name Changes in Israel". *Names* 2 (1954): 38–39.

[Alfred]. *Account of a Shooting Excursion on the Mountains near Dromilly Estate, in the Parish of Trelawny, and Island of Jamaica, in the Month of October, 1824!!!* London: Harvey and Darton, 1825.

Algeo, John. "The Australianness of Australian Placenames". *Names* 36 (1988): 173–85.

———. "Trans-Atlantic Street Names". *Names* 47 (1999): 205–14.

Allen, Irving Lewis. "Some Informal Neighborhood and Street Names in Manhattan: From *Alphabet City* to *The Dead End*". *Names* 41 (1993): 219–27.

Armstrong, Douglas V. *The Old Village and the Great House: An Archaeological and Historical Examination of Drax Hall Plantation, St Ann's Bay, Jamaica*. Urbana: University of Illinois Press, 1990.

Ashley, Leonard R.N. "The Spanish Placenames of California: Proposition 1994". *Names* 44 (1996): 3–40.

Augustins, Georges. "Naming, Dedicating: Street Names and Tradition". *History and Anthropology* 15 (2004): 289–99.

Azaryahu, Maoz. "Street Names and Political Identity: The Case of East Berlin". *Journal of Contemporary History* 21 (1986): 581–604.

Azaryahu, Maoz, and Arnon Golan. "(Re)naming the Landscape: The Formation of the Hebrew Map of Israel 1949–1960". *Journal of Historical Geography* 27 (2001): 178–95.

Bacon, Edgar Mayhew, and Eugene Murray Aaron, *The New Jamaica*. New York: Walbridge and Co., 1890.

Baird, Robert. *Impressions and Experiences of the West Indies and North America in 1849*. Philadelphia: Lea and Blanchard, 1850.

Beckford, William. *A Descriptive Account of the Island of Jamaica*. London: T. and J. Egerton, 1790.

Berg, Lawrence D., and Robin A. Kearns. "Naming as Norming: 'Race', Gender, and the Identity Politics of Naming Places in Aotearoa/New Zealand". *Environment and Planning D: Space and Society* 14 (1996): 99–122.

Berleant-Schiller, Riva. "Hidden Places and Creole Forms: Naming the Barbudan Landscape". *Professional Geographer* 43 (1991): 92–101.

Bilby, Kenneth M. *True-Born Maroons*. Kingston: Ian Randle Publishers, 2006.

Black, Clinton. *The Story of Jamaica from Prehistory to the Present*. London: Collins, 1965.

Blome, Richard. *A Description of the Island of Jamaica*. London: J. Williams, Jr, 1672.

Brathwaite, Edward. *The Development of Creole Society in Jamaica, 1770–1820*. Oxford: Oxford University Press, 1971.

Brodber, Erna. *Woodside, Pear Tree Grove P.O.* Kingston: University of the West Indies Press, 2004.

Brothers, Timothy S., and Lisa M. Kennedy. "The Changing Geography of Vegetation Placenames in the Indiana Prairie Border Region". *Names* 40 (1992): 17–32.

Brown, Geof. "The Truth about PRIDE". *Gleaner* 20 February 1998.

Browne, Patrick. *The Civil and Natural History of Jamaica*. New York: Arno Press, 1972 [reprint of 1789 edition].

Brunn, Stanley D., and James O. Wheeler. "Notes on the Geography of Religious Town Names in the US". *Names* 14 (1966): 197–202.

Buisseret, David, ed. *Jamaica in 1687: The Taylor Manuscript at the National Library of Jamaica*. Kingston: University of the West Indies Press, 2008.

Burenhult, Niclas. "Streams of Words: Hydrological Lexicon in Jahai". *Language Sciences* 30 (2008): 182–99.

Burenhult, Niclas, and Stephen C. Levinson. "Language and Landscape: A Cross-Linguistic Perspective". *Language Sciences* 30 (2008): 135–50.

Burnard, Trevor. "European Migration to Jamaica, 1655–1780". *William and Mary Quarterly* 53 (1996): 769–96.

———. "Slave Naming Patterns: Onomastics and the Taxonomy of Race in Eighteenth-Century Jamaica". *Journal of Interdisciplinary History* 31 (2001): 325–46.

Burrill, Meredith F. "Toponymic Generics I (and II)". *Names* 4 (1956): 129–37, 226–40.

Burton, Richard D.E. "Names and Naming in Afro-Caribbean Cultures". *New West Indian Guide* 73 (1999): 35–58.

Buscaldi, Davide, and Paulo Rosso. "A Conceptual Density-Based Approach to the Disambiguation of Toponyms". *International Journal of Geographical Information Science* 22 (2008): 301–13.

Cameron, Kenneth. *English Place-Names*. London: B.T. Batsford, 1996 [1961].

Campbell, Mavis C. *The Maroons of Jamaica 1655–1796: A History of Resistance, Collaboration, and Betrayal*. Granby, Mass.: Begin and Garvey Publishers, 1988.

Campbell, Jon C. "Stream Generic Terms as Indicators of Historical Settlement Patterns". *Names* 39 (1991): 333–65.

Carey, Bev. *The Maroon Story: The Authentic and Original History of the Maroons in the History of Jamaica 1490–1880*. Gordon Town, Jamaica: Agouti Press, 1997.

Cassidy, Frederic G. "The Earliest Placenames in Jamaica". *Names* 36 (1988): 151–61.

———. "The Etiology of Place Naming". *Names* 32 (1984): 402–6.

———. *Jamaica Talk: Three Hundred Years of the English Language in Jamaica*. London: Institute of Jamaica, 1961.

Chapman, Esther, ed. *Pleasure Island: The Book of Jamaica*. Kingston: Arawak, 1952 [1951].

Chenoweth, Michael. *The 18th Century Climate of Jamaica: Derived from the Journals of Thomas Thistlewood 1750–1786*. Philadelphia: American Philosophical Society, 2003.

Chevannes, Barry. "Rastafari: Towards a New Approach". *New West Indian Guide* 64 (1990): 127–48.

Christie, Pauline. *Language in Jamaica*. Kingston: Arawak Publications, 2003.

Christopher, A.J. *The British Empire at Its Zenith* . London: Croom Helm, 1988.

Clarke, Colin. *Decolonizing the Colonial City: Urbanization and Stratification in Kingston, Jamaica*. Oxford: Oxford University Press, 2006.

———. *Kingston, Jamaica: Urban Development and Social Change, 1692–2002*. Kingston: Ian Randle Publishers, 2006 [1975].

Clarke, Lorna. "My Favourite Jamaican Place Names". *Gleaner, Outlook*, 11 November 2001.

Cohen, Saul B., and Nurit Kliot. "Israel's Place-Names as Reflection of Continuity and Change in Nation-Building". *Names* 29 (1981): 227–48.

———. "Place-Names in Israel's Ideological Struggle over the Administered Territories". *Annals of the Association of American Geographers* 82 (1992): 653–80.

Crampton, Jeremy W. "Maps as Social Constructions: Power, Communication, and Visualization". *Progress in Human Geography* 25 (2001): 235–52.

Cruickshank, J. Graham. "Field Names in Barbados". *Journal of the Barbados Museum and Historical Society* 2 (1935): 166.

Cundall, Frank. *Historic Jamaica*. London: Institute of Jamaica, 1915.

———. *Place-Names of Jamaica*. Revised by Philip M. Sherlock. Kingston: Institute of Jamaica, 1939.

Curtin, Philip D. *The Atlantic Slave Trade: A Census*. Madison: University of Wisconsin Press, 1969.

Dallas, R.C. *The History of the Maroons*. London: T.N. Longman and O. Rees, 1803.

Davies, K.G. *The Royal African Company*. London: Longmans, 1957.

Davis-Daly, Verna Lee. "What's in a Name?" *Gleaner*, 5–7 August 1994.

Day, Michael. "Limestone Valley Systems in North Central Jamaica". *Caribbean Geography* 2 (1985): 16–32.

DeCamp, David. "Cart Names in Jamaica". *Names* 8 (1960): 15–23.

Dickison, Roland. "Onomastic Amelioration in California Place Names". *Names* 16 (1968): 13–18.

Dillard, Joe. "Names or Slogans: Some Problems from the Cameroun, the Caribbean, Burundi, and the United States". *Caribbean Studies* 9 (1970): 104–10.

Dorion, Henri. "L'homonymie et l'autoreproduction des noms de lieux". *Names* 47 (1999): 223–32.

Duckert, Audrey R. "Gutter: Its Rise and Fall". *Names* 4 (1956): 146–54.

———. "Place Nicknames". *Names* 21 (1973): 153–60.

Duckson, Don W., Jr. "A Creek Is a Creek . . . or Is It?" *Names* 31 (1983): 51–61.

Dunlap, A.R. "Gat and Gut". *Names* 5 (1957): 248.

Earle, William. *Obi; or, the History of Three-Fingered Jack*. Edited by Srinivas Aravamudan. Peterborough, Canada.: Broadview Editions, 2005.

Elliott, J.H. *Empires of the Atlantic World: Britain and Spain in America 1492–1830*. New Haven: Yale University Press, 2006.

Evans, Lance. "Interesting Jamaican Place Names". *Weekly Gleaner (N.A.)*, 28 July–3 August 1995.

Eyles, R.J. "When Is a Stream Not a Stream?" *Malaysian Journal of Tropical Geography* 1 (1980): 1–11.

Eyre, L. Alan. "Biblical Symbolism and the Role of Fantasy Geography Among the Rastafarians of Jamaica". *Journal of Geography* 84 (1985): 144–48.

———. "James Robertson: Jamaica's Mapmaker Superlative". *Jamaica Journal* 17, no. 4 (1984–85): 57–63.

Fairclough, G. Thomas. " 'New Light' on 'Old Zion' ". *Names* 8 (1960): 75–85.

Fermor, Patrick Leigh. *The Traveller's Tree: A Journey through the Caribbean Islands*. London: John Murray, 1950.

Field, John. *A History of English Field-Names*. London: Longman, 1993.

Fincham, Alan. *Jamaica Underground: The Caves, Sinkholes, and Underground Rivers of the Island*. Kingston: The Press, University of the West Indies, 1997.

Fischer, David Hackett. *Albion's Seed: Four British Folkways in America*. New York: Oxford University Press, 1989.

Fisher, Peter, and Jo Wood. "What Is a Mountain? Or the Englishman Who Went Up a Boolean Geographical Concept but Realised It Was Fuzzy". *Geography* 83 (1998): 247–56.

Fisher, Peter, Jo Wood, and Tao Cheng. "Where Is Helvellyn? Fuzziness of Multi-Scale Landscape Morphometry". *Transactions of the Institute of British Geographers* 29 (2004): 106–28.

Ford, Robert E. "Toponymic Generics, Environment, and Culture History in Pre-Independence Belize". *Names* 39 (1991): 1–26.

Fraser, Ian A. "Placenames of Scottish Origin in Nova Scotia". *Names* 34 (1986): 364–72.

Geggus, David. "The Naming of Haiti". *New West Indian Guide* 71 (1997): 43–68.

Gelling, Margaret. "Place-names and Landscape". In *The Uses of Place-Names*, edited by Simon Taylor, 75–100. Edinburgh: Scottish Cultural Press, 1998.

———. *Place-Names in the Landscape*. London: J.M. Dent and Sons, 1984.

———. *Signposts to the Past: Place-Names and the History of England*. Chichester, UK: Phillimore and Co., 1997 [1978].

Girouard, Mark. *Life in the English Country House: A Social and Architectural History*. New Haven: Yale University Press, 1978.

Gosse, Philip Henry. *A Naturalist's Sojourn in Jamaica*. London: Longman, Brown, Green, and Longmans, 1851.

Goulbourne, Jean L. "Same Name, Different Places". *Gleaner, Outlook*, 18 October 1998.

Gritzner, Janet H. "Seventeenth-Century Generic Place-Names: Culture and Process on the Eastern Shore". *Names* 20 (1972): 231–39.

Groenke, Ulrich. "Spurious Attribution of Meaning in Place-Name Traditions". *Names* 15 (1967): 119–25.

Gudde, Elisabeth K. "Mocho Mountain". *Names* 5 (1957): 246–48.

Gudde, Erwin G. "Naming Storms". *Names* 3 (1955): 34–37.

———. "Sugarloaf". *Names* 4 (1956): 241–43.

Gulley, Harold E. "British and Irish Toponyms in the South Atlantic States". *Names* 43 (1995): 85–102.

Guppy, H.B. *Homes of Family Names in Great Britain*. London: Harrison, 1890.

Gurney, Joseph John. *A Winter in the West Indies, Described in Familiar Letters to Henry Clay, of Kentucky*. London: John Murray, 1840.

Hakewill, James. *A Picturesque Tour of the Island of Jamaica*. London: 1825.

Hall, Douglas. *In Miserable Slavery: Thomas Thistlewood in Jamaica, 1750–86*. London: Macmillan, 1989.

Hall, Richard N. "Recent Progress in the International Standardization of Geographical Names". In *Proceedings of the Eighth International Congress of Onomastic Sciences*, edited by D.P. Blok, 224–29. The Hague: Mouton and Co., 1966.

Hamlin, Frank R. "Numbers in Placenames". *Names* 47 (1999): 233–42.

Hamp, Eric P. "The Linguistic Evidence of Placenames for History". *Names* 43 (1995): 131–34.

Handler, Jerome S., and JoAnn Jacoby. "Slave Names and Naming in Barbados, 1650–1830". *William and Mary Quarterly* 53 (1996): 685–728.

Heck, Lewis. "Geographic Names in the US Coast and Geodetic Survey". *Names* 1 (1953): 103–11.

———. "The Problem of a National Gazetteer". *Names* 1 (1953): 233–38.

Herman, R.D.K. "The Aloha State: Place Names and the Anti- Conquest of Hawai'i". *Annals of the Association of American Geographers* 89 (1999): 76–102.

Heuman, Gad. *"The Killing Time": The Morant Bay Rebellion in Jamaica*. London: Macmillan Caribbean, 1994.

Hickeringill, Edmund. *Jamaica Viewed: With All the Ports, Harbours, and their Several Soundings, Towns, and Settlements*. London: John Williams, 1661.

Higman, B.W. *Jamaica Surveyed: Plantation Maps and Plans of the Eighteenth and Nineteenth Centuries*. Kingston: Institute of Jamaica Publications, 1988.

———. *Montpelier, Jamaica: A Plantation Community in Slavery and Freedom 1739–1912*. Kingston: The Press, University of the West Indies, 1998.

———. *Plantation Jamaica, 1750–1850: Capital and Control in a Colonial Economy*. Kingston: University of the West Indies Press, 2005.

———. *Slave Population and Economy in Jamaica, 1807–1834*. Cambridge: Cambridge University Press, 1976.

Holmer, Nils M. "Indian Place Names in South America and the Antilles I (and II and III)". *Names* 8 (1960): 133–49, 197–219; 9 (1961): 37–52.

Homiak, John P. "Dub History: Soundings on Rastafari Livity and Language". In *Rastafari and Other African-Caribbean Worldviews*, edited by Barry Chevannes, 127–81. The Hague: Institute of Social Studies, 1998.

Hough, Carole. "A Database for English Placenames". *Names* 43 (1995): 255–74.

Howard, David. *Kingston: A Cultural and Literary History*. Kingston: Ian Randle Publishers, 2005.

Howard, Robert Mowbray, ed. *Records and Letters of the Family of the Longs of Longville, Jamaica, and Hampton Lodge, Surrey*. London: Simpkin, Marshall, Hamilton, Kent and Co., 1925.

Hudson, Brian J. *The Waterfalls of Jamaica: Sublime and Beautiful Objects*. Kingston: University of the West Indies Press, 2001.

———. "Waterfront Development and Redevelopment in the West Indies". *Caribbean Geography* 2 (1989): 229–40.

Hudson, Pat. "The Regional Perspective". In *Regions and Industries: A Perspective on the Industrial Revolution in Britain*, edited by Pat Hudson, 5–38. Cambridge: Cambridge University Press, 1989.

Hunn, Eugene. "Columbia Plateau Indian Place Names: What Can They Teach Us?" *Journal of Linguistic Anthropology* 6 (1996): 3–26.

The Importance of Jamaica to Great Britain, Consider'd. London: A. Dodd, [1740].

Ingram, K.E. *Sources of Jamaican History 1655–1838: A Bibliographical Survey with Particular Reference to Manuscript Sources*. Zug, Switzerland: Inter Documentation Company Ag, 1976.

Jacob, Christian. *The Sovereign Map: Theoretical Approaches in Cartography throughout History*. Chicago: University of Chicago Press, 2006.

Jacobsson, Mattias. *Wells, Meres, and Pools: Hydronymic Terms in the Anglo-Saxon Landscape*. Uppsala: Uppsala University Library, 1997.

Jennings, J.N. *Karst Geomorphology*. Oxford: Basil Blackwell, 1985.

Kari, James. "Some Principles of Alaskan Athabaskan Toponymic Knowledge". In *General and Amerindian Linguistics: In Remembrance of Stanley Newman*, edited by Mary Ritchie Key and Henry M. Hoenigswald, 129–49. Berlin: Mouton de Gruyter, 1989.

Karras, Alan L. *Sojourners in the Sun. Scottish Migrants in Jamaica and the Chesapeake, 1740–1800*. Ithaca: Cornell University Press, 1992.

Kenny, Hamill. "Place-Names from Surnames". *Names* 18 (1970): 137–54.

Kuper, Adam. *Changing Jamaica*. London: Routledge and Kegan Paul, 1976.

Lasker, G.W. *Surnames and Genetic Structure*. Cambridge: Cambridge University Press, 1985.

Laurence, K.M. "Continuity and Change in Trinidadian Toponyms". *New West Indian Guide* 50 (1975): 123–42.

Law, Robin. *Ouidah: The Social History of a West African Slaving "Port" 1727–1892*. Oxford: James Currey, 2004.

Leighley, John. "Biblical Place-Names in the United States". *Names* 27 (1979): 46–59.

Leslie, Charles. *A New and Exact Account of Jamaica*. Edinburgh: A. Kincaid, 1739.

Levinson, Stephen C., and David P. Wilkins, eds. *Grammars of Space: Explorations in Cognitive Diversity*. Cambridge: Cambridge University Press, 2006.

Lieberson, Stanley. *A Matter of Taste: How Names, Fashions, and Culture Change*. New Haven: Yale University Press, 2000.

Lind, Ivan. "Geography and Place Names". In *Readings in Cultural Geography*, edited by Philip L. Wagner and Marvin W. Mikesell, 118–28. Chicago: University of Chicago Press, 1962.

Long, Edward. *The History of Jamaica, or, A General Survey of the Antient and Modern State of that Island, with Reflections on its Situation, Settlements, Inhabitants, Climate, Products, Commerce, Laws, and Government*. 3 vols. London: T. Lowndes, 1774.

Lyew-Ayee, P., H.A. Viles, and G.E. Tucker. "The Use of GIS-Based Digital Morphometric Techniques in the Study of Cockpit Karst". *Earth Surface Processes and Landforms* 32 (2007): 165–79.

Lynch, Mrs Henry. *The Wonders of the West Indies*. London: Seeley, Jackson, and Halliday, 1856.

Macdonald, Alastair. *Mapping the World: A History of the Directorate of Overseas Surveys 1946–1985*. London: HMSO, 1996.

Macmillan, Mona. *The Land of Look Behind: A Study of Jamaica*. London: Faber and Faber, 1957.

Malpas, Jeff. *Heidegger's Topology: Being, Place, World*. Cambridge, Mass.: MIT Press, 2006.

Marsden, Peter. *An Account of the Island of Jamaica; with Reflections on the Treatment, Occupation, and Provisions of the Slaves*. Newcastle, UK: the author, 1788.

Maxwell, James. *Remarks on the Present State of Jamaica*. London: Smith, Elder and Co., 1848.

McCartney, Paul J. *Henry De la Beche: Observations on an Observer*. Cardiff: Friends of the National Museum of Wales, 1977.

McDavid, Raven I., Jr. "Linguistic Geographic and Toponymic Research". *Names* 6 (1958): 65–73.

McDavid, Raven I., Jr, Raymond K. O'Cain, George T. Dorrill, and David Fischer. "Names *Not* on the Map". *Names* 33 (1985): 216–24.

McMahon, Benjamin. *Jamaica Plantership*. London: Effingham Wilson, 1839.

McMullen, Edwin Wallace, Jr. *English Topographic Terms in Florida 1563–1874*. Gainesville: University of Florida Press, 1953.

Millward, Celia. "Place-Name Generics in Providence, R.I., 1636–1736". *Names* 19 (1971): 153–66.

Minkel, Clarence W. "Names in the Mapping of Original Vegetation". *Names* 5 (1957): 157–61.

Minton, Arthur. "Names of Real-Estate Developments: I (and II and III)". *Names* 7 (1959): 129–53, 233–55; 9 (1961): 8–36.

Möller, Lucie Alida. "Metadata for South African Geographic Names Databases". *Names* 47 (1999): 297–311.

Monmonier, Mark. *From Squaw Tit to Whorehouse Meadow: How Maps Name, Claim, and Inflame*. Chicago: University of Chicago Press, 2006.

Morales Padrón, Francisco. *Spanish Jamaica*. Translated by Patrick E. Bryan. Kingston: Ian Randle Publishers, 2003 [1952].

Morgan, F.W. *Ports and Harbours*. London: Hutchinson University Library, 1958 [1952].

Morison, Samuel Eliot. *Admiral of the Ocean Sea: A Life of Christopher Columbus*. Boston: Northeastern University Press, 1983 [1942].

Mozley, Geraldine, ed. *Letters to Jane from Jamaica*. London: Institute of Jamaica, 1938.

Mufwene, Salikoko S. *The Ecology of Language Evolution*. Cambridge: Cambridge University Press, 2001.

Nelson, R.J. *Naming and Reference: The Link of Word to Object*. London: Routledge, 1992.

Nicolaisen, W.F.H. "Scottish Place Names as Evidence for Language Change". *Names* 41 (1993): 306–13.

———. *Scottish Place-Names: Their Study and Significance*. London: B.T. Batsford, 1976.

Nilsen, Don L.F. "American Proper Noun Reference: The Humorous Naming of Persons, Places, and Things". *Names* 30 (1982): 171–82.

Norris, Darrell A. "Unreal Estate: Words, Names, and Allusions in Suburban Home Advertising". *Names* 47 (1999): 365–80.

Nuessel, Frank. *The Study of Names: A Guide to the Principles and Topics*. Westport, Conn.: Greenwood Press, 1992.

Nugent, Maria. *A Journal of a Voyage to, and Residence in, the Island of Jamaica, from 1801 to 1805, and of Subsequent Events in England from 1805 to 1811*. London, 1839.

Olschki, Leonardo. "The Columbian Nomenclature of the Lesser Antilles". *Geographical Review* 33 (1943): 397–414.

Orth, Donald J. "The US Board on Geographic Names: An Overview". *Names* 38 (1990): 165–72.

Owens, Jeffrey Alan. "Naming the Plantation: An Analytical Survey from Tensas Parish, Louisiana". *Agricultural History* 68 (1994): 46–69.

Pawson, Michael, and David Buisseret. *Port Royal, Jamaica*. Oxford: Clarendon Press, 1975.

Payne, Roger L. "Development and Implementation of the National Geographic Names Database". *Names* 43 (1995): 307–14.

Pearce, Ruth L. "Welsh Place-Names in Southeastern Pennsylvania". *Names* 11 (1963): 31–43.

Phillippo, James M. *Jamaica Its Past and Present State*. London: John Snow, 1843.

Pielke, Roger A. *The Hurricane*. London: Routledge, 1990.

Pillsbury, Richard. "The Street Name Systems of Pennsylvania before 1820". *Names* 17 (1969): 214–22.

Randall, Richard R. "A Report and Summary of the Fourth United Nations Conference on the Standardization of Geographical Names, Geneva 1982". *Names* 32 (1984): 343–46.

———. "The United States Board on Geographic Names and International Programs". *Names* 39 (1991): 249–56.

———. "The United States Board on Geographic Names and Its Work in Foreign Areas". *Names* 38 (1990): 173–82.

Randel, William. "Survival of Pre-English Place Names in Jamaica". *Names* 8 (1960): 24–29.

Raper, Arthur. "Gullies and What They Mean". *Social Forces* 16 (1937): 201–7.

Rayburn, Alan. "The Transfer of Scottish Placenames to Canada". *Names* 47 (1999): 313–23.

Redmonds, George. *Names and History: People, Places, and Things*. London: Hambledon and London, 2004.

Relph, E. *Place and Placelessness*. London: Pion, 1976.

Rennick, Robert. "How to Study Placenames". *Names* 53 (2005): 291–308.

Rentenaar, Rob. "How Danish Is Tivoli?" *Names* 24 (1976): 24–29.

Richardson, Ruth E. "Using Field-Names". *Landscapes* 3 (2002): 70–83.

Robb, John G. "Toponymy in Lowland Scotland: Depictions of Linguistic Heritage". *Scottish Geographical Magazine* 112 (1996): 169–76.

Robb, Kenneth A. "Names of Grants in Colonial Maryland". *Names* 17 (1969): 263–77.

Robe, Stanley L. "Caribbean Words in Mexican Toponymy". *Names* 8 (1960): 6–14.

Roberts, J. Timmons. "Power and Placenames: A Case Study From the Contemporary Amazon Frontier". *Names* 41 (1993): 159–81.

Roberts, Peter A. *West Indians and Their Language*. Cambridge: Cambridge University Press, 1988.

Robertson, James. *Gone is the Ancient Glory: Spanish Town, Jamaica, 1534–2000*. Kingston: Ian Randle Publishers, 2005.

———. "Stuart London and the Idea of a Royal Capital City". *Renaissance Studies* 15 (2001): 37–58.

Rubenstein, Hymie. " 'Bush', 'Garden', and 'Mountain' on the Leeward Coast of St Vincent and the Grenadines, 1719–1995". In *Islands, Forests, and Gardens in the Caribbean: Conservation and Conflict in Environmental History*, edited by Robert S. Anderson, Richard Grove and Karis Hiebert, 194–213. Oxford: Macmillan Caribbean, 2006.

Savage, Victor R., and Brenda S. Yeoh, eds. *Toponymics: A Study of Singapore Street Names*. Singapore: Eastern Universities Press, 2004 [2003].

Sawkins, James G. *Reports on the Geology of Jamaica; or, Part II of the West Indian Survey: Memoirs of the Geological Survey*. London: Longmans, Green and Co., 1869.

Schnakenbourg, Christian. *Histoire de l'industrie sucrière en Guadeloupe aux XIXe et XXe siècles: Tome I, La crise du système esclavagiste (1835–1847)*. Paris: L'Harmattan, 1980.

Seacole, Mary. *Wonderful Adventures of Mrs Seacole in Many Lands*. New York: Oxford University Press, 1988 [1857].

Sebba, Mark. *Spelling and Society: The Culture and Politics of Orthography Around the World*. Cambridge: Cambridge University Press, 2007.

Senior, Bernard Martin. *Jamaica, As It Was, As It Is, and As It May Be*. London: T. Hurst, 1835.

Sheridan, Richard B. "The Role of the Scots in the Economy and Society of the West Indies". *Annals of the New York Academy of Sciences* 292 (1977): 94–106.

Sherlock, Philip, and Hazel Bennett. *The Story of the Jamaican People*. Kingston: Ian Randle Publishers, 1998.

Shreve, Forrest. *A Montane Rain-Forest: A Contribution to the Physiological Plant Geography of Jamaica*. Washington, DC: Publication No. 199, Carnegie Institution of Washington, 1914.

Sistren, with Honor Ford Smith, ed. *Lionheart Gal: Life Stories of Jamaican Women*. London: The Women's Press, 1986.

Sloane, Hans. *A Voyage to the Islands Madera, Barbados, Nieves, S. Christophers, and Jamaica, with the Natural History of the Last of Those Islands*. London, 1707–25.

Smith, Grace Partridge. "They Call It Egypt". *Names* 2 (1954): 51–54.

Smith, Grant. "Describing Types of Placename Information". *Names* 40 (1992): 299–306.

Smyth, William J. *Map-making, Landscapes, and Memory: A Geography of Colonial and Early Modern Ireland c. 1530–1750*. Notre Dame: University of Notre Dame Press, 2006.

Stark, James H. *Stark's Jamaica Guide (Illustrated)*. Boston: James H. Stark, 1898.

Steers, J.A. "The Cays and the Palisadoes, Port Royal, Jamaica". *Geographical Review* 30 (1940): 279–96.

———. "The Coral Cays of Jamaica". *Geographical Journal* 95 (1940): 30–42.

———. "Sand Cays and Mangroves in Jamaica". *Geographical Journal* 96 (1940): 305–11.

Stewart, George R. "A Classification of Place Names". *Names* 2 (1954): 1–13.

———. *Names on the Globe*. New York: Oxford University Press, 1975.

———. *Names on the Land: A Historical Account of Placenaming in the United States*. San Francisco: Lexikos, 1982 [1945].

Sweeting, Marjorie M. *Karst Landforms*. London: Macmillan, 1972.

Taylor, Christopher. *Fields in the English Landscape*. Stroud, UK: Sutton Publishing, 2000 [1975].

Taylor, Douglas. "Names on Dominica". *Names* 2 (1954): 31–37.

Taylor, Frank Fonda. "From Hellshire to Healthshire: The Genesis of the Tourist Industry in Jamaica". In *Trade, Government, and Society in Caribbean History 1700–1920: Essays Presented to Douglas Hall*, edited by B.W. Higman, 139–54. Kingston: Heinemann Educational Books Caribbean, 1983.

Taylor, Mark Patrick, and Robert Stokes. "When Is a River Not a River? Consideration of the Legal Definition of a River for Geomorphologists Practising in New South Wales, Australia". *Australian Geographer* 36 (2005): 183–200.

Taylor, Simon, ed. *The Uses of Place-Names*. Edinburgh: Scottish Cultural Press, 1998.

Thornton, John. "Central African Names and African-American Naming Patterns". *William and Mary Quarterly* 50 (1993): 727–42.

Tole, Lise. "Measurement and Management of Human-Induced Patterns of Forest Fragmentation: A Case Study". *Environmental Management* 37 (2006): 788–801.

United States Board on Geographic Names. *Directions for the Treatment of Geographical Names in Jamaica*. Washington, DC: Board on Geographic Names, 1947.

Viner, Jacob. *The Role of Providence in the Social Order: An Essay in Intellectual History*. Princeton: Princeton University Press, 1972.

Waddell, Hope Masterton. *Twenty-Nine Years in the West Indies and Central Africa*. London: T. Nelson and Sons, 1863.

Waibel, Leo. "Place Names as an Aid in the Reconstruction of the Original Vegetation of Cuba". *Geographical Review* 33 (1943): 376–96.

Walter, Henriette. *Honni soit qui mal y pense: L'incroyable histoire d'amour entre le français et l'anglais*. Paris: Robert Laffont, 2002.

Wesche, Marjorie Bingham. "Place Names as a Reflection of Cultural Change: An Example from the Lesser Antilles". *Caribbean Studies* 12 (1972): 74–98.

White, William B. *Geomorphology and Hydrology of Karst Terrains*. New York: Oxford University Press, 1988.

Williams, Wilma. "Early Kingston". *Jamaica Journal* 6, nos. 2–3 (June–September 1971): 3–8.

Wilmot, Swithin. " 'A Stake in the Soil': Land and Creole Politics in Free Jamaica – the 1849 Elections". In *In the Shadow of the Plantation: Caribbean History and Legacy*, edited by Alvin O. Thompson, 314–33. Kingston: Ian Randle Publishers, 2002.

Wilson, Kathleen. "Empire, Trade, and Popular Politics in Mid-Hanoverian Britain: The Case of Admiral Vernon". *Past and Present* 121 (1988): 74–109.

Withers, Charles W.J. "Authorizing Landscape: 'Authority', Naming, and the Ordnance Survey's Mapping of the Scottish Highlands in the Nineteenth Century". *Journal of Historical Geography* 26 (2000): 532–54.

Wood, Betty, ed. *The Letters of Simon Taylor of Jamaica to Chaloner Arcedekne, 1765–1775*. Cambridge: Cambridge University Press for the Royal Historical Society, 2002. Camden Miscellany vol. 35, *Travel, Trade and Power in the Atlantic 1765–1884*.

Wright, Philip, and Paul F. White. *Exploring Jamaica: A Guide for Motorists*. London: Andre Deutsch, 1969.

Zelinsky, Wilbur. "Classical Town Names in the United States: The Historical Geography of an American Idea". *Geographical Review* 57 (1967): 463–95.

———. *Exploring the Beloved Country: Geographic Forays into American Society and Culture*. Iowa City: University of Iowa Press, 1994.

———. "Nationalism in the American Place-Name Cover". *Names* 31 (1983): 1–28.

———. *Nation into State: The Shifting Symbolic Foundations of American Nationalism*. Chapel Hill: University of North Carolina Press, 1988.

———. "Parsing Greater Washington's Namescape". *Names* 41 (1993): 344–60.

———. "Some Problems in the Distribution of Generic Terms in the Place-Names of the Northeastern United States". *Annals of the Association of American Geographers* 45 (1955): 319–49.

Zinkin, Vivian. "The Syntax of Place-Names". *Names* 17 (1969): 181–98.

Index

Aaron, Eugene Murray, 29, 102, 120
Abbey, The, 220
Abbey Court, 220
Abbey Farm, 220
Abbey Green, 42, 220
Abbeydale Pen, 220
Abbeydale Road, 220
Aberdeen, 41–42, 79, 220
Aboukir, 50
Abraham, 86
Abrahams, Peter, 27
Abu, 185
Accompong, 191, 202–3
Accompong, Negro-Town, 202
Accompong's Town, 203
Ackee Walk, 181, 213, 244
Adelaide Street, 233
Adelaide Village, 198
Adelphi, 55
Admiral's Mountain, 185
Admiral's Pen, 185, 255
Aeolus Valley, 55
Africa, 22, 24, 28, 50–52, 129, 175, 203, 253–54, 258
Afrikaans, 175
Agriculture, 155–56, 165, 167, 171, 180, 249, 251
Agua Alta, 26, 120
Aguacadiba, 26
Aintree, 215
Airy Mount Plantation, 167
Albany, 41
Albert, Prince, 237
Albert Street, 237

Albert Town, 185, 200
Albert Village, 198
Albion, 54, 82, 247
Albion Hill, 93
Alderton, 99, 198
Alderton Village, 198
Aleppo, 54
Aleppo Estate, 53
Alestro, 146
Alexander the Great, 52
Alexandria, 50, 223
Algeo, John, 239
Algeria, 50
Allerdyce Gardens, 244
Alley, 227, 243–44
Alley, The, 152, 227
Alligator Hole River, 117, 121
Alligator Pond, 135–36, 193, 228
Alligator Pond Bay, 135, 141
Alligator Pond Kay, 152
Alligator Pond River, 117, 121, 135
Alps, The, 45
Altamont, 43
Alves, 42
Ambience Jamaica, 194
Amby, 45
American Revolution, 47, 53, 237
Americas, 88, 234
Amerindians, 23–24
Ameyro, 26
Amity, 68
Amity Cross, 68, 225

Amity Hall, 68, 79, 82, 161, 209
Amity Hall Pen, 68
Amity Mountain, 68
Amsterdam, 45
Amsterdam Settlement, 179–80
Anchovy Bottom, 97
Anchovy Estate, 159
Anchovy Gully, 127–28
Anchovy River, 117, 120
Anchovy Valley, 95
Anchovy Valley River, 117, 120
Andes, 48
Angels, The, 29, 59
Anglesea, 247
Angola, 50
Angwins Crawle, 175
Annamaboe, 51–52
Annotto Bay, 228
Anotta Bay, 141
Antigua, 241
Antillia, 255
Appleton, 205
Apprenticeship, 30, 65–66, 200
Apricot Villa, 222
Arabia, 53
Arabia Felix, 53
Arawak, 26–27, 120
Arawak Hotel, 27
Arawak Inn, 194
Arcadia, 55, 79, 247
Arcadia Estate, 228
Arcadia Junction, 228

Ardenne, 44
Argyle, 41
Arm, 116
Armadale, 42
Arnett Gardens, 216
Arthurs Seat, 42
Ascot, 215
Ashley, 162
Ashley Hall, 162
Ashley Road, 213
Asia, 22, 51–52, 247, 253
Auchinbeddie, 42
Auchindown, 49
August Town, 201, 240, 242
Aurora, 55
Australia, 52
Avenue, 238–42
Axe and Adze, 180
Axe and Adze Settlement, 179

Baalbec, 53–54
Babylon, 53
Bacchus Run, 55
Back o' Wall, 214, 258
Back River, 114, 117
Bacon, Edgar Mayhew, 29, 102, 120
Bagnolds District, 230
Bahamas, 25
Bahia de la Vaca, 28
Baillieston, 205
Baird, Robert, 126, 182
Balaclava, 46
Bald Pate Way, 244
Baldwin's River Gully, 128
Ballards Vale, 96
Ballards Valley, 95
Ballast Bay, 141
Balmagie, 241
Bamboo, 200
Bamboo Pen, 255
Bamboo Pond, 136
Banana, 155, 193, 229
Banana Grounds, 184
Banana River, 117

Banana Walk, 244
Banana Way, 244
Banbury Cross, 203
Banff, 42
Bangalore, 51
Bank, 153–54
Bank Mountain Land, 189
Barbadoes Valley Cockpits, 49, 100
Barbados, 16, 49, 126–27, 220, 251
Barbados Avenue, 241
Barbary Coast, 28, 50
Barbary Hall, 50
Barbary Hill, 50
Barbary Hill Wharf, 50
Barbecue, 1, 187
Barbecue Bottom, 97
Barbecue Bridges, 232
Barbecue River, 118
Barbican, 221
Barbican Road, 234
Barcelona, 28
Barebush Cay, 152
Barkerswood, 108
Barry Street, 236
Bartons Plantation, 211
Bartons Wharf, 211
Basie, Count, 241
Bath, 202, 247
Bath at Milk River, 122
Bath of St Thomas the Apostle, 122
Bath Spring, 123
Battles, 30, 41, 45–47, 50
Bauxite, 29, 134, 148, 193
Bay, 140–43
Bay of Waterfalls, 29
Bay Vista Village, 199
Baypoint Villas, 221
Beach, 154, 194
Beanbird Lodge, 218
Beckford, William, 180–81, 186, 220
Beckford Kraal, 175
Beckford Street, 236

Beckford Town, 202
Beeston Street, 236
Beethoven, Ludwig van, 241
Belcour Lodge, 49
Belgium, 45
Belgrave Mews, 217
Bellas Gate, 230
Belle Air, 72
Belle Castle, 72
Belle Claire, 72
Belle Piece, 191
Belle Plain, 72, 103
Belle View, 1
Bellefont, 32
Bellers Moat, 146
Bellevue (Belle Vue), 72–73, 78–79, 81–82, 168
Bellevue Settlement, 179
Bellwood, 42
Belmont, 62, 67, 72, 78, 82
Belmont Beach, 145
Belmont Heights, 242
Belmont Road, 242
Belthazar, 57
Belvedere, 72, 81–82, 159
Belvidere, 73, 81
Benin, 50–51
Benlomond, 42
Bennett, Hazel, 255
Bensonton, 205
Berkshire, 40
Berkshire Hall, 209
Berlin, 44
Bermuda, 49
Bermuda Mount, 49
Bernard Lodge, 163
Bernard Street, 236
Berrydale, 41
Bert Road, 213
Bethany, 53, 56
Bethel, 53
Bethel Town, 53
Bethlehem, 53, 56
Beulah Park, 57
Beverly Hills, 234
Biafra, 51

Biblc, 52–53, 56–59
Biddeford, 188
Biddeford Pen Land, 188
Big Bottom, 97
Big Bridge, 231
Big Half Moon Cay, 153
Big Level, 86
Big Woods, 109
Bird River, 121
Birdsucker Mews, 217
Birnamwood, 108
Bitterwood Villa, 221
Black, Clinton V., 199
Black Grounds, 123, 184–85
Black Lands, 102
Blackheath (Black Heath), 162
Blackmoor Street, 236
Black Morass, 132, 134
Blackness, 41
Black River, 6, 29, 114, 117, 119–20, 133–34, 202, 211, 247
Black River Bay, 228
Black River Harbour, 147
Black River Morasses, 133
Black Shop, 207
Black Spring, 122
Black Spring Mountain, 88
Blackwood, 108
Blake, Sir Henry, 90, 120
Blake Bridge, 231
Blake Mountains, 90
Blake River, 120
Bleauwearie, 131
Blenheim, 44, 247
Blome, Richard, 104, 145, 180
Bloody Bay, 142
Blowing Point, 149
Blue Hole, 79, 82, 125, 145, 246
Blue Lagoon, 145
Blue Mountain, 88
Blue Mountain Peak, 87, 245

Blue Mountain Valley, 95
Blue Mountains, 86–89, 126, 210–11
Bluefields (Blue Fields), 28, 49, 62, 145, 247
Bluefields Bay, 145
Bluefields Mountain, 66
Boar Island, 134
Boar River, 118
Boatmans Bay, 141
Bochart, Charles, 14
Bog, 82
Bog Estate, 136, 151
Bog Islands, 151
Bog Walk, 4, 119, 182, 191, 206
Bog Walk Gorge, 206, 231
Bog Walk Tavern, 206
Bog Walk Village, 206
Boggy Gut, 130
Bogle, Paul, 130, 257
Bogue Hill, 92
Bogue Islands, 151, 153
Bold Attempt, 75
Bolivia, 48
Bombay, 51
Bonavista, 73
Bon Hill, 73
Bonneville, 44
Bonny Gate, 230
Bonny Pen, 180, 230
Bonny Pen Settlement, 180
Booby Kay, 152
Boroughbridge, 231
Boscobel Beach, 194
Bossue River, 121
Boston Beach, 154
Boston Settlement, 180
Boswell, James, 66
Botany Bay, 52
Bottom, 97
Boulevard, 242–43
Boundbrook, 47, 131
Bourdon Street, 236
Bournemouth Gardens, 184, 216

Bowen, Richard, 58
Bower Hall Settlement, 180
Bradshaw, Sonny, 241
Braeton, 215
Bragging Tom River, 120
Branch, 114, 116, 130
Brandon Hill, 79
Brathwaite, Kamau, 253
Brazil, 51
Brazilletto Mountains, 89
Breadnut Bottom, 97
Breadnut Hill, 96
Breadnut Island, 134
Breadnut Tree Piece, 191
Breadnut Valley, 96
Breaker Shoal, 153
Breezy Hill, 93
Bremen Valley, 44
Brid Port, 148
Bridge, 231–32
Bridgeport, 215
Bridgeview, 215
Brighton, 40, 78
Bristol, 38
Britannia, 54
British America, 38, 41
Broadgate, 230
Broadmouth River, 120
Broad River, 114
Broad Stone River, 117, 120
Brodber, Erna, 108
Bronte, 45
Brooklyn, 47
Brothers Union, 69
Brougham Village, 198
Broughton Lane, 237
Brown, Hamilton, 7, 200
Browne, Patrick, 13, 97
Browns Lane, 213
Browns Pasture, 192
Browns Town, 6, 7, 200, 204, 212
Brunswick, 44
Brussels, 45
Bryan Castle, 42–43
Bucknor's Reef, 153

Buff Bay, 247
Buff Bay River, 114
Bugaboo River, 121
Bugádoo, 185
Bull Bay, 141
Bull Bay Pen, 171
Bull Bay River, 118
Bull Dead Mountain, 94
Bull Head Mountain, 89, 94
Bull Head River, 118
Bull Hole, 145
Bull Savanna, 106–7, 228
Bulls Pen, 171
Bump, 94
Bunkers Hill, 47
Bunkers Hill Estate, 47
Bunkers Hill Mountain, 185
Burial Ground Point, 150
Burnside, 42
Burnt Savanna, 105, 107, 232
Burnt Savanna Mountains,
   89
Burnt Shop, 207
Burnt Sugar Work, 164
Burying Cay, 152
Bush Cay, 152
Bushy Park, 79, 172
Bustamante Highway, 257
Butlers, 61
Buxton Village, 198
Bybrook, 131, 210

Cabarita Island, 151
Cabarita Plantation, 165
Cabarita (Cabarito) Point,
   149
Cabaritta River, 118, 254
Cabbage Bottom, 97
Cabbage River, 120
Cabbage Valley, 95
Cabo de Farol, 28
Cacoon Castle, 177
Cacoon Castle Pen, 180
Cacoon River, 117, 120
Cacoon Settlement, 180
Caguay (Caguaya), 26–27

Cairo, 50
Calabar, 50–51
Calabar Mews, 217
Calabash Gully, 129
Calabash Bottom River, 117
Calabash Ridge, 88
Caledonia, 41, 54, 78, 82
Calibash Bottom, 97
Callabash Bay, 141–42
Callaloo Gutters, 129, 131,
   221
Callaloo Meadows, 217
Callaloo Mews, 217, 221
Callaloo Piece, 191
Cambridge, 40, 79, 82, 231
Cambridge Back Lands, 189
Cambridge Estate, 189
Cambridge Farm, 177
Cambridge Gut, 130
Campbell Piece, 191
Camps Hill, 91
Canaan, 57
Canaan Estate, 57
Canaan Valley, 57
Canada, 47–48
Canberra Avenue, 241
Candlefly Peak, 241
Cane River, 117
Canoe Bay, 141
Cape Cod, 51
Cape Trafalgar, 30
Capture Land, 254
Cardiff, 42, 247
Cardiff Hall, 209, 217
Careening Island, 151
Careening Key, 152
Caribbean, 22–25, 43,
   49–50, 73, 156–57, 165,
   185, 241, 251, 256
Caribbean Avenue, 241
Caribbean Close, 241
Caribbean Isle, 194
Carining Coi, 153
Carlisle, 247
Carlisle Bay, 202
Carlsruhe, 44

Carmichael's Run, 190
Carpenters Mountains, 89
Carrickfoyle, 43
Carrion Crow Bay, 141
Carthagena, 31
Cartography, 8, 10, 13–14,
   16, 35, 85, 150, 153, 184,
   244
Casa Maria, 194
Cascade, 60, 137
Cascade Plantation, 167
Cascade River, 137
Cashew Pen, 169
Cashmans River, 119
Cashoo River, 120
Cassava River, 117
Cassidy, Frederick G.,
   26–27, 132, 174, 180, 185
Castile Fort Pen, 31
Castle, 6, 17, 40–43, 80,
   160–63, 168, 172, 176,
   208–10, 221, 247, 249–50
Castle Fort Villa, 221
Castleton Gardens, 182
Catherine Mount
   Mountain, 185–86
Catherine's Peak, 88
Cathkin, 42
Cave, 98–99, 126
Cave Bottom, 97
Cave Hill Estate, 218
Cave River, 98, 114, 226
Cave Valley, 119, 223
Cave Valley River, 98
Caves Island, 134
Cay, 151–53
Cayman, 25
Caymanas Estate, 8, 218
Caymanas Park, 218
Cedar Grove, 108
Cedar Grove Pen, 171
Cedar Gully, 128
Cedar Valley, 79, 82, 95–96
Central America, 48–49
Central Village, 6, 198, 225
Chalets, The, 219

Chalky Hill, 93
Chalky River, 117
Chancery Lane, 237
Channel, 154
Chantilly, 44
Chapel (The Chappel), 202
Chapelton, 135, 158, 202, 223, 232
Charing Cross, 225
Charlemont, 42
Charles I, 256
Charles II, 205, 256
Charles Pasture, 192
Charles Square, 256
Charles Street, 236
Charlestown, 202–3, 254
Charlotte Lane, 237
Charlottenburgh, 44
Charlton Alley, 244
Chateau (Chatteau), 163
Chateau Estate, 163
Chateau Morant, 163
Chaucer, Geoffrey, 241
Chedwin, 215
Cheese, William, 10
Cheesefield, 10
Cheesefield Pen, 10
Cheesefield Plantation, 10
Chepstowe, 42
Chereras, 29
Chestnut Lane, 237
Cherry Garden, 42–43, 183–84
Cherry Garden Estate, 183
Cherry Garden Mountain, 183
Cherry Gardens, 219
Chester Castle, 210
Chesterfield, 79
Chigoe Foot Market, 208
Chigury Hut, 210
China, 52, 253
Chocolata Bay, 142
Chocolata Gully, 129
Chocolata Hole, 145
Chocolata Ridge, 88

Chovey, 230
Christmas Island, 151
Church Corner, 226
Church Street, 234, 236
Church Pasture, 192
Churchill Corner, 227
Ciboney Ocho Rios, 194
Cindy Villa, 222
Cistern Gully, 128
Cistern River, 117, 120
City, 206, 212–17, 250
Claremont, 40, 78
Clarence Villa, 221
Clarendon, 31–32, 38, 230
Clarendon Park, 172
Clarke, Lorna, 3
Clarks Town, 200, 233
Clarkson, Thomas, 200
Clarkson Town, 200, 237
Clarkson Village, 198
Clarksonville, 199
Classical names, 17, 45, 50, 52–55, 91, 221
Clay River, 117, 120
Clifton, 1, 40, 78, 82
Clifton Hill, 79
Clifton Pen, 79
Clive, Robert, 41
Clones, 42
Clonmell, 43
Close, 238–41
Close Harbour, 147
Cluny, 44
Clydesdale, 42
Clydeside, 42
Coastal features, 138–40
Coates Ford, 231
Cockburn Gardens, 244
Cockpit, 99–102
Cockpit Country, 35, 97, 99–102, 184–85
Cockpit Point, 149
Cockpit River Head, 100, 124
Coco River, 117
Cocoa Bay, 141

Cocoa Ridge, 88, 230
Cocoa River, 120
Cocoa Walk, 79, 181
Cocorocoe (Cocrocoe) Gully, 128
Coddringtons Creek, 145
Codrington Hole, 145
Coffee, 15, 30, 108, 131, 155–56, 167, 178, 186–87
Coffee Ground Pass Piece, 191
Coffee Grove Plantation, 167
Coffee River, 120
Coffee Tree Piece, 191
Coffee Walk, 181
Coffee Walk Mountain, 181, 187
Colbeck, Colonel John, 162
Colbeck Castle, 162, 250
Colbecks Estate, 162
Colchis, 54, 247
Cold Harbour, 145–46
Cold Ridge, 88
Cold Spring (Coldspring), 79, 122, 134
Cold Spring Plantation, 167
Cole Gate, 229
Colombo Close, 241
Colonial Church Union, 200
Colonies, The, 35
Columbus, Christopher, 23–24, 26–29, 52
Columbus Heights, 29
Columbus Park, 29
Come See Plantation, 168
Comfort, 66
Comfort Castle, 66
Comfort Hall, 66, 79, 209
Comfort Village, 66, 198
Concord, 47
Concordia, 55
Concrete Jungle, 216
Congo, 51, 203
Congo Bottom, 51

Congo Bridge, 51, 232
Congo Mountain, 51, 188
Connolley (Connolly)
    Avenue, 244
Constable, John, 40
Constant Spring, 60, 71, 239
Constant Spring Estate, 159,
    220
Constant Spring Gully, 240
Constant Spring Road, 226,
    242
Content, 62, 67, 78–83, 168,
    173, 248
Content Avenue, 242
Content Estate, 63, 65, 83
Content Gap, 62
Content Garden, 63, 65
Content Mountain, 63
Content My Own, 66
Content Pen, 63, 65, 83
Content Plantation, 63, 65,
    79
Content River, 113
Content Settlement, 63, 65,
    179
Content Village, 62, 198
Cony River, 121
Cook, 230, 254
Cook, Captain James, 52,
    230, 254
Cookell, 254
Cooks Bottom, 97
Cooks Gate, 229
Cooks Hill, 254
Coolie Shop, 207, 255
Coolshade, 79
Cooper Hill, 43
Cooreville Gardens, 241
Copper River, 120
Copse, 108
Coquar Bay, 142
Coquar Plumb Bay, 141
Coral Cliff, 194
Corn Husk River, 117
Corn Puss Gap, 94
Corner, 226–28

Corner Forty-Four, 227
Corner Pen, 226–27
Corner Shop, 207
Cornhill, 236
Cornwall, 14, 31, 247
Cornwall College, 31
Cornwall Court, 218
Cornwall Estate, 31
Cornwall Mountain, 31
Cornwall Pen, 31
Cornwall Regional
    Hospital, 31
Cornwallis, General
    Charles, 47
Coronation Market, 35
Cottage, 79, 82, 163–64
Cottage Pen, 79, 172
Cottage Settlement, 180
Cotterwood, 108, 254
Cotton Tree Gully, 129
Cotton Tree Spring, 85, 122
Counties, 2, 31–34, 215
Couples, 195
Court, 160–63, 210, 218–21,
    243
Courtleigh, The, 195
Courtleigh Manor Hotel,
    220
Cousins's Cove, 143
Cove, 114, 140, 142–44, 146,
    148, 158
Cove Harbour, 146
Cowards Ridge, 88
Cow Bay, 141
Cow Bay Point, 149
Cow Park, 172
Cow Park Pen, 171–72
Coyaba, 27
Crab Hole Bay, 142
Crab River, 121
Crab Lanthorn Gully, 127
Craig Head, 42
Craigie, 42
Crane Corner, 227–28
Craskell, Thomas, 14–15
Craul Bay, 141

Crawfish Spring, 122–23
Crawford, 202
Crawford Town, 202–3
Crawl, 174–76
Crawle, 168–69, 174–76,
    181, 249, 251
Crawle Estate, 175
Crawle Ford, 231
Crawle Halt, 176, 230
Crawle Pen, 175, 178
Crawle Piece, 191
Crawle Pond, 175
Crawle River, 175
Crawles, The, 176
Creek, 140, 145–46
Creighton Hall, 161
Cremona, 45
Creole, 7, 20, 246, 249,
    252–54
Crescent, 238–40
Criterion Hall, 10
Crofts Mountain, 89
Crooked Gut, 130
Crooked River, 114
Crooked Spring, 122
Cross, 202
Cross, The, 224–25
Cross Keys, 225
Cross Pass, 232
Cross Roads, 224–25
Cross-Path, 203
Crotona Court, 219–20
Crown Tavern, 207
Crystal Waters Villas, 221
Cuba, 24–25, 49, 245, 257
Cuba Mount, 49
Cuckolds Point, 149
Cudjoe Hill, 91
Cudjoes Town, 203
Cuffee Gully, 129
Cuffee Spring, 85, 121
Cuffees Town, 203
Culloden, 41, 49
Cumberland, 215
Cumberland Pen, 178
Cumberland Road, 233

Cuna Cuna Pass, 95
Cuna Cuna Trail, 211
Cundall, Frank, 81
Cunhacuna Pass, 95
Cuni Cuni, 88, 95
Cunningham Mews, 217
Cunu Cunu Wood, 211
Cushmans River, 119
Cut Throat Gully, 127–28
Cut Throat Hill, 92
Cut Through Hill, 92
Cutting Grass Spots River, 117

Dahomey, 51
Dallas, 90
Dallas, R. C., 99–100, 112–13, 121, 186, 254
Dallas Castle, 90
Dallas Mountain, 89–90
Dalvey, 42
Danbottom, 97
Darien, 49
Databases, 13–17
Davis Cove Wharf, 211
Davis's Cove, 143
Dawkins Bog Farm, 177
Dawkins Caymanas, 83
Dawkins Caymanas Estate, 8
Dawkins Salt Pond Pen, 177
Dawkins Spring, 121
Daytona, 215
De Camp, David, 3
Dead Sea, 57
Deanery Road, 242
Dee Side, 41, 79
Deep Ford, 231
Deep Gully, 128
Denbigh, 42
Denbigh Crawle, 175
Denham Town, 213, 237
Derby Ford, 231
Derry, 42, 58
Develders Pass, 95, 232
Devils Hole, 125, 145
Devils Race Course, 86

Devils River, 113
Dias, 182, 229
Dicks Pasture, 192
Dignum Mountain, 55
Dinner Time, 86
Dionysus, 55
Dirty Spring, 122
Discovery Bay, 29, 198
Distress, 173
Districts, 5, 8, 13, 16, 20, 32–35, 100, 107, 125, 156, 174, 187–88, 234, 245–46
Dobsons Farm, 177
Dockyard Lane, 234
Doctors Cave, 154
Doctors Cave Beach, 154, 192
Dog War a Mattuse Lane, 237
Dolphin Head, 94, 171
Dolphin Island, 151
Dolphin Pen, 171
Dominica, 24
Dominica Drive, 241
Dominican Republic, 25
Don Christopher's Cave, 98
Don Christopher's Cove, 143
Donald Sangster Airport, 257
Donegal, 42
Don Figuerero's Mountains, 89
Dornoch Head, 124
Dornock, 42
Dorrels Island, 151
Douglas Castle, 210
Dove Cote Park, 172
Drax, William, 162
Drax Hall, 161–62, 208
Dream Scape Villa, 221
Drive, 238–41
Drunkenmans Key, 152
Dry Gut, 130
Dry Harbour, 146, 178
Dry Harbour Mountains, 89

Dry Harbour Wharf, 211
Dry Hill, 93
Dry River, 117–18
Dry River Pasture, 192
Dry Shoal, 153
Dry Sugar Works, 164
Dublin, 55, 205
Dublin Castle, 42
Duckenfield Hall, 161
Duff House, 42
Duhaney Park, 240
Duke Street, 236
Dulce Domum, 55
Dumbarton, 41
Dumblane, 42
Dumfries, 41
Dumfries Street, 237
Dun Laoghaire, 205
Dunbar, 41
Dunbar Ground, 191
Dunbars Corner, 227
Duncans, 176
Dundee, 1, 41, 83
Dungle, The, 255
Dunkeld, 41
Dunkirk, 53
Dunns Hole, 145
Dunns River, 137
Dunns River Falls, 137
Dunns River Falls and Beach, 154
Dunrobin, 41
Duplin, 42
Duppy River, 121
Dutch, 175
Dyke Road, 258

East Branch, 114, 116
East Kingston, 35
East Queen Street, 35–36, 236
East Street, 236
Eastwood, 42
Easy Mind, 66
Ebenezer, 57
Eden, 56, 58, 247

Eden Estate, 56, 169
Eden Hill, 56
Eden Mount, 56
Eden Mountain, 56
Eden Park, 56
Eden Pen, 169
Eden Vale, 56
Eden Wood, 56
Edgewater, 215
Edinburgh, 41
Edinburgh Castle, 42
Edmund's Valley Mountains, 89
Ed's Lost Rack Pit, 99
Eel River, 117, 120
Eglinton, 42
Egypt, 50, 58, 214, 254, 258
Egypt Estate, 191, 232, 254
Egypt Pen, 50
Elderslie, 42
Eleven Mile, 225
Elgin Street, 237
Elim Estate, 57
Elim Mountain, 57
Elizabeth II, 192
Ellen Street, 233
Ellerslie, 42
Elletson, Thomas Hope, 71
Ellington, Duke, 241
Elphinstowe, 42
Elysium, 55
Emerald Island, 151
Emmaus, 57
Enchanted Gardens, 194
Endeavour, 74–75, 78, 82
Enfield, 79
Enfield New Works, 164
Enfield Old Works, 164
England, 23–24, 36–41, 45, 72, 77, 130, 163, 204, 210, 224, 241, 255
English Place-Name Society, 11
Envy, 173
Envy Not, 69
Envy Valley Pen, 69

Eponyms, 7–10, 21–22, 60–61, 64, 67, 71–73, 77, 114, 120–23, 127–30, 142–43, 149–50, 157, 170–71, 197–200
Essex Valley, 95
Essex Valley Mountains, 89
Estate, 64, 80, 92, 156–72, 174–75, 190, 211–12, 216, 218, 249, 251
Ethiopia, 258
Eureka, 55
Europe, 19, 21–28, 43–46, 52, 234, 253
Evans Piece, 191
Excellent Town, 200
Exeter, 247

Fall, 136–37
Fall River, 136–37
Falls River, 1
Falmouth, 134, 247
Fantasy Resort, 195
Far Enough, 168
Farquhars Beach, 154
Farm, 82, 177–78, 181
Farm Hill, 178, 187
Farm Mountain, 178
Farm Pen, 79, 178
Farm Plantation, 178
Farm Turn, 228
Fat Hog Quarter, 4, 35
Fat Hog Quarter Estate, 159
Fat Hog Quarter River, 118
Fellowship, 67
Fellowship Hall, 67, 79, 209
Fellowship Hall Pen, 67
Feriagua Channel, 154
Fermor, Patrick Leigh, 191
Fern Gully, 129, 229
Fetter Lane, 237
Field, 5, 13, 190–92
Figtree Bay, 141
Figurary Gully, 128
Finn, The, 43
First Street, 236

Fish River, 117
Fishermans Bay, 141
Fishers Row, 234
Five Fall Spring, 122
Five Miles, 225
Flamingo Pond, 135
Flat Bridge, 231
Flatt Cove, 143
Fleet Street, 236
Flemington, 42
Fletchers Land, 189
Fletchers Lane, 189
Flint Bay, 141
Flint River, 117
Flint River Estate, 158
Florence, 45
Florida, 104, 132
Flower Hill, 42
Flowers Town, 213
Folly, 173
Folly Bay, 143, 150
Folly Pen, 79
Folly Point, 150
Font Hill, 220
Font Hill Estate, 220
Fontabelle, 73
Fontabelle Spring, 125
Fontainbleau Plantation, 44
Fonthill Abbey, 220
Ford, 231
Foreshore Road, 257
Forest Hut, 82, 210
Forges Point, 149
Forked River, 116
Fort Clarence, 135
Fort Stewart Pen, 170
Fort William Estate, 229
Foster Lane, 237
Founts (Harbour), 146
Four Mile, 225
Four Paths, 207, 225, 229–30
Four Roads, 225
Fowl House Spring, 123
Fowle Point, 149
France, 23–24, 30, 43–45, 73
Frankfield, 223, 228

Frankfort, 247
Frankfurt, 44
Franklin Town, 212
Free Point, 149, 201
Free Towne, 201
Freedom, 201
Freedom Village, 199
Freefield, 42
Freeman, 201
Freemans Bay, 201
Freetown, 81–82, 201
Frenchmans Island, 134
Frenchmans River, 134
Fresh River, 132
Fresh Water Spring, 122
Friars Cap Point, 150
Friendship, 62–63, 66–68,
   78, 81–83, 160, 173, 248
Friendship Cross, 67, 225
Friendship Estate, 67
Friendship Farm, 67
Friendship Gap, 67
Friendship Hall, 67
Friendship Lane, 242
Friendship Mountain, 67, 79
Friendship Park Avenue,
   242
Friendship Park Road, 242
Friendship Pen, 67, 79
Friendship Plantation, 67
Friendship River, 113
Friendship Valley, 67
Frome, 229
Furrys Town, 202, 203
Fustic Grove Pen, 171
Fyffe and Rankin, 61

Gallinepa River, 118, 120
Galleon Harbour, 147
Galloway, 41
Gallows Point, 149
Gap, 94–95
Garden, 182–84, 215–17
Garden Boulevard, 240
Garden Hall, 182
Garden Hill, 182, 184

Garden Hill Plantation, 182
Garden Valley Settlement,
   182
Gardens of Arcadia, 55, 219
Garland Grove, 108
Garvey, Marcus, 18, 209, 257
Garvey Maceo School, 257
Garveymeade, 216, 257
Gate, 229–30
Gazeland Meadows, 218
Generic terms, 3, 8, 12, 18,
   60, 83–86, 148, 155–57,
   166, 177, 235, 249–52
Geneva, 45
Geneva Mountain, 89
Geographical Names,
   Committees, 11–12, 16,
   96, 198, 200
George V Park, 257
Georges Lane, 237
Georges Pen, 218
Georges Plain, 103
Georges Plain Estate, 188
Georges Plain Estate
   Mountain, 83
Georges Plain Mountain,
   188, 251
Georges Valley, 96
Georgia, 46
German Town, 44
Germany, 30, 44–45, 200
Gethsemane, 57
Getz, Stan, 241
Ghana, 50, 256
Ghost Town, 213
Gibraltar, 30–31, 78, 247
Gimme-Me-Bit, 4, 252
Ginger Hill, 93
Ginger Hill Settlement, 180
Ginger Ridge, 88
Ginger River, 117
Glade Gate, 229
Glasgow, 41, 79, 82, 224
Glen Abbey, 219–20
Glen Islay, 42
Glenmore, 42

Glock Corner, 227
Gloucestershire, 195
Goat Gully, 129
Goat Hill, 92
Goat Isle, 151
Goat Pen Hole, 145
Godfreys Spring Farm, 177
Gold Street, 236
Golden Grove, 78, 82, 108,
   246–47
Golden Grove Village, 198
Golden River, 113
Golden-Spring Estate, 228
Goldsmiths Villa, 221
Golfo de bien Tempo, 28
Good Hope, 71–72, 79, 191,
   194
Good Hope Mountain, 72,
   89
Good Intent, 72, 79
Goodwill, 72
Goomers Town, 203
Gordon, George William,
   257
Gordon Castle, 42
Gordon House, 257
Gordons Farm, 177
Gordons Store, 207
Goshen, 50, 56–57, 82, 247
Goshen Estate, 56
Goshen Pen, 56
Gossamer, 86
Gosse, Philip Henry, 62, 145
Government Pen, 169, 186
Graemes Corner, 226–27
Grames's, 226
Gran Oran, 50
Grand Cairo, 50
Grand Cascade, 137
Grand Cave, 98
Grand Tour, 43, 45
Grange Lane, 233
Grants Pen, 216
Grants Pen Road, 216
Grass Piece Hill, 92
Grass Quit Glade, 244

Grass River, 117, 133
Grassy Pond, 135
Gravel Hill, 93
Grays Inn Halt, 230
Great Britain, 22–26, 29–43, 46, 51, 54, 60, 158, 162–63, 166, 170, 194, 204, 234, 238, 241, 248–49, 252–53
Great Cascade, 137
Great Cave, 98
Great Fall, 136
Great Goat Island, 151
Great House Close, 219
Great Morass, 132–33, 145
Great Pelican Key, 152
Great Pond, 136
Great Pond of Fresh Water, 135
Great River, 114
Great Salt Island, 151
Great Salt Pond, 135
Great Salt Ponds, 136
Great Sea, 135
Great Spanish River, 118
Greater Portmore, 236, 240, 258
Greece, 54–55, 199, 221, 234
Greek Pond Spit, 150
Green Bay Bank, 153
Green Park, 172
Green Pond, 135–36
Green Vale, 79
Green Walk, 181
Green Hill, 79, 82, 93
Green Island, 151, 247
Green Island Harbour, 146
Green Isle, 151
Greenfield, 79
Greenfield Town, 213
Greenock, 42
Greenwich Park, 172, 247
Greenwich Pen, 213
Greenwich Street, 237
Greenwich Town, 213, 234
Gregory Park, 215, 258
Grenada, 24

Grenada Crescent, 241
Ground, 184–85
Grove, 1, 104, 107–8, 159, 167, 171, 180, 184, 228, 243
Guadeloupe, 49
Guanaboa, 26
Guanaboa Vale, 26, 97
Guantanamo, 24
Guatemala, 49
Guava Park, 172
Guava River, 116–17
Gully, 126–29
Gully Piece, 191
Gun Key, 152
Gun Point, 149
Gunne Cay, 152
Gurney, Joseph John, 104, 169
Gurney Village, 198
Gut, 129–31
Gutter, 131–32
Gutterez, 132
Gutters, 131
Gutters Lane, 237
Gutters Pen, 132
Guys Hill, 86

Haddington, 41
Haiti, 25, 49, 256
Hakewill, James, 224
Halberstadt, 44
Hales Hole, 145
Half Moon Bay, 141–42
Half Moon Kay, 152
Half Way Tree, 202, 225–26, 239, 255
Half Way Tree Road, 224
Half-a-Bottle, 86
Hall, 160–62, 208–10
Hall, Douglas, 254
Hall Green Content, 64
Hall's, 209
Hall's Delight, 66
Halse (Hals) Hall, 161, 169–70, 208

Halse Hall Crawle, 175
Halse Hall Pen, 170
Halt, 230–31
Ham Walk, 181
Hamilton Town, 7
Hampden Sugar Estate, 190
Hampshire Lane, 233
Hampstead, 40, 79
Hampton Court, 163
Hand Dog Bump, 94
Hannah Town, 212
Hannah's Pen, 212
Hanover, 32, 143–44, 224, 247
Hanover Street, 233, 236
Happy Content, 66
Happy Grove, 79, 108
Happy Hut, 210
Happy Retreat, 168
Harbour Street, 224, 234, 236
Harbour View, 206, 241
Hardwar Gap, 94
Harmony Farm Pen, 68
Harmony Hall, 68, 78, 209
Harmony Hall Mountain, 68
Harmony Hall Pen, 68
Harmony Hill, 68
Harmony Pen, 68
Harmony Plantation, 68
Harmony Vale Plantation, 68
Harper, Charles, 14
Harris Savanna, 106–7
Harris Street, 213
Harrison, Thomas, 15
Hastings, Warren, 51
Harvey Village, 198
Hato de Liguanea, 103
Haughton Court, 163
Haughton Court New Works, 63
Haughton Court Old Works, 63
Haughton Hall, 208

Haven Walk, 244
Havendale Heights, 244
Hawai'i, 256
Haycock Hill, 92
Hays (Hayes) Savanna,
  106–7
Hazard Estate, 159
Hazard Plantation, 168
Head, 94, 124
Healthshire Hills, 92
Heartease, 5–6, 226
Heath Hall, 161–62
Hectors River, 54
Hedonism, 195
Heights, 216–19, 243
Helicon, 55, 198–99
Heliopolis, 53
Hellshire Hills, 92
Hellshire Hummock, 94
Hellshire Park North, 218
Hellshire Park North Estate,
  218
Hellshire Point, 149
Henderson, John, 148, 202
Henry VII, 40
Hermitage, 62–63, 67, 76,
  78, 80–82, 173
Hermitage Reservoir, 76
Hermitage Road, 242
Heywood Street, 236
Hibernia, 42, 54
Hibiscus Lodge, 194
Hickeringill, Edmund, 174
Hideaway Villa, 222
Higgin Land, 189
Higgin Town, 189
Highgate, 40, 79, 230
High Fall, 136
High Holborn, 236
High Land of Pedro Point,
  149
High Peak, 88
High Street, 234
Highway, 243
Hillary, Sir Edmund, 174
Hill, 12, 86–88, 91–97, 158,

167, 171, 185–86, 216, 243,
  254–55
Hill Middle, 191
Hill Crest Villa, 221
Hillaby, 49
Hillcrest, 219
Hillside, 79
Hispaniola, 24, 26, 256
Hobby's Hole, 145
Hoddars (Hooders) River,
  119
Hog Grass Bump, 94
Hog Hole River, 118
Hog House Hill, 92
Hog Meat Bottom, 97
Hog River, 118
Hogghole Bay, 141
Hoggs Run, 190
Hole, 125–26, 144–45
Holiday Inn Jamaica, 194
Holland, 45, 51, 190, 247
Holland, Lord and Lady, 45
Hollywell, 125
Holy Mount Plantation, 57,
  168
Holywell, 125
Home Castle, 42
Homers Cove, 143
Homer's Mountain, 54
Hope, 70–72, 160, 173
Hope, Richard, 242
Hope, Major Roger, 71
Hope Aqueduct, 71
Hope Bay, 72, 146
Hope Botanical Gardens,
  71, 192, 242
Hope Boulevard, 71, 242
Hope Estate, 71, 192
Hope Mews, 217
Hope Pastures, 71, 192, 234,
  242
Hope River 29, 113, 241,
  242
Hope Road 242
Hope Zoo, 71
Hopefield, 72

Hopefull Valley (Vally), 71,
  95
Hopeton, 72
Hopeton Mews, 217
Hopewell, 41, 62–63, 67, 72,
  78, 82–83, 125
Hopewell Lane, 242
Hopewell Mountain, 180
Hopewell Pen, 79
Hopewell Settlement, 180
Horse Savana, 106–7
Horse Savanna River, 118
Hot Salt Spring, 122
Hot Spring, 122
Hotel, 27, 193–95
Hudson River, 205
Hudsons Bottom, 97
Hudsons Hole, 145
Hull, 204
Hummock, 94
Hungry Gully, 129
Huntley, 82
Hunts (Hunt's) Bay, 130,
  145, 148
Hut, 210–11
Hydrological features,
  110–11

Ida, 50
Independence City, 206,
  215, 250
India, 51–52, 94
Industry, 75, 78
Industry Mountain, 180
Industry Settlement, 179–80
Industry Village, 198
Inverness, 41
Ipswich, 230
Ipswich Cave, 98
Ireland, 22, 37–38, 42, 54,
  158, 166, 170, 233, 238
Irish Town, 43
Iron River, 117
Irons Mountain, 188
Island, 134, 151–53, 245
Islington, 205

Israel, 52–53, 56, 256
Italy, 45
Iter Boreale, 55, 170
Ivy Green Mews, 217
Ivy Store, 207

Jack Tar Village, 199
Jackass Hill, 93
Jackass River, 121
Jacks Hill, 93, 219
Jacks Hole, 145
Jack's Place, 218
Jack's View Heights, 218
Jacksons Valley, 95
Jacob Hut, 210
Jamaica, 24–25, 36, 102, 218,
    221, 245, 255–56
Jamaica Automobile
    Association, 16, 27, 81
Jamaica Grande, 194
Jamaica Hilton, 27
Jamaica Inn, 194
Jamaica International
    Exhibition, 193
Jamaica Jamaica, 194
Jamaica Omnibus Services,
    214
Jamaica Palace, 194
Jamaica Pegasus, 194
Jamaica Place Names
    Committee, 12, 96, 198,
    200
Jamaica Safari Village, 199
Jamaica Survey
    Department, 16, 198
Jamaica Tourist Board,
    194
Jamba Spring, 50
James Hill, 93
James Street, 236
Java, 51
Jenny's Gutt, 130
Jericho, 53, 56
Jerusalem, 53, 56
Jew Spring, 121
Jews, 53

Jocks Lodge, 42
John Crow Hill, 92
John Crow Mountains, 86,
    89–90, 203
John Crow Peak, 88
John Robinson, 61
Johns Hall, 208
Johns Lane, 237
Johns Peak, 95
Johns Rock, 154
Johnson, Dr Samuel, 66
Johnson Mountain, 188
Johnson's Pen, 212
Jointwood, 109
Jones Pen, 213
Jones Town, 213
Jordan, 52–53, 56–57
Jose Marti School, 257
Juan de Bolas, 61
Juan de Bolas River, 114
Jubilee Pen, 57
Judgement Cliff, 74
Junction, 224–25, 228–31
Junction Road, 228, 231
Juno Pen, 55
Jupiter Ford, 231

Kapp, Kit S., 14
Karachi Avenue, 241
Kay, 152–53
Keats, John, 40
Keith Hall, 41
Kemps Hill, 93
Kenco Spring, 122
Kenmure, 42
Kenmure Ridge, 88
Kensington, 40, 78, 82, 205,
    215
Kentucky, 46
Kettle Spring, 121
Key, 152–53
Kildare, 9, 42
Killiekrankie, 42
Kilmarnock, 42
King Avenue, 213
King Gate, 229

King Street, 36, 209, 224,
    233, 236–37, 248
King's Highway, 243
Kings Mews, 217
Kingston, 17, 31, 35, 53,
    169–70, 174, 198–99,
    204–6, 209–20, 223–28,
    232–45, 247, 255, 257–58
Kingston Gardens, 215
Kingston Harbour, 25–26,
    36, 103, 119, 122, 146–48,
    150, 154, 205–6, 212, 216,
    235
Kingston Lane, 237
Kingston on Thames, 204,
    247
Kingston on Hull, 204
Kingston Pen, 212, 214
Kingston Racecourse, 257
Kingston Road, 224
Kingstown, 205
Kinloss, 42
Kirkvine, 193
Kiwi Villa, 222
Knapdale, 42
Knight Street, 236
Knockpatrick, 43
Knollis, Humphrey, 14
Knowles, Sir Charles, 256
Konigsberg, 44
Kremlin, 46

La Caridad, 31
La Mirage, 195
Labour Content, 64
Labour in Vain Savana, 106
Lacovia, 29, 89, 202
Lacovia Gut, 130
Lacovia Mountain, 89
Lacovia (Wild Slip)
    Mountains, 89
Ladds Lane, 237
Lagoon, 136
Lagoon River, 120, 132
Lake, 134
Lambkin Hill Pen, 171

Lambs Valley, 95
Lancaster, 79
Lancewood, 109
Lancewood Pen, 171
Land, 188–89
Lane, 233–238
Language, 7, 19–20, 23–30, 43, 50, 104, 112, 118–20, 129, 152, 175, 253–54, 258
Languedoc, 44
Lapland, 45
Last Street, 237
Latinuna (Harbour), 146
Latium, 45
Laughlands, 189, 202
Launceswood Spring, 121
Lawes Street, 236
Lawrence Tavern, 206
Lebanon, 52, 56, 79, 213, 253
Left Arm, 116
Left Branch, 114
Leith, 41
Lennox, 42
Leogan, 49
Le Page, R.B., 132, 174, 185
Leslie, Charles, 27, 104, 112
Lesser Portmore, 258
Lethe, 55
Level Bottom, 97
Lewis Store, 207
Leyden, 45
Liberty, 210
Liberty Castle, 210
Liberty Content, 66
Liberty Hall, 209–10
Liberty Hill, 210
Liberty Pen, 210
Liberty Tree, 210
Liberty Valley Village, 198, 210
Life Styles Resort, 195
Liffy Side, 43
Light Hole, 99
Light Hole Cave, 99
Ligon, Richard, 126

Liguanea, 25–26, 220, 227, 234
Liguanea Avenue, 227
Liguanea Mews, 217
Liguanea Pen, 255
Liguanea Plain, 103, 238–39
Liguanea Plaza, 26, 227
Liguanea Ridge, 26
Liguanea Villa, 26, 221, 227
Lilys Rock, 154
Lima, 48
Lime Bush River, 117
Lime Hall, 227
Lime Key, 152
Lime Kiln Bay, 143
Lime Savana, 105
Lime Street, 234
Lime Tree Garden Pen, 167, 171, 183
Lime Tree Garden Plantation, 183
Lime Walk, 181
Limerick, 43
Limestone Gully, 128
Lincoln Pen, 180
Lincoln Pen Settlement, 180
Line Gate, 229
Linton Park, 172
Little Cove, 143
Little Ease, 66
Little Gate, 229
Little Goat Island, 151
Little Half Moon Cay, 153
Little Pelican Kay, 152
Little Port Royal Street, 236
Little Prospect, 173
Little River, 114
Little Salt Island, 151
Little Sand Bay, 141
Llandewey, 42
Llandovery, 42, 193, 247
Llandovery Beach, 222
Llangibby, 42
Lock Land, 190
Logans Junction, 229
Logwood, 104, 109, 178, 207

Logwood Tavern, 207
Lombard Street, 236
London, 38, 40, 237, 239, 243, 247
Long, Edward, 27–29, 46, 49, 87, 89, 92, 105–7, 117–18, 137, 175, 199, 201–2, 208
Long Bay, 140–43
Long Fish River, 117
Long Hill, 91–92, 229
Long Island, 151
Long Kay, 152
Long Lane, 233, 244
Long Mountain, 88
Long Mountain Country Club, 219
Long Point, 149–50
Long Pond, 136
Long River, 120
Long Savana, 105
Longlands, 190
Longville, 199
Longville Crawle, 175
Longville Park, 172, 199
Longwood, 109
Look Behind, District of, 34–35
Look Out, 79, 82
Lorrimers, 185
Los Angeles, 29, 59
Lottery, 74
Lottery Estate, 251–52
Lottery Mountain, 74
Lottery Pen, 74, 173
Louisiana, 46
Lousy Point, 150
Louzy Bay, 143, 150
Love Lane, 213, 237
Lovely Grove Plantation, 167
Lovenor Pen, 258
Low Ground, 158
Low (Lowe) River, 119
Lower King Street, 35
Lower St Andrew, 35

Lower Works, 164
Luana Mountain, 89
Luana Pen, 50
Luaetree Pond, 135
Lucea, 202, 224, 229
Lucky Hill, 74
Lucky Hill Plantation, 168
Lucky Valley, 74, 79, 95–96
Lucky Valley Estate, 95
Luglatchet, 149
Luidas River, 113
Luidas (Lluidas) Vale, 96–97, 119
Luke Lane, 237
Lydford, 193
Lymetree Bay, 141
Lynch, Mrs Henry, 126
Lynch, Sir Thomas, 14
Lynch Island, 151
Lynchs Vale, 96

Macauley Village, 198
Macca Land, 213
Macca Sucker, 86
Macmillan, Mona, 35
Macungo Hill, 203
Madeira, 29
Madras Plantation, 52
Madrid, 31
Maggotty Estate, 164
Magotty Cove, 143
Mahoe Bay, 142
Mahoe Garden, 184
Mahoe Gardens, 183
Mahoe (Moho) River, 119–20
Mahogany Hill, 92
Maiden Lane, 237
Maiden Valley, 95
Maima, 26
Main Branch, 114, 116
Main Channel, 154
Main Gully, 128
Main Morass, 133–34
Main Ridge Gap, 94
Main Savanna Gully, 128

Mais, Roger, 241
Majesty Pen, 206
Mali, 256
Mallard Hole, 145
Mammee, 1, 159, 167, 171
Mammee Bay, 27, 141–42
Mammee Gully, 128
Mammee Hill, 92
Mammee Ridge, 88
Mammee River, 117
Mammee Spring, 122
Manatee Bay, 141
Manatee Hole, 125, 145
Manatee Valley, 95
Manchanil Harbour, 146
Manchester, 32–33, 38, 52, 188, 199
Manchester, Duke of, 199
Manchester Street, 233
Manchineel Gully, 128, 130
Manchioneal (Manchineel), 145, 202
Mandela Highway, 243, 257
Mandela, Nelson, 18, 243, 257
Mandela Park, 257
Mandeville, 199, 227
Mangrove Bay, 141
Mangrove Point, 149–50
Manheim, 44
Manley, Norman, 257
Manley Avenue, 257
Manley Meadows, 217
Mannings Town, 204
Man of War Keys, 152
Manor Centre, 220
Manor House Gully, 220
Manor House Hotel, 219
Manor Park, 219–20
Manor Park Close, 220
Manor Park Estates, 219–20
Manor Park Plaza, 220
Manor Park Road, 220
Mantica Point, 149
Maps, 8–18, 26, 60, 85–87, 94–95, 98–100, 104, 121,

129, 138, 140, 153–54, 157, 165, 197, 200
Marchmont, 42
Marcus Garvey Avenue, 257
Marcus Garvey Drive, 257
Marengo Park, 45
Marescaux Road, 244
Margaret Town, 203
Margarets Bay, 51
Marigold Way, 240
Mark Lane, 237
Market, 207–8, 224, 250
Market Street, 237
Marl Pit Piece, 191
Marlborough, Duke of, 44
Marley, 32
Marley, Bob, 241
Marlie Hill, 93
Marlie Mount, 91
Maroon Town, 1
Maroon Village, 198
Maroons, 99, 114, 184, 191, 202–4, 211, 254, 258
Martello Drive, 241
Martha Brae Harbour, 147
Martha Brae River, 97, 116
Marthabrae, 202
Martinique, 49
Martyr, Peter, 27
Mary Browns Corner, 226
Mary Gales Run, 190
Maryland, 46, 230
Maryland Settlement, 180
Mason River Runs, 190
Mason Yard, 215
Matildas Corner, 226–27, 241
Mattee (Mattys) River, 119
Matthews Lane, 237
Maxfield Avenue, 228
Maxwell, James, 88
May Day Hill, 91
May Day Mountains, 89
May Pen, 7–8, 61, 168, 170, 216–17, 224, 229, 243, 251–52

May Pen Cemetery, 213, 216
Maybole, 42
McMahon, Benjamin, 187
McMahons Tavern, 207
McMullen, Edwin Wallace,
 104, 132
Meadowbrook Mews, 217
Meadows, 217–18
Meagre Tavern, 207
Melilla, 28
Melrose, 42
Melrose Hill, 92
Me No Sen You No Come,
 4, 35, 77, 99, 252
Meribah, 57
Merrimans Point, 150
Merry Isle, 151
Mesopotamia, 53, 56
Mesopotamia Mountain, 53
Metcalf Street, 237
Metcalfe, 32
Mews, 217
Mexico, 24, 46, 89
Michaels Hole, 145
Michelton Halt, 230
Mickleton Pen, 231
Middle Channel, 154
Middle East, 52–56, 258
Middle Quarter River, 35
Middle Quarters, 35
Middlesex, 31, 202, 247
Mile Gully, 129
Mile Gully Mountain, 89
Milford, 42
Milk River, 128
Milk River Bath, 207, 229
Milk Street, 236
Milkwood Piece, 191
Mine (The Mines), 193
Mine Pen, 193
Mineral Spring, 122–23
Minimus, 55
Mint Estate, 157
Minto, 42
Miranda Hill, 49
Miskito, 49, 149

Miss Miller's Cave, 98
Mistress Bell Cave, 98–99
Moat, 146
Mocho, 50, 82, 207
Mocho Mountains, 89
Modifords Salt Pond, 135
Mona Estate, 251
Mona Heights, 240
Mona Mews, 217
Mona Road, 226, 234
Moncrieff's Gully, 129
Moneague Hotel, 206
Moneague Lake, 134
Moneague Tavern, 206
Monmouth, 42
Montego, 202
Montego Bay, 28, 118, 141,
 146, 151, 193–94, 221, 229,
 233, 243, 245, 256–58
Montego Bay Point, 149
Montego Freeport, 148, 151
Montego River, 118
Montes de las Uves, 89
Montgomery, 18
Montpelier, 32, 43, 82
Montpelier Estate, 211
Montpelier Wharf, 211
Montreal, 47
Montrose, 41, 79
Montrose Road, 42
Monza, 215
Moonlight City, 206, 250
Moonrise Villas, 221
Moor Park, 172
Moore Town, 170, 202–3
Moors (Moore's) Reef, 153
Morant, 201–2
Morant Bay, 201, 257
Morant Bay Rebellion, 130,
 208
Morant Cays, 153
Morant Point, 28
Morant River, 116, 201, 208
Morass, 132–33
Morass Gut, 130
Morass River, 120

Morces Gap, 94–95
Mordant Street, 236
Morgan, Henry, 232
Morgans Pass, 232
Morgans Valley, 232
Morocco, 50
Morrant Harbour, 146
Morvan, 44
Moses, 56–57
Mosquito Bay, 149
Mosquito Cove, 49, 146
Mosquito Cove Mountain,
 89
Mosquito River, 118
Mossmans Peak, 88
Mount, 73, 90–93
Mount Airy, 91
Mount Alta, 79
Mount Ararat, 91
Mount Atlas, 55
Mount Augusta, 55
Mount Bethel, 53, 56
Mount Blow, 42
Mount Carmel, 53, 56
Mount Cromwell, 90
Mount de las Uvas River,
 90
Mount Diablo, 90, 107
Mount Diablo Gully, 127
Mount Diablo River, 90
Mount Eagle, 43
Mount Egypt, 50
Mount Envy, 69
Mount Ephraim Pen, 57
Mount George, 43
Mount Gilead, 57
Mount Hermon, 53, 56
Mount Holstein, 44
Mount Horeb, 91
Mount Ida, 90
Mount Lebanon, 52, 79
Mount Lebanus, 52
Mount Libanus, 52, 90, 247
Mount Manna, 57
Mount Maria, 90
Mount Misery, 90

Mount Moriah, 53, 56
Mount Moses, 57
Mount Nebo, 53, 56
Mount Olive, 57, 79
Mount Olivet, 57
Mount Olympus, 55
Mount Ossa, 55
Mount Parnassus, 55
Mount Pleasant, 62–63, 67, 72–73, 78, 82, 91, 242
Mount Pleasant Mountain, 186
Mount Salus, 55
Mount Sion, 57, 79
Mount Telegraph, 90
Mount Unity, 69
Mount Vernon, 41–42
Mount Zion, 56, 79, 91
Mountain, 2, 6, 12, 86–92, 90, 95, 178–79, 185–88, 249, 251
Mountain Pond, 135
Mountain River, 118
Mountain Spring, 79, 124
Mountain Valley, 87
Mountain View Avenue, 241, 257
Mountainside, 232
Moy Hall, 42
Mozart, Wolfgang Amadeus, 241
Muirhead, 42
Muirton, 42
Muirton Back Land, 189
Muirton Estate, 189
Mulatto Pen, 169
Murmuring Brook, 113
Murray's Plantation Walk, 181
Musquito Cove, 143
Musquito Point, 149

Naggo Head, 50
Nain, 228
Nairn, 42
Nanny, 203, 257

Nanny Town, 203, 257
Nannyville, 257
Nanse Pen, 216
Napoleon Bonaparte, 30, 45
Naseberry Garden, 182
Nassau, 44
Nassau Mountains, 89
Nassau Valley, 95
National Heroes Park, 257
National Housing Trust, 218
Navarre, 31
Navy Island, 151
Negril, 174, 194, 221
Negril Harbour, 143, 146
Negril Hills, 91
Negril Point, 150
Negro River, 255
Negroe Town, 202
Nelson, Horatio, 30, 50
Nelson Street, 237
Ness Castle, 210
Netherlands, 45
Nethersole Place, 234
New Amsterdam, 49
New Bermuda, 49
New Bethany, 53
New Canaan, 57
New Castle, 17, 79
New Crawford Town, 202
New Eden, 56
New England, 226
New Forest, 247
New Garden, 182
New Haven Gap, 95
New Jerusalem, 53, 56
New Kingston, 220, 241
New Liguanea, 26
New Lumber Road, 191
New Nanny Town, 257
New Paradise, 58
New Paradise Estate, 160
New Providence, 66
New Savanna, 107
New Savana Mountains, 89
New Savana Pen, 171
New Savane River, 134

New Street, 234
New Town, 203
New Works, 164
New York, 46, 49, 205, 215, 239, 244
Newcastle, 17, 198
Newmarket, 134, 208
Newport, 38, 42, 148, 215
Newry, 43
Newton, 17
Niagara, 47, 137
Niagara River, 47
Nicaragua, 49, 149
Nigeria, 50–51
Nigger House Corner, 226
Nightingale Grove, 108
Nightingale Grove Pen, 171
Niles, The, 50
Nine Turns, 228
Ninth Street, 236
Norman Gardens, 241
Norman Manley Airport, 257
Normanby Village, 198
Norris, 226
North America, 6, 22–23, 41–43, 46–48, 71–72, 77, 103, 126, 130–31, 141, 144–45, 209, 219
North Branch, 116
North Coast, 36
North Coast Highway, 243
North Kingston, 35
North Negril, 150
North Street, 235–37
North West Point, 150
Norway, 45
Norwood, 53
Nose Point, 150
Nottingham Pen, 170
Nugent, Maria, 3, 58, 186
Nuttall Street, 237
NW 7th Street, 236
Nyere Community Farm, 177, 257

Oaxaca, 24
Oberlin, 47
Occasion Call, 200
Occasion Town, 200
Ocean Boulevard, 234
Ocean Sands Resort, 194
Ocho Rios, 27, 29, 129, 194, 218, 221, 258
Ocho Rios Gully, 129
Old Cashue Pen, 169
Old Crawford Town, 202–3
Old England, 190
Old Harbour, 146, 148, 202, 208
Old Harbour Bay, 130, 161, 208
Old Harbour Glades, 218
Old Harbour Market, 202, 208
Old Harbour Mews, 217
Old Hope Road, 71, 218, 226, 234, 242
Old Man Bay, 143
Old Market Street, 233
Old Montpelier, 246
Old Mill, 191
Old Nanny Town, 202–3
Old North Harbour, 146
Old Woman's River, 106
Old Woman's Savana, 105–7
Olim Port, 148
Olive Park, 172
Olivier Bridge, 231
One Bush Cay, 152–3
One Bush Reef, 153
One Hundred (100) Lane, 237
One Hundred and Twenty (120) Feet Fall, 136
Operation Friendship, 214
Oran, 50
Oran Plantation, 50
Orange Bay, 141
Orange Cove, 143, 247
Orange Grove, 79, 244
Orange Grove Pen, 171

Orange Grove Plantation, 167
Orange Hall, 209
Orange Hill, 78, 82, 93
Orange River, 117, 232
Orange Street, 236
Orange Valley, 78
Orchard Estate, 108
Orchard Plantation, 108
Oristan, 28
Osborne Mountains, 89
Osborne Store, 207
Ottawa Avenue, 241
Ouida, 51
Owen Piece, 191
Oxford, 40, 82, 89, 247
Oxford Street, 236

Paisley, 41
Palermo (Harbour), 146
Palermo, The, 45, 220
Palestine, 213
Palisades, 150
Palisadoes, 150, 152, 257
Palléta, 29
Palm Beach, 154
Palmers, 225
Palmers Cross, 225
Palmers Hut, 210
Palmeto Point, 149
Palmeto Savana, 105
Palmetto Gully, 127–28
Palmetto Gut, 130
Palmetto River, 117
Palmyra, 53
Palmyra Estate, 53
Palmyra Pen, 53
Panama, 49
Pan de Botillo, 29
Pans Lodge, 55
Papine, 42, 226, 252
Papine Corner, 226
Papine Estate, 251
Parade, 215, 256
Parade Gardens, 215
Paradise, 58, 82, 173, 247

Paradise Bridge, 58
Paradise Estate, 160
Paradise Park, 58–59
Paradise Pen, 79
Paradise Street, 236
Paris, 44
Parishes, 2, 31–34, 215, 246
Park Lane, 237
Parnassus, 55, 247
Parnassus Estate, 55
Parratee Bay, 29
Pass, 95, 232
Pass Water, 133
Passage, The, 202
Passage Fort, 202, 215
Passmore Town, 212
Pasture, 191–92
Path, 225
Patrick City, 206
Patricks Creek, 145
Pattons Spring, 121
Paul Bogle Square, 257
Paul Island, 134
Paved River, 117
Payton Place, 240
Peak, 87–88, 245
Pear Tree Gut, 130
Peck Street, 236
Pedro Cays, 153
Pedro Cross, 225
Pedro Plains, 103
Pedro Point, 150
Pedro Pond, 135
Pedro River, 98, 119
Pedro Valley, 95
Pedros Cockpits, 100
Pegg Point, 150
Pelican Point, 149–50
Pelican Spit, 150
Pellew Island, 151
Pembroke, 42
Pembroke Estate, 186
Pen, 168–74, 211–13
Pen Hill, 170
Pen Hill Plantation, 170
People's Railway, 223

People's Theatre, 213
Pepper Bush River, 117, 120
Pera, 29
Percey Lane, 237
Percy Street, 237
Perexil Isle, 151
Perth, 42
Peru, 48
Peru Cave, 98
Peters Creek, 145
Peters Lane, 237
Petersfield, 79
Petrifying Springs, 122
Petunia Way, 240
Pharaoh, 57
Phillippo, James Mursell, 69, 197–98, 200
Phillips family, 192
Phillipsfield, 192
Phoenix Park, 42, 55
Pidgeon Island, 151
Piece, 190–91
Piedmont, 45
Pig Bay, 141
Pilgrim Plantation, 58, 168
Pilgrimage Plantation, 58, 168
Pimento, 165, 167, 178
Pimento Grove Plantation, 167
Pimento Tree Piece, 191
Pimento Villa , 221
Pimento Walk, 251
Pindars River, 98
Pindus Range, 55
Pineapple Villa, 221
Pipers Corner, 227
Pisgah, 57
Pizarro, Francisco, 48
Place, 4, 238–40
Plain, 102–3
Plant, 192–3
Plantain Garden River, 117
Plantain Garden River Estate, 183

Plantain Garden River Harbour, 147
Plantain River, 117
Plantain Spring, 121
Plantain Walk River, 117, 120
Plantation, 156–57, 165–74, 180, 218, 249–51
Plantation Heights, 218
Planters Hall, 165
Planters Retreat, 165
Planters View, 165
Platform Bay, 141
Pleasant Farm, 177
Pleasant Happy Content, 64
Pleasant Hill, 78
Plinlimmon, 38, 42
Plowden Hill, 91–92, 207
Plumb Point, 149
Plumtree Bay, 141
Plum-Tree Tavern, 228
Poinciana Place Villa, 221
Point, 148–50
Point Estate, 149
Point Hill, 228
Point Hill Plantation, 149
Point Pen, 149
Pomegranate Villa, 222
Pomfret Run, 190
Pond, 135–36
Poor Man's Corner, 66, 226
Porras, 52
Port, 147–48
Port Antonio, 148, 164, 193
Port Esquivel, 148
Port Henderson, 148, 202
Port Kaiser, 148, 193
Port Maria, 28, 148, 202, 204
Port Maria Bay, 148
Port Morant, 148, 229
Port Rhodes, 148
Port Royal, 26, 31, 66, 74, 148, 150, 152, 202, 204–5, 234, 237, 239
Port Royal Cays, 153
Port Royal Harbour, 146–47

Port Royal Street, 236
Port St Frances, 148
Port St Thomas, 148
Portland Bight, 28
Portland Cave, 98
Portland Gap, 94, 220
Portland Ridge, 88, 202
Portmore, 17, 148, 206, 215, 240
Porto Bello, 41, 49
Portsmouth, 215
Portugal, 23, 28–29, 51, 53
Porus, 52, 229, 232
Pot Gully, 129
Potato Piece, 191
Potosi, 48, 247
Potsdam, 44
Practise Street, 242
Pretty Bottom, 97
Primrose Cottage, 66
Princess Street, 236
Prospect, 62–63, 67, 69–70, 75, 78, 82–83, 159–60, 168, 242, 248
Prospect Farm, 177
Prospect Hill, 70, 79
Prospect Hill Plantation, 167
Prospect Pen, 79
Providence, 59, 63, 67, 73–74, 76, 78, 82, 242
Providence Estate, 160
Puerto Bueno, 27
Puerto Grande, 24
Puerto Rico, 25
Pump Spring, 121
Pumpkin Hill, 92, 114
Pumpkin House River, 117
Purgatory, 58
Put Together Corner, 227
Pye Corner, 227

Quaco Point, 150
Quamina's Pasture, 192
Quao, 203

Quasheba Mountain, 89, 188

Quaws Pond, 135

Quebec, 47, 247

Quebec Estate, 47

Quebec Lodge, 47

Queen of Spains Valley, 95, 97

Queen Street, 234, 236, 242

Queen's Park, 215

Queens (Queen's) Town, 202–3

Queensborough, 240

Queensbury, 240

Queensbury Ridge, 88

Quick Step, 35

Rabys Corner, 226

Rachaels Farm, 178

Rachaels Farm Pen, 178

Radnor, 42

Raes Town, 204

Railways, 193, 223

Ram Goat Channel, 154

Ramble, 79, 82, 173, 229

Ramble Pen, 79, 173

Range Crescent, 241

Rastafarians, 214, 258

Ravenswood, 42

Ravinia Court, 220

Ravinia Road, 220

Recess, 43

Red Church Street, 233

Red Hill, 93

Red Hills, 27

Red Hills Road, 237

Redgate, 230

Reef, 153

Refuge Cay, 153

Regent Street, 236–37

Reid, Jane, 1

Republic, The, 258

Resource, 74, 79

Rest, 66, 173

Rest Pen, 79

Rest Store, 207

Rest and Be Thankful, 66

Retirement, 62–63, 67, 75–76, 78, 82, 168, 173

Retirement Crescent, 242

Retirement Estate, 251

Retirement Pen, 79

Retirement River, 113

Retirement Road, 242

Retirement Settlement, 179

Retreat, 63, 67, 75–76, 78, 80, 82–83, 168, 248

Retreat, The, 76

Retreat Avenue, 242

Retreat Lane, 242

Retreat Pen, 76, 78

Retrieve, 79

Rhine, 44, 247

Richmond, 38, 40, 81, 82

Richmond Castle, 38

Richmond Estate, 38

Richmond Hill, 38, 40, 78, 82, 247

Richmond Hill Estate, 38

Richmond Hill Lodge, 40

Richmond Hill Mountain, 40

Richmond Hill Park, 40

Richmond Hill Pen, 40

Richmond Hill Plantation, 40

Richmond Vale, 40

Ridge, 87–88

Right Arm, 116

Right Branch, 114

Riley's River, 224

Rinchin Island, 134

Rio Blanco Village, 194

Rio Bronte, 119

Rio Bueno, 27, 118, 124, 128, 232

Rio Cobre, 28, 118–19, 136, 231, 233

Rio de Cobre, 112

Rio de Flora, 112

Rio de Pedro, 112

Rio d'Ora (d'Oro), 118–19, 130

Rio Grande, 112, 114–15, 118, 204

Rio Hoa, 112

Rio Hoe (Hoja), 118, 136

Rio Magno, 118–19

Rio Magno Gully, 119

Rio Minho, 28, 114, 118, 158, 162, 227, 230, 232

Rio Montando, 118

Rio Novo, 118

Rio Nuevo, 112, 202

Rio Pedro, 118, 119

Rio Sambre, 112, 118

Rio Zautaco, 29

Ripleys Shoals, 153

Riswick, 45

River, 111–21

River Head (Riverhead), 79, 119, 124

River Rises, 124

Riversdale, 43

Riverside Drive, 241

River Styx, 113

Riverton City, 206, 217, 250

Riverton Meadows, 221

Riverton Mews, 217

Rivoli, 45

Roads, 223–44

Roaring Reef, 153

Roaring River, 114, 116, 120, 137, 199

Roastmeat Hall Savana, 105

Robertson, James, 15

Robertson's Shoal, 153

Roby, John, 247

Rock, The, 154

Rock City, 213

Rock Edge Bay Villas, 221

Rock Hall, 79, 209

Rock Hall Plantation, 209

Rock River, 117

Rock River Estate, 159

Rock Spring, 79, 124

Rockfort, 154

Rocky Bay, 141
Rocky Cay, 152
Rocky Cove, 143
Rocky Gully, 128
Rocky Hill, 93
Rocky Point, 149
Rocky Point and Spit, 150
Rocky Point Bay, 142
Rocky River, 117
Rodons Store, 207
Rollington Pen, 212, 255
Roman Hall, 45
Rome, 45, 54–55, 214, 221, 234
Rome Pen, 45
Rose Garden Estate, 183
Rose Garden Mountain, 183
Rose Hall, 32, 79, 249
Rose Hill, 78, 82, 93
Rosemary Lane, 237
Rosemount, 79
Rosetta, 50
Ross's Content, 64
Rotten Gut River, 121
Round Hill, 24, 79, 82, 91
Round Hill Gully, 128
Round Savana, 105
Rowes Corner, 227
Roxbro (Roxburgh), 42
Royal Court, 195
Rudds Corner, 227
Ruinate River, 120
Rum Lane, 237
Run, 190
Runaway Bay, 141, 202, 221
Running Gut, 130–31
Running Gut Estate, 188
Running Gut Land, 188
Rush Ponds, 135
Russia, 45–46, 256
Ruthven, 42

Sabina Park, 45, 215
Sail Rock, 154
Salem, 47

Salina, 132
Salt Creek, 145–46
Salt Gully, 128
Salt Gut, 130, 202
Salt Island, 153
Salt Island Pond, 135
Salt Pond, 135, 171
Salt Pond Hill, 91
Salt Pond Hut, 210
Salt Ponds, The, 135–36
Salt River, 117, 132
Salt River Head, 124
Salt Savanna, 107
Salt Spring, 122, 124, 170
Salt Spring Estate, 158
Salt Spring Pen, 228
Salt Swamp, 132
Salt Water Gut, 130
Salta Marsh, 135
Salters Moat, 146
Saltpan Hill, 27
Saltspring Junction, 228
Sam Sharpe Square, 256
Sambo Bottom River, 121
Samphir Savana, 105
Sancta Maria Savana, 105
Sandals Inn, 194
Sandals Negril, 194
Sandals Royal Caribbean, 194
Sand Hills, 91–92
Sandown, 215
Sandy Bank, 154
Sandy Bay, 141
Sandy Cay, 152
Sandy Gully, 127–30, 171, 206
Sandy Hill, 93
Sandy River, 117
Sangster, Donald, 257
Sanguinetti's Land, 189
Sans Souci, 195
Santa Ana, 28
Santa Cruz, 59
Santa Cruz Mountains, 89
Santa Cruz Park, 172

Santa Cruz Village, 198
Santa Fe, 29, 221
Santa Gloria, 28
Santa Maria, 59
Santa Maria Gully, 127–28
Santa Maria Island, 151
Santa Maria Savanna, 104, 107
Santiago, 27
Santiago de Cuba, 24
Saratoga, 46
Sardinia, 28
Saucy Train Cross-roads, 191
Savanna, 103–7
Savanna, The, 202
Savana Bay, 141
Savana Channel, 154
Savana Point, 149
Savanna la Mar, 28, 31–32, 104, 202–3, 229, 258
Savanna la Mar Harbour, 147
Savanna River, 106, 121
Savanna Spring, 106, 122
Savoy, 247
Sawkins, James, 66, 88, 94, 99, 118–19, 125, 150, 184
Saxetum, 55
Scandinavia, 45–46
Scarlett Hall Estate, 229
Scarlettfield, 192
School House Corner, 227
Schwallenburgh, 44
Scotch Grass Gully, 128
Scotland, 36–38, 41–43, 72, 151, 190, 210
Scotland Gate, 230
Scots Cove, 49, 143–44
Scots Hall (Town), 202–3
Scotts Ford, 231
Scotts Pass, 232
SE 5th Street, 236
Sea Well, 125
Sea Chalet Villas, 221
Sea Esta Villa, 222
Seacole, Mary, 46

Seafield, 42
Seaford Town, 44, 200
Seals Cove, 144
Seasplash Resort, 194
Seaview Avenue, 213
Sedge Pond, 135–36
Sedgy Bay, 141
Selvon, Samuel, 241
Sentiment, 17, 38, 47, 61,
    65–69, 77–83, 158–59,
    166, 170, 173, 209, 236,
    242–44, 248–49, 252
Serge Island, 134
Serpentine River, 114
Settlement, 178–80
Seven Corners, 228
Seven Mile, 225
Seven Mile Walk, 181–82
Seven Plantations, 165
Sevens, 165
Sevilla Nueva, 26, 28
Seville, 31, 247
Seymour Park, 218
Shakespeare, William, 241
Shanty Rock, 254
Shanty Town, 217, 221
Sharpe, Sam, 256–57
Sharpnose Point, 150
Shaw Park, 172
Shearer, Hugh, 53
Sheffield, 192
Shell Bay, 142
Sherlock, Sir Philip, 255
Sherwood Content, 62
Shickles Pasture, 192
Shickles Pen, 192
Ship Island, 151
Ship Rock, 154
Shoal, 153
Shooters Hill, 78
Shop, 207
Short River, 114, 120
Shorthaul Point, 150
Shortwood, 109, 241
Show Meself Corner, 227
Shreve, Forrest, 90, 94

Siberia, 46
Sibley, Inez Knibb, 27, 90,
    94, 131, 205
Silent Hill, 79
Silver Grove, 108
Silver Hill Peak, 88
Simmers (Sinners) Valley, 10
Simpson, James, 14–15
Singles Negril, 195
Sistren Theatre Collective,
    213
Sivila (Harbour), 146
Six Miles, 225, 243
Sixteen Mile Walk, 107, 182
Sixty (60) Feet Fall, 136
Skyline Chalets, 219
Skyline Drive, 219
Slave trade, 30, 38, 50–51,
    156
Slavery, 31–32, 56–57, 64–65,
    75–76, 157, 165, 184–89,
    196–97, 200–202, 209,
    237, 246, 248, 250–52
Sleepy Tree Gully, 127
Sligoville, 198–99
Slipe Pen, 169
Slipe Pen Road, 168
Slipe Road, 244
Slippery Gut, 4, 130
Sloane, Sir Hans, 175
Slype Pen, 169
Smart Castle, 162
Smith Village, 181, 213, 237,
    244
Smiths Lane, 237
Smokey Vale, 244
Snake Gully, 127
Snowdon, 38, 42
Sod Hall Estate, 158
Somerset, 79, 82
Soursop Turn, 228
South Africa, 256
South America, 22, 24, 26,
    48–49
South Branch, 116
South Camp Road, 36

South Coast, 36
South Negril Point, 150
South West Point, 150
Southfield, 41, 79, 228
Southside, 36
Sovereign Plaza, 227
Spain, 20, 23–30, 43, 104,
    112, 118, 120, 152–53,
    175–76, 194, 233–34, 255
Spanish Crawle River, 120
Spanish Harbour, 146
Spanish Lookout River, 120
Spanish Pond, 135
Spanish River, 120
Spanish Town, 29, 31, 53,
    124, 127, 169–70, 182, 186,
    202, 204, 217, 223, 233,
    249, 255
Spanish Town Road, 198,
    213–14, 224–25, 233–34,
    242–43
Spanish Town Street, 237
Spice Grove, 108
Spicy Grove, 108
Spit, 148, 150, 152
Spitzbergen, 45
Spot Valley Estate, 229
Spring, 82, 121–24
Spring Estate, 79
Spring Garden, 42, 62, 67,
    77–78, 81–82, 182–84, 242
Spring Garden Estate, 79,
    183
Spring Garden Pen, 183
Spring Garden River, 136
Spring Gardins, 81
Spring Grove, 108
Spring Gut, 129–30
Spring Head, 124, 135
Spring Hill, 79
Spring Mount, 89
Spring Plain, 103
Spring Vale, 96, 136, 171
Spring Valley Plantation, 167
Spring Village, 198
Springfield, 5–6, 9, 32,

Springfield (*continued*)
62–63, 67, 77–78, 81–82,
183, 192, 242
Spur Tree, 89
Spur Tree Hill, 92, 131
St Andrew, 31–32, 211–12,
215
St Ann, 32, 59
St Anne, 202
St Anns Bay, 26–28, 64, 202,
204, 227
St Ann's Gully, 128
St Anns Gut, 130
St Anns Harbour, 146
St Anns Run, 190
St Bridget, 9
St Catherine, 31, 38, 187,
247
St Catherine's Peak, 88
St Christopher, 32, 89
St D'Acre, 59
St David, 210, 247
St Domingue, 256
St Elizabeth, 32, 38, 254
St Faith, 59
St George, 32
St Helen, 59
St Helena, 49
St Iago, 27
St Jago, 59
St Jago de la Vega, 202, 204
St Jago Ponds, 135
St James, 32
St James's Isle, 27
St John, 31–32, 59
St Joseph, 32
St Kitts, 49, 241
St Leonard, 59
St Lucia Avenue, 241
St Lucy's Harbour, 146
St Margaret, 59
St Margarets Bay, 51, 204
St Mary, 32, 38, 59, 143, 191
St Nicholas Abbey, 220
St Paul, 32, 59
St Peter, 32, 59

St Thomas, 31–32, 87
St Thomas in the East, 32,
246
St Thomas in the Vale, 86,
107
St Thomas Road, 218
St Toolis, 59
St Vincent, 59
Stanfield, E.D., 12
Stanhopes Creek, 145
Stanton Street, 236
Starvegoat Island, 141
Starvegut Bay, 141
Starvegutt Point, 149
Status, 160–64
Steers, J.A., 153
Stennetts Town, 204
Stephens Lane, 237
Stettin, 44
Stewart Castle, 162–63
Stewart, George R., 19
Stewart, James, 162
Stewarton, 42
Stillwell Mews, 219
Stirling, 42
Stirling Castle, 41, 78
Stoddarts Peak, 88
Stokes Hall, 161–62, 208
Stonefield, 42
Stony (Stoney) Gully,
127–28
Stony Gut, 130, 208
Stony (Stoney) Hill, 32, 93,
171, 223, 228, 242
Stony Hill Heights, 219
Stony Point, 149
Stony River, 117, 164, 232
Store, 207
Strand Street, 233
Strathbogie, 42
Strathdon, 42
Street, 233–38
Stringers Moat, 146
Stubbs Bridge, 231
Sturge Town, 200
Sturge Village, 198

Style Hut, 210
Styx River, 113, 247
Succabus Bay, 143
Sugar, 15, 22, 30, 58, 65, 74,
80, 155–69, 175, 178–79,
186–88, 191, 211, 251
Sugar Loaf Bay, 142
Sugar Loaf Peak, 88
Sulphur Hot Spring, 122
Sulphur River, 117
Sultana Villa, 222
Summer Hill Yard, 215
Summit, The, 219
Sunderland, 190
Surinam, 49
Surinam Quarters, 35, 49
Surrey, 31, 247
Surrey Meadows, 215
Sutton, 17
Suttons Estate, 192, 227
Suttons Pasture, 192
Sutton Street, 236
Swallowfield Pen, 169
Swamp, 132
Swampey Gully, 127
Swansea, 42, 247
Sweeting, Marjorie, 97, 100
Swept Away Resorts, 194
Swift River, 114
Swimmers Bay, 143
Switzerland, 45, 219
Syria, 52–54, 253

Tabernacle, 58
Tainos, 20, 23–27, 30, 104,
152, 194, 255–56
Tamarind Tree Grove Pen,
171
Tangier, 50
Tangle River, 114
Taranto, 55
Tarentum, 45, 55
Target Street, 241
Tavern, 206–7
Taylor, John, 146
Taylor Hut, 210

Taylors Caymanas Estate, 8
Teak Savanna, 106
Tel Aviv, 53
Tellus, 55
Temple Hall, 187
Temple Lane, 237
Tensing Pen, 174
Tern Cay, 153
Terra Nova Hotel, 195
Terrace, 238–40
Tewan Crescent, 213
Thames Street, 234, 236
Thatch River, 117, 120
Thatch Walk, 181
Thistlewood, Thomas, 58,
    191, 232
Thomas, Herbert, 90
Thompson Town, 228
Thompson Village, 198
Thornhill Settlement, 179
Three Bush Cay, 152
Three Fathom Bank, 154
Three Finger Jack, 210–11,
    218
Three Finger Jacks Huts,
    210, 218
Three Finger Woman
    Tumble, 211
Three Head Shoal, 153
Three Hills Plantation, 167
Three Mile, 225
Three Roads, 225
Thrills, 195
Tick Savana, 106
Timbuctoo, 50
Tims Hill, 92
Tinson Pen, 216
Tinson Pen Aerodrome, 244
Titchfield, 202
Tivoli, 137, 221
Tivoli Gardens, 214, 216
Tobago, 24–25
Tobago Avenue, 241
Tobolski, 46
Toll Gate, 207, 229
Toneys Hutt, 210

Too Good Gully, 127
Top Hill, 78, 82, 93
Topography, 85–109
Torrington Bridge, 244
Tory Turn, 228
Tourism, 145, 154, 193–95,
    199
Tower Island, 151
Tower Street, 234, 236
Town, 200–205, 213
Town Gully, 127
Townhouses, 218–19
Trafalgar, 30–31, 79
Trafalgar Road, 220, 241
Transfer names, 8–9, 21–22,
    36–53, 236–37, 247–48
Trelawny, 32, 102
Trelawny, Negroe Town,
    202
Trelawny Town, 203
Trench Pen, 212
Trench Town, 213, 234
Trenton, 47
Trigger Road, 241
Trinidad, 23–24
Trinidad Terrace, 241
Trinity, 32
Trinity Estate, 160
Trinity Ville, 199
Tripoli, 50, 54
Troja, 54
Troy, 54
Trout Hall, 209
Trumpet Tree Gully, 127
Trumpet Tree Gut, 130
Truro Gate, 229
Truro Pen, 229
Try See Spring, 121
Tucker Piece, 191
Tuckers Turn, 228
Tulip Lane, 237
Tulloch, 41
Turkey, 54
Turn, 228
Turners Four Paths, 225
Turtle Crawle Harbour, 147

Turtle Crawle River, 118
Turtle Ponds, 135
Turtle River, 117
Tuscany, 45
Tweedside, 79, 180
Tweedside Settlement, 180
Twi, 254
Twickenham, 79
Twickenham Park, 172
Two Claw Peak, 88
Two Falls, 136
Two Mile Wood Crawle,
    175
Two Paths, 225
Two Roads, 225
Tyre, 54

Ugly River, 113
Umbrella Point, 150
Union, 69, 173
Union Hill, 69
Union Lodge, 69
Union Mountain, 69
Union Pen, 69
Union Plantation, 69
Union Run, 69, 190
United Kingdom, 22, 37,
    40–46, 51, 54, 158, 162–63,
    166, 170, 238, 241
United Nations, 12, 16
United Negro
    Improvement Association,
    209
United States, 10–12, 18–19,
    46–47, 54, 72, 77, 94, 113,
    116, 168, 219–20, 241
Unity, 68–69, 79, 82
Unity Grove, 69
Unity Hall, 69
Unity House, 69
Unity Pen, 69
Unity Valley, 69
University of the West
    Indies, 240
Up Park Villa, 221
Upper King Sreet, 35

Upper Mount Atlas, 50
Upper Musgrave Manor,
220
Upper Regent Street, 237
Upper Waterloo Road, 45,
220–21

Valdemosa Villa, 221
Vale, 96–97
Vale Lionel Village, 198
Vale Royal Cottage
Settlement, 180
Vale Royal Mountain, 180
Valhalla Villa, 222
Valley, 95–96
Venezuela, 49
Vera Mahollis Savanna, 107
Verdun, 44
Vere, 32, 192, 227, 230
Vernon, Admiral, 41
Victoria, Queen, 237
Victoria Park, 215
Victoria Street, 237
Victoria Town, 200
Victoria Village, 198
Villa, 221–22
Villa Bella, 195
Villa Caribe, 221
Villa Carmel, 221
Villa D'Este, 221
Villa Field, 221
Villa Harlequin, 223
Villa La Alba, 221
Villa Pen, 221
Village, 196–99
Village Plaza, 199
Ville, 196–99
Virginia, 42, 46

Waa Wee Gully, 128
Wagner, Richard, 241
Wag Water, 26
Wag Water River, 120, 230
Wait-a-Bit, 4, 185
Wailers, The, 241
Wakefield, 40, 78, 82, 192

Wakefield Hall, 161–62
Walde-Vaca-Morass, 133
Wales, 37–38, 42, 47, 96,
149–50, 247
Walk, 180–82
Walkerswood, 108
Wallywash Great Pond, 136
Waltham, 217
Waltham Park Road, 228,
242
War, 12, 31, 46–47, 53–54,
148, 192, 211, 237
Wareika Hill, 258
Warrior's Hill, 258
Washington, 47
Washington, George, 42
Washington Boulevard, 225,
242
Watch Hill, 114
Water Lane, 233, 237
Water Street, 236–37
Water Valley, 96
Watercress River, 120
Waterfall Plantation, 167
Waterloo, 45
Waterloo Lane, 233
Waters Valley, 95
Waterton, 42
Waterworks, 219
Way, 238–40
Webbers Valley, 95
Wedemire, Howard, 33
Welch Womans Point,
149–50
Welcome, 69
Welcome Hall, 69
Well, 124–25
Wellington, Duke of, 45
Wellington Drive, 241
Wellington Street, 233, 237
West Bay Farm Road, 241
West Branch, 114, 116
West End, 150
West Harbour, 146
West Indies Federation, 241,
255

West Kingston, 35
West Middle Shoal, 153
West Point, 150
West Street, 236
Westchester, 215
Western Kingston, 214
Westmoreland, 32–34, 241
Westmoreland Plain, 103
Weston, 17
Weston Park, 217
Westphalia, 44
Wharf, 211
White Church Street, 233
White Cliff Bay, 141
White Hall Gardens, 237
White River, 1, 117, 137
White River Cascade, 137
White Sands Villas, 221
White Shop, 207
White Street, 236
White Wing Walk, 244
Whitehall, 79, 82, 247
Whitehall Cross, 225
Whithorn Village, 198
Whitney Estate, 228
Whitney Turn, 228, 232
Whittakers Corner, 226–27
Whydah, 50–51
Whydah Bay, 51, 204
Wilberforce Village, 198
Wild Cane River, 117
Wild Pen Piece, 191
Wildman Street, 236
William Street, 233
Williamsfield, 62, 67, 77,
81–82, 192
Williamsons Crawle, 175
Wilsons Shop, 207
Winchester, 82, 246
Winchester Negro
Grounds, 184
Wind Hill Plantation, 167
Windsor, 40, 79, 82, 125,
247
Windsor Castle, 40, 79
Windsor Castle Estate, 40

Windsor Castle Farm, 40
Windsor Castle Mountain, 40
Windsor Castle Pen, 40
Windsor Estate, 40
Windsor Farm, 40, 177
Windsor Forest, 40
Windsor Forest Estate, 40
Windsor Forest Pen, 40
Windsor Lodge, 40
Windsor Mountain, 40
Windsor Park, 40
Windsor Park Pen, 40
Windsor Pen, 40, 102
Windsor Plantation, 40
Windward Road, 234, 242
Withy Wood, 227
Witwyck, 205
Wivel Gut, 130
Woman Town, 203
Wood, 108–9
Woods Island, 151
Woodlands, 78, 82

Woodpecker Grove, 108
Woodstock, 79, 247
Wordsworth, William, 66
Worlds End Gully, 128
Works, 164
Worthy Park, 98
Worthy Park Cave, 98
Worthy Park Estate, 231
Wreck Bay, 141
Wreck Reef, 153

Xamaye, 24
Xamayca, 27

Yallahs, 26, 135, 202, 226, 230
Yallahs Ford, 231
Yallahs River, 137, 220
Yanky (Yankee) River, 119
Yard, 214–15
Yard Theatre, 215
Yates Savanna, 107
Yaws Spring, 123

Yerry Yerry Gully, 129
York, 10
York Castle, 210
York Pen, 217
York Street, 233–34
York Town, 217
Yorkshire, 40
Yoruba, 50, 129
Young Gal Hill, 203
Young Gal Town, 203
YS, 230
Ysassi, Don Cristóbal Arnaldo de, 141
Ythanside, 42

Zebra Alley, 244
Zelinsky, Wilbur, 54
Ziadie Gardens, 219–20
Zimbabwe, 256
Zion, 258
Zion Hill, 57, 93